PHENOMENOLOGY AND LACAN ON SCHIZOPHRENIA,
AFTER THE DECADE OF THE BRAIN

R

FIGURES OF THE UNCONSCIOUS 2

Phenomenology and Lacan on Schizophrenia, after the Decade of the Brain

Alphonse De Waelhens
Catholic University of Leuven
Wilfried Ver Eecke
Georgetown University

Leuven University Press
2001

Published with the Support of
"K.U.Leuven Commissie voor Publicaties"

Published by arrangement with Editions Nauwelaerts, Louvain, and Duquesne University Press, Pittsburg.
Chapters II-VIII and Conclusion were originally published in French as A. De Waelhens, *La Psychose*. Copyright 1972, Editions Nauwelaerts.
The Introduction, Chapters II-VIII and Conclusion were published in English as A. De Waelhens, *Schizophrenia* (W. Ver Eecke, Trans.). Copyright 1978, Duquesne University Press.

ISBN 90 5867 160 7
D / 2001 / 1869 / 67
Cover: Lejon Tits
Illustration cover: Bosco, Extracción de la piedra de la Locura. Derechos resercados © Museo Nacional del Prado - Madrid.

Distribution in the USA and Canada: Coronet Books Inc., 311 Bainbridge Street, Philadelphia PA 19147

In Memory of
Alphonse De Waelhens
An Exceptional Teacher

CONTENTS

FOREWORD

A. De Waelhens

From now on it is unthinkable that one should construct a philosophical anthropology without the input of psychoanalysis, psychopathology, and psychiatry. Yet this assertion immediately triggers an immense debate. This debate concerns method: How will phenomenology enter into dialogue with and
permit itself to be instructed by forms of knowledge which are developed from
a perspective not at all its own? Indeed psychoanalysis, psychopathology and
psychiatry are guided by different principles and different methods of investigation than philosophy; the former also are confronted with other problems
and they have other duties and other goals than the latter. There seems to be
almost no common ground. A further difficulty lies in the fact that there exists
almost as many radical differences among the views which these diverse clinical disciplines take towards a single object. This has the result that, if the debate is to be rigorous, it must thoroughly consider each problem. The debate
concerns the different levels of the phenomena and the theories: should the
data and the questions offered by these sciences be integrated just as they are,
or should their assimilation be preceded by a hermeneutical interpretation such
as the one which Merleau-Ponty presented before using the work of Goldstein
and Gelb? But what interpretation is the correct one? Moreover, the debate
concerns the structures of intelligibility: that which psychiatry calls *comprehension* does not dovetail with the usage which psychoanalysis makes of this
term, and phenomenology's usage differs from both of the above. The notion
of delirium, or, in another perspective, that of normality would furnish the
theme for a significant exegesis. And, finally, or really in the first place, the
debate concerns the status of consciousness. In regard to this question, not
only do the positions of the various disciplines vary considerably, but, in addition, each discipline, while not necessarily badly informed about the other's
point of view, experiences difficulties in producing an exact translation of
someone else's terminology.

   We do not propose, and with good reason, to solve these preliminary difficulties. We will simply attempt to never lose sight of them, and to make, on
each occasion, remarks which appear to us to be enlightening, and which,
perhaps, may serve as a preparation for a later, systematic treatment. We are
not unaware of the extent to which the risks of such an endeavor, already so
precarious, will be aggravated by such a procedure. We only hope that our
reflection will have the result of offering a better chance for success to those
who follow. But what, precisely, is our endeavor? If, in the past few years,
confrontations between philosophers, psychoanalysts and psychiatrists have
been numerous, varied, and fruitful, it is nevertheless far from true that all the
paths which converge on that immense and decisive intersection which is

anthropology have been explored, or really, have even been embarked on. It would appear that even the joint exploration of this domain by phenomenology and psychoanalysis has of yet certainly neither yielded all its fruit nor explored all its possibilities. We would like to make a fresh effort in this regard. This effort, the fruit of long preparation, attempts to avoid the twin pitfalls of ignorance and repetition. We do not propose either to rehash that which has already been acquired, nor to practice a "wild" phenomenology whose pseudo-discoveries would have no other origin than a quite evident lack of information. Our project, therefore, will be to reflect, from a philosophical and phenomenological perspective, but with the help of psychoanalysis, on several dimensions of behavior which, in brief, we will call here "irrational," but which, in fact, will be mainly psychotic behavior. We will work toward a comprehension along the lines just sketched out, while continually enriching this perspective with the insights of the principle schools of psychiatry, and with the interpretation given by psychoanalysis, as it is expressed in the works of Freud and Lacan.

It is our wish that this interpretation should clarify the potentiality for madness lying at the very heart of the structures that are constitutive of the human condition. The philosophers would desire from such a work a clarification of these structures, which in, and often because of, their usual or normal functioning are hidden. In spite of all past attempts to disengage these structures, only banal results have been obtained. As was said above, this project necessitates a minimum explication of psychoanalytic and psychiatric thought. This explication will determine the formal framework of this work. A final chapter will attempt to clarify how this interdisciplinary research and its eventual acquisitions can modify the notion of "comprehension."

* * *

We are aware that such a project is ambitious almost beyond hope of success. We also know that we have not completely succeeded in this undertaking. We know that it is far from perfect. Our excuse is the hope of perhaps opening up the terrain in some small way for those who may attempt, at a more opportune time, and with better means, to take up the task. Beyond this, our excuse is the very great interest which we have brought to the project, and, to put it simply, the pleasure which we have received in composing it. It is for our reader to judge whether this joy be an illusion.

PREFACE

Ver Eecke

The translation of the contribution by A. De Waelhens would not have been possible without the help of a number of my students. First translation of chapters or parts of chapters were made by Kenneth Caldwell, Claudine Speyer, Octavio Roca, Devra Simiu, Bonnie Ferguson, Iseult Honohan, Magdalina Holquin, Anne de Renzo, William Pitt, John Donovan, and Arnold Davidson. Before and during the translation, regular discussions were held to provide uniformity in the translation. I then checked and corrected the translations. Some of the corrections were extensive. In order to check the English, the corrected version was once more read by two students: John Donovan and Arnold Davidson. All corrections were discussed, and I read the final translation once more, so that I accept the responsibility for the final version.

For the explanatory footnotes, I received valuable suggestions from Joseph H. Smith, M.D. (Chairman of the Forum for Psychiatry and the Humanities at the Washington School of Psychiatry) who read the entire manuscript. I also received many suggestions from my colleague Mario del Carril, who was willing to listen many times to the philosophical problem for which I wanted references in analytic philosophy. Other colleagues were as helpful as Dr. del Carril, but I pressed them less frequently. Having done it nevertheless, I hope they accept my expression of gratitude in return.

Georgetown University provided a summer grant for the project and I continued work on it during the first month of my research grant in Bonn, provided by the A. von Humboldt Foundation of West Germany.

A manuscript is not a manuscript without typing service. My wife, Josiane Ver Eecke-Berten and Ms. Alneater Gilliam of the philosophy department, had the skill and the patience to turn an impossible handwritten product into a neat final product.

In the main text, the translator's explanatory notes by W. Ver Eecke are indicated by alphabetical symbols (a, b, c) and appear as footnotes. The notes written by the original author of the book (De Waelhens/Ver Eecke) are indicated by regular arabic numbers and appear as endnotes. Almost all section-titles in the main text are the translator's. The bibliography, too, was made by the translator.

For writing the Chapter: *The Usefulness of the theory of De Waelhens/Lacan for an effective approach to schizophrenia, after the decade of the brain*, I (W.V.E.) wish to thank the many colleagues who gave me important advice: Bertram Karon, Michael Teixeira, William Richardson, Palle Villemoes, Paul Desan, Ann-Louise Silver, John Muller, Frank Marotta, and Pat Crowe. I also wish to thank the Graduate School of Georgetown University for a publication subsidy, the office of the Dean of Faculty for partially subsidizing attendance at conferences on psychosis and schizophrenia and the department of Philosophy for defraying additional expenses to make the manuscript ready.

Introduction

SITUATING THE CONTRIBUTION OF A. DE WAELHENS

Ver Eecke

This introduction has three parts. In the first, an attempt is made to relate the work of De Waelhens to the work of Sartre and that of Wittgenstein. De Waelhens presents as his thesis the fact that one's self-identity or one's self-presence is related to the desires of others. In order to argue that Sartre's position on the relation between one's selfhood and others is defective, and should include as de Waelhens does, a reflection upon the desires of others, we will use a report on the discovery by our own children of the possibility that they once did not exist. De Waelhens also develops the idea that one's name is very important for one's selfhood. We hope that we have found in Wittgenstein's reflections on one's own name, in *On Certainty*, a way of showing the philosophical importance of De Waelhens' reflections.

In the second part of the introduction, we will present the crucial contributions made by De Waelhens in this book.

In the third part, we will formulate some critical remarks.

I. DE WAELHENS, SARTRE AND WITTGENSTEIN

A. Sartre and De Waelhens: The Origin of the Self

On a Sunday afternoon in 1975, my wife, my children and myself drove in our car along Constitution Avenue in Washington, D.C. In the back of the car, the children found constant occasion to quarrel with each other. In order to divert their attention and thereby create peace I drew their attention upon the Washington Memorial and told them that when my wife and I first arrived in Washington, we walked up the nine hundred or so steps to the top. The children looked at the Memorial. The height of the monument and the fact that we had walked up all those steps seemingly impressed them. Then came the question: *Where were we?* As a matter of fact—and I must confess, not without some secret enjoyment—I told them that they did not yet exist. Still remembering what they had learned during my wife's last pregnancy, a couple of months before, the children replied also in a matter of fact "Yes, but we were in your tummy, is it not mammie?" My wife truthfully replied, that they were not. In my mirror, I could see consternation on the faces of the children. I heard a long silence. Finally, our oldest daughter asked: "But, did you like to have children?" We replied that we did. Satisfied, our daughter produced a contented face and appropriated in silence the words that had been spoken. Our boy, three years younger, then broke the silence and said: "And when I then came back, was I then with you in the Monument?"

On this Sunday afternoon, our attempt to create peace in the rear of the car had resulted in confronting our children with the fact that once they had not existed. Becoming aware of this fact was for both clearly puzzling. The oldest child solved the puzzle by accepting her parents' desire for children—i.e., their desire for her—as a substitute for her existence. She solved the riddle of her origin by a reference to the level of desires. The younger child had not yet worked out a positive solution for the problem, and therefore denied and repressed the problem: he talked as if he had been only temporarily absent, but had in effect always existed.

Sartre is one philosopher who has explicitly posed the question which our children faced that Sunday afternoon in the presence of the Washington Monument. The question is: how can a self conceive of its own origin. His answer is that for consciousness it is impossible to conceive of its own origin except by projecting to be its own foundation.(1) He expresses this even metaphorically as follows: "man is a being whose project it is to be God," or "to be man is to desire to be God."

It is clear from the attitude of our daughter that there is an alternative answer possible. This alternative answer involves making other persons indispensable for my own self-presence. Sartre is aware of this alternative. He writes towards the end of *La Transcendance de l'Ego*(2) that one must evade solipsism, and that one can do that only by heeding the intuition of Hegel. This intuition, writes Sartre, consists in realizing that I depend upon the other for my being.

In *Being and Nothingness,* Sartre is indeed capable of developing a concept of personhood which gives to the other a fundamental role: i.e., I am a body for the other. This is revealed to me, says Sartre, in the look. The function of that other is that he is a threat, because in his look he reduces me to an object, while revealing to me my objective dimension (my body). My only strategy therefore is to look back and reestablish my subjectivity (my for-itself) by reducing the other to objectivity.

Sartre is forced to take this position because he does not allow for a dynamic relation in the self between the self as consciousness and the self as body. Indeed, if he were to allow for such a dynamic relation, it would be possible to see that the others can be a threat to me (they can objectify, ridicule, or even torture me), but they can also be helpful (they can smile, embrace, or kiss me). It should be noted that a smile, an embrace, or a kiss do not remain something external to my self. On the contrary they make me happy; they make me appear to myself as a desirable person. In certain circumstances, the relation to another might even lead one to change one's relation to one's body. For my children getting teeth was a painful process. They often cried. In such moments, it was helpful for them if we took them in our arms and cud-

16

dled them. Through this cuddling, our children seemed to be able to learn to accept their hostile body—hostile because it caused them pain.(3)

As Sartre has clearly seen, the other has a constitutive function for my selfhood. But the function of the other is not limited to the threat of his look.(4) This is so because as a self I am in a dynamic relation with my body. For such a self the other can be a threat or a help. Whether he is a threat or a help can only be clarified by analyzing the desires involved. A smiling look does not have the same effect as an objectifying look.

The introduction of desires of others as constitutive for my selfhood allows us to have an intuitive understanding of why a child can be content by knowing that when (s)he did not yet exist, (s)he was already expected.

Clearly, such an intuitive understanding is not sufficient for professional philosophical reflection. The difficulty is to know how to proceed further. The solution chosen by De Waelhens is to interrogate psychoanalysis. In this book, the author concentrates on the problem of schizophrenia. Through this interrogation De Waelhens learns that the schizophrenic is a person for whom the question "who he is" is not answered satisfactorily. He therefore creates a hallucination to redefine his own self in terms which are more acceptable and more meaningful for him.

If one now accepts that hallucinations are an attempt of the patient to redefine his own selfhood, we might hope to get a step further in the elucidation of the problem of selfhood. De Waelhens argues that two dimensions are crucial for the constitution of the self. One is intuitively familiar from the present discussion: i.e., the desire of others.(5) The other dimension has not yet been introduced intuitively: i.e., language.

B. Wittgenstein and De Waelhens. Selfhood and One's Name

On Certainty by L. Wittgenstein is a very puzzling little book. The author uses the peculiar technique of proving nothing in the strict logical sense of proof, but he succeeds in presenting plenty of stimulating insights. It is then left to the readers to find the logical arguments and the framework whereby the insights that emerged during the reading of the book are presented and defended.

Such an attempt has been undertaken by the co-editor of the book, G. H. von Wright in his article "Wittgenstein on Certainty." There G. von Wright introduces the concept of *Vorwissen* 'pre-knowledge'(6) to make sense out of the main line of argumentation used by Wittgenstein in *On Certainty*.

When reading *On Certainty*, I have been struck by the line of argumentation which von Wright has clarified for us. I have also been impressed by Wittgenstein's stubborn insistence that *a person's relation to his own name is a unique kind of relationship*. I am not aware of any commentary clarifying this point. Let us look at this problem, because in psychoanalysis the problem of a person's name also has a central position. I hope to relate Wittgenstein's reflection on a person's name to the theses presented in psychoanalysis on the same problem.

The problem of one's own name is a crucial problem in *On Certainty*. It is mentioned from no. 328 on, until almost the end (no. 668; the last number of the book is 676). The theme thus runs through about half the book. It is mentioned or discussed explicitly in at least 32 numbers.(7) In all these texts, Wittgenstein is asking the simple question: why am I certain of my own name? The technique used by Wittgenstein to answer this question is that of trying out stronger and stronger statements until he reaches a climax in his formulation in no. 628-29. The four numbers in which he still discusses the problem afterwards are anti-climatic in that they just echo some weaker statements made in the earlier numbers.

In 328-30, Wittgenstein equates a person's certainty about his own name with the certainty that a person has about several other facts: that the earth existed before he was born, that his life has taken place on earth or close to it, that he was not on the moon, etc. (327). In all these cases, it makes no sense to doubt. Presumably, Wittgenstein continues, a reasonable man cannot doubt everything. In order to doubt certain things, he must have grounds (323). Those things that one cannot doubt without grounds *must be believed* (330). They must be believed because they are a precondition to learn other things (games) (329). This belief is a kind of necessary *Vor-wissen*. It cannot be known; it cannot be abandoned; it must thus be safeguarded in another mode. Wittgenstein proposes to call this mode a *willingness to believe* (330).

In 425 Wittgenstein affirms that it is improper to say that the grounds by which I know my own name are belief or surmise. Wittgenstein compares it with the statement: "I am in England" or "This is a tree." I am as certain about these statements as I am of my own name, and vice versa (417-424). About three phenomena, it is proper, says Wittgenstein, to maintain not just that I believe them, but that I *cannot make a mistake about them*. Still, says Wittgenstein, I *am not infallible* about them. He has indeed suggested possibilities in which the statement "I am in England" could be an error (420-421).

One is thus forced to interpret Wittgenstein as saying that someone is right in claiming *that he is certain what his name is, even though he might be in error*. Between a person and his name there are thus two legitimate epistemological relations. The one maintained by the person himself, and the one maintained by others who might have superior information.

The epistemological validity of the opinion of others can be rightfully tested objectively: i.e., arguments can be presented, discussed, accepted or rejected. Depending on whether certain arguments are accepted or rejected it is possible to arrive at the statement "yes, Mr. X's name is L. W." or "no, Mr. X's name is not L.W." This conclusion might be in accordance with the belief of Mr. X; it need not be. Thus others have a knowledge of the relation between Mr. X and his name which is relative to the arguments that are brought forth.

I take it that Wittgenstein maintains that Mr. X is right in refusing to accept that his certainty about his own name is relative to arguments. He is thus right in claiming *subjective certainty.*

In 464 and 470 Wittgenstein adds a new thought. The two numbers are written with one day's difference, but they are clearly related. The meaning of naming is related in both numbers to a well-wish ("Good morning" in 464; or "I wish you luck" in 469) and to the sentence "[...] that's a tree" (465, 467, 468).

Wittgenstein argues that the well-wishes or the sentence identifying a tree are useless and superfluous sentences (464) if they are not pronounced within a certain context in which they become *meaningful* and *informative.* In 464, Wittgenstein claims that suddenly mentioning someone's name does not add anything if his identity is already fully known from the context. (He is my friend, and I know it because I have talked for some time to him as my friend.) *Knowledge of someone else's identity and of his name are thus one and the same thing.* However, in 470 Wittgenstein claims that this line of argumentation is problematic for my own name. Indeed, my certainty about my own name is not grounded in arguments. Between me and my name, there is no distance, because as Wittgenstein says, there is no other (thing) which can be used as the ground for my certainty about my own name (470).

I take it that Wittgenstein means to say that "I" and "my belief in my name" are more the same than "my knowledge of some one else's identity" and "my knowledge of his name." The latter refers to the same subject. Are we to say that the first ("I" and "my belief in my name") *are* the same?

In 486-493 Wittgenstein reinforces our interpretation of the close relation between "I" and "my belief in my name." He does it by approaching the problem from a new angle. He asks what kind of reaction one can expect from a person whose belief (or certainty or surmise) in his name one wants to falsify (492). Wittgenstein's reply is that such a person could simply *refuse* to give up his belief (492) or that he even could *admonish* his partner for his whole attempt (495). The reason for such a reaction says Wittgenstein approvingly is that the revision of one's belief or certainty in one's name would amount to the destruction of all yardsticks (492), or of all authority to which one can appeal for justifying any judgments (493).

Thus the relation between me as a person and *my belief in my name is* a precious relation. It contains the ground for all yardsticks and for all authority by which judgments can be justified. It then makes sense that a person *refuses* that a wedge be inserted between himself and his belief in his name, or that one *admonishes* some one who tries it.

With the concept of 'refusal,' we approach Wittgenstein's central thought about the relation between a person and his certainty about his own name. Indeed this theme is repeated (577) just before Wittgenstein's crucial statement about the problem of the proper name (579). The refusal theme is again connected with the one of the authority to ground truth (578). The theme is repeated once more towards the end of the book where Wittgenstein argues that concerning my own name, I "do not *need* to give way before any contrary evidence (657)."(8) This theme is also formulated in the expression: that "the assumption that I might be making a mistake has no meaning" (659).

Now that Wittgenstein has shown the very special nature of the relation between me and the belief in my name, it is natural that he asks why this is the case.

The first step is to see if that special relation is based on memory. Indeed, our name is so often used that if we are not certain of it we cannot trust our memory on any other matter (568). Wittgenstein rejects this possibility. Indeed, we need no statistical proof that our name has been used more than any other concept in order to say that if I am not certain of my name, then I am crazy (572).

Wittgenstein's second step is then to affirm that the proposition "I know my name" is not an empirical proposition (569). This is the case, because it is reasonable that a person refuses possible arguments against his belief about his own name (577). It is thus *a form of a priori*. Or in Wittgenstein's language: to be certain of one's name is part of the language-game with names of people (579).

Wittgenstein is now ready to summarize his views on the problem of names of persons (628-629). The problem has two aspects. On the one hand, it is essential for the language game with personal names that *everybody is certain of his own name*. On the other hand, this certainty is but subjective certainty. It has no universal, objective or logical validity (628). Thus it makes sense if others question the validity of the necessary and solid belief in someone's own name.

The mysterious function and precious nature of a person's name for his personhood can be illustrated by a central symptom of judge Schreber. In anticipation of his release from the asylum Schreber wrote his *Memoirs* in order to explain to his wife and acquaintances various oddities in his behavior (p. 1. Pagination of original German edition). These oddities are: first, his desire or his need to wear female ornaments (ribbons, necklaces etc.) and to look half-naked at himself in a mirror (p. 429). Second, there is compulsive bellowing (p. 429). This bellowing is mentioned by the medical officer's report to the court deciding about his possible release (p. 388). The officer mentions that these voices disturb the *nightrest of* patients (p. 388), that it disturbs even people outside the asylum (p. 399). Franz Baumeyer went through the case records of Schreber's asylum. He found an entry describing what Schreber was screaming: he was screaming insulting words, or "I am Schreber, the President of the Senate."(9) Thus one central symptom of judge Schreber is the bellowing, which at the height of his illness involved screaming in the middle of the night through an opened window: his *name* and *the title of his job* (i.e., the two signifiers of his identity).

According to Wittgenstein, the relation of a person to his own name is characterized by a degree of certainty which poses epistemological problems.

It cannot be proven or verified in the normal sense. It is here that G. von Wright's concept of pre-knowledge is helpful. Indeed, he interprets Wittgenstein as maintaining that every language-game has a foundation which is part of a person's pre-knowledge.(10) The certainty by which a person relates to his own name is part of one's pre-knowledge.

The question which now arises is whether the domain of pre-knowledge is a domain that is absolutely and categorically outside the field of experience upon which philosophy can reflect? Does the domain of pre-knowledge constitute a limit to philosophical reflection? Is there any human experience which is beyond the field that philosophy can reflect upon? A straightforward negative answer would have great implications for philosophy. It appears to me more correct to say that the domain of pre-knowledge can be made available to philosophy, but only indirectly. Philosophy must first be informed about the domain of pre-knowledge before it can start to reflect. About the special and precious relation that exists between a *person* and the *belief in his own name,* we can get information from writers such as Joseph Conrad *(Lord Jim),* from mentally ill patients such as judge Schreber and from anthropologists such as Levi Strauss who analyze the function of the name in the social structure of primitive tribes.

Informed by the study of mental illness, philosophy of psychoanalysis has developed some insights into the function of the name for a person.(11) These insights can best be understood by using a reductionist model of human beings by way of contrast. Suppose that people could be described as atomistic physical bodies. One could then say that procreation would require the copulation between a male and a female and the fruit of such a union. This fruit when it has reached sexual maturity could participate in the random encounter of mates for copulation, and then participate in turn in procreation.

It is clear that such a model would leave out what is most typically human. Human procreation is not reduced to random copulation. Human sexuality is guided, prepared and supported by phantasies, by prohibitions, institutions and laws.

Human sexuality is only in its borderlines promiscuous. Normally human sexuality is submitted to a norm, it is made the expression of respect, trust, commitment. If this norm is violated in reality, it is nevertheless upheld in poetry, literature and the dreams of people.

Human sexuality is also restricted by prohibitions. The prohibitions can be extensive, as they are in primitive societies. They can be minimal, as is the case in our society. Or they can be lifted symbolically to show the divine nature of this particular person, as was the case with the Pharaoh.

Human sexuality is also imbedded in institutions. There is marriage, its public celebration, the criteria by which the choice of marriage partners leads to joy, disappointment or trouble.

Finally there are laws. The fruits of one's labor, i.e., one's income and one's property is not fully at one's disposal. Society stipulates that those whom it recognizes as someone's descendants have claims upon the fruits of the labor of the ancestor that are beyond the control of the ancestor.

The name is the crucial element by which, human procreation is transformed from a physical relation to a human relation. Naming creates the possibility of relating one's sexual desire to a person (i.e., someone with a name) instead of purely to a body. In effect, names are a necessary condition for any form of incest prohibition. With one's name also arises the privileges and duties which are stipulated by human institutions and the laws.

Those obligations, prohibitions, and rights or promises, are not given in general terms. They are given as concrete guidelines. Without *concrete* obligations and prohibitions, a person does not insert himself into the human world of signification. As the name is the signifier which by definition defines the obligation and rights of a person, it is necessary that a person is certain of his name. It is by identifying with his name that he becomes part of the human world.

Psychoanalysis teaches us that this is emotionally a very difficult task. Philosophy of psychoanalysis reserves for itself precisely the task of reflecting upon the insertion of an individual into the human world of signification. Its conclusion is that this insertion cannot be separated from the disappointment that the child experiences when it recognizes that it is not any more the significant other for the mother. It also teaches us that such an insertion requires the presence of a father figure who can transform this disappointment into a promise.

Philosophy of psychoanalysis teaches us also what the consequences are if this insertion in the human world of signification is but partially successful, i.e., if the relation between me and my name is but a signifier of a threat, and not of a promise.

II. THE CRUCIAL CONTRIBUTIONS OF DE WAELHENS

In this book De Waelhens helps to remedy an anomaly in psychoanalytic theory. The anomaly is the fact that psychoanalytic theory seems to put the sources of mental illness in the vicissitudes of the instincts (libido and aggressivity). However, in practice psychoanalytic therapy does not interfere directly with the instincts; in psychoanalytic therapy one only talks; one talks about the representatives of the instincts. It is thus also not surprising that psychoanalytic theory produced a number of studies about aspects of language, i.e., on jokes, on slips of the tongue, on dream stories. It is also not surprising that a crucial step forward was made by Freud in his therapeutic techniques when he introduced systematically a technique involving language: "free association."

It is natural that a philosopher will want to ask the question: what is the relation between instincts and language? Which one is primary for a concept of a human being? The answer of De Waelhens is that to be a human subject is to insert oneself into language. But the process of the insertion into language is the story of the vicissitudes of instincts. De Waelhens defends this thesis in two ways. First, he defends it by presenting a hypothetical reconstruction of the child's insertion into the world of language. The constraints for this hypothetical reconstruction are that this reconstruction must be able to explain the symptoms of mental illness. He does this in Chapter V. Chapters III and IV are preparatory for Chapter V. In Chapter VI the author exhibits the power of his theory by showing how the different symptoms of mental illness can be structurally derived from his theory. The second way in which De Waelhens defends his thesis on the relation between language and instincts is through his analysis of the crucial technique used in psychoanalysis, i.e., free association. This is done in Chapter VII.

The central thesis that De Waelhens is defending is that to be a human subject is to be capable of inserting oneself in the world of language. Mental illness is then seen as a failure or a deficiency in this insertion. The forces that account for this failure or this deficiency are multiple. De Waelhens analyses the structural ones.

With mental illness there is a loss of metaphoric understanding of language. The classic example is the case of a patient of Tausk (Vienna) by Freud.(12) This girl reports that she has been deceived by her boy friend. She explains this by saying that her boy friend is a hypocrite, that he appears every time different to her. To summarise her opinion about him she then uses a German expression: *Augenverdreher,* someone who twists eyes. This expression in German is not used in its literal meaning; it is used as a metaphor, i.e., some one who twists the eyes of someone else is a deceiver, a hypocrite. The complaint of the patient, however, is not just that her boy friend is a hypocrite, *but also* that her eyes are not quite right, they are not straight any more, they are "twisted."

The explanation that De Waelhens defends—and in this he follows Lacan—is that words have lost part of their symbolic dimension. It does not mean that words have disappeared. They remain, but as non-symbolic signifiers which appear as a part of the real. This real has, however, no objective or inter-subjective validity. It exists only in the imagination of the patient. It is but an *imaginary real.*

Language and words are, according to Lacan, metaphorical. They refer to something other than themselves. It now happens that some words have a second kind of metaphorical power. (She is a rose; he is a chicken). Such words have a dictionary definition, which allows us to understand what they normally refer to. This dictionary definition does not tell us, however, to what this word *metaphorically* refers to.

In order to use language, one must be able to grasp that words stand for something else. In order to understand metaphors one must be able to see that a metaphor is not used literally but only metaphorically.

The expression: "She is a rose" means something only if one knows that the scribble on this paper refers to something in the world. Furthermore, one must grasp that this expression does not mean that the girl one is talking about is a plant, or has flowers that one can cut off, or has thorns. Instead, one must understand that the expression means that the girl is as nice as a rose.

Understanding metaphorical language thus requires that one can *make distinctions* in the dictionary definitions of a word. One must be able to disregard certain features as irrelevant, and retain other features as highly relevant. Thus, in the expression "she is a rose," one must be able to see that she is not a rose in the sense of being a plant, that she is not a rose in the sense that she is thorny, that she is not a rose in the sense that she has a nice smell, but only in the sense that she is *nice*. Understanding the metaphorical meaning of the expression "she is a rose" can be reduced to the capability of seeing that the girl in question is in one sense a rose, but in another sense not a rose.

It is clear that the patient of Tausk has lost the prerequisites for understanding the metaphor: *Augenverdreher*, 'hypocrite.' She takes *Augenverdreher* 'twister of eyes' *in all its senses* and thereby *equates hypocrite* with physical *trouble with her own eyes*. In fact, the patient loses sight of the metaphorical meaning (the signified of the metaphor) and gets fixated upon the literal meaning (the signifier which should convey the metaphorical meaning.) Lacan summarises the loss of metaphorical power of a patient then as follows: there is a *confusion* of *signifier* and *signified*, and instead of grasping a metaphorical meaning the patient produces an *imaginary real* symptom. The patient complains about her eyes.

We should keep in mind that Lacan claims that the loss of metaphorical power (this is called the symbolic in Lacanian terminology) is not a final equilibrium for a patient. He substitutes the *lost meaning by* an *imaginary real:* his *symptom.*

The above should prepare us for the Lacanian linguistic reinterpretation of the central thesis of psychoanalysis: the castration complex. The reinterpretation begins by stressing the total dependence of the child upon a mother-figure. Such a situation is psychologically unacceptable for the child. But it cannot change the situation except fictitiously. And that is what the child is supposedly doing. It *imagines* that it is indispensable for the mother; it acts as if it is the significant other upon whom the mother must rely. This might explain the exaggerated rage of small children when they are refused something. Their rage is out of proportion to what they are enraged about. Their rage is very understandable if one sees that what they are enraged about is not the refusal of the one piece of candy, but the mere fact that they were refused something at all. Such a refusal threatens their imaginary solution to their feeling of dependency. If their mother can refuse them something, it must be that, contrary to the child's fiction, the child is not for the mother that which totally fulfills her. Indeed, she is capable of putting distance between her and her child by refusing things to it. From the point of view of the child, it means that it is again confronted with the problem of how it is certain that the other, the mother, will not abandon him but will necessarily care for him.

The imaginary solution of the child is radically challenged when the child notices that its mother has a significant relation with someone else, i.e., the father-figure. Children will indeed show resentment when parents talk to each other and will try to disturb them. The discovery of such a relation between mother and father means for the child that, contrary to its fiction, not it but the father is for the mother the significant other.

There are logically several different reactions available to the child. It can react by rejecting this challenging experience. It can react by abandoning the imaginary solution which is now destroyed. It can react by a creative solution that must still be described.

Abandoning its imaginary solution is for the child unacceptable because it would leave her in the unacceptable position which forced her to create the imaginary solution in the first place.

Rejecting the new experience is an option that is open to the child. This would mean that the child rejects out of its awareness any significant relation between the mother and father-figures. As the child has already a relation to the mother it means that the child must refuse any significant reference to the father. The child must refuse to learn that the father is for the mother-figure a significant other.

Lacan emphasizes that it is not necessary that the father be alive. What is important is whether his word or his name is held in respect or in disrespect. This is one way to illustrate how Lacan could construct his theoretical term "name-of-the-father." It is that which forces the child to see that it is not the significant other for the mother. It is also that which the child must reject in order to maintain fictitiously that it is the only significant other for the mother. This solution is according to Lacan the origin of schizophrenia.

The third reaction available to the child is a creative reaction to this challenge. It is according to Lacan a reaction which establishes *metaphor* as the basis for *self-identity* and *self-presence*. Indeed, the solution for the child is to recognize that it is *in one sense* not the significant other it thought it was, but that *in another sense* it is a significant other (in the next generation). The child thus accepts that it is *now* a *partial* significant other. It thus establishes a metaphoric method of *self-definition*.

Psychoanalysis now adds a scandalous dimension to this innocent discussion of self-identity as defined by metaphoric self-presence. Psychoanalysis claims that the child *represents* its relation to its mother figure. The child *does not think* this relation. The image used by the child to create its fictitious solution to its feeling of dependency is the image of the phallus. Indeed, Lacan claims that the way in which the child fictitiously thinks it is the significant other for the mother figure is by thinking that it is the phallus of the mother.

The grounds for such a scandalous claim by psychoanalysis are the words of patients who retroactively remember their childhood desires with the help of the phallic symbol,(13) and the universal presence of the phallic symbol in literature, and cultural artifacts.

Refusal to accept the thesis of psychoanalysis would however amount to saying that the child *thinks* its relations with others rather than that it *represents* them. Alternatively opponents of psychoanalysis, who accept the thesis that the child *represents* its relation to its mother, must find *another representation* (a non-phallic representation).

The triangular relation between mother-father-child can thus be represented in phallic terms as follows. In order to overcome its real dependence, the child imagines itself to be the phallus of the mother. However, the mother relates to the father and thus signifies to the child that the phallus of the mother is the father.

The child's imaginary self-presence was grounded on the fictitious belief that it was the phallus. This imaginary solution is now destroyed. The child is not the phallus of the mother, it is not the significant other of the mother. The child finds itself *dislocated* from the privileged position it has assigned to itself in imagination. If the child wants to hold on to some form of self-presence it must maintain that it is significant for some other, or that it is partially significant for another, i.e., that it has *some phallic significance for another*. Within the terminology established this means that the child accepts that its phallic value is *metaphorical*, i.e., the child learns that it may be of some significance now, but that its real significance lies in the future. It learns that *it is* and is *not* significant. It learns that *it is* and is not a phallus for someone else. It is however certain of one thing: its imaginary self-presence has been destroyed; in imagination the child has been *dislocated*.

The crucial problem for the development of the child is how it reacts towards this *imaginary dislocation*. The deficient reaction is a reaction which lacks the capability to transform this imaginary dislocation into a positive experience. This deficient reaction simply takes the dislocation as dislocation and expresses the fact that one's self-presence is a *wounded self-presence*. Typical for this deficient reaction is that the *wound is* not expressed metaphorically but as existing *imaginatively* in *the real*.

Before Schreber was ill he had a thought in his dreams: "It must be nice to be a woman at the moment of intercourse." During his illness, Schreber thinks that God is miraculously *unmanning him*. (p. 51). Furthermore, Schreber gives an extraordinary significance to a small cut in his face caused by the barber (p. 297-98).(14)

This leads us to affirm with De Waelhens that hallucinations should not be understood in terms of false perceptions. Hallucinations are not perceptions to which nothing corresponds. Hallucinations are *false attempts* by a subject *to insert himself* in the human world of meaning creation. Indeed, hallucinations are by the patients themselves clearly understood as *being different from the real;* the patients provide clues for understanding that hallucinations are efforts at the *imaginary level*.

Thus Judge Schreber is absolutely convinced that he is becoming a woman, that his body is changing and that everybody can see this if they watch him half-naked before his mirror. However, Schreber adds two remarks which situate his subjective certainty *outside the real* ("a brief glance however would not suffice, the observer would have to go to the trouble of spending 10 or 15 minutes near me" p. 280) and *in the imaginary* (the undoubted impression that he has a female trunk would come "especially when the illusion is strengthened by some feminine adornments" p. 280). But a real woman needs no feminine adornments to be perceived as feminine; and one does not need 10 to 15 minutes to see that a naked woman is a woman.

An even more extraordinary testimony to the fact that hallucinations are disconnected from the real and are thus better looked at as unsuccessful attempts to deal with human meaning creation is to be found in Schreber's successful legal appeal for his release from the asylum.

Schreber quotes (p. 430-31) a text written by his physician as part of the medical officer's report about Schreber to the court (p. 401). In that text the medical officer summarizes his arguments against releasing Schreber as follows: "What objectively are delusions and hallucinations are for him absolute truth and fully adequate reasons for action" (p. 401).

Schreber comments upon this text by saying that "yes" he has unshakable certainty in what his physician calls his delusions, but that it is absolutely false to say that his delusions are for him adequate reasons for action. And he adds, "they can never in any way influence my behavior in any worldly matter" (p. 431). He prefaces this by a statement that in this context creates almost a poetic melodrama: "Just as Jesus Christ, I can say: My kingdom is not of this world." In writing their judgement, the court approvingly refers to this firm distinction established by judge Schreber (p. 483-84) to build the grounds for releasing him.

It is the thesis of Lacan that the imaginary dislocation which occurs in the Oedipus complex can be solved creatively if the name-of-the-father, i.e., the phallic power of the father is accepted by the child. It is the task of the mother to make the father (or better the name-of-the-father or the word of the father) a significant other for the child such that the child can create a positive self-presence beyond the imaginary dislocation of the Oedipus complex. How the word of the father helps the child to overcome this imaginary dislocation is a story which De Waelhens presents in a very pedagogical manner. By reducing the story to one paragraph I could only confuse the reader. I hope that I succeeded in hinting at the philosophical significance of the first and most central thesis of De Waelhens' book, i.e., to be a subject is to acquire metaphorical capacity. Such a capability is acquired with the help of another (the name-of-the-father).

The thesis about the metaphorical capacity of the subject is built upon another thesis of De Waelhens. This thesis also tries to understand the human subject from the point of view of language. The thesis is that for a subject to be a subject he must be able to distinguish himself from the first love object (the mother). This occurs in the game of the child. De Waelhens introduces this thesis by a reflection upon the concept of 'primal repression.'

The term 'primal repression' is for Freud a theoretical term. Freud was forced to introduce this term in order to make coherent his explanation of repression. Indeed, he explained repression by a double mechanism: repression is seen to be the result of a repressing activity (by the superego, for instance) *and* of the attraction exercised by what is already unconscious. Only this dual origin of repression, according to Freud, could explain the persistence of repression. Such a theory, naturally, poses the problem of how does one explain the first repression. Clearly this process must be of another nature, because there is no repressed to attract the newly repressed. Freud describes the 'primal repression' as being a first inscription of the instinct into a representation, but at an unconscious level.(15)

The further clarification of this theoretical term occurs in two steps. The first step has been made by Lacan. This author noticed that Freud was looking for a mechanism to explain the difference between psychosis and neurosis. For the mechanism of psychosis Freud uses different words such as *Verwerfung* 'repudiation,' *Ablehnung,* 'refusal,' *Aufhebung,* 'suppression' and *Verleugnung,* 'disavowal.' The two terms that Freud used most frequently are: *Verwerfung* and *Verleugnung.* He uses the second term mainly towards the end of his life. These two terms are however used in other contexts as well.(16) Indeed, *Verwerfung* is sometimes used for a normal repression or even for conscious rejection. *Verleugnung* is often used to refer to the refusal to accept the absence of the penis in a female. Lacan's merit is to have seen Freud's emerging intention to find a specific mechanism for explaining psychosis. He chose the term *Verwerfung* and translated it by *forclusion,* 'foreclosure.' Having established foreclosure as a failure, Lacan then searched in Freud's work for the positive phenomenon of which foreclosure was the failure. Lacan thinks he found such an indication in Freud's study on *Negation.* There Freud calls this phenomenon *Bejahung,* 'affirmation.'(17) Lacan interprets this term to mean: acceptance of the symbolic process or of the symbolic order.

The second step in the clarification of the concept of 'primal repression' is then taken by De Waelhens. He refers to a passage within one of Freud's most crucial publications on metapsychology: "Beyond the pleasure principle."(18) In that passage Freud analyses the actions of a child of 1½ years old, who is capable of tolerating, accepting and transforming into a game the frustrating experience of the disappearance of the mother. Freud calls it a great cultural achievement for the child. The crucial elements of the achievement are that the child is capable of replacing the mother by a toy and even by words (*Fort-da*), such that it—the child—is the one who decides about the disappearance of the mother (through the substitute of the mother: the toys or the words). Thus the child is capable of seeing the mother as other than itself. De Waelhens interprets the mastery of language (or of games) by the child as a confirmation of the fact that the symbolic order has been conquered. Foreclosure has been avoided. De Waelhens' next question is this: what are the prerequisites that allow the mastery of the symbolic order. Negatively, this becomes the question as to what one can consider causes for its failure, i.e., for foreclosure.

The answer of De Waelhens is formulated with the help of a study by Aulagnier. The thesis is that the child must be presented with a system of signifiers (the phantasms of the mother) from where it can signify its own self as an autonomous body.

The full thesis about primal repression becomes thus the following: Primal repression is the process whereby the instincts are attached to a representation. Formulated positively, primal repression is the nonconscious insertion of the subject's instincts into the world of psychic representation. For this to be possible, the child needs the support of its own mother. She must present the child with the signifiers through which the child can signify its body as different from the coenesthetic experience that it makes of it, and also different from the body of the mother. The mother performs this task, among others, by the mixture of care and distance she shows to the baby by feeding and cuddling, or alternatively by not panicking when the child experiences his autonomy in his acts of crying. It is clear that this behavior of the mother finds its explanation at the level of the mother's conception of herself, her child and their mutual relation. Clearly this conception is not fully conscious. It is for the most part expressed in phantasms. Language (phantasms) is thus the instrument to avoid foreclosure or to achieve 'primal repression.' To be a full subject and not a mentally ill person is understood by De Waelhens as being able to insert oneself into the world of language *and* to comprehend its metaphorical dimension. This thesis of De Waelhens allows him to explain why the talking-cure of psychoanalysis can be theoretically grounded. It is to this problem that the author turns in his last chapter.

III. CRITICAL REMARKS

In this last part of the introduction, we want to present a number of points in which further research is necessary to complement the thesis defended by De Waelhens, and a number of points in which the solutions should be sought in a direction that is different than the one suggested by De Waelhens.

There are two areas in which research is needed beyond the ones presented by De Waelhens. The first area is that pertaining to the relation between the mother and the child. It is the thesis of De Waelhens—and in this he follows Aulagnier(19)—that the mother must be capable of creating during pregnancy an image of the child that she will give birth to. She must also be capable of investing this image with the narcissistic feelings that emerge during pregnancy. The logic of the argument is convincing, but the empirical evidence from which the argument is extracted is open to attack. Indeed, Aulagnier does not present a statistical analysis of the images produced by pregnant mothers about their future child. And about the mothers of psychotic children she presents the *reported memory* of their relation to their future child while pregnant. It is clear that a reported memory need not coincide with the actual experience. Aulagnier does not bridge this possible discrepancy by statistical material. The use of research on the self-conception of pregnant woman done in the United States can serve as empirical confirmation of Aulagnier's thesis. Still the existing studies of which we are aware do not present the empirical confirmation that the theory asks for.(20)

The second area in which more research is needed concerns the cause for foreclosure of the name-of-the-father. In Lacan and De Waelhens, one has the impression that the cause for the foreclosure of the name-of-the-father is to be found in the mother who undermines the word and the law of the father;(21) such a mother may even repress the sexual origin of her child which would remind her of the husband.(22)

De Waelhens seems to be aware that the mother's attitude towards the word of the father cannot be the whole story. Indeed, at the end of chapter V, De Waelhens summarizes his position on the relative role of the mother and the father in the causation of schizophrenia in their off-spring.

In that passage De Waelhens adds that it must be *possible* for the mother to respect the father, his word and the law he represents.(23) He further adds that facts in this area cannot be considered causally related, because the real origin of schizophrenia is to be found at the level of imaginary perception of the structures.

These remarks are interesting. De Waelhens does not further elaborate upon them. They in effect mean that the influence of the name-of-the-father is not solely determined by the mother's attitude, but by what the father himself is and how the child perceives the name-of-the-father in imagination.

The original description was as follows:

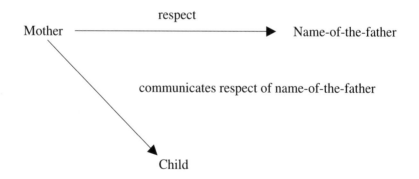

Clearly, the central figure is the mother in this model.

The corrected description is as follows:

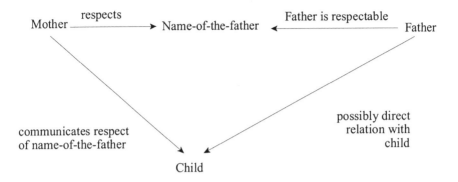

Clearly in this model the father is somebody respectable and thus promotes respect. De Waelhens can easily incorporate this aspect of the new model. However, it is not clear how he can incorporate the possible direct influence of the father on his child.

Research done on the father of judge Schreber (who served for Lacan and De Waelhens as proof for their theory) has shown that the father of Schreber was very present in his family, that his law was very much enforced.

Niederland mentions that Schreber's father proposed in his educational books that all striving for independence should be suppressed. One method was to have a blackboard in the children's room. On this blackboard their misbehavior and violations of rules were written down. Schreber senior suggested that a family session should be held at the end of the month before the blackboard, discussing the merits and faults of the child. Niederland mentions that Schreber senior boasted of the results this method had with his own children.(24)

In another paper, the same researcher mentions the art of renouncing as proposed by Schreber senior. This method consisted in the child sitting in the lap of a lady (nurse, nanny), while this latter eats or drinks what she wants. The child is not allowed to eat or drink until it is time for the regularly scheduled meals. Niederland mentions that Schreber wrote that one nurse had given a piece of a pear to a crying child. After her dismissal, the word spread to the nurses of Leipzig. Afterwards, Schreber senior writes, he had no trouble with nurses.(25)

In Germany of his time, Schreber senior has not been insignificant. He was a physician, an orthopedist, a writer, a lecturer, educator and inventor. In 1958 there were still two million members of the "Schreber Vereine."(26)

Thus Schreber senior was everything but a non-existent figure as De Waelhens refers to him.(27) Thus, we would like to propose that the *real father* has an influence too upon the child's acceptance of the name of the father. We would also like to distinguish in the father two forms of presence towards his child. First, there is the father as he imposes the law. This presence is frustrating (or in psychoanalytic language castrating). Second, there is also the father as a promise or a guide or an invitation (Erikson and Loewald call it the non-castrating presence of the father).(28)

Our new model would thus become:

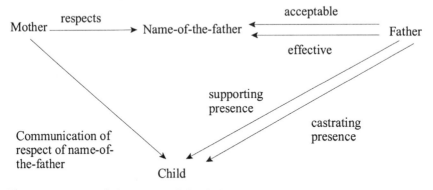

The acceptance of the name-of-the-father is dependent of both the mother's respect for the father and the father's real presence to his child (castrating and/or supporting). The respect of the mother is dependent upon the father's effective but acceptable presence to the mother.

Within the theory of De Waelhens (Lacan) the function of the mother and the father are reduced to the respect for the name-of-the-father. In this theory, the function of the two parents is not clearly delineated. This fits well with one of the three major criticisms of Vergote, who wants to keep the dual union with the mother as much of a primary signifier as the paternal metaphor.(29)

We now want to turn to the areas in which the solution should be sought in a different direction than the one suggested by De Waelhens.

The first area is worked out already by Vergote. The argument of Vergote is made in two steps. The first step is set by discussing the reasons for the psychotic breakdown of Schreber. Contrary to De Waelhens, Vergote argues for a dual level causality for such a break-down. Indeed, according to De Waelhens, judge Schreber was since his childhood a latent schizophrenic. Only an occasion was needed for this latent schizophrenia to erupt. This occasion was provided when Dr. Flechsig took on the role of "A-Father" for judge Schreber, after his ideal ego was wounded because of the repeated stillbirths of his wife. Vergote, on the contrary, wants to elevate the occasion to a *network of real causes*. He mentions three facts: judge Schreber's illness erupted at about the age that his own father had died; at a time too when he saw himself deprived of normal paternity; and at a time finally when he was elevated to presiding Judge to a Court of Appeals, i.e., a function which is very paternal.(30)

The second step set by Vergote is to argue for the organic dimensions in mental illness. He stresses that the psychotic break-down is described even by De Waelhens as a withdrawal of emotional energy. This inevitably leads to the economic point of view related to psychic events. For Freud this was expressed by the dual nature of his concept of instinct (drive), which was neither a purely biological nor a purely psychological concept.

The position of Vergote is reinforced by recent research done on the life of father and son Schreber. Indeed, two of Judge Schreber's three breakdowns are connected with overwork. The first occurred after an exhausting campaign for political office *(Reichstagsabgeordnete* 'candidate for the German parliament'). The second (which is described in the *Memoirs*) occurred at the moment when Judge Schreber had mastered the role of presiding Judge, where the other judges were up to 20 years his senior. Judge Schreber writes that he was very exhausted in both cases. (The third illness is more directly related to the women in his life: his mother had died and his wife had had a stroke). Thus the economic point of view seems relevant.

Furthermore, the Lacan-De Waelhens analysis does not include an analysis of the anal symptoms of Judge Schreber. These anal symptoms are mentioned in Schreber's *Memoirs*, but also in the medical report discovered by Franz Baumeyer (p. 63, b; 66, a). Within the theoretical system of Erikson it is possible to incorporate these symptoms.(31) But it means giving weight to the *intentional transformation* or *fixation* of the *libido*. Erikson relates the anal form of libido to a special bodily relation to oneself and to others. The bodily relation to the self in the anal stage is that of "holding-on." The relation to the others is that of autonomy. Erikson also argues that child-rearing practices at that stage will permanently reinforce a sado-masochistic duality in the libido. (His preferred example is that of the Sioux Indians). Such a theory, however, must (in accord with Vergote but in contrast to De Waelhens) accept that the history of the libido has a dimension that is not grasped by the structural theory of Lacan-De Waelhens.

The second area in which future research might have to look in a direction that is different than the one suggested by De Waelhens is the problem of the real, and thus of the truth. De Waelhens has three theses concerning this problem. The first is that the real can be revealed in degrees which are correlative to the level of constitution of the subject. To say it in a reverse perspective: the earlier the subject is fixated in his development, the less of an access to the real will be available to that subject.(32) The second thesis is that the real is available only because of and only through language. Language creates the distance necessary for the subject to experience the real as other of the self,(33) but language is also that which reveals the real. It reveals it as the other of itself.(34) The third thesis is that the guarantor of the truth is the symbolic Other. This symbolic Other is not a concrete other but a kind of transcendent Other, for whom I must justify my conception of the real. Thus my truth is always precarious, momentary and partial.(35) This leads De

Waelhens to affirm that each part of the perceived real can be debated, but only in order to accept another perception.(36)

It is possible that we do not represent correctly the intentions of the author in interpreting his theses. Then De Waelhens might have an easy task in extracting himself from the difficulties we will now develop. We will however try to develop our interpretation from the texts as they are written.

De Waelhens defends the thesis that the real is only available to the subject if he has successfully gone through the different stages leading to the Oedipus complex. The real is not available except if the subject has been introduced to the paternal metaphor and has enjoyed the imaginary support of a mother figure for the appropriation of the body. The other is therefore seen as the mediator between the subject and the real (first thesis). From such a point of view it easily follows that the truth is precarious (third thesis) or that the real needs a mediator, a revealer (language) (second thesis).

Against such a position one should argue that the paternal metaphor only presents the child with the distance necessary to interrogate *in his own right* the real. This interrogation must occur with *principles available to the subject himself,* (otherwise the subject would not know how to convince a "transcendent Other"). This means that in order for the real to be the real, *not everything is debatable.*

The presence in the child of autonomous principles of judging the real is a necessary condition for the possibility of De Waelhens' theory to be correct. Indeed, De Waelhens interprets the cause of schizophrenia to be the foreclosure of the name-of-the-father. This in turn is produced because of the lack of respect of the mother for the word and the law of the father. But for such a lack of respect to have any effect, the child, the infant, must be capable of "perceiving correctly" the parents.

This capacity to perceive the real as real is only partially destroyed in the schizophrenic, as De Waelhens himself argues. Indeed, the patients do not treat their own hallucinations as they treat their perceptions. For the patients hallucinations are not "false perceptions." Hallucinations are inscribed in another register.(37) Let us return to the two examples of De Waelhens. A girl accuses her physician of burning her face during the night. Another lady hallucinates that she gives birth several times a week. To the first De Waelhens asked: "Did you ever notice the burns on your face in the mirror in the morning?" To the second De Waelhens asked how she could pay for the gynecological services. The replies of the two ladies implied that these were nonsense questions.

We should remember here the comment of Judge Schreber to the report of the medical officer to the Court. The officer had written that Judge Schreber had hallucinations in which he firmly believed and which were sufficient motivation to act. Judge Schreber replied that "yes" he believed firmly in what were called "his hallucinations," but that "no" he did not take them to be motivations to act. He thought that, just as for Jesus Christ, his kingdom (his hallucinatory self) was not of this world.

We therefore want to argue that some awareness of the real is preserved in the schizophrenic and is already present in the infant. The real remains that to which a Kantian causality and his other categories apply.(38) There can be a problem on how a subject is thought, is trained or is helped in accepting this real. But such a problem is totally distinct from the problem of what is the real. This distinction does not seem preserved in the approach of De Waelhens.

NOTES

(1) Sartre, Being and Nothingness, p. 693-94.
(2) Sartre, La Transcendance de l'Ego, p. 84. n. 77.
(3) For an article length debate in which data of child psychology are used extensively, see: W. Ver Eecke: "The look the body and the other."
(4) For an analysis of the positive function of others for the self, see Aristotle's analysis of the question: 'Why does the happy man need friends.?" p. 1169b-1172a.
(5) See p. 213.
(6) In "Wittgenstein on Certainty." May be a better translation for "Vor-Wissen" would be the concept used in the phenomenological tradition: pre-reflective knowledge.
(7) They are: 328, 425, 464, 470, 486, 491-92, 515, 567-79, 594-98, 628-29, 642, 656, 660, 668.
(8) Wittgenstein mentioned this idea already in no. 494.
(9) Franz Baumeyer, "The Schreber Case," p. 63. "President of the Senate" is the literal translation of Schreber's title as president of the Appeals Court to which he was appointed just before his illness.
(10) G. Von Wright: "Wittgenstein on Certainty," p. 57.
(11) In this work A.D.W., p. 90-91. Also M-C and E. Ortigues: Oedipe Africain, p. 57-73 and p. 151ff.
(12) Freud, G.W.X., p. 296-98; S.E. XIV, p. 197-99.
(13) Freud's case study of "little Hans" gives the opportunity to see the production of phallic symbols by a child.
(14) Franz Baumeyer found in Schreber's case records the statement that Schreber claimed that "his penis had been twisted off by an instrument which he called 'a nerve probe'" in "The Schreber case," p. 63.
(15) Laplanche and Pontalis, The Language of Psychoanalysis, under the index word: primal repression. Text in Freud, G.W.X., p. 250; S.E., XIV, p. 148.
(16) For references see Laplanche and Pontalis: The Language of Psychoanalysis, under the appropriate index word.
(17) Freud, G.W., XIV, p. 15; S.E., XIX, p. 239. Lacan, Écrits, 386ff. Laplanche and Pontalis, The Language of Psychoanalysis , under the index word: foreclosure.
(18) Freud, G.W., XIII, p. 11-15; S.E. XVIII, p. 14-17.
(19) Aulagnier: "Remarques sur la structure psychotique."
(20) We are referring to: Lucie Jessner: "On Becoming a Mother" and Lucie Jessner, Edith Weigert and James L. Foy: "The Development of Parental Attitudes during Pregnancy." Other research that is relevant is that done on the families of the schizophrenics. Studies did find peculiar defects in the communication system in families of schizophrenics (peculiar language, overexactness, blurred meanings). (See Freedman

et al.: Comprehensive Textbook of Psychiatry, p. 868, 872, 987). This is, however, but indirect research of the problem. One can indeed postulate that a different imaginary relation towards the future child by the pregnant mother will lead to different behavioral relations after the child is born. But what is required is research about this imaginary relations during pregnancy.

(21) See p. 154-156; 224-25.
(22) A.D.W., p. 154, quoting Aulagnier.
(23) A.D.W., p. 218.
(24) Niederland, "Schreber's Father," p. 497.
(25) Niederland, "The 'Miracled-up' World of Schreber's Childhood," p. 387-88.
(26) Niederland, "Schreber's Father," p. 492.
(27) A.D.W., p. 224.
(28) See the use made of this insight by White in "The Schreber Case Reconsidered... ," p. 219.
(29) Vergote, "Raisons de la déraison," p. 782.
(30) Vergote, "Raisons de la déraison," p. 784.
(31) Erikson, Childhood and Society, p. 72-97, 247-274.
(32) A.D.W., p. 302.
(33) A.D.W., p. 145.
(34) A.D.W., p. 264-65.
(35) A.D.W., p. 237.
(36) A.D.W., p. 264-65.
(37) A.D.W., p. 303.
(38) Within the neo-Kantian terminology of H. Wagner, this is called the secondary constitutive a priori (Philosophie und Reflexion, # 19, p. 160ff.).

Chapter One

THE USEFULNESS OF THE THEORY OF DE WAELHENS/LACAN AS AN EFFECTIVE APPROACH TO SCHIZOPHRENIA, AFTER THE DECADE OF THE BRAIN

Ver Eecke

De Waelhens' presentation of Lacan's theory of schizophrenia is an excellent tool for understanding the subjective position of the schizophrenic. However, two points in De Waelhens' presentation need correcting. First, I will argue against De Waelhens' seemingly exclusive explanation of schizophrenia by psychological causes that there are also genetic and biological causes for it. Second, I will also argue against De Waelhens' pessimistic view about the prospects of psychological treatment of schizophrenics by pointing out that such treatment can sometimes improve dramatically the quality of life of schizophrenics. These two corrections are substantial but are not grounds for rejecting De Waelhens' theory, because the corrections can be introduced from within De Waelhens' own theoretical position. The genetic and biological causal origin of schizophrenia can be incorporated because De Waelhens' theory argues that schizophrenia can result from a deficiency in any corner of the Oedipal triangle (the father, the mother, or the child). All one therefore needs to do in order to incorporate genetic and biological causes in De Waelhens' theory is demonstrate that these factors have a negative influence on the child's development and in particular on the process of Oedipal triangulation. As for De Waelhens' pessimism about the positive outcomes of psychological treatment of schizophrenics, it should be noted that De Waelhens presented a dual psychological theory of schizophrenia without completely unifying these two explanations. I will show that when De Waelhens' dual psychological theory is unified it can give an account of the effectiveness of successful psychoanalytically inspired therapies, thereby making therapeutic practices theoretically better understood. In this chapter I will argue for these two corrections to De Waelhens' theory. My response to the first weakness in De Waelhens' theory is to propose a dual form of causality for schizophrenia (both biological and psychosocial). My response to the second weakness is to make use of recent developments in Lacan and Schreber studies and to argue that schizophrenia is not just a failure in the symbolic system (the functioning of language) but a failure in the imaginary system as well (body image). Treating this double failure—so I will argue—is the key for successful psychotherapy with schizophrenics.

This chapter consists of two parts. As these two parts employ quite different methodologies, each can profitably be read on its own. In the first part, I

will present facts and arguments for the proposition that genetic and/or biological factors do play a role in the development of schizophrenia. I will also
argue that a genetic or biological explanation of schizophrenia does not exclude the thesis that psychosocial factors *also* play a role in *causing* schizophrenia. I am sympathetic to what I consider to be a sophisticated judgment
and review of the different models of causality in schizophrenia presented by
Gottesman. He writes: "I would allocate the lion's share of causes to various
multifactorial-polygenic (oligogenic) models that require a dynamic and epi-
genetic interplay of various moderate-to-high-risk genetic combinations and a
number of 'toxic environmental' factors/experiences.... [T]he greater the genetic loading or liability, the more likely it is that the environmental factors
operating on a particular person to trigger a schizophrenic episode are subtle.
The lower the genetic liability, the more likely it is that the environmental
factors will be obvious. The remaining territory of causes could be allocated
to multifactorial mixed models, to an unknown number of individually rare
single major loci, and to apparent sufficient environmental causes" (Gottesman 1993, 239-40). Such a view of causality in schizophrenia clearly lends
importance to the environmental factors that De Waelhens considers. In the
first part of this chapter, I will also argue that regardless of the genetic-
biological origins of schizophrenia, it remains crucial for forensic psychiatry
and psychology to understand the psychic dimension of severe mental illness.

In the second part of this chapter, I will report on some developments in
Lacan's thought and in Lacan scholarship since the publication of De Waelhens' book on schizophrenia. I will point out how these developments elaborate a suggestion already made by De Waelhens. Furthermore, I will show
how the elaboration of that suggestion is useful for understanding existing
successful therapeutic approaches to schizophrenia. I will finish by pointing
out some important developments in Scheber scholarship—Schreber being the
main case for the theory of De Waelhens and Lacan—that confirm and go
beyond the suggestion made by De Waelhens. This part contains many theoretical reflections on several practical problems encountered in the treatment
of schizophrenics.

PART ONE
A DIALOGUE WITH THE PSYCHIATRIC AND THE
PSYCHOTHERAPEUTIC COMMUNITIES

I. The problem of the cause of schizophrenia

A. Epistemological dualism: its reasonableness

Let us turn to my first claim: i.e., that a biological explanation of schizophrenia does not exclude the thesis that psychosocial factors *also* play a causal role in schizophrenia. The idea of some form of dual explanation for an effect is not new. Historians, for example, distinguish between the background causes and the occasion for the outbreak of World War I. Consider the following statement: "Among more obvious general causes, the alliance system may be singled out. Europe was divided into two camps. Every incident tended to become a test of strength between the two. A given incident, such as German intervention in Morocco, or the assassination of Francis Ferdinand, could not be settled on its own merit, merely by the parties concerned;... Each power felt that it must stand by its allies whatever the specific issue" (Palmer & Colton 1970: 669). Thus any incident could become the occasion for igniting a war.

The medical profession, too, approaches psycho-somatic illnesses by means of a dual causality model. Interestingly, psycho-somatic theorizing has taken the additional step of interrogating the dynamic *interaction* of psychic, social, and biological factors. Consider the following description: "A six-week, structural psychiatric group intervention for postsurgical patients with malignant melanoma reduced psychological distress and enhanced long-term effective coping" (Kaplan & Sadock 1995:1469). "When patients were evaluated for recurrence and survival six years later, those control patients [with no psychiatric therapy]... showed a trend for cancer recurrence and a significantly greater rate of death than patients who did receive such therapy"(Ibid.). In between these two statements the following facts were mentioned: "At six-month follow-up, the patients [with psychiatric therapy]... showed increases in the percentage of large granular lymphocytes and natural killer cells and increased natural killer-cell (NK) cytotoxic activity" (Ibid.). Thus in psycho-somatic medicine, the question is not whether psychological factors aggravate or heal somatic illnesses, but rather how psychological factors *interact* with somatic conditions. One researcher, Besse van der Kolk puts it this way: "It is thus no longer scientifically justifiable to make clear distinctions between psychologic and biologic processes; rather we need to define our understanding of the degree to which genetic, developmental, toxic, and social factors converge to result in certain clinical syndromes!" (Ibid., 1471-2). Pekka Tienari takes the same epistemological position for schizophrenia by claiming that it is time "to move forward to attack the question of *how* genetic and envionmental influences transact to influence development" (Tienari 1992, 155, and also168-9).(1)

Accepting dual causality with reference to schizophrenia would establish an opening for psychosocial theories of schizophrenia without yet determining whether the psychosocial factors are only occasions, or instead contributing or primary causes. There are several approaches to the study of schizophrenia which could lead to the claim that a neurobiological cause is the sole cause of the disease. I will survey them and show that their proponents do not really make such a strong claim; that their evidence would not support it if they did; and that in many cases the evidence argues positively against such a strong claim.(2)

A first candidate for being the exclusive cause of schizophrenia is genetics. An important argument for the genetic hypothesis is a series of twin and family studies. In twin studies, "the concordance rate for schizophrenia [is] between 40 and 50 percent [for monozygotic twins]... [and] is four to five times the concordance rate in dizygotic twins or the rate of occurrence in other first-degree relatives.... [Furthermore, there is] a higher rate of schizophrenia among biological relatives of an adopted-away person who develops schizophrenia than among adoptive, non-biological relatives who rear the patient" (Carpenter & Buchanan 1995: 891). In studies not concentrating on twins but on relatives of schizophrenics, "on average the first-degree relatives of schizophrenic probands had a risk for schizophrenia 5-fold to 10-fold higher than that found in the relatives of the control group" (Ibid., 944). These studies are impressive indicators of the claim that genetics presents a vulnerability. The studies do not prove that genetics is the sole cause of schizophrenia because there is only a 40 to 50 percent concordance for monozygotic twins. If they have the same genetic endowment, why wouldn't both monozygotic twins become schizophrenic rather than one of them? Further doubt about genetics as the sole cause of schizophrenia is raised by the following consideration: "Schizophrenia persists as an illness despite the fact that the majority of its victims do not marry or procreate" (Andreasen, 647).

Several surveys support the thesis that genetics alone cannot explain schizophrenia. P. Portin and Y. Alanen analyze twin studies, adoption studies, environmental studies, and brain imagining findings and write: "In light of the evidence provided by the epidemiological studies of the genetics of schizophrenia, it seems that the present-day conclusion is that genes are neither sufficient nor a necessary cause of schizophrenia, but a risk factor for it. Interaction between genetic factors on the one hand and physical, psychological and psychosocial factors on the other appears to be important in the aetiology of this disease". Kenneth Kendler and Scott Diehl write: "Schizophrenia is clearly a complex disorder in that gene carriers need not manifest the illness (incomplete penetration), affected individuals need not have the gene (environmental forms or phenocopies), diagnostic uncertainties cannot be avoided, and different families may carry different susceptibility genes (genetic heterogeneity)" (1993, 261). Summarizing their findings about family, twin, and adoption studies they write: "These conclusions... are not inconsistent with the hypothesis that in some individuals, schizophrenia is largely environmental in origin, while in others, the disorder is caused largely by genetic factors" (Ibid., 266).

Several studies provide direct proof that genetics is not the sole cause of schizophrenia. A Danish study demonstrates that even though "a history of schizophrenia in a parent or sibling is associated with the highest relative risk of having the disease, the place and season of birth account for many more cases on a population basis" (Mortensen et al. 603). That same study finds that there are also cultural factors that increase the risk of getting schizophrenia. For example, "the risk of schizophrenia was... increased for children born to Danish mothers in countries other than Denmark... or in Greenland" (the relative risk was respectively 3.45 and 3.71 compared with rural areas in Denmark in which the risk was 1.00) (Ibid., 605). Also, "the risk of schizophrenia for persons with unknown fathers and no maternal history of schizophrenia was twice the risk for persons with no parental history of the disorder (the reference group)" (Ibid., 605) . The hypothesis that schizophrenia in the unknown fathers could account for all the difference was discounted. Rather, two cultural hypotheses were proposed: the "difference might be explained by the lower socioeconomic status of the mothers of these offspring or by difficulties in growing up in a family without a father" (Ibid., 606). A Finnish study proves a further point: genetics creates only a vulnerability because genetics alone is not a sufficient condition for getting schizophrenia. The second condition necessary for the appearance of schizophrenia is the psychological characteristics of the adopting family (Tienari 1992, 163).

A second mono-causal hypothesis is based on the idea that schizophrenia could be caused by a virus or by autoantibodies. The hypothesis of viral infection is encouraged by the fact that patients with tertiary neurosyphilis can present schizophrenia-like psychosis and by the fact that schizophrenia is more likely to occur in people born in late winter or early spring. The hypothesis of an autoimmune disorder is supported by the fact that systemic lupus erythematosus, an autoimmune disorder, causes a schizophrenia-like illness (Wyatt & al., 1995: 927, 939, 940). The studies in support of this hypothesis do not make strong claims. They report that "schizophrenics may have an increase in one subset, CD5 + B-lymphocytes, which might be consistent with a state of autoimmune activation." The authors add: "Those findings are preliminary" (Ibid., 940). On viral infection, they write that "no investigators have conclusively proved the existence of a transmissible, infectious particle in schizophrenia" (Ibid. 940).

A third monocausal explanation can be found in the thesis that schizophrenia results from structural and/or functional brain abnormalities. The first candidate for such an explanation is the dopamine hypothesis. While there are solid arguments for some form of dopamine hypothesis, there is no satisfactory formulation of the hypothesis yet. Positive arguments suggest that the dopamine hypothesis is compatible with the claim that psychosocial factors also have a function in schizophrenia. A primary argument in favor of some form of dopamine hypothesis is the fact that medications which block dopamine type 2 (D2) receptors diminish schizophrenic symptoms and that dopamine agonists worsen them (Wyatt & al., 928, 929). A second argument in favor of the dopamine hypothesis is the discovery of a strong correlation between the effectiveness of a medication for alleviating schizophrenic symptoms and an increase in brain 3-MT, a major metabolite of dopamine. Presumably, effective antipsychotic medications block dopamine receptors and thereby increase the production of dopamine metabolites (Ibid., 929). Similarly, another metabolite of dopamine, HVA, was found in higher levels in the plasma of schizophrenics than in that of control groups, and antipsychotic medications seem to reduce those levels in patients that improve.

As of now the facts about dopamine have been integrated into two alternative hypotheses, neither of which is completely satisfactory. The neurodegeneration hypothesis includes the presence of a degenerative process—either of a neurological order or of the dopamine system—which then, under repeated stress, creates a neurological degeneration. Although this hypothesis can explain the fact that patients who originally have mainly positive symptoms later often develop negative symptoms, as well as the fact that stress factors play a role in the origin of schizophrenia, this hypothesis cannot easily account for the age of onset and the season of birth in schizophrenia. Also, the hypothesis lacks solid evidence of neurological degeneration (Ibid., 932). The alternative hypothesis, the neurodevelopmental hypothesis, suggests the occurrence of an early insult or trauma (possibly in utero or at birth) which in turn causes deficiencies in the maturation of brain structures. The illness becomes manifest when the cognitive possibilities of the mature brain need to become operative. This hypothesis can explain the age of onset of schizophrenia but not so easily the course of the illness, which manifests important negative symptoms within the first few years of the illness. This hypothesis also cannot explain child psychosis (Ibid., 932).

*

Let me turn now to the positive arguments for the possibility of co-causality of the dopamine hypothesis and some other cause. With reference to antipsychotic medications, clinicians have observed "that at times those medications work minimally or not at all.... [and] many patients continue to have cognitive deficits and negative symptoms despite having had marked response to treatment" (Ibid., 929). Also, "amphetamine-induced psychoses... lack a number of features commonly associated with schizophrenia, such as the presence of negative symptoms, the specific kinds of auditory hallucinations that occur in schizophrenia, and a chronic course" (Ibid.). Finally, animal research leads scientists to conclude that "stress-induced dopamine release could play a role in psychotic decompensation" (Ibid., 931). In such a version of the dopamine hypothesis, stress is conceptualized as a causal factor in which dopamine is the mechanism. The theory of schizophrenia presented by the authors reviewed implies that persons with a prepsychotic structure are vulnerable to the consequences of stress. This claim goes hand in hand with claims made by Lacanian-inspired therapists that prepsychotic persons are prone to create repeated self-inflicted stress (Calligaris 1991, 26-7, 51-53, 61-66, 73; Moyaert, 270-1).

The second and third candidates for the thesis that schizophrenia is the result of structural or functional abnormalities in the brain are norepinephrine and serotonin, respectively. Richard Wyatt and his colleagues conclude their survey of studies about norepinephrine by writing that those studies "do not contain sufficient evidence to suggest that a defect in the norepinephrine system is primary to the development of schizophrenia... however, the studies implicate an alteration in norepinephrine metabolism or response to stress in at least some schizophrenic patients. The noradrenergic system not only is integral to the body's response to stress but is also involved in modulating the dopaminergic system" (Wyatt et al., 933). About seratonin the same authors write: "Studies of patients with schizophrenia have failed to convincingly demonstrate that abnormalities in 5-HT [serotonin] neurotransmission mediate the expression of symptoms. Nevertheless, some data are suggestive" (Ibid., 935). The authors then summarize the most promising data. Thus, regarding the second and third candidates for an exclusive biological explanation for schizophrenia, it is important to remember that serotonergic neurotransmission is not believed to be a causal explanation of schizophrenia and that the possible function of the noradrenergic system is explicitly linked to the body's response to stress. One can therefore conclude that consideration of the function of these two systems in the brain includes psychological stress as a possible factor in schizophrenia.

A fourth candidate for the thesis that schizophrenia is the result of structural or functional abnormalities in the brain is glutamate. Phencyclidine (PCP, angel dust), which blocks one glutamate receptor (NMDA), produces a schizophrenia-like syndrome including "hallucinations, thought disorder, negative symptoms, and cognitive deficits" (Ibid., 935). Postmortem studies found an increased number of NMDA receptors in the putamen (Ibid., 936). The thinking is that "neurochemical abnormalities could result in the altered functioning of th[os]e neural circuits.... Damage (presumably prenatal) to the hippocampus and amygdala could result in increased glutamatergic activity in neurons projecting from those structures... to the nucleus accumbens. Consequently, dopaminergic transmission in the nucleus accumbens altered. When the person becomes stressed, dopamine turnover increases in response to stress; the result is an acute psychotic state from excess dopamine transmission" (Ibid., 936-7). Thus (again as part of the neurobiological explanation), appeal is made to the psychological factor of stress.

There are many other chemical agents which have been used to prove a biological basis for schizophrenia. I will examine one example from each of the four categories into which these agents are classified. About biogenic amines, studies show that agents (for example, physostigmine, DFP) which increase cholinergic activity increase negative symptoms, whereas anticholinergic agents improve negative symptoms. About endogenous psychotogenes, studies show that schizophrenics have a relatively low incidence of allergies as well as decreased responses to histamine. As for neuropeptides, investigators have noticed high levels of CCK (creatinine phosphokinase) in the limbic system of schizophrenics. Among the miscellaneous agents, studies noticed that gluten-poor diets decrease psychiatric admissions (as was the case during World War II) or correlate with improvements in psychiatric patients (Wyatt et al., 938). These facts are not used by Wyatt and his colleagues in the most recent *Comprehensive Textbook of Psychiatry* to present a theory of schizophrenia that excludes psychosocial factors.

Finally, there is the curious fact that the sex of the person makes a difference in the age of onset and possibly in the course and outcome of schizophrenia (Karno & Norquist, 908; Wyatt et al., 941). Commenting on the sex factor, Wyatt and his coauthors write that "some estrogens appear to have antipsychotic effects, and estrogens are known antagonists of D2 receptors. Conversely, dopamine regulates the biological effects of estrogens by decreasing the binding of that hormone to its receptors"(Wyatt et al., 941). However, the authors continue by noting that "there are numerous social demands that could interact with an already altered substrate to increase the risk of developing schizophrenia" (Wyatt et al., 941).

In the *Comprehensive Textbook of Psychiatry*, Wyatt and his coauthors conclude their overview article, "Schizophrenia: Neurochemical, Viral, and Immunological studies," as follows: "The overwhelming beneficial effect of antipsychotic medications in schizophrenia cannot be overlooked. Regardless of the original cause of the illness, the neurochemical outcome appears to be a perturbation of the dopamine neurotransmitter system" (Ibid.). However, when analyzing the evidence in support of the dopamine system, these same authors explicitly discuss stress as one of the variables. A critical evaluation of the argument for a neurobiological basis of schizophrenia needs to distinguish between, on the one hand, non-interpreted facts and, on the other hand, theoretical explanations of the facts. The survey articles that summarize the theories which attempt to understand the neurobiological basis of schizophrenia do not exclude psychosocial factors. Rather, psychosocial factors are included in the reasoning of how the major neurobiological factor (dopamine system) works. With reference to non-interpreted facts such as the beneficial influence of a gluten-poor diet for schizophrenia or the low incidence of allergies among schizophrenics, most researchers do not consider that evidence as proof that schizophrenia is caused solely by a gluten diet or by being highly sensitive to histamine. Rather, these non-interpreted facts indicate that there is a neurobiological factor at work in schizophrenia. But such a claim can co-exist with claims derived from other observations in both the neurobiological and the psychosocial domains. An example of a claim in the neurobiological domain is the one that "regardless of the original cause of the illness, the neu-rochemical outcome appears to be a perturbation of the dopamine neurotrans-mitter system" (Wyatt et al., 941). An example of a claim which allows for the role of the psychosocial domain is: "None of the high-genetic-risk pro-bands raised in healthy adoptive families had psychosis" (McGlashan & Hoffman 1995, 963). Thus, theoretically, the neurobiological explanation for schizophrenia does not exclude the possibility of psychosocial factors. In some neurobiological explanations, positive appeal is made to these other factors.

B. Epistemological dualism: positive arguments

I now want to survey some of the claims that argue in favor of the thesis that psychosocial factors are in some way involved in schizophrenia. I want to distinguish between the arguments concerning a first episode and those con-cerning recurrence.

1. General conditions and/or first episode occurrence

a/ Statistical studies
The most important study proving that both genetic and psychosocial factors play an important role in the creation of schizophrenia and psychosis is the Finnish adoption study directed by Tienari. That study reports that children of biological mothers with functional psychosis (index adoptees)(3), given up for adoption, are more often psychiatrically disturbed (16 out of 155, or 10.3%) than the children of control parents given up for adoption (2 out of 184, or 1.1%) (Tienari 1992, 161-62). That same study also reports that no adopted child of a functionally psychotic biological mother acquired a functional psy-chosis if the adoptive family was "psychologically healthy" (Ibid., 163).(4, 5) Of the index adoptees, 58 ended up having "healthy" adoptive families, 38 "neurotic" adoptive families, and 47 "severely disturbed" ones. The ratios of functional psychoses for the index adoptees were: 0 out of 58 in healthy adop-tive families; 4 out of 39 in neurotic adoptive families; and 9 out of 47 in se-verely disturbed adoptive families. The same ratio of functional psychoses for control adoptees were: 0 out of 74 in healthy adoptive families; 0 out of 58 in neurotic adoptive families; and 2 out of 44 in severely disturbed adoptive families.

Let me review the research methods of Tienari and his collaborators. In

Finland, they collected a sample consisting of all women who were hospitalized for schizophrenia and paranoid psychosis on January 1, 1960, augmented by all those admitted with a similar diagnosis through 1979. Of the 19,447 schizophrenic women, 264 had given up 291 children for adoption. Of the 291 children given up for adoption, 94 were excluded from the study because the children were adopted by a relative, adopted abroad, or adopted after age four. During field work, 18 more children were excluded.(6) Twenty adoptive families refused to be interviewed and four more biological mothers were not considered schizophrenic after the personal interviews were completed.(7) The index offspring of the final sample was thus 155 (Tienari 1992, 159-161).

The biological index mothers were selected because they were hospitalized for schizophrenia and paranoid psychosis. The hospital diagnosis was evaluated by two experienced psychiatrists using Finland's traditional diagnostic criteria (corresponds closely to G. Langfeldt's criteria). Two other researchers applied the Research Diagnostic Criteria (RDC) to the hospital records of the mothers. When possible, the biological parents were given a psychiatric interview, a 10-card Rorschach, and the Minnesota Multiphasic Personality Inventory (MMPI) (Ibid., 160). Tienari explicitly notes that the criteria for including biological index mothers did not exactly correspond to the *Diagnostic and Statistical Manual of the Mental Disorders III* (DSM III) criteria for schizophrenia. Mothers who had schizophrenia, paranoid psychosis, and atypical psychoses were included. Mothers who had affective psychoses or schizotypal or non-psychotic disorders were not included (Ibid., 161).

The control group was created by adopted-away children of biologic parents who had not been hospitalized because of psychosis. The control group was pair-wise matched case-by-case, using seven criteria, by persons outside the research department (Wahlberg et al. 1997, 357).

The index and control children and their adoptive families were randomly numbered so that the four psychiatrists studying them were not aware whether they studied an index or a control family. The study took two days for each family (14-16 hours). The family relations were studied by family and couple interviews, Consensus Rorschach, and the Interpersonal Perception Method. Furthermore, adoptive parents and children were individually interviewed, individual Rorschachs were given after the Consensus Rorschach and MMPI was given to adoptive children. For a sub-sample of adoptees, additional tests were given: the Continuous Performance Test (CPT), Span of Attention Test (SOA), and Smooth Pursuit Eye Movement Test (SPEM) (Tienari 1992, 160-161). The interviews and tests were tape-recorded which makes possible blind ratings, reliability checks, and reclassifications by other investigators in a later phase of the investigation.

Additional studies, such as a 33-item family rating scale (OPAS), were done on the adoptive families. Four of the thirty three items in the rating scale had poor reliability. Using the twelve items with the highest reliability (between .068 and 0.84) there was a significant correlation between these independent ratings of the adoptive families and the individual diagnoses of the offspring (from personal interviews) (Ibid., 164). The highest correlation was for empathy, disrupted communication, and conflict between parents and offspring (Ibid., 164-66).

Tienari writes that the results of the Finnish adoption study "are consistent with the hypothesis that healthy rearing families have possibly protected the vulnerable child" (Ibid., 162-3). Another study also indicates that a happy family experience protects children from serious mental illness, including schizophrenia (Rutter 1985).

In twin studies, the higher concordance rate for schizophrenia among monozygotic twins as opposed to dizygotic twins is normally understood to be proof of a genetic factor in the illness. However, there is also a higher concordance among dizygotic twins than among ordinary siblings. Because dizygotic twins and ordinary siblings are genetically equally different, the genetic factor cannot be used to explain the higher concordance among dizygotic twins. A possible explanation is that dizygotic twins can be assumed to share, on the average, more similar environments than ordinary twins share. Furthermore, the fact that affected concordant monozygotic twins were not more severely psychotic than affected discordant twins is not what a pure genetic theory of schizophrenia would predict under a pure genetic model of schizophrenia.

Some statistical studies show a correlation between schizophrenia and some psychological factors, while not quite pointing to a causal mechanism. A number of indicators of vulnerability to schizophrenia were retrospectively derived from the study of childhood records for 24 schizophrenia cases out of a sample of 1000 boys. The indicators were: "unusual anxiety [but not inappropriate aggression or anger], lack of historicity [sense of self continuing over time and goal-directed behavior], difficulty in interpersonal relationships and lack of competency" (Hartmann et al. 1984; Teixeira 13). One retrospective study of the developmental histories of schizophrenics found that "affection was less characteristic of the rearing of the schizophrenics; there was a high frequency of negative parental attitudes such as rejection, overprotection, and domination" (Schofield & Balian, 1959; discussed in Gottesman 1991; Teixeira 12). Also, a Finnish study shows a significant increase in risk for later schizophrenia among children of unwanted pregnancies as compared with children of wanted or mistimed pregnancies (Myhrman et al. 1996). That study deserves description.

Myhrman and his group took the birth cohort of 1966 in Northern Finland. Ninety-six percent of all births in the area were covered. Data collection started during prenatal visits at the sixth or seventh month of pregnancy, at which time midwives administered a standard questionnaire. A questionnaire item determined the mother's attitude towards the pregnancy during the first visit to the perinatal clinic. It asked whether the pregnancy had come at a good time, whether later would have been better, or whether the pregnancy was not wanted at all (Ibid., 637). No questions were asked about the possible reasons for the unwantedness of the pregnancy, making it impossible for the study to distinguish between purely psychological reasons for not wanting the pregnancy or psychological reasons that were founded on physical or biological grounds (e.g., mother's illness or pregnancy complications) (Ibid., 638). The sample consisted of the 11,017 children still alive at age 16 and living in Finland. In a second stage of the research, all hospital records with diagnoses for psychosis, personality disorder, or addiction were gathered from the Finnish Hospital Discharge Register up to 1993. DSM-III-R criteria were used to identify cases of schizophrenia and other psychoses. Two senior researchers then rechecked the cases against the clinical records (Ibid., 637).

There were 76 cases of schizophrenia (sample size:11,017, representing a risk of 0.7% for the age range of 16 to 28 years). The attitude towards pregnancy was known for 10,769 (98%) of the total sample and included all schizophrenics. The results are presented in Table 1.(8)

Table 1.

	Percent of Total Population	Total Number of Pregnancies	Number of Schizophrenics	Percent Schizophrenic
Wanted Pregnancies	62 %	6,858	44	0.6 %
Mistimed but wanted Pregnancies	24 %	2,628	13	0.5 %
Unwanted Pregnancies	11 %	1,238	19	1.5 %
Unknown	2 %	248	0	0.0 %
Total Population	100 %	11,017	76	0.7 %

The cumulative incidence of schizophrenia for children from unwanted pregnancies is thus more than twice as high than it is for children from wanted pregnancies, including wanted, but mistimed, ones. The children from unwanted pregnancies were then compared according to sociodemographic and perinatal criteria to the pooled group of children from mistimed, but wanted, pregnancies and from wanted pregnancies. The cumulative incidence of schizophrenia was greater in each of the criteria: maternal age (below 20; 20-34; above 35); mother's parity; father's social class; marital status; mother's frame of mind (normal; depressed); birth weight (below or above 2000g); gestational age (below or above 37 weeks); perinatal brain damage and admission to childrens' hospital during first 28 days of life (Myhrman et al., 639).

Let us now turn to studies that look for a causal psychological mechanism for schizophrenia. Summarizing the research from the UCLA Family Project as presented by D. Miklowitz and LymanWynne and their respective co-authors, Michael Teixeira writes: "At 15-year follow-up, 28% of the adoles-

48

cents had developed broad schizophrenia spectrum disorders, defined by DSM-III criteria, for schizophrenia, schizotypal, paranoid, or borderline personality disorder. Those adolescents whose parents were initially high in TAT-communication deviance were far more likely to have developed schizophrenia spectrum disorders at 15 year follow-up than adolescents whose parents had intermediate or low levels of baseline TAT-CD [communication deviance]. Families with high communication deviance *and* negative affective style were the most likely to have children who subsequently developed schizophrenia spectrum disorders" (Teixeira, 2). The studies are not able to assert whether communication deviance is a risk factor for severe mental disorders in general or for schizophrenia in particular (Teixeira, 3). A Finnish study by Eeva Aronen can be used to confirm the line of thinking present in communication deviance studies. Indeed, Aronen's study found that providing family counseling to families with children from birth until five years of age "once every 4-6 weeks, i.e., about 10 times a year" (Aronen, 158), diminished the number of psychiatrically classified children once they became 10-11 years old. Furthermore, at 10-11 years of age, 5 children in the control group of 19 and 1 in the counseling group of 21 were classified as "definitely mentally disturbed children" (Ibid., 160). A similar result is obtained under similar conditions when the children reach 14-15 years of age (Aronen, et al.).

A study by Denise Fort directly challenges the above communication deviance argument regarding schizophrenia. I will first present the findings and the author's conclusions. I will then argue that Fort both brings a welcome new theoretical perspective, but draws the wrong conclusion.

In Fort's experiment, the subjects were normal sons and their parents and schizophrenic sons and their parents. The subjects were alternatively speakers and listeners. As speakers they were asked to make a tape recording describing the meanings of four proverbs. They were told that the listeners would be asked to select the correct proverbs from a list provided to them on the basis of the tape they were about to make. The listeners were given three tapes. Parents were given the tape of their son and sons were given the tape of their parents. (Both groups were told whose tape they were given). Parents also received a tape of two other sons, a normal and a schizophrenic one. Sons also received two more tapes of parents. One tape was from parents with a schizophrenic son and the other tape was from parents with a normal son. One tape was obviously specific to each son and his parents. The other tapes were standardized and no one received the same proverbs twice.

The following results were obtained: In proverb identification, parents perform less well after listening to a schizophrenic son and sons perform less well after listening to parents of a schizophrenic son. These results confirm Fort's main hypothesis between schizophrenics and their parents: there is communication deviance in *both directions*. However, schizophrenic sons were more impaired when responding to parents of schizophrenics than normal sons were and *schizophrenic sons responding to parents of a normal son improved so much that there was no difference between their performance and that of normal sons* (Fort, 87). These results confirm the defective communication of parents of schizophrenics.

In proverb interpretation, parents were clearly impaired after listening to a schizophrenic son. Sons listening to parents of schizophrenics were impaired but the result was not statistically significant (Ibid., 89).

In a third measure, Fort scores the attentional distractors present in the interpretation of the chosen proverb by the listeners. Both parents of normal sons and of schizophrenic sons had a significantly higher proportion of attentional distractors after listening to a schizophrenic son than after listening to a normal one (Ibid., 89-90). However, both normal and schizophrenic sons did not have a significantly higher score for attentional distractors after listening to parents of a schizophrenic son than after listening to parents of a normal son (Ibid., 90). "Yet another finding, and a completely unexpected one, was that parents of normals had a significantly higher proportion of attentional distractors present in their speech than the parents of schizophrenics irrespective of the type of speaker to whom they were responding" (Ibid., 90).

Fort concludes correctly that in some cases (in proverb identification and also, but to a lesser degree, in proverb interpretation) there is both an impairing influence of the schizophrenic son on adults and an impairing influence by parents of schizophrenics on children. Fort's research demonstrates that the claim of unidirectional impairment (parents impair children) is incomplete. The complete story is that there can be reciprocal impairment of parent and child (also Wachs 1983).

Fort also draws another conclusion based on the results of her attentional distractors measurements: "The validity of theories espousing an etiological relationship between deviant parental communication and deviant communication in the schizophrenic is seriously challenged. The disruptive impact of the schizophrenic son was strongly confirmed in the present study while at the same time no evidence was found in support of the view that parents of schizophrenics have a disorganizing influence on the communications of sons" (Ibid., 90). Based on her findings, this conclusion is in error. In her experiment, Fort is not measuring communications deviance as it occurs in the daily lives of families—which is the intended measurement of the theories she attacks. Rather, Fort is measuring attention distractors—which is different from communications deviance—and she is measuring it in an experimental setting which has no life-damaging consequences—which is what communications deviance measures. Fort is thus comparing apples and oranges. My claim is confirmed by the second result of Fort's attentional distractors measurements: "parents of normals had a significantly higher proportion of attentional distractors present in their speech than the parents of schizophrenics irrespective of the type of speaker to whom they were responding" (Ibid., 90). Parents of normal sons can be assumed to be non-pathogenic. Still, they score significantly higher in attentional distractors. One must suppose that in this case "attentional distractors" measure something innocent or something desirable such as the capability to reflect or to be humorous. As I do not have the raw material of her experiment, I cannot pinpoint what it measures. Thus, Fort is incorrect in claiming that her experiment disproves the communication deviance factor in schizophrenia.

Notwithstanding her one wrong conclusion, Fort makes some sensible suggestions at the end of her article. Researchers, according to Fort, should not ignore the impact of schizophrenics on their families; clinicians should not blame parents because it compounds the defeat of parents; education, social support, and management techniques should be given [to schizophrenics and their families] (Ibid., 95). I agree with these recommendations. The rest of my essay will show that also other positive steps can be undertaken in order to heal schizophrenics if one accepts my dual epistemological theory, which I will now further argue.

Severity of thought disorder in unmedicated schizophrenics has been recognized as a criterion of the severity of schizophrenia (Cancro 1969a and 1969b) and of predicted outcome (Harrow & Marengo). Teixeira reports that a study by M. Shenton and coauthors, using the Holzman-Johnston Thought Disorder Index (TDI) "found that only 10% of normal control subjects had TDI scores greater than 9 compared with 75% of the relatives and/or families of the manic patients, 50% of the relatives or families of the schizophrenic patients, and 100% of the relatives or families of the schizoaffective manic patients, [who] had TDI scores above 9. Moreover, patients with high TDI scores tended to have relatives with high TDI scores, and the quality of thought disorder found in patients was mirrored in attenuated form in their first-degree relatives" (Teixeira, 4; Shenton et al.).

The Yale group of investigators headed by Theodore Lidz observed that the families of schizophrenics were always markedly disturbed and distorting. The investigators related parental conflict, egocentricity, and communication disturbance to egocentricity, thought disorder, and difficulties with boundaries or differentiation between self and other, subjective and objective, and between thoughts and feelings (Teixeira, 5; Lidz 1978; Lidz & Fleck 1985).

The connection between psychological family trauma and schizophrenia is supported by the observed increase of incidence of schizophrenia in families in which the husband died during pregnancy (Huttunen & Niskanen 1978) and in which a grandparent died within about two years of birth (Walsh 1978; Teixeira, 5).(9)

Bertram Karon has identified a pathogenesis intrafamilial risk variable, using a TAT-based scoring system. The pathogenesis variable is defined as "the degree to which the parent, when there is a potential conflict between the needs of the child and the needs of the parent, unconsciously acts in terms of the parent's needs without regard to the potentially conflicting needs of the child" (Karon & Widener, 47, 52-3). And statistically, 35% of scorable stories told by parents of non-schizophrenics were scored as pathogenic whereas 75%

of scorable stories told by parents of schizophrenics scored as pathogenic (Teixeira, 6; Karon & Widener, 47, 53; Meyer & Karon; Mitchell 1968). Also a mother's pathogenesis score correlated with the degree of illness in adult male schizophrenic patients (Nichols 1970). Finally, pathogenesis scores of therapists treating schizophrenic patients correlate negatively with patient improvement in the first half-year of treatment (VandenBos & Karon 1971; Teixeira, 6).

One further argument in support of family trauma as a risk factor for schizophrenia can be derived from one of many facts known about schizophrenia and sexuality. The rates for schizophrenia are higher for unmarried than for married persons, except for widowed persons (Karno & Norquist, 908; Jablensky et al.). This statistic tends to confirm what is known clinically: schizophrenics have difficulties both in building intimate relationships and in assuming their sexuality. More troubling is the following statistic: lifetime prevalence of rape for two samples of women, one with schizophrenia and the other with bipolar disorder, appeared to be 23% compared with an estimated 7%-8% prevalence in the general population. (Darves-Bornoz et al.; Teixeira, 7). Experienced psychiatrists point out that women in mental hospitals are defenseless victims of an unsavory environment: male mental patients and unscrupulous staff. Furthermore, they are locked up in their wards and when they complain they are discredited. More obviously related to the family of birth and indicating a possible contributing factor for severe mental illness are the following observations: "36% of a sample of women with schizophrenia and 28% of a sample of women with bipolar disorder were victims of sexual abuse in childhood. For these two patient groups, intrafamilial sexual abuse accounted for approximately 50% of total sexual abuse for both clinical groups compared with 30% incidence... in the general population" (Ibid.)

Finally, the idea that schizophrenia is at least sometimes also related to intrafamilial factors is compatible with the claim that there are also biological factors at work. This view is proposed by Grotstein when he claims that even if one were to accept the idea that the deficit in the schizophrenic is "ultimately attributable to a precocious abruption of the mother's physical and psychical presence from the infant—[as experienced by the infant]" it could still be the case that the cause could be "hereditary, congenital, perinatal, and continuing developmental reinterpretive elaborations [in the child itself]" (Grotstein, 43). According to this view, the immediate cause of schizophrenia would be a psychological one [the mother-child relation], but the psychological cause in turn could be explained by any number of other factors (biological, environmental (e.g., painful operations in infancy without anesthesia, as will be discussed later) or psychological (e.g., a father concealing from the daughter that the deceased mother was Jewish and also committing incest with the daughter, as mentioned later)) which have little or nothing to do with the mother.

The compatibility of psychic and biologic causality is made more plausible by the research of neuroscientists who demonstrate that psychic interaction is required to keep or even to promote the growth of certain neural connections. For instance, "At about 6 to 9 months, the *multimodal* (including vocalization, body movement, smiling, and eye contact) high intensity positive affect exchanges that occur between mother and infant, specifically stimulate growth of *dopaminergic* circuits. Dopaminergic circuits subserve the infant's ability to sustain the high levels of sympathetic nervous system arousal that can be considered as the neural basis of emotional excitement and joy" (Pally 1998, 573). Research by G. Dawson and K. Fisher indicates that stimulation of the mother not only activates certain brain circuits, but that the mental health of the mother is a factor in determining what part of the brain is activated. Their research is summarized as follows: "Non-depressed mothers who play the game 'peekaboo,' elicit *left* frontal activity in the infant. When non-depressed mothers leave their babies it elicits *right* frontal activation and signs of distress in the infant. By contrast, when depressed mothers play the game 'peekaboo,' their infants exhibit *equal* activation of both hemispheres. When infants are separated from depressed mothers they exhibit a relative rise in *left* frontal activity and fewer signs of distress. They hypothesize that alteration of the 'normal' asymmetric pattern for affect may underlie the clinical finding of avoidant attachment and may predispose these children to later clinical pathology" (Pally, 574). The latest research in neuroscience would thus tend to give psychic states a causal role in both activation and formation of brain circuits. That in turn might suggest a biological mechanism for intrafamilial psychic factors contributing to mental illness.

A number of studies also point to cultural risk factors for schizophrenia. First, the incidence of schizophrenia in Swedish conscripts was 1.65 times higher for conscripts coming from the city as it was for those from rural areas (Lewis et al. 1992). Second, according to a World Health Organization Study with two and five year follow-up, individuals living in developing countries can expect better outcomes for both schizophrenia and affective disorders (Sartorius et al, 1986, 1996). Third, the *China Daily* of June 23, 1988 reported a survey by China's Public Health Ministry that the incidence of schizophrenia had increased from 7 per thousand in the 1970s to 10.4 in the late 1980s—an increase of almost 50% incidence in just over a decade, one characterized by many cultural changes (Teixeira. 9).

Finally, using reviews of studies about psycho-social stress in life events for schizophrenia and bipolar affective disorder, Teixeira concludes that "overall, despite inconsistencies and methodological difficulties in both retrospective and prospective life events studies, an independent role is suggested for stressful events in the onset and course of schizophrenia as well as bipolar disorders" (Bebbington et al. 1995; Teixeira, 13). While Teixeira considered that there was empirical evidence for the connection between stressful events and the onset of schizophrenia, there Lacan's theory, first, presents a theoretical reason for that connection and, second, specifies the kind of stress that can provoke a schizophrenic breakdown (Lacan 1977, 217; De Waelhens 1978, 133ff; Fink 1997, 106).(10)

b/ Causal arguments

Statistical evidence points to a possible causal relation between psychosocial factors and severe mental illness. However, statistical correlations do not by themselves constitute a causal theory nor do they reveal a causal mechanism. Progress can be made in formulating a causal psychosocial mechanism for severe psychopathology by incorporating the following theoretical claims backed by many scientific studies.

First, Teixeira cites a long list of prospective and longitudinal studies that "demonstrate that children with attachment insecurity ('anxious/avoidant,' 'anxious/resistant,' 'disorganized/disoriented'), compared with secure attachment, are less competent in relations with adults and peers, are more fearful of strangers, prone to behavioral problems including anxiety and social withdrawal, show over-dependence on teachers, and have lower self-confidence and ego resilience" (Teixeira, 10).

Second, both mother and father can contribute, although in different ways, to an insecure mother-child attachment. Again, Teixeira quotes a long list of studies which reveal a number of maternal characteristics connected with secure attachment as opposed to insecure attachment. Those maternal characteristics are: "sensitive/attuned responsivity, emotional availability, and warm, positive, affectionate, comforting, and accepting attitude (Teixeira, 11). One study even reports that the mothers' representations of attachment during her pregnancy predicted the organization of infant-mother attachment found at one year of age (Fonagy et al. 1991; Teixeira, 12). One NIMH study analyzed the attachment in two- and three-year-olds of mothers with bipolar, major and minor unipolar depressive, and non-psychiatric control mothers. The study concludes that "mothers' expressed emotions (positive versus negative) predicted patterns of attachment, *independent of diagnosis* (Radke-Yarrow et al. 1985; Teixeira, 11). That same study shows that the absence of the father increased the risk of insecure mother-child attachment for mothers with major affective disorder (Radke-Yarrow et al. 1985; Teixeira, 11).

Third, a follow-up analysis on the Finnish adoption study analyzed the gene-environment interaction leading to some unexpected results for causal thinking about schizophrenia. A subsample of 154 adoptive families (58 index and 96 comparison ones) were chosen from among the original sample with the stipulation that at least one adoptive parent be available and the adoptee not be older than 36 years. The reasoning was that older adoptees would have older adoptive parents whose communication habits would possibly differ from the communication experienced during rearing (Wahlberg et al., 357). The putative adoptee vulnerability was measured by the Rorschach Index of Primitive Thought which was independently scored by two research psychologists with an intraclass correlation coefficient of 0.91 (Ibid.). "Environmental risk was measured by using frequency of communication deviance as a continuous variable, scored independently from Rorschach assessments of the adoptive parents" (Ibid., 355).

The study found that the putative risk for schizophrenia as measured by the Index of Primitive Thought was almost evenly distributed among the high risk adoptees and the control adoptees. Among the high-risk adoptees (children of a schizophrenic mother), 41.4% showed no evidence of the putative schizophrenic genotype. At the same time, "56.2% of the comparison adoptees showed at least some evidence of this rather extreme form of schizophrenic thought disorder" (Ibid., 358). As for the communication deviance scores, there is a wide range of scores in the rearing parents of both the index and comparison adoptees, with the scores of index adoptive parents slightly higher. This support for the hypothesis that offspring influence rearing parents was not statistically significant (Ibid., 359-60).

When analyzing the *interaction* of high genetic risk (being the biologic child of a schizophrenic mother) with the communication deviance of the adoptive parents, the study made two interesting findings. First, increasing communication deviance on the part of the adoptive parents steeply increases the positive scores on the Index of Primitive Thought for high genetic risk adoptees (the scores go from 40% to 90%), but does not at all increase the positive scores for control adoptees (these scores stay in the range between 40% and 60%, and actually decrease with increased scores in communication deviance of adoptive parents) (Ibid., 358-9). Second, when exposed to adoptive parents with low levels of communication deviance, the high genetic risk adoptees "have a lower proportion of positive scores than do the comparison adoptees" (Ibid., 359, 361). Thus, high genetic risk adoptees are hurt more by a defective environment than comparison adoptees, but they end up with a better measure on the Index of Primitive Thought than the comparison adoptees when both kind of adoptees have a "protective" environment. It is as if the comparison adoptees develop more according to their own scheme whereas high genetic risk adoptees either drown or flourish depending on the environment, here defined as high or low communications deviance in adoptive parents.

Fourth, several cases have been reported in which the attachment to the mother became difficult or disturbed because of external factors. In one case, the external factor was the decision by the medical staff to operate on the child without anesthesia and without telling the mother. "Not having been told [that it was normal for an infant, operated on without anesthesia, to reject the mother—as an expression of anger], the mother felt that either the child or she was defective; she withdrew defensively and told her child for many years, 'You could never love me'" (Karon & Widener, 49). To read this case as an illustration that the mother should not have blamed the child is to miss the point of the case. What mother is divine enough to be able to overcome such a sudden rejection? The mother did not reject the child. The child rejected the mother because of the actions of the medical staff. In not telling the mother about their procedure, they deprived the mother of information useful to her in overcoming the baby's rejection. Still, the tragic consequence in this case is that a failing attachment to the mother is harmful. In another case, the external factor was the allergic reaction of the baby to the formula after being weaned at the age of four weeks. The mother misinterpreted the crying of the child as misbehavior and only a couple of months later told the pediatrician about the child's difficulties. In the meantime, the child "was no longer placid and happy as he had originally been; he was anxious-looking, whined a lot, and was very irritable when he came in contact with any human being" (Pao, 148-9). In still another case, an 18-month-old girl, Margie, developed a treatment-resistant rash. "Her pediatrician hospitalized her and had her restrained spread-eagle under heat lamps. He forbade her mother's visits, after which Margie would cry inconsolably. After three weeks she came home a changed person: now very clingy, sucking her thumb, and no longer a chatterbox" (Silver 1992b, 117). One can sympathize with the no-win situation of the pediatrician, but the psychiatrist-psychoanalyst treating the adult Margie interprets the hospital experience as possibly crystallizing her "preverbal sense of having a tenuous place in the family" (Silver 1992b, 126) and thus contributing to her severe mental illness.

To the objection that I have accepted studies about both affective disorders and schizophrenia to prove the presence of a psychosocial dimension in schizophrenia, I like to refer to a number of studies (Taylor 1992; Farmer et al. 1987, 1988; McGuffin et al. 1982) that argue against a clear "dichotomy between schizophrenia and affective disorders, and... instead suggest a continuum model of psychopathology" (Teixeira, 2). In conclusion, the different studies about attachment thus present a causal mechanism for theories which emphasize a failure in the dyadic relation of mother and child as a sign of vulnerability to schizophrenia (e.g., the theories of Pao, Bion, Winnicott, and Aulagnier—authors belonging to quite different traditions). The causal mechanism—failure in the proper attachment to the maternal figure—can be triggered by many factors, some of which have nothing to do with the mother (painful operation, separation from the family for medical reasons, or undiagnosed allergic reactions, for example).

2. Arguments concerning the recurrence and course of schizophrenia

Let me now turn to the arguments about the recurrence and course of schizophrenia. Emil Kraepelin created the idea of a natural course of schizophrenia. His suggestion was that schizophrenia was an incurable disease with a progressively worsening symptomatology. Kraepelin used the claim of progressive worsening as the criterion for distinguishing schizophrenia from paranoia, which he considered an illness with a stable plateau. De Waelhens points out the many epistemological difficulties with Kraepelin's idea of a natural course of schizophrenia: ad hoc hypothesis, inability to distinguish schizophrenia from paranoia, prognosis confirming diagnosis, and empirical falsity:(11) De Waelhens then uses these epistemological difficulties discovered in Kraepelin's position to organize the chapter in which he surveys some of the great psychiatrists' theories about schizophrenia. The idea of schizophrenia having an unavoidable natural and progressive worsening course limits—if true—the potential of any treatment that aims at healing. If schizophrenia has, on the contrary, a psychosocial component, the diagnosis of schizophrenia as having a negative natural course deprives the patient of a potent, if not crucial, psychological factor in healing: hope. I therefore seek to support with empirical studies De Waelhens' epistemological claim that schizophrenia cannot be understood as an illness with a necessary negative natural outcome.

In his review of long-term follow-up studies of schizophrenia, Thomas McGlashan concludes that schizophrenia "does not appear to be progressively dementing as originally described. On the average, functional deterioration appears to plateau and even to relent somewhat after 5-10 years of manifest illness" (McGlashan 1988, 538). About psychotherapy, he writes that it has "positive potential if applied in a supportive, rehabilitative mode in the context of *stable and unlimited* continuity of care" (Ibid.). Thus McGlashan's review flatly contradicts the idea of an unavoidable, natural, and progressively worsening course. The alternative view sometimes associated with McGlashan's studies (Ibid.; Dingman & McGlashan) that the psychodynamic aspect of schizophrenia is minimal and that psychoanalytic therapy is mostly dangerous and not helpful is rejected as invalid in a methodological analysis of McGlashan's work (Bechgaard, 1990, 1994). Thus Birgitte Bechgaard writes: "The basic framework of design and method of this study has been arranged in a way corresponding to a course of illness study in the field of biological psychiatry and... within this framework it is not possible to draw any conclusions of the outcome of psychotherapy for patients" (Ibid. 1994, 9). Bechgaard reaches this conclusion about McGlashan's Chestnut Lodge study after evaluating four requirements for studies on outcome of treatment: 1. Baseline-data. In the Chestnut Lodge study there are no before-study data since the so-called baseline-data "are a mixture of data from before and during treatment" (Ibid., 7). 2. Outcome-variables should be in accordance with the standard of treatment. "Even though the work of scoring the dynamic outcome standards has been performed [in the Chestnut Lodge study], they will never appear in any statements of results" (Ibid., 8). 3. The baseline-variables should be in accordance with the outcome-variables. However, "the baseline-variables [in the Chestnut Lodge study were]... determined by their known or anticipated ability to predict courses of illness"(Ibid., 8). 4. Treatment-variables must be included. "The Chestnut Lodge study does not include a single variable dealing with treatment" (Ibid., 8). Bechgaard thus concludes: "Methodologically the study does not fulfill any of the demands for a study of outcome of treatment" (Ibid., 18).

In her review essay, Courtenay Harding stresses that the Vermont Longitudinal Study analyzed "the poorest prognostic group, yet more than two-thirds of these subjects, all of whom met DSM-III criteria for schizophrenia, went on to demonstrate significant improvement and even recovery" (Harding, 658). Results from ten world studies indicate "significant improvements and a wide heterogeneity of outcome for patients with schizophrenia" (Ibid.). The author points to several studies that suggest that psychosocial factors have an influence upon negative symptoms such as, among others, "apathy based in loss of hope," resistance to "giving up patienthood," or "guilt over past dysfunction" (Ibid., 661). The author points to a crucial psychosocial factor that contributes to amelioration: the "'low turning point'—the point at which [the patients] decided to reorganize their lives towards recovery" (Ibid., 665). This leads the author to search for ways in which an active role for the patient can be discovered. She finds this active role in what she calls "rehabilitation crises," i.e., attempts "to go back to school, to ask someone for a date, leave the parental home, or get a job" after stabilization of the psychotic breakdown (Ibid., 666). Several studies allow her to support the claim that "10-20 years after acute hospitalization, 60% of patients will be socially recovered as well as part-time employed" (Ibid., 667). Programs aiming at social integration and vocational rehabilitation can help such recovery as is clear from a comparison between a Maine group of patients without rehabilitation and a Vermont group with a rehabilitation program. About 30 years after the initial study, the patients of the Vermont group were 40% employed, which was statistically significantly more than the employment rates of the Maine group. This difference in employment rates between the two groups is all the more significant because "both cohorts were equivalent in work histories" (Ibid., 670). The idea of improved social integration seems to explain why it is that family psychoeducational programs lead to a dramatic reduction in relapse rate, or why the Program for Assertive Community Treatment in Madison, Wisconsin "demonstrated considerable effectiveness" (Ibid., 668). Furthermore, the author points out that the patients in the Vermont study pointed to hope as an important factor in their improvement or recovery by saying: "Someone believed in me, someone who told me I might have a chance to recover, and my own persistence" (Ibid., 672). This might explain why several long-term follow-up studies argue "that the best treatment for schizophrenic patients is 'therapists relating constantly and actively to the healthy aspects of the psychotic patient'" (Ibid., 673, quoting M. Bleuler 1978, 297).

Finally, many studies show that high Expressed Emotion (EE) of a key relative leads to earlier relapses, pointing again to a psychic dimension in schizophrenia (Straube & Oades, 409). In the original studies by Brown and associates, EE measures three variables in persons: critical comments, hostility, and overinvolvement. Several studies demonstrated a correlation between relapse rate and EE in environment when the schizophrenic patient returned after hospitalization. Surveying the studies of EE, P. McKenna writes: "the

58

studies of EE provide compelling evidence that psychological factors contribute to exacerbations of schizophrenia" (233). McKenna adds, however: "It may not be EE itself which promotes relapse, but rather some unknown factor; this might be some specific aspect of family life, or it might merely be generally high level of stress and strain" (Ibid.).

II. The meaning of what schizophrenics say and do

With reference to the question of the meaning of the behavior and speech of schizophrenics, two completely separate problems need to be addressed. The first is the question of whether the patients are to be considered legally competent. The second question concerns understanding the patients.

A. *Forensic psychiatry and psychology*

The question of legal competence occurs sometimes with suspicious patients, particularly paranoiacs or paranoid schizophrenics. The question of legal competence occurs typically with regard to two problems: inheritance and permission for surgical interventions. Let us concentrate upon the legal problem of judging whether a person is legally competent to make a will. It may occur that a person is suspicious of her children. The person may even be paranoid about them and might decide to exclude them from her will. The generally accepted criterion for whether a person has the legal right to make a decision, even if it is an unwise one, is determining whether the person is free enough to decide. A neurobiological approach to paranoid schizophrenia might claim that, ultimately, dopamine is a partial cause of schizophrenia. Even if that were true, it is difficult to envision that courts would currently accept a neurobiological test of dopamine or of metabolites of dopamine as decisive for the question of legal competence, regardless of the psychic capabilities of the person. Rather, the courts want to decide the question of legal competence on the basis of the person's psychic freedom.

Informed by Lacan's theory of mental illness and phenomenology, De Waelhens, presents a clear criterion for deciding the legal competence of paranoiacs and paranoid schizophrenics (See Chapter Six: *Concluding Reflections on the Problem of Psychosis. Psychoanalytic and Existential Criteria of Psychosis*). According to phenomenology, truth is a claim that implies the idea that it is intersubjectively provable. One particular person might not be convinced or might not be persuadable, but the one making a legitimate claim to truth is convinced that others can be shown the validity of his or her truth claim. It is possible that one person might be too suspicious of her children, or that another one might contemplate too big a punishment for the suspicions she has. These two options are some of the possible options of a free person, even if they are, from some points of view, regrettable options. If, however, these persons with regrettable options are willing to provide proofs to convince others of their point of view, then they differ radically from others (paranoiacs) who do not see the need for any proof of a truth claim. Such paranoid persons have structurally lost the possibility of freedom because they are totally enthralled by their fixed imaginary ideas. Not seeing the need for any proof to other persons (to a third, as De Waelhens calls it) means that the patient has lost the sense that evidence needs to be evaluated, not just imagined. This criterion should permit the distinction between regrettable decisions that are legally permissible and decisions that legally make no sense (Godderis, 11ff).

B. The meaning

On the problem of discerning the meaning of the behavior and speech of schizophrenics I agree generally with the authors of the following statement which appeared in a survey article on schizophrenia and psychodynamic theories: "Generally, psychoanalytic theories of schizophrenia, especially those with a descriptive-homeostatic [sic] perspective, continue to inform the clinical eye and help the clinicians understand the patients they encounter" (McGlashan & Hoffman, 962). The authors define descriptive-homeostatic theories as those that stay close to the manifest phenomenology. They oppose them to etiological-facilitative theories—such as that of Melanie Klein. These latter theories try to explain the psychic genesis of schizophrenia. Lacan's theory is certainly psychogenetic. Meanwhile, De Waelhens is a phenomenologist and he combines both approaches: he stays close to the phenomena but uses Lacan's structural theory in order to choose and clarify the meaning of five structural characteristics of schizophrenia.

De Waelhens chooses the following phenomena as characteristics of schizophrenia (Chapter Six of this book): 1. The body image is consciously or unconsciously experienced as fragmented in some way; 2. There are many difficulties with language in which there seems to be a deficiency in the relation between signifier and signified, leading to neologisms, as De Waelhens notes, but also leading to incomprehensibility, mutism, and stilted language (Lipton & Cancro, 974-5); 3. These patients desire to beget themselves with their own mother, which in turn indicates that the Oedipal triangle is deeply disturbed; 4. These patients often have difficulty situating themselves with reference to sexual difference; 5. There is often a confusion between death and birth leading to all kinds of difficulties with reference to the experience of time. De Waelhens then makes use of Lacan's structural theory to select those language difficulties as the most profound difficulties of the schizophrenic. The practice of using the interpretation of proverbs as a test for schizophrenia is intuitively using the same idea. De Waelhens then proceeds to clarify the four other characteristics of schizophrenia as consequences of the language difficulties. Post-Lacanian therapists then use Lacan's theory of schizophrenia to design therapies for schizophrenics.

III. Treatment of schizophrenia

In this section, I want to discuss some problems regarding the treatment of schizophrenics. The presentation of Lacan's theory of schizophrenia by De Waelhens implies that schizophrenia can not be fully undone. Some contemporary followers of Lacan still hold that view and believe that therapy consists of providing substitute anchors for the search for meaning by the schizophrenic (Fink 1997, 82). Other followers of Lacan believe that more can be done, provided that one works explicitly with the language deficiency of the patient. To the best of my knowledge, all believe that listening to the schizophrenic is helpful and necessary. This claim clarifies why it is that schizophrenics with explicit delusions have a better future than those without them: they communicate.

A. Limits to the use of medication

As I did in my discussion of causality, here too I wish to engage in a dialogue with the psychiatric and the therapeutic community. In the medical and the psychiatric community, the belief in the efficacy of medication is strong. I want to report on some facts that should introduce some reservation regarding what medication can achieve.

First, nearly one third of schizophrenics remain psychotic even after an adequate trial of medication (Schulz, 991).

Second, the negative symptoms of schizophrenia, such as lack of affect, anhedonia, and a-motivation are not so amenable to treatment by medication. Antipsychotic medication may result in either improvement or worsening of these symptoms (Ibid., 989).

Third, it is well known that there is a risk for a considerable range of side effects, from mild discomfort to permanent movement disorders (Ibid., 994), or to the sometimes lethal neuroleptic malignant syndrome (this occurred in 0.1% to 1% of patients treated with neuroleptics or, according to some reports, in even more cases) (Ibid., 995).

Fourth, medication of schizophrenics aims at symptom reduction. It sometimes neglects to consider the quality of life of the treated patients (Awad). Two consequences have been linked to an exclusively pharmacological approach to schizophrenics. Notwithstanding the serious side-effects, the belief in the efficacy of medication led to a practice in the US in which the patients were given much higher doses than in other countries (Schultz, 990); they were even given more medication than was needed to keep the symptoms under control (Ibid., 991). This defective approach now seems to be counteracted by the search for the lowest effective dose (Ibid., 990). The other consequence of failing to pay attention to the quality of life of the schizophrenic patient is the high rate of suicide (10% to 17 %), mainly attributed to their experiencing the hopelessness of their illness (Ibid., 989).

Fifth, schizophrenics treated by medication or by electro-convulsive therapy (ECTC) complain about their subjective experience (Awad, 743; Kafka, 25-6). In developing my philosophical argument, I will rely upon Lauren Slater (1998), who describes herself as a severely depressed person, with self-mutilation and suicide attempts leading to five hospitalizations. Her diagnosis was obsessive-compulsive disorder. The example of a severely depressed person works to make a philosophical point about schizophrenics as well, if one accepts either that there is a continuum among the severe mental illness forms or if one accepts that, in general, medication is not aimed at fine-tuning the subjective experience. Through medication, Slater improved so much that she obtained a doctorate, became a director of a clinic, published a book, and married—all within 10 years. Slater complains that after a year of using medication, she "cracked up" and had to increase her dosage without ever feeling as good as before. She also complains about her loss of libido, which leads her to worry that without her sexuality, she is not in touch with her deeper self. She complains that she cannot get anything creative done. She feels pain at having lost her identity in which her illness was a crucial component. A common sense remark might be that one cannot have it both ways: being well and maintaining one's identity as a sufferer of a severe mental illness. Such a remark misses, however, something essential. The now improved person feels a need to make connections between her psychic view of every detail of the world when she was ill and her psychic view of the world in her improved situation. Making these connections is a form of psychic work in which all newly acquired crucial concepts, by which one organizes one's psychic world, must be changed and connected with the old ones. Whereas before she had to develop the courage to accept help and develop self-worth by trusting others, now she needs to care for others and develop self-worth by being self-reliant. Furthermore she needs to tell herself a story of how these two strategies are the strategies of one person. Making these psychic connections is psycho-therapeutic work.

B. Dualist approach to treatment of severe mental illness

Given the less-than-total satisfaction provided by a pharmacological approach, it might be useful to report on some forms of a dual approach to the treatment of severely mentally ill persons.

A prime example of a dualist approach to the treatment of severe mental illness can be found in Felix and Loretta Loeb's proposal for the treatment of manic attacks. They hypothesize that "the primary and underlying... disturbance in manic-depressive illness is a biologically determined increase in phallic sexual instinctual drive... This biological determinant is counteracted by lithium therapy" (Loeb & Loeb, 891; also 892). The authors point to the fact that the same dose of lithium taken by the patient does not produce a stable level of blood lithium. To maintain a stable therapeutic level of blood lithium, the lithium actually taken by the patient must be increased, sometimes dramatically, during manic episodes (Ibid., 881-83). The authors draw attention to another series of facts they observe: the manic phase was preceded by socially unacceptable aggressive sexual advances; those in turn were preceded by marked verbal sexual expressions. Loeb and Loeb postulate that the increase in phallic sexual thoughts was mainly unconscious. Psychoanalysis or psychoanalytically-inspired therapy deals with the unconscious. With the help of such treatment, the patients were able to become aware of their sexual thoughts and could even diagnose themselves as having an undue increase in sexual thoughts and fantasies. The patients so treated were now able to inform their therapists about such phantasy changes in their lives. The therapist was then able to order a blood test and, when necessary, he could increase the lithium dose. That dose could then be diminished if a blood test, ordered after the patient reported diminished sexual phantasies, showed that the blood lithium level was rising above the therapeutic range (Ibid., 883). For Loeb and Loeb, psychoanalytic treatment allows the patients to be accurate predictors of a coming manic attack. The prediction can then be verified by checking the blood lithium level. Loeb and Loeb thus provide an example in which one approach (the biological one) is considered to be dealing with causes, whereas the second approach (the psychological one) is given an important function in that it creates a warning mechanism. The second approach is encouraged and applauded because it provides an additional diagnostic tool.

We find another example of a dualist approach in Antoine Vergote's recommendation of treatment of depression. In this example, the relation between the two approaches (the biological and psychological) are the reverse of our first example. Vergote argues that the cause of at least some depressions is psychological and that treatment consists in doing psychic (psychoanalytic) work. Comparing depressives with melancholics, Vergote observes that melancholics accuse themselves whereas depressives complain about themselves. Since Freud, excessive self-accusation is attributed to a defect in the superego. Complaining about oneself, according to Vergote, indicates a defect in some psychic entity other than the super-ego. To complain is to express the feeling that one is less than what one wants to be. What one wants to be is defined by one's ideal-ego or ego-ideal. Vergote then concludes that the depressive whose main symptom is complaint about oneself has been unable to mourn the loss of an impossible ideal. His recommendation is to help such patients to mourn this loss. However, in order to be able to do the necessary psychic work, patients must satisfy two conditions. They must be able to concentrate and pay attention. They also must have some narcissistic investment in their own psychic products (dreams, memories, feelings) in order to have the energy and interest to work with them. Medication might be mandated in order to provide enough sleep for the patient to be able to do the necessary psychic work demanded by psychoanalysis. Vergote explicitly criticizes those who would refuse to make use of medication as an instrument for psychoanalysis (Vergote 1993, 124-5). That same dualist approach of assigning medication a subsidiary role for the psychotherapeutic treatment of schizophrenics is argued for by an experienced therapist of schizophrenics (Karon & VandenBos, 209-10, 436; Karon 1999, 5). Willy Apollon, the principal psychoanalytic therapist in a Montréal clinic for the treatment of severely mentally ill people, formulates the subsidiary role of medication as follows: medication should be used to prevent the illness from damaging the organic body (e.g., by preventing sleep) (Apollon, 95).

However, some might argue that a successful dualist approach to other mental illnesses is not a valid argument for a dualist approach in the treatment of schizophrenia. One strong argument against a dualist approach and in favor of a pure medical treatment of schizophrenics is the study conducted by P. May and associates at the Camarillo State Hospital in California. Five methods of treatment were compared. "1/ psychotherapy without medication, 2/ psychotherapy with medication, 3/ medication alone, 4/ ECT [Electro-Convulsive Therapy], 5/ milieu therapy (Karon & VandenBos, 376). The study concludes "that medication was the treatment of choice, that improvement on their criteria up to day of discharge showed an advantage to patients receiving medication over those not receiving medication, and that all other differences were trivial" (Ibid., 377).

In their publication, Bertram Karon and Gary VandenBos argue that the California study is not a proper comparison of good medication with good psychotherapy for the following reasons: First, each therapist had to perform all five methods of therapy, including psychotherapy, even if they did not believe in the efficacy of a particular therapy. Belief in efficacy of psychotherapy by the therapist is essential for the success of the therapy whereas that is not so much the case for biological treatments (Ibid., 376). Second, most of the supervisors of psychotherapy described as experienced therapists had little experience with schizophrenics—and some had none beyond their residency (Ibid., 376-7). Third, improvement was measured on the day of discharge, not at preset time intervals. Discharge meant interruption of psychotherapy, which is known to be anxiety producing. Furthermore, whereas follow-up psychotherapy was not routinely provided, medication was maintained after discharge (Ibid., 377, 463). Fourth, the study notes greater insight into their own psychology in patients who had received psychotherapy, but the study dismissed this observation as having minimal importance (Ibid., 377). Fifth, in a four year follow-up study, less than half the sample is included, so that differences in mean hospitalization of 200 versus 600 days become statistically insignificant even though the study started with a large sample of 288 patients (Ibid., 376-78). Sixth, the study eliminated the least and the most ill schizophrenics and kept the middle third. This led to a sample that was mainly lower middle class white, with above-average intelligence. This is not representative of the known population of schizophrenics (Ibid., 376).

One can thus conclude that the California study ends up with statistical anomalies (reason 5 and 6); dismisses a benefit of psychotherapy (reason 4); makes a comparison at a time known to be negatively impacting patients receiving psychotherapy (reason 3); and compares standard medication with psychotherapy done by inexperienced therapists, some of whom lacked motivation, in turn supervised by therapists who in some cases had no prior experience with schizophrenics. The comparison made in the California study was therefore in actuality a comparison between good medication and bad psychotherapy (reason 1 and 2).

The project of Bertram Karon and associates at Michigan State University developed a research design that was free of the major defects of the California project. First, in the Michigan State project there were no reluctant therapists. The two supervisors were therapists, experienced in the treatment of schizophrenic patients, knowledgeable of the subculture of the patient group (inner-city of Detroit), and known to their colleagues to be clinically efficient (Ibid., 396). They trained and closely supervised their trainees. The study also differentiated the impact of the experienced therapists from that of the trainees (Ibid., 448, 455). Second, the Michigan State project included a test (the Feldman-Drasgow Visual-Verbal Test (VVT)) specifically designed to measure schizophrenic thought disorder, which according to Eugen Bleuler is the primary symptom of schizophrenia. The Michigan State project used the VVT both as a major index of imputed deep-structure improvement of the patient and as a predictor of long term condition as defined by other measures such as hospitalization days (Ibid., 431). Third, improvement was measured at preset times (six, twelve, and twenty months) not at the time of discharge which is presumed to be biased against measuring improvement caused by psychotherapy.

The findings of the Michigan study after 6 months were that in comparing the hospital group, called Group C (treated with medication), with the combined psychotherapy groups, psychotherapy contributed little (Ibid., 425). The psychotherapy groups were called Group A and B (Group A was treated psychoanalytically without medication; Group B used ego-analytic therapy with adjunctive medication progressively decreased; both groups used about 70 sessions over a 20-month period) (Ibid., 391, 399), However, if the psychotherapy group is subdivided between experienced and inexperienced therapists, then the patients of the experienced therapists did significantly better than the patients of both the inexperienced therapists and those of the hospital group treated by medication (Ibid., 425), as measured by both thought disorder tests and days of hospitalization (Ibid., 423, 425).

The findings after a twelve month period were: the pooled psychotherapy patients were hospitalized less, exhibited less thought disorder (VVT), and were judged to be functioning healthier (Clinical Status Interviews (CSI)) than the hospital patients treated by mediation. Looking specifically at the patients treated by inexperienced psychotherapists (trainees), the authors of the Michigan State project noted imbalanced improvement of these patients as a group. Indeed, patients of Group A's trainees had longer hospitalization and much improvement in thought disorder; whereas patients of Group B's trainees had much less hospitalization but their thought disorder remained similar to that of the control Group C treated by medication (Ibid., 428).

The findings at 20 months were that the patients of the psychotherapy group had 31% to 51% less hospitalization days, and had less thought disorder than the control group using medication only, and the patients of the experienced therapists had improved more than the patients of the trainees (Ibid., 430-3).

Karon and VandenBos confirm their conclusion that psychotherapy is more helpful than medication alone by quoting the results of a Wisconsin and a Massachusetts studies that reported more hospital days for patients on medication than for psychotherapy patients the year after termination of therapy (Ibid., 440). They reconcile the apparent contradiction between their findings and those of the California study as follows: "The California project has little to say about the effectiveness of psychotherapy, with or without medication. It does answer the question: 'Is psychotherapy provided by inappropriately trained but medically qualified residents of much use?' The answer is 'no.' The Michigan State Project asks the question: 'Is psychotherapy provided by appropriately trained professionals (psychiatrists *and* psychologists) useful?' The answer is 'yes.' The fact that the trainees in the Michigan State Psychotherapy Project really did learn to do psychotherapy effectively, as evidenced by the actual progress of their patients during the project, clearly indicates that psychotherapy with schizophrenic patients is a skill that is both teachable and learnable" (Ibid., 460).

Having argued that medication alone is not the treatment that produces the best results for schizophrenics, do the authors of the Michigan State Project advocate psychoanalysis or psychotherapy only? They do not. Rather, they provide arguments for a dualist approach by writing: "It would be a mistake to cite our position as objecting to all uses of medication. Medication is better than no treatment at all, and it may even be better than treatment provided by inappropriately trained and unmotivated therapists. As an adjunct to psycho-therapy, it may be helpful to some psychotherapists in the beginning of treat-ment, or as an adjunct to weather a particularly upsetting crisis" (Ibid., 436; also 209-10).

One statistical result in the Michigan study not pointed out by its authors is that the VVT statistic (measuring thought disorder) indicated a greater effi-ciency of the approach by Supervisor A (psychoanalytic therapy) than the approach by Supervisor B (ego-analytic approach) after six, twelve, and twenty months of treatment and in the two year follow-up study (Ibid., 423, 427, 430, 438).

Notwithstanding the success in the Michigan study of psychoanalytic-oriented psychotherapy in Group A, many remain skeptical about psycho-analysis because it is difficult to create valid empirical studies of psychoana-lytic treatments. S. Fisher and R. Greenberg write in their book *Freud Scien-tifically Reappraised*: "In fact, there is no study of psychoanalysis as a treat-ment that cannot be dismissed because of seriously contaminated or compro-mised data" (Fisher & Greenberg, 201). However, Rolf Sandell and coauthors of the *Stockholm Outcome of Psychoanalysis and Psychotherapy Project*, write: "The requirements of this [Fisher and Greenberg's] gold standard is that patients be randomized to treatment groups, either comparative therapy groups or to a therapy group and a non-treated group, and that the ensuing treatment should be strictly controlled and monitored, so that one may be sure that the treatment in question was really delivered the way it was intended to. This in turn requires a thorough standardizing training of therapists in adhering closely to a therapy manual.

Unfortunately, it will never be possible for an outcome study on psycho-analysis to be conducted so as to satisfy these requirements. This is not only a matter of the fact that psychoanalysis could not ever be manualized without ceasing to be psychoanalysis or that psychoanalysts in general could never be expected to accept being manualized, in any case. It is also a matter of the fact that such degrees of control are inevitably impossible for such long dura-tions as are typical of psychoanalysis. Not only would we have to control the practices of analysts for years; if we had a non-treatment control group, we would also have to control the adherence of the non-treated patients to this condition. Or, if we had a comparative treatment group, we would have to enforce that the patients stayed in their respective therapies during the whole trial, let alone that we would have had to enforce their compliance with the randomized treatment assignments to begin with. That is not a realistic plan. Patients actively seek out their therapies, interrupt those they are not satisfied with and seek other, new ones. So, as some scholars argue... self-selection is part and parcel of psychotherapy and psychoanalysis, not only to begin with but all the way through, that is, in choosing to stay in treatment, to go to to-day's session, day after day" (Sandell et al. 1998, 1-2).

If one cannot provide empirical proofs that meet the "gold standard" of empirical research for the usefulness of psychoanalysis, it does not mean, however, that there are no empirical proofs at all. Studies by Sidney Blatt and his co-workers provide evidence, first, of the therapeutic efficacy of psychodynamic treatment of severely disturbed young adults and, second, of the greater efficacy of psychoanalysis than brief pharmacological and psychological outpatient treatment for the subgroup of introjective pathologies.

First, in *Therapeutic Change. An Object Relations Perspective,* Sidney Blatt and Richard Ford studied 90 patients at the Austen Riggs Center, Stockbridge, Massachusetts at admission and some 15 months later, having received during the interim period "psychodynamically informed treatment, including psychotherapy at least four times a week" (Blatt & Ford 1994, 197). According to a *Diagnostic and Statistical Manual of the Mental Disorders III*R (DSM-IIIR) diagnostic, "approximately 20% (n=29) of the sample were considered psychotic, 70% (n=50) as severe personality disorders (including borderline and narcissitic disorders), and 10% (n=11) as primarily depressed" (Ibid., 32). Blatt and Ford conclude that "evidence for significant progress in these patients was observed in systematic and reliable ratings made on clinical records... and on variables independently derived from several different types of psychological assessment procedures (i.e., Rorschach, Thematic Apperception Test [TAT], human figure drawings, and Wechsler intelligence tests)" (Ibid., 197; 149-57 for the statistics). The progress took different forms for two different categories of patients—anaclytic versus introjective ones (Ibid., 201).(12)

Second, in an article "The destructiveness of perfectionism," Blatt, surveying a wealth of research distinguishes between anaclytic forms of psychopathology (nonparanoid schizophrenia, borderline personality disorder, infantile—or dependent—character disorder, anaclitic depression, and hysterical disorders) and introjective pathologies (paranoid schizophrenia, overideational—or guilt-ridden, self-critical—borderline personality disorder, paranoid and schizoid personality disorders, obsessive-compulsive disorders, introjective—guilt-ridden—depression, and phallic narcissism) (Blatt 1995, 1013). The anaclytic disorders involve an exaggerated concern with interpersonal relations and use "avoidant defenses ranging from withdrawal and denial to repression to cope with psychological conflict and stress" (Ibid.). The introjective pathologies are overly concerned with autonomy and control and "primarily use counteractive defenses (e.g., projection, rationalization, intellectualization, doing and undoing, reaction formation, and overcompensation) (Ibid.). Blatt argues that a dialectic between those two strategies is necessary in human development. This remark hints at a profound reason for dealing with the psychic side of the treatment of mentally ill people: developmental balancing acts that were not performed or were performed badly need to be allowed to occur for the first time or need to be allowed to be redone and corrected.

Blatt further reports that introjective pathologies do not respond as well to brief pharmacological and psychological outpatient treatment for depression [the specific illness upon which the article is focused, though its arguments are generalizable] as other patients do. They do better than other patients in long-term, intensive, psychodynamically-oriented therapy. Furthermore, "a reanalysis of the data of the Menninger Psychotherapy Project (MPRP) indicated that introjective outpatients made significant greater therapeutic gain in intensive (5 times weekly) psychoanalysis than in long-term (twice weekly) psychotherapy.... Their therapeutic gain in psychoanalysis was also significantly greater than was that of anaclitic patients who were also treated with psychoanalysis" (Ibid., 1015).

Thus, at least in some cases, there is indication that psychoanalysis is more effective than other forms of psychotherapy. This is confirmed in one of the reports from the Stockholm Outcome of Psychotherapy and Psychoanalysis Project. In that report the authors study the "capacity to prevent the return of symptoms after treatment" rather than "the sheer reduction of acute symptoms" (Blomberg, 1). The report documents the finding that both "psychotherapy and psychoanalysis produce highly stable effects" (Ibid., summary), but "patients who—for whatever reason—did not undergo the recommended *psychoanalysis* were significantly worse off than patients who did not undergo the recommended psychotherapy" (Ibid., 3). Stability means that the patient did not fail a Clinically Significant Outcome (CSO) once he had achieved the CSO in one of three measurements at twelve-month intervals (Ibid., 1). A clinically significant outcome was defined as scoring "better on the SCL-90, Social Adjustment Scale, and the Sense of Coherence Scale, than the worst or lowest scoring 10% in a norm group consisting... of psychology students and a random community sample" (Ibid., 2). If psychoanalysis is in some cases the treatment of choice, then the therapeutic community can benefit from a dialogue with updated psychoanalytic theory.

PART TWO
DEVELOPMENTS IN LACAN AND SCHREBER SCHOLARSHIP
SINCE THE PUBLICATION OF *SCHIZOPHRENIA* BY DE WAELHENS

I. Development in Lacan Scholarship

I now want to propose De Waelhens' theory of Lacan as a theory that is close to empirical phenomena and can serve as a means by which to understand different successful approaches to the treatment of schizophrenics.

A. From an apparent inconsistency in De Waelhens' presentation to a fuller understanding of schizophrenia

One can find in De Waelhens two versions of a psychological causal explanation of schizophrenia. The first causal explanation is derived from a student of Lacan: Piera Aulagnier (Chapter Three, Section III: Failure of Primal Repression). De Waelhens presents his explanation as a variant of the theory of the schizophrenogenic mother, even though he then adds that schizophrenia must be understood as the result of a *failure in a triangular structure in which each of the three angles (maternal figure, paternal figure, and child) can play a role* (Chapter Five, Section VII: The Relative Role of the Mother and Father in Psychosis).(13) Compared with some Anglo-American variants, the causal explanation by De Waelhens has two unique features: it concentrates upon the *desire* (as opposed to the behavior) of the mother and it begins its analysis of the influence of the maternal figure as early as the *period of pregnancy* (not just from the period after birth).(14)

The study points to a number of observations of mothers of normal children: the narcissistic investment of the pregnant woman in her pregnancy, the transformation of that narcissistic involvement into expectation of a child by the work of the imagination, the unconscious acceptance of the sexual origin of the child, the rather quick overcoming of the post-partum depression, the delicate balance of feeling of oneness-in-otherness with the baby, and the support provided by the mother for the child to learn to live with its body, even a body that causes displeasure or pain (hunger, teething).(15)

Mothers of schizophrenic children tend, according to Aulagnier's report, to lack the work of imagination that transforms the narcissistic involvement into expectation of the future child, tend to repress unconsciously the idea of the sexual origin of the child, and tend to imagine themselves as the creator of the child. They also have a harder time overcoming the post-partum depression and show a disturbance in the delicate balance of the feeling of oneness-in-otherness with their children.(16) This latter disturbance is conceptualized as leading to difficulties for the child in inhabiting its own body since the child needs to deal with the paradox of experiencing its own body as other from but still desirable to the mother.

One strain of thought in this explanation—which De Waelhens will be able to use legitimately to diminish the apparent contradiction of having two different causal explanations—is the claim that the mother represses the sexual origin of the child which in turn leads to difficulties in recognizing the otherness of the child. As a consequence, the mother does not do the necessary work of imagination to provide the desirable balance in the feeling of oneness-in-otherness with the baby. Using Lacanian language, De Waelhens summarizes this situation as pointing to "the mother's incapacity to construct a corporeal signifier" which "must result in a 'massive castration' of the future subject... . The foreclosure of the name-of-the-father has here its point of origin" (De Waelhens 1978, 64). Castration here does not mean the Oedipal castration of classical psychoanalysis. Rather, it means that the child is deprived of the benefit of a mediating structure in its relation with the mother. That mediating structure is thought to be helpful for the child in appropriating its own body. As this mediating structure—the imaginary work of the mother creating pictures of herself relating to her child as separate from her—is promoted by the mother unconsciously accepting the sexual origin of the child, De Waelhens can claim that the presence or absence of this mediating function has an implicit connection with the *unconscious acceptance by the mother of the function of the father.*(17)

Thus one strain of thought in the causal explanation of schizophrenia as tied to the function of the maternal figure leads to the claim that the *maternal figure helps to lay the groundwork for a failure in the paternal function.* This explanation thus has a connection with the second explanation which claims that schizophrenia results simply from a failure in the paternal function. This second causal explanation presented by De Waelhens is one derived directly from Lacan—more specifically from Lacan's interpretation of Judge Schreber. This explanation starts by accepting the notion that the child has a symbiotic relation with its mother. In that relation, the child creates an imaginary and illusionary solution to its problem of dependence upon others for its survival. That illusion can be conceptualized as the child's attempt to situate itself in a maternal space characterized by the possibility of fusion with the mother. If the fusion is not total, the child still imagines itself to be the sole object of the desires of a mother considered omnipotent.

Lacanian theory argues that the normal way for a child to correct its illusionary vision of others and itself is for the mother to show respect for a third, normally the father. That third—the father—need not be physically present. He need not even be alive. Therefore, Lacan summarized his views with the formula that the mother must show respect for the name-of-the-father. Such respect by the mother gives a double message to the child. It shows the child both that the mother is not omnipotent and that the child is not the only object of the mother's desires. After first trying to destroy the mother's message by interrupting the communication between mother and father or by wishing that the father be gone (or dead), the child then moves in the direction of a more constructive solution. The child borrows the insignia of the father and carries them as regalia (glasses, hat, shoes) before selecting unconsciously a mark in the father with which to identify in the hope of thereby maintaining some of the esteem of the mother. That mark is the signifier which, from then on, will unconsciously organize the desire of the child.

Of the many consequences created by that move, two are important to mention explicitly. First, by that move—which corresponds to the Freudian Oedipus complex—the *child substitutes mediation for immediacy*. Indeed, the child in the post-Oedipal period unconsciously aims at maintaining the esteem of the mother—not by being directly present to the mother but by incorporating in itself something for which the child guesses that the mother has great affection: some mark in the father. Second, the child has made a move in which identity and difference are united. Indeed, whereas the child situated itself as the object of the mother's desire, now the child situates itself differently: it situates itself as *wanting to be like the father respected by the mother*. Still, the child feels itself to be the same child in both positions. As the child shifts its position while still feeling that it is the same person, the child synthesizes identity and difference. Because such a synthesis is typical for metaphors and because the whole process originates in the introduction of the father figure in the emotional life of the child, Lacan refers to that process as the introduction of the paternal metaphor (Lacan 1977, 200; This book, Chapter Five; Ver Eecke 1988). The absence of such a move is considered the structural cause of schizophrenia, which is expected to erupt if the proper occasion presents itself. Lacan conceptualizes that occasion as the appearance of an "A-Father" figure in the emotional life of the patient (This book, Chapter Five; Section VI; Lacan 1977, 217; Laplanche 1969, 125).

De Waelhens senses the problem of his dual causal explanation of schizophrenia when he writes in a special section of *The Relative Role of the Mother and Father in Psychosis*: "Could we not be reproached for having located the origin of psychosis both in the child's relationship to the mother, and in his relationship to the father?" (De Waelhens 1978, 137). De Waelhens answers his own rhetorical question by arguing that the two causes are in effect not two separate causes but two causes which reinforce each other and thus become part of one more general cause. Thus the schizophrenogenic mother who during pregnancy omits the work of the imagination does not create a chain of signifiers into which the child will be introduced. If the child has not been introduced to the world of signifiers, then it cannot effectively internalize a paternal signifier, because the child has remained alien to the world of signifiers. On the other hand, if the father is "a caricatural personage" (Ibid., 138), how can she show respect for him and introduce him to the child?

Thus De Waelhens presents the overall psychological cause of schizophrenia to be both a defective maternal and a defective paternal role. As the maternal role consists, among others, in creating (by fusion, by mirroring) the basis of self esteem for the child and the paternal role consists, among others, in introducing a sense of finitude, of limit, of separateness, and of law(18) (and conceptualized by Freudians as the imposition of castration), the schizophrenic seems to be in need of help from two contradictory directions. But how can one claim that a patient needs at the same time fusion and separation, for instance? This claim is a paradox only if one has a static view of human development in which one claims that a child can either miss fusion or separation. It is not a paradox if one has a dynamic view of human development in which one postulates the need for the simultaneous healthy presence of both. This is similar to the view developed by Blatt (presented earlier) which argues that human beings need both "the development of satisfying interpersonal relationships and a well-differentiated sense of self" (Blatt 1995, 1012) and that "these two developmental processes evolve in an interactive, reciprocally balanced, mutually facilitating fashion from birth through senescence" (Ibid.).

The view that both the maternal and the paternal function have been defective in the schizophrenic goes a long way in explaining the advice of experienced and successful therapists of schizophrenics. Harold Searles, for example, advises that, first, it is mandatory to "foster the necessary emotional atmosphere in the sessions for the development of the contented, unthreatened emotional oneness to which I refer by the term 'therapeutic symbiosis'—a form of relatedness of the same quality as that which imbues the mother-infant relatedness in normal infancy and very early childhood" (Searles 1986, 598). He advises, second, that "limit-setting is one of the major dimensions of therapeutic technique in this work" (Ibid.). Furthermore, Searles' claims point to a dialectic connection between the two above requirements: "The analyst is able firmly to set and maintain limits to the extent that he is aware of, and accepting of, his own individual limitations. But the very nature of the work with schizophrenic patients, who themselves have so much unresolved infantile omnipotent striving, is such as powerfully to evoke the analyst's unconscious fantasies of omnipotence" (Ibid., 601).(19) And, "An analyst who, for whatever unconscious reasons, cannot become able to live comfortably with the possibility that his patient may never become free from psychosis cannot, by the same token, foster the necessary... 'therapeutic symbiosis'" (Ibid., 598). Thus the therapists who cannot control their own sense of omnipotence in healing schizophrenics will not only be incapable of setting the necessary limits to their patients (thus being defective in their paternal function) but they will also not be able to create the necessary therapeutic symbiosis (thus being defective in their maternal function). In summary, a successful maternal function (e.g., therapeutic symbiosis) requires the incorporation of a paternal function (acceptance of finitude and limit setting).

The above reading of Searles allows me to make two points. The first point is a practical one: if effective therapy requires such contradictory capabilities, it is no wonder that Blatt can conclude: "Significant differences exist in therapeutic efficacy among therapists, even the experienced and well-trained therapists in the TDCRP [Treatment of Depression Collaborative Research Program]" (Blatt et al. 1996, 1281-2). All indications are that a similar statement can be made for therapists of schizophrenia. A psychiatrist, with administrative responsibility for treating schizophrenics, will have to make choices between different therapists. One would hope that he or she would be able to select effective psychotherapists. Searles presents us with a test, a criterion for effectiveness in psychotherapy. De Waelhens' theory, as it is informed by Lacan, can provide a reason as to why the criterion given by Searles is necessary.

My second point is theoretical: for the maternal function and the paternal function to be effective, feelings of grandiose omnipotence must be checked. When De Waelhens wrote *Schizophrenia*, Lacan had articulated that requirement explicitly for the maternal function by insisting that a mother needs to acknowledge her own lack by showing respect for the name-of-the-father. Lacan had not yet articulated that requirement as well for the paternal function. He does that later (Evans, 64-5), when he writes that the father should be a symbolic father, i.e., a subject himself submitted to the law and thus subject to finitude (death) and limitation rather than an imaginary omnipotent figure (Lacan Seminar III, 293; Evans, 62).

Since the original publication of De Waelhens' book, several of Lacan's seminars have become available, and Lacan scholarship, too, has developed. Scholars and therapists studying the ideas of Lacan have pointed out that his definition of psychosis and of schizophrenia by foreclosure of the name-of-the-father is a very important conceptual achievement, but it remains a *negative* definition (Calligaris 26; Vergote 1998, 227). One can find in Lacan's thoughts elements that go beyond his own negative definition when he points to schizophrenia as the failure of the symbolic system to get hold of the imaginary (Fink 1997, 89), because both the symbolic and the imaginary are deficient. As a result, the stitching of the symbolic to the imaginary, the creation of anchoring of meaning, is defective. In Lacan's technical language, the schizophrenic lacks "button ties"—also called "anchoring points" or "quilting points" (Fink 1997, 93-4; Moyaert 1993, 271). Consequently, the patient is confronted with the horror of the Real that can neither be imagined nor symbolized (Evans, 77, 155).(20) This line of thinking is explicitly taking the road suggested by De Waelhens: i.e., the failure of the symbolic is also a failure of the imaginary. However, the solution suggested by De Waelhens can now be better articulated because recent theoretical developments have made us aware of the multiple failures that are possible in both the imaginary and the symbolic.

The possibility that the imaginary system may fail in many ways becomes obvious if one recalls that Lacan twice revised his mirror stage theory. In his original presentation, Lacan located the achievement of the child and the reason for its jubilation in the fact that it now had created a unified total body image instead of experiencing itself as body parts. In a first revision, Lacan located the reason for the jubilation of the child in the child's discovery of the mother's emotional involvement with the child. The mother's involvement is noticeable in the child's search for the mother's eye when it sees itself in the mirror. According to this reading, it is the involvement of the mother's desire with the child which allows the child to invest libidinally in its own body (Fink 1997, 88; Simiu, Ch 1: *Sea-change: The Theory Transformed*, 3-27; Ver Eecke 1984, 70ff). In a second revision, Lacan accepts the idea from one of his students, Rosine Lefort, that the child not only needs to create a unified body image but it also has to create a body image that performs the role of container to some contained (Lacan Seminar I, 104). Lacan explicitly connects the idea of the body as container to a contained with his theory of the mirror stage by means of his famous flower vase in which a concave mirror allows a person to see flowers separated from a vase as being in a vase.(21) For a human being, the body image as container needs to have a place for needs, feelings, faeces, urine, food, and even pain. The baby's task of creating a body image as container requires the skilled help of a maternal figure.

Similarly, the multiple ways in which the symbolic system may fail can also be better understood in light of later publications of Lacan's thought. Indeed, De Waelhens reconstructs Lacan's thesis on the basis of Lacan's summary of his seminar on psychosis, published in his *Écrits*. In that summary, Lacan presents as the major reason for the failure of the symbolic the fact that the mother shows no respect for the word of the father (Lacan 1977, 218). It is true that Lacan there adds one paragraph about the deficiencies of the father himself, but it is almost presented as an afterthought. However, in the full seminar, Lacan stresses at length that the paternal function requires a symbolic father not an imaginary father (Lacan Seminar III, 215, 292-3). He defines an imaginary father as someone who "manifests himself simply in the order of strength and not in that of the pact" (Ibid., 205). He describes the consequences of such a paternal figure as follows: "We are all familiar with cases of these delinquent or psychotic sons who proliferate in the shadow of a paternal personality of exceptional character, one of these social monsters referred to as venerable" (Ibid., 204). Later on Lacan will conceptualize this notion of the symbolic father as the "barred Other" (Evans, 15). Thus in light of the full development of Lacan's thought, we can argue that the father too can contribute to the failure of the symbolic order in a child. He can do so because he presents himself more as an imaginary rather than as a symbolic father.

Finally, the failure of the symbolic may not just be the result of a deficiency in the symbolic or in the imaginary; it may also be attributed, in some cases, to traumas, to the horror of the Real itself. This possibility arises because Lacan seems to accept two moments in the development of the child in which language emerges. On the one hand, Lacan describes the result of the Oedipal complex as the establishment of the symbolic order, thereby creating an effective signifier. On the other hand, he also comments on Freud's analysis of his grandchild who, as an infant, did not cry when his mother left him, because he had, first, created a transitional object (the spool) and then, second, replaced the spool with the words "fort-da" (away-here) (Lacan 1977, 103). Thus, through his dual theory of the origin of language, Lacan allows for the possibility that something might go wrong in the use of language (the symbolic) in the pre-Oedipal period, a time when the imaginary seems to dominate. Indeed, children may not succeed in using either transitional objects or words to deal with a departing mother or they may do so in a radically defective way.

There are multiple reasons for failures of the symbolic. Furthermore, these multiple reasons may exert their influence independent from or in addition to maternal and paternal influences. Two cases illustrate my claim. Gary VandenBos presents the case of a child whose parents were going through a difficult divorce. However, the family physician played unwittingly a major role in creating a psychotic-like symptom in the child. Indeed, the boy was sent to the family doctor because he was quite "nervous" and was placed on mild tranquilizers. The boy had asked for explanations from his doctor who had told him that he had bad nerves. To further questions the doctor had answered that nerves were like worms under the skin. The boy was sent to VandenBos because he "was compulsively splashing water on his face and soaking his hands... as many as 20 to 30 times a day. He would wake up in the middle of the night to do the same thing" (Karon & VandenBos, 159). VandenBos found out that the boy knew about worms from fishing. He knew that if they dried, they burst open. He was therefore afraid that his bad nerves were going to burst open and hence he tried to keep them wet. The nervousness had changed into compulsive behavior because of the explanation from an outsider (the family doctor) about the child's nervousness.

Rosine Lefort presents another case, that of Robert, who was grossly neglected by his mother (twice he was brought to the hospital in a state of acute wasting before he was one year old). However, a surgical team greatly contributed to the child's developmental difficulties, because they administered an antrotomy at the age of five months without anaesthetics, while forcing a bottle of sweetened water in the boy's mouth to prevent it from crying. Lefort writes that she had the impression that his horror "fantasies had become reality" (Lacan, Seminar I, 100). In the case presented by VandenBos, the family physician unwittingly helped create the horror of the Real by making a connection between the boy's nervousness and worms. In the case presented by Lefort, the encounter with life itself created too much of a horror (not being fed and having caretakers who brutalized him by operating without anaesthesia).

As mentioned before, the later Lacan argues that psychosis is the reaction towards the Real which cannot be signified by the imaginary or by the symbolic. As the Real is horrifying, the lack of its mastery by signifying it leads to very defensive strategies. In presenting psychosis as a reaction to a developmental failure at two levels, an opening is created for a more complex definition of schizophrenia. Indeed, a psychotic reaction is not a reaction to the failure of the symbolic alone (failure of the paternal metaphor). It is a reaction to the joint failure of the imaginary and the symbolic. I will therefore articulate the connection and the difference between the functions of the imaginary and the symbolic.

Let me start by clarifying the imaginary as it is created in the mother-child relationship. The challenge in the mother-child relation is for the mother to introduce distance between herself and the child while creating a deep form of caring unity with her child. The child's challenge is to use the gift of caring unity with the mother as the basis for accepting itself as embodied and to use the gift of distance offered by the mother as the means for separating itself from its mother.

The challenge of the symbolic is for both the mother and the father to introduce and make acceptable to the child the idea of finitude, which implies that the child must accept its place in the legitimate order of human beings. The painful dimension in this challenge is that the symbolic displaces the child from its imagined privileged position with its mother. This displacement involves the experiencing of a narcissistic wound on the part of the child. However, it also results in the child discovering an identity and a direction for its own desire. Both, the identity and the direction of the desire, result from the child borrowing through identification a basic mark from the father. The identity of the child is signaled by the name given to the child, but is only significant if the child accepts that identity which in turn means that the child in its unconscious has been marked and grounded in a central meaning-giving signifier. The early Lacan called that meaning-giving signifier: the name-of-the-father. The later Lacan splits the two moments involved in his original concept of the name-of-the-father. He differentiates the fact of receiving a name from the phenomenon of accepting the meaning associated with it (my name is John Smith and I have the choice of honoring or dishonoring that name). Lacan keeps calling the first moment the fundamental signifier, now referred to as S1 and he calls the second moment S2. The first moment is associated with the negative experience of alienation (my name is something different from the inner feeling of my selfhood and is imposed on me without my consent). The second moment is associated with separation (how I choose to individuate myself—as honoring or dishonoring my given name) (Fink 1996). With this move, Lacan connects his original idea of the name-of-the-father as the fundamental signifier with his other idea of meaning consisting of a chain of signifiers. S1 and S2 are seen to be the beginning of an infinite series of signifiers: S1, S2, S3, S4.

The case of Robert presented by Lefort in a seminar given by Lacan illustrates the claim that psychosis is not just the failure of the symbolic but rather the failure of the symbolic because of an already failed imaginary. In the case of Robert, we do not hear about the father. The mother was, at the time of Robert's treatment, diagnosed as a paranoiac and confined (Lacan, Seminar I, 91). His mother kept him with her, moving from house to house. She neglected his essential needs so much so that at five months he arrived in a hospital with acute "hypertrophy and wasting"(Ibid.). After an infection which necessitated an operation he was isolated and "fed on a drip"(Ibid.) At nine months he was returned to his mother, only to come back to the hospital, two months later, "again in a state of acute wasting" (Ibid., 91). Five months later the mother legally abandoned the child. As a foster child, Robert changed residence twenty-five times before he was four years old (Ibid.). Furthermore, as indicated before, the therapist discovered that Robert had undergone an antrotomy at the age of five months without anaesthetics (Ibid., 100).

Some of Robert's symptoms were: his extreme lack of coordination in movement; his hyper-agitation; his lack of coordinated speech (he would frequently utter screams and guttural, discordant laughter, and he yelled two words: Miss and wolf); his prehensive activity was un-co-ordinated—"he would throw his arm out to take hold of an object and if he didn't reach it, he couldn't correct it, and had to start the movement all over again from the beginning" (Ibid., 92); he had convulsive fits of agitation without real convulsions, "during each of the routine moments of his daily life—the pot, and above all the emptying of the pot, undressing, feeding" (Ibid., 92). "One evening, after going to bed, he tried to cut off his penis with a pair of plastic scissors, while standing on his bed in front of the other terrified children" (Ibid., 93). "The business of undressing was for him the occasion for genuine crises... one [episode of undressing] having lasted three hours, during which the staff described him as possessed. He howled—Wolf!, running from one bedroom to the next, smearing the other children with feces that he found in the pots. It was only once he was tied up that he calmed down" (Ibid., 96).

Using Lacan's three categories, Lefort, as Robert's therapist, writes this about him: "I had the impression [that] it was Robert's tragedy that all his oral-sadistic fantasies had been realised in the actual events of his life. His [horror] fantasies had become reality... the image that Robert had constructed of a starving, paranoiac, dangerous mother, who certainly attacked him. Then the separation, a bottle held by force, making him swallow his cries. The force-feedings with the tube, twenty-five moves in succession" (Ibid., 100). Lefort continues: "I had the impression that this child had sunk under the real, that at the beginning of the treatment there was no symbolic function in him, still less an imaginary function" (Ibid.). Lacan corrects Lefort by adding: "But he did have two words" (Ibid.). The treatment consisted in restoring the imaginary and the symbolic so that the horror of the Real diminished, if it did not disappear.

Lefort's effort at restoring the imaginary could be described almost completely with object-relations terminology. The body had to be accepted as a container with reference to milk, faeces, and urine. Lefort remained present to

Robert as a stable object even though he was aggressive or peed on her (Ibid., 95). Her tolerant presence—so writes Lefort—helped Robert create a self-image. However, it only allowed him to create a bad self-image as is evident from the following: "When I had to frustrate him—he ran to the window, opened it and cried out—Wolf! Wolf!, and seeing his own image in the glass, he hit it, crying out—Wolf! Wolf! That is the way Robert represented himself, he was the Wolf!" (Ibid., 95).

Then, in two phases, Robert reconstructed a good self-image using two forms of mirroring separated by a symbolic act. Robert first projected his bad image onto the therapist and separated himself from her. Lefort writes: "I was made to swallow the bottle of dirty water and was on the receiving end of the aggressive pee. So I was the Wolf! Robert separated himself from it during one session, by shutting me in the toilets, then returned to the room where we had the sessions, all alone, climbed into the empty bed, and started to moan. He could not call me, yet I did have to come back, since I was the permanent person. I came back. Robert was stretched out, pathetic, his thumb now within an inch of his mouth. And, for the first time in a session, he held out his arms to me and let himself be consoled" (Ibid., 97).

In the second phase of constructing his good self-image, Robert used a symbolic act in which he renamed himself. Lefort describes it this way: "Robert, completely naked and facing me, collected up the water in his cupped hands, raised it to the level of his shoulders and let it run the length of his body. He started afresh several times, and then he said to me, softly—Robert, Robert" (Ibid., 98). He then repeated the scene with milk.

The separation of the good boy (Robert not Wolf!) from the therapist was performed in another form of mirroring: "He first tried to differentiate himself from me by sharing with me. He gave me everything to eat, saying, while touching himself—Robert, then touching me—Not Robert. I made great use of this in my interpretations to help him and me" (Ibid., 99).

In Robert's case, there is not just a failure of the symbolic: there is also abuse of the symbolic—the patient calls himself Wolf instead of Robert—in order to structure an already deficient imaginary. Let us start with the deficient imaginary. Robert had not only failed at separating himself as a good object from a maternal figure; he had not yet established himself as a good object. Robert beat his own image and called it Wolf. He had created a bad self-image. But the creation of the bad self-image was an achievement of the therapy. Prior to therapy, Robert's self-image had no place for the things that go in and out of the body: milk, urine, and feces. The milk and the bottle had been so much connected with deprivation and pain that the imaginary assumption of his body must have become unacceptable. The digestive body is for Robert one horror story. As reported by Lefort, Robert uses all digestive functions aggressively (the milk, the urine, and the faeces). Robert then uses the symbolic order to create some distance between himself and his digestive body that is unacceptable. He gives up his Christian name Robert and calls himself Wolf, signifying his radical badness. Thus the obvious failure of the symbolic order in which Robert does not call himself Robert but Wolf is more than a failure of the symbolic. It is first of all the failure to imaginarily inhabit his body because that body has been made the source of pain by others, and Robert needed to be a loved body for those others in order to be able to accept himself as embodied (Moyaert, 267).

Lacanian theory does not require that physical pain be inflicted on the child in order for the child to fail in its imaginary effort to inhabit its body. Crucial for its healthy development is that the child experiences itself as lovable by others in its own right. In a case presented by Bertram Karon, there is no indication that physical pain was inflicted upon the child—with one possible exception: the toilet training was completed early. There was, however, evidence that the child was not really loved for its own sake. Indeed, while trying to praise the child, the mother proudly focused upon trivial achievements and did not applaud real achievements. Karon writes: "Consciously, she was attempting to impress people with the accomplishments of her son; unconsciously, she was convincing them of his worthlessness by presenting the worthless productions first and the worthwhile productions later or not at all" (Karon & VandenBos, 340). In the case of Robert too, the physically inflicted pain was occurring within a context in which Robert experienced himself as worthless and unlovable. Let us be clear: Lacanian theory does not make pain as such the cause of failure in the imaginary. It is the dialectic between the experience of pain and the experience that one is not lovable which creates a difficulty for the child in properly constructing a body image it can inhabit. Dealing with a body which has been constructed as an unlovable and paining one sometimes also leads to distortions of the symbolic world. Sometimes these symbolic distortions are as visible as the imaginary distortions.

Compared with object-relations theory, Lacanian theory is better able in Robert's case to point to the crucial usage made by Robert of one of the two words he knew: "wolf." Robert lets go of his bad self by abandoning his self-given name "wolf." He creates a good self identity by publicly accepting his Christian name. Words and the symbolic organize progress in the imaginary.(22)

B. Implications and applications of Lacan's developed theory of schizophrenia

1. Implications

Recently, interest has developed in the question if psychotic break-downs can be prevented. This raises the question of the status of a person before his or her psychotic breakdown.

Can Lacanian theory be used to address the puzzling question as to whether one can say that a particular person has a psychotic (schizophrenic) personality even though he or she has not yet had a breakdown. The Lacanian answer is a definitive yes (Fink 1997, 82). In theory, Lacan requires two conditions for a schizophrenic breakdown: a cause and an occasion. The cause is foreclosure of the name-of-the-father. The occasion is a psychological stress which hits the weak point of the psychic structure. As the weak point in the psychotic personality is the foreclosure of the name-of-the-father, Lacan argues that the occasion for the breakdown will be the encounter with a figure (an A-Father) who calls upon something in the subject which he does not possess (Lacan 1977, 217). When discussing the recent research in the Schreber case we will be able to give an example of the occasion for a breakdown. Thus, according to Lacan's view, all manifest schizophrenics have, even before their breakdown, a schizophrenic structure.

In the work of Contardo Calligaris we find the description of a person who never experienced a breakdown but who is said by the author to have a psychotic structure. It concerns an American who moved in several totally different social situations and was in each of them very successful (Calligaris, 13). He had fought in Vietnam and had been decorated (Ibid., 11, 14). He then decided to return to the United States, but, as did many veterans, he went first to India and Burma where he got involved in drugs (Ibid., 11). He had no ideological stance on either the Vietnam war or the drug culture (Ibid., 13). He then came to Paris where he met and married the daughter of an important industrialist. After his wedding, he became director of the administrative division of his in-laws's enterprise—a function which he apparently performed smoothly (Ibid., 12). He was sent to analysis by his wife because he had fallen in love with his mother-in-law. This was a problem for his wife but apparently not for the American. The analysis stopped because he was arrested. His wife called the psychoanalyst and explained that he had gone to a bar. There he had met a group of people who were planning a robbery. They thought he might be able to help and asked him for his participation. He agreed. The robbery failed. One robber was killed and the American was jailed. Commenting on the case, Calligaris observes that this person had been able to insert himself successfully in several totally different cultural environments: the Vietnam war, the hippy culture in India, and the high bourgeoisie in Paris. He did well in all of them, apparently without experiencing transition shocks. Evidently in the same spirit of easily moving between extremes, he reacted to the proposal for participating in the bank robbery with: "Why not?" (Ibid., 12).

Calligaris uses the case of this American as an example of a personality with a psychotic structure but no psychotic breakdown. Such a person is somebody for whom there is plenty of meaning in life, but no particular meaning is assumed as a meaning for him. In Lacanian terminology, this person lacks a primary signifier around which he can construct the meaning of his life—which in turn allows him to take root. His life is similar to that of an actual psychotic who spent his week-ends from Friday evening until Monday morning traveling by train without goal, without direction (e.g., visiting a friend or going to a place to ski). Rather, he stepped down from one train to mount another, assembling information about changes in departure time, lateness of trains, etc. According to Calligaris, this absence of basic signifier in the person reveals itself in the kind of transference produced in a psychoanalytic session and is of a different nature than the one produced by a neurotic. Lacanian theory thus complements neurobiological research trying to find neurobiological markers for identifying potential psychotics before the actual psychotic breakdown. Lacanian theory points to a psychological marker of a psychotic personality before the psychotic breakdown. This is similar to the findings of Felix and Loretta Loeb, who discovered a psychological criterion—which then could be biologically confirmed—for an approaching manic crisis (890, 892).

2. Usage of Lacanian theory for an analysis of successful treatments of schizophrenics

In this section, I want to present techniques and advice given by therapists—both Lacanians and non-Lacanians—who have had success in treating schizophrenics. I will try to see if Lacanian theory—as presented by De Waelhens—can clarify why these techniques and advice are successful.

a/ Lacanian-inspired therapy of schizophrenics

Of the many techniques presented at the 1998 Lacan Clinical Forum at the Austen Riggs Center in Stockbridge, Massachussetts, by Françoise Davoine and Jean-Max Gaudillière, a Parisian couple treating schizophrenics, I will sample some of the most interesting ones. Gaudillière reported that he regularly starts his treatment by requesting that the patient bring into the office an object from the crazy world in which he or she lives. Thus, a male who had stayed about eight years in his room was asked to bring an object from that room into the office. He brought a seventy-pound lamp stand. Another patient who worked in Paris but was originally from Bruges was diagnosed as having his crazy world not in Paris but in Bruges. The patient associated Bruges with death: suicides on the canals and the historical expression: *Bruges la morte* (Bruges the dead one), which originated when the port closed after the North Sea receded. Thus Gaudillière told the patient that there was an exposition in Bruges about Memling, and that he could not go; would the patient make sure to bring Gaudillière a catalogue from the exposition? Gaudillière's theory is that if an object is taken away from the crazy world in which the patient lives, then the patient will start to talk because of the hole created in his crazy world (Gaudillière 1998). The efficacy of this technique can be explained by the Lacanian thesis that psychosis is an attempt to cover up the lack that cannot be signified by the paternal metaphor (Lacan 1977, 201, 211, 217). Re-introducing a lack in the crazy world can, therefore, potentially open up the possibility for a signifying process because it creates an opening in the psychotic defenses.

A second strategy of Gaudillière's dealt with the suicidal thoughts of the patient who had been in his room for about eight years. Gaudillière had to travel to Alaska. He told the patient that he would be away for a week and that he would call him everyday. Upon arrival in Alaska, he called his patient and told him that it was nine in the morning there, that it was Wednesday, and that he would call back the next day, at the same time. The patient did not commit suicide. Gaudillière had successfully played the role of a "stable object" providing in a mirroring action stability to the patient. He explicitly did not ask the patient how he felt. He addressed only the primary imaginary need of the patient.(23)

Gaudillière addressed the symbolic deficiencies in this same patient when, after some therapy, the patient forgot his pipe in the waiting room. In French one says about a soldier who just died in the war: "*Il a cassé sa pipe* (He broke his pipe)." This metaphorical saying was well known to the patient. Gaudillière decided to use this moment of forgetfulness to start the work of creating a paternal metaphor. He decided to use it as the first signifier by which to let the patient organize his world symbolically. He told the patient: "You forgot your pipe, you did not break your pipe [i.e., you did not kill yourself]. You had a choice and you chose to forget, not to break your pipe" (Gaudillière 1998). Gaudillière repeated several times that the patient had forgotten and not broken his pipe. This intervention was not the end of the treatment but it reportedly resulted in significant improvements: the suicidal ideas disappeared. Gaudillière claims that he consciously aims at using with his patients the two techniques of asking for one object from the crazy world in which the patients live out their craziness and of searching for a means to create a grounding signifier. Both techniques aim at restoring the symbolic function in the schizophrenic, but in doing so Gaudillière pays close attention to the imaginary dimension of the needs and gestures of the patient (calling the patient every day from Alaska; translating in words the imaginary meaning of the actual forgetting of a pipe).

At the same conference at the Austen Riggs Center, Françoise Davoine reported that she gives her telephone number to her patients. Sometimes they call her late at night. If it is not an emergency, she tells them that they cannot call her that late because after being called at night she cannot sleep anymore and then the next day she cannot do her work and thus cannot help the patient (Davoine 1998). This example was given to illustrate that one may impose reasonable limits even on schizophrenics. Imposing reasonable limits is introducing an aspect of the symbolic order: i.e., imposing the law and thus imposing limits. However, Davoine did not just introduce the symbolic by imposing limits. She introduced the symbolic within a relation that expressed maternal care which in turn captured the imaginary of the patient. She presented as motivation the fact that the therapist would not be able to help the patient if she had been awakened the night before. That argument reassures the patient that the therapist is available for help and also makes an effort to be fit to help. The argument gives a further suggestion to the patient. It tells him or her that the therapist too is a human being with limited capabilities which she respects in order to be able to do therapy. This intervention addresses the imaginary because it makes the possibility of care for the patient the central issue. However, it introduces symbolic limits and symbolic lack as a condition for imaginary importance.(24)

John Muller, the Director of Education at the Erikson Institute for Education and Research of the Austen Riggs Center, defends the use of a general technique for dealing with psychotic patients struggling with the loss of boundaries or what he calls "dedifferentiation" (Muller 1999, 8). He describes those patients as having problems with the three Lacanian registers of the Symbolic, the Imaginary, and the Real. For those patients, words (the symbolic) are experienced as real things and, therefore, rather than clarifying the situation, an attempt at communication by using words promotes imaginary fusion between patient and therapist and/or provokes hostility. Sometimes patients' faces show that they are in terror confronting the horror of the "Real"—in Lacan's sense. In those circumstances, Muller regularly asks the patient to draw or paint what they face. He then asks the patient to bring the painting or the drawing into his office.

Muller reports that this exercise often results in the amelioration of psychotic symptoms. His interpretation of the success of this technique is that it seems to allow the patient to imaginarily construct themselves as separate enough from the horror of the "Real" so that they become capable of naming the elements of the horrible "Real." Words by themselves are powerless to master the horror of their experience. Words can gain their therapeutic effect if first supported by appropriate imaginary products (a drawing or a painting, for example). Sometimes patients use that technique themselves, as was the case with a patient who was afraid of committing suicide one night. He put his bed sheet in the corridor and painted on it for the rest of the night. In the morning, he hung the bed sheet on his wall. When he saw the therapist he said: "I hanged the painting instead of myself" (Muller 1999, 8-12). In this case, the patient seems to have used two imaginary moves to save himself from committing suicide. These moves were actions in which the Real, the Imaginary, and the Symbolic are inchoatively knotted together. Before pointing to the symbolic in the second move, let me describe the imaginary dimensions of both moves. First, he painted (expressed himself) in the corridor instead of staying in his room. Second, feeling that a hanging had to happen, he hung the painting rather than himself. Notice that this second imaginary act of hanging the painting instead of himself was made possible because of the symbolic order in which the verb "to hang" has two meanings. Imaginarily, the patient allowed the one to stand in for the other. One might conclude that if the psychotic faces the horror of the "Real" because of failures in both the structure of the imaginary and of the symbolic, it is natural to expect that liberating the patient from the horrors he or she experiences will require the help of *both* the imaginary and the symbolic. Muller has suggested one way of doing that.

I now wish to turn to non-Lacanian therapists who are successful in treating schizophrenics in order to see if their methods can also be interpreted as dealing with both the imaginary and the symbolic, even if they do not use that terminology.

b/ Non-Lacanian therapists

Let us first turn to some general advice given by experienced therapists such as Karon and VandenBos. They write: "Aside from the importance of rapidly establishing and maintaining the emotional contact, the principles of treatment for acute reactions are the same as those we have discussed in general. Particularly important are making the distinction between thoughts and actions, and the acceptability of all feelings, but particularly [of] anger" (Karon & VandenBos, 197; also 168). In order for the therapist to establish emotional contact with the patient, the authors recommend providing protection and gratification (Ibid., 145). Concerning protection, they go so far as to say: "For many schizophrenic patients, it is extremely useful somewhere in the first hour to say that you will not let anyone kill him (or her)" (Ibid., 153). They report that for many schizophrenic patients they treated: "an overwhelming conscious fear of death immediately preceded the psychotic break" (Ibid., 143).(25) Concerning the provision of gratification they write: "The therapist must talk freely, and try to be helpful on the verbal level. Even words may be experienced by the patient as a medium of exchange which can be given and taken. The therapist must be seen as someone who does not demand, but gives" (Karon & VandenBos, 165).

The general recommendations by Karon and VandenBos deal with a mixture of imaginary and symbolic problems. Lacanian theory claims that schizophrenics unconsciously have great difficulty in dealing with death (This book, Chapter VI, Section I & III). That same theory claims that successfully establishing the paternal metaphor is dealing with the psychological implications of death. Lacanian theory also sees a schizophrenic as someone who is horrified by the Real (of which the unavoidability of death is one crucial element), because it implies the failure of the imaginary and the symbolic. Karon and VandenBos do not deal with the defective way in which the schizophrenic deals symbolically with death; rather they deal with the problem in a maternal and protective way: i.e., they address the imaginary. They address the *fear* of death, take that fear seriously, and provide assurances against threats of death.

Two things they do not do: they do not install real protection against murderers by buying guns. They also do not give arguments to prove that the fear is unfounded. All they do is to give personal assurances against murderers, thereby addressing the imaginary fears of their patients.

Karon and VandenBos address another aspect of the imaginary when they advocate that all emotions must be accepted, even anger. In terms of the later Lacan, such an approach allows the patients to create a body image that is allowed to contain what belongs to the person. Karon and VandenBos even advocate that same maternal approach in their talk: talking to schizophrenics must be experienced by the schizophrenic as *giving* not as taking. However, Karon and VandenBos also advocate the introduction of the work of the symbolic when they advocate that a *distinction* must be made between thought and action. In so doing, they thus address, in their general advice, both the imaginary and the symbolic needs of their schizophrenic patients.

When they address concrete issues, these same authors do not just address the imaginary and the symbolic separately; they seem to address the intersection of the two as well. One of the most dramatic examples is that of a patient who had both nightmares and hallucinations of his stepmother beating him. The patient asked: "What I want to know is, if I run away from here and kill her, will the dream stop?" (Karon & VandenBos, 198). The therapist, Karon, used that question to address a challenging imaginary task of the patient: i.e., to accept himself as embodied with all the detestable feelings he had. Karon replied: "Who told you it was wrong to kill her?... Somebody must have told you it was wrong. Who says it's wrong to *want* to kill a bitch like that. The old bitch deserves to die, for what she did to you" (Karon & VandenBos, 198). The patient reacted by recounting the cruel treatment he had received as a child from his stepmother. At that point, Karon introduced the symbolic order by making the distinction between the thought of wanting to kill—which the therapist approved—and actually killing—which he called stupid. Note however, that Karon used imaginary motives to make a symbolic distinction stick: "The only reason for not killing her [the stepmother] is that you get caught. If you're willing to die in order to kill her, she must be more important than you [appeal to a narcissistic motive]. That sounds stupid to me [mirroring move]. (But note—I did not say 'bad.') It would be stupid to do it, but you certainly should *want* to kill a bitch like that" (Ibid., 198).

It is worth asking why Karon warns therapists not to use the motive of badness to make the distinction between thoughts and actions. To me, it looks as if Karon sometimes makes use of imaginary motives but avoids them at other times. He makes an appeal to an imaginary motive when he points out that killing will put the patient in a position in which he might be executed. If the patient is willing to die for doing something to his stepmother then she must be more important than he is. For Lacan, the question of who is more important, I or the other, is a question generated by an imaginary position. Karon makes another move in the imaginary domain when he says: "That sounds stupid to me." In that move he actually gives no arguments. He simply makes a mirroring move: to me it sounds stupid. He could also have made that mirroring move by saying: to me that is bad. This brings us to what Karon is willing to mirror. He is willing to mirror that the patient is considering doing something that the therapist regards as stupid. He advises explicitly against mirroring that the patient is considering doing something that he regards as bad. Why? We might get some clarification from analyzing the purpose of the intervention.(26)

Karon wants a symbolic distinction to stick: it is acceptable to want to kill; it is not acceptable to actually do the killing. For that distinction to stick it must get a hold of the imaginary. Thus, in forceful ways, Karon makes it clear that it is permitted, that it is reasonable, that it is even good to *want* to kill in the given circumstances. Then Karon wants to convey the idea that actual killing is another matter. In order to make that distinction effective he first points out that, in killing, the patient risks dying himself (the death penalty), thus risking making his stepmother more important than himself. Karon then uses a second strategy to make the distinction stick by tying the act of killing to a negative judgment on the part of the therapist (the mirroring other). Two things Karon does not do: He does not simply say: killing is stupid or killing is bad. That would be to present the distinction (the symbolic) without ties to the imaginary—unless the context were by itself very much a mirroring context. Karon explicitly embeds his judgment in a mirroring sentence: that sounds... (stupid or bad)... to me. In his second strategy, Karon explicitly rejects the use of moral condemnation. Why? What are the relative advantages of saying: "that sounds stupid to me" as opposed to "that sounds bad to me?"

To say that something is stupid is to make an intellectual judgment. To say that something is bad is to locate a problem in a domain where feelings (e.g., guilt or feeling bad about oneself) run high. Feelings are in the domain of the imaginary. Things need to be repaired in the imaginary (Karon helped the patient accept his hatred for his stepmother). Can that which needs repair be used as a reliable motive for introducing an important distinction? I think not. The Lacanian reason is not so much that the imaginary of the schizophrenic needs repair as it is that in the imaginary there is a tendency to fuse and not to distinguish. Thus feelings might be expected to diminish the distinction between wanting to kill and the act of killing. Furthermore, the imaginary includes the domain of guilt and thus patients might already feel bad about themselves. To label something bad might therefore not provide patients with the grounds for actually separating themselves from the bad thing. On the other hand, patients generally do not feel that they are stupid. Calling something stupid might then provide patients with the grounds for separating themselves from that stupid thing. But providing patients with the grounds for separating themselves from an undesirable thing is making the symbolic adhere. In order to make his intervention effective, Karon repeated several times his approbation of the desire to kill and his idea that actually killing was stupid. By the fourth day of his therapy, the patient's nightmares stopped.

When dealing with sexuality, Karon and VandenBos again address both the imaginary and the symbolic. They lift moral bans that might prevent patients from accepting their bodies or from accepting the pleasurable body. At the same time, they introduce a subtle symbolic restriction. Thus when discussing masturbation, they write that "the therapist should unequivocally indicate that it is neither harmful nor morally wrong. Masturbation is simply something people do if they do not have anything better to do" (Ibid., 203). When discussing heterosexual relations they write: "The therapist should point out in no uncertain terms that sexual intercourse is fun and that it is part of the pleasure of being alive. This is the only reason for having intercourse. The patient should be told emphatically that if he or she enjoys it, he or she should engage in intercourse; if they will not enjoy it, they need not engage in it... . Of course, it is unjustified to hurt an innocent person. Therefore, the patient should take precautions against having children unless the couple wants them, and, of course, rape is no more justified than beating someone for any other purpose" (Ibid., 204).

Through the above interventions, the therapists seem to have as their primary purpose the promotion, in their patients, of the process of forming an imaginary body that includes sexuality. Karon and VandenBos say as much when they write: "We have found that... the unconscious significance of masturbation is not incest but treason—that is, there is the fantasy that their body, genitals, and/or (in the case of the male) their sexual products rightfully belong to the overwhelming demanding mother" (Ibid., 203). Or with reference to intercourse they write: "Female patients... may be concerned with the fear of being ripped open by the fantasied huge penis" (Ibid., 204).

Still, Karon and VandenBos introduce symbolic limits to the permission they give to their patients to assume imaginarily their sexuality. As with the feelings of hatred, here too they introduce the symbolic limits without appealing to an imaginary feeling (guilt or the idea that something is bad). Thus they write that masturbation is what people do "if they do not have anything better to do," and about intercourse they write that intercourse is fun but that "it is unjustified to hurt an innocent person [have unwanted children or rape someone]" (Ibid., 204).

Another way to describe in Lacanian terms what Karon and VandenBos are trying to achieve is to say that they are addressing the problem of pleasure for the patient. Within the imaginary position, the right to pleasure does not belong to oneself. One exists in an imaginary symbiotic unity with another. In naming (I am John; she is Jane), the symbolic order creates separate individuals. By naming (some sex acts are called consensual; others are called rape), the symbolic order also makes distinctions between pleasures. Some pleasures are forbidden (the therapists mention that some sex is rape). Others are not just not forbidden, they are called "good' or "fun" and are thus legitimized.

From a Lacanian point of view, I wonder if the success of Karon and Vanden-Bos' intervention here is not just the support of the imaginary effort of the patient to create a body image that includes sexuality, but also the fact of making that imaginary effort possible by introducing symbolic limits to sexuality without tying these limits to imaginary motives (feelings of guilt or talk of badness). Lacanians call this move the linking of pleasure to law, thus making pleasure a legitimate satisfaction of desire (Strauss, 59; see also Apollon et al., 102-105). In Schreber's case this was a crucial challenge for him.

Three other examples from Karon and VandenBos illustrate the Lacanian insight that therapy requires addressing both the imaginary and the symbolic. In the therapeutic relation, the therapist needs to do two things. He or she needs to allow imaginary projection to occur. In order to be helpful, the therapist must then move to a symbolic position. (Schema L: Lacan 1977,193; Fink 1997, 34). In a first example, Karon and VandenBos write: "The voice of God is an hallucination to be dealt with tactfully. Direct challenges that the voice really is not that of God can provoke violent attacks on the therapist... Listen to the material carefully. Sometimes one can say, without directly referring to the 'Godly' experience, 'I wonder if your mother used to say... [whatever it is that 'God' said].' Often a patient who would resent a direct challenge will immediately accept the statement as true, sometimes adding, 'But how did you know?'" (Karon & VandenBos, 184). A bit further, they write: "If a voice is challenged, it should only be because it has said something clearly destructive and you (the therapist) cannot believe that God is destructive" (Ibid.). In the above examples the patient is each time allowed to hold on to his or her imaginary projection while the therapist slightly corrects that projection, signaling that he or she (the therapist) is positioned elsewhere. Each time, the patient is not frontally contradicted. In the first instance, he or she is allowed to believe that God said what he said and is asked if his or her mother said that also. In the second instance, the patient is corrected on the basis of an internal argument: the God who is talking to you is, for you and me, a good God (mirroring move), and thus he cannot command bad things.

In the second example a patient somatized his illness. He said: "there is something wrong with my head and I need an operation." In replying, the therapist did not belittle or contradict the patient. Still the therapist did not simply mirror the patient's position. Here is the therapist's reply: "Of course there's something wrong with your head, if you hear voices. The only operation you need is to talk to someone about your problems and what makes the voices appear. Are you interested?" (Ibid., 186). The supposedly uncooperative patient said: "Yes, that sounds like a good idea" (Ibid., 187). Again, the therapeutic intervention is an artful mixing of mirroring and moving out of that mirroring position into what Lacanians call the symbolic position.

The third example illustrating that therapy requires addressing both the imaginary and the symbolic concerns Karon and VandenBos' general advice on how to be helpful to schizophrenic patients. They start by making it explicit that therapy with schizophrenics requires "giving" as in the mother-child relationship, thus demanding from therapists that they situate themselves for their patients in the imaginary. They argue further that: "The typical schizophrenic patient has felt deprived all his life. It is important that the therapist do whatever possible to be perceived as a giver and not a taker and to be perceived as a nonpunisher and nonpoisoner" (Ibid., 164-5). They argue that "[a]ll patients, but in particular schizophrenic patients, do not think of themselves as basically human. They think they are something different from all other people, and that other people could never comprehend their defects, difficulties, and anxieties" (Ibid., 167). Therefore one can tell such patients: "All I have to offer you is understanding, but that's really a great deal" (Ibid.). The request to offer and give understanding is here made with the explicit hope that the patient's experience of being understood will create the mirror effect that if the other can understand him or her, he or she must be just as human as the other.

When we look at how Karon and VandenBos propose to be helpful in the concrete, we discover several proposals that introduce the symbolic dimension as a controlling factor for the imaginary position taken by the therapist. Thus, in a first concrete proposal, the authors claim it to be useful to offer the patient a cup of coffee at the beginning of a session because they both like to drink coffee themselves during the session. They explain their advice as follows: "The patient thus gets direct oral gratification without interpretation" (Ibid., 165). The gift of a cup of coffee is thus explicitly placed in the context of maternal gratification, which in Lacanian terms is in the imaginary domain. But then the authors point out that frequently the patients refuse the offer and feel good about it. They suggest that such a rejection allows "a therapeutic working-through of the separation-individuation process" (Ibid.). But a tolerated rejection as part of a planned separation-individuation process is a symbolic process. That same symbolic goal of creating separation is behind the following advice: "When a patient chooses to do something different from what the therapist has suggested and it proves to be a better choice, it is an extremely therapeutic experience, if the therapist is genuinely delighted with it" (Ibid., 170).

Karon and VandenBos also suggest concrete ways to helping when the patient mentions problems. The authors suggest that the therapist should offer help [an imaginary step]. However, the offer of help should be presented in the following form: "Well, any decent therapist should be able to help you with that," (Ibid., 167). The authors explain their reasoning this way: "Such comments implant the idea that not only is help being offered, but the help is not magical, it is just the result of adequate training" (Ibid.). In Lacanian terms, this means that the help is not given within an imaginary framework (it is not magic, and the therapist is not omnipotent); instead, the help is offered from a symbolic point of view (it is the result of training, and the symbolic order is able to make the distinction between adequate and inadequate training, between a competent and an incompetent therapist).

Thirdly, Karon and VandenBos give concrete advice on how to deal with mistakes made by the therapist (and the patient). They write: "It is important early in therapy to introduce the idea that 'mistakes' are extremely useful" (Ibid., 169). Using a mirroring technique of we (the clever ones) against them (the dumb ones), they suggest telling the patient: "You know, our society is crazy because it doesn't teach that bright people make more mistakes than stupid people. Stupid people make a mistake and say, 'Oh my God, I'm stupid' and stop doing it. Bright people make more mistakes, because they do something new; then they learn, which means they make fewer mistakes. Once they learn to do something, they start doing something else and start making mistakes all over again. There is no way not to make mistakes other than to stop doing things" (Ibid., 169). For Lacan, the symbolic can only emerge if a natural tendency in the imaginary mirroring relation is overcome: the tendency to cover up gaps. This is done by acknowledging deficiencies, which is achieved by using words to articulate impossible dimensions of imaginary efforts. Without familiarity with Lacanian theory, Karon and VandenBos explicitly create room for this idea in their handling of the problem of therapist's (and the patient's) mistakes.

Among the therapists of Chesnut Lodge, Rockville, Maryland, both Frieda Fromm-Reichmann and Ann-Louise Silver give concrete examples of dealing with schizophrenics. Of the many forms of sublimation such as writing, composing music, or dancing, Frieda Fromm-Reichmann singles out dancing as having special capabilities for preventing manifest psychotic behavior (Fromm-Reichmann, 69-70). Fromm-Reichmann gives no explanation for her intuitive appreciation of dancing. On the other hand, we find an explicit argument made by a student of Fromm-Reichmann, Ann-Louise Silver for the practice of putting cold, wet sheet packs on patients—a practice now discontinued (Silver 1991, 49). The cold, wet sheet packs in combination with therapeutic talking were credited with "Margie's self-mutilations and her assaults on others stopp[ing] completely," after one week of hospitalization (Silver 1992 b, 119). The cold, wet packs are credited with having provided her with "a dependable physical boundary" (Ibid., 127). Dancing, similar to the cold, wet packs is credited with creating a boundary for the body self when the psychic bodily self is defective. Establishing a sense of bodily self is the work of the imaginary. Ann-Louise Silver points out, without reference to Lacanian theory, that as a therapist she then replaced the cold wet packs with "increasingly successful attunement.... . Her [the patient's] relationship with me [Silver] and with others then became real, mutually validating" (Ibid., 127). Silver thus continued her effort of establishing a body boundary with mirroring work that allowed the body self to contain emotions and thoughts, even the patient's own active assertiveness (Ibid., 121). The patient confirmed later that what helped her the most was: "You [Silver, the therapist] taught me that it is all right to hate, and that it will not hurt the other person or myself" (Ibid., 124). That work also involved the symbolic work of differentiating thought from action, which itself was done within the context of much imaginary work (Ibid., 125).

From a theoretical point of view, it is worth observing that Silver often describes her work in categories belonging to the domain of Lacan's imaginary. Still, she, like her teacher, Fromm-Reichmann, is aware of the need to anchor the mirroring work with psychotic patients in symbolic triangularity: She quotes Fromm-Reichmann that supervision is important "especially in therapy with a psychotic patient... not because of what the supervisor may have to offer, but for the very fact that the privacy of two is changed into a relationship of three" (Silver 1991, 3).

This same mixture of imaginary presence and minor symbolic limit setting is present in the way A-L. Silver handles her availability to her patients over the phone. Silver is mainly concerned with being a permanent mirroring presence for her patients, who easily disorganize when they feel angry. When feeling angry, they become ashamed for feeling angry, then turn their anger against themselves, and then feel panicky over their impulses to punish themselves in a brutal way (self-mutilation, overdose of drugs, etc). Sometimes, leaving a message on the therapist's answering service is, for the patients, enough to be reassured. Sometimes the patients request a call back from the therapist. Sometimes they need to talk to her. Dr. Silver tells such patients her approximate schedule and gives a phone number where she can be reached. This quasi-permanent imaginary presence comes with a soft symbolic limitation: she tells those patients that she is a light sleeper and can't get back to sleep easily once awakened. And a sleepless night means that she cannot work well the next day (Oral communication).

Repeatedly, Gaetano Benedetti stresses what a Lacanian would call the need for mirroring in treating schizophrenics: i.e, the need for the therapist to affirm or accept that he or she is a substitute or mirror for the patient. He writes: "The patient understands himself bit by bit inasmuch as he is understood by us. The fragments of his ego are reconstructed through our act of understanding him" (Benedetti 1995, 199).(27) Thus a patient had the fantasy of renting an apartment with two rooms, one intended as a music room. The patient feels trapped because in trying to realize her fantasy, she feels that she will lose her desire for it and the unused, empty room will be a perpetual reminder of the loss of her desire. On the other hand, if she tries to keep her desire for music by staying in touch with her fantasy she fears that the fantasy will disappear. Benedetti simply asked the patient if she would "deposit her fantasy with him?" (Ibid., 265). Benedetti comments that his intervention allows the patient to both liberate herself from a fantasy she does not want without killing it. Benedetti interprets himself as playing the other part of the patient for her. She can now forget about her fantasy while being sure that the fantasy does not die. The fantasy remains available for her to reclaim it when she wants. In reference to this intervention, the patient says that the previous day she had a dream that she bought a house and gave Benedetti the key. In the dream, Benedetti came to the empty house and gave it a soul (Ibid., 265).

In another example, the therapist, presumably supervised by Benedetti, dealt with a patient who expressed the split in herself with the delusion of two armies trying to destroy each other. Her effort to maintain her unity consisted of her watching the hostile armies so that they would not destroy everything. The therapist related the hostile armies to her inner conflicts. The decisive intervention, however, was when the therapist told the patient that she could close her eyes and sleep since the therapist would watch in her place (Ibid., 364).

Benedetti summarizes his ideas by writing that a "therapist can become in this way the mirror of the disintegrated parts of the patient" (Ibid., 367). The question raised by the Lacanian framework is: where is the symbolic in Benedetti's technique? The answer is given by Benedetti himself: it is in the aim of the process. Benedetti writes: "' the therapeutic confusion of identity' is, paradoxically, a method of overcoming the pathological confusion of identity which is the essence of psychosis" (Ibid.,365).

A further articulation of the intertwining of the imaginary and the symbolic comes from a study using the theories of both Lacan and Peirce to investigate mother-infant relations. In that study, John Muller (1996) accepts the thesis of the psychologist Jerome Bruner that culture is the major factor when trying to understand human beings and their interactions. This thesis implies that even the most intimate relations between human beings are regulated by internalized cultural norms. Muller then proceeds to demonstrate that thesis in the mother-infant relation. Using a study by Brazelton, Koslowski, and Main, he shows that the interaction between mother and child consists of a cycle of attention and withdrawal in which the mother is attentive to the cues of the child. That interaction has thus a "conversation-like pattern" (Muller 1996, 20) which is subject to cross-cultural variation. About the mothers, studies have shown that "American mothers combined facial expressiveness with vocalization, whereas Japanese mothers combined facial expressiveness with leaning close" (Ibid.). About the children, those same studies noticed that "infants in both cultures smiled overall about the same proportion of time, but the American infants smiled three times as often as the Japanese infants, while the Japanese smiled for longer average durations" (Ibid.). J. Cohn and E. Tronick asked mothers of three-month-old infants to artificially alter their normal interaction pattern with their children by showing depressed reactions. The infants tried repeatedly to elicit normal reactions from their mothers. After a while the infants gave up. When the mothers later started the communication game again, the children showed signs of anger.

Muller interprets these studies as demonstrating that the mother-child relationship obeys (cultural) norms. Without the mother's adherence to those norms, the child does not feel recognized. As a consequence, writes Muller:

"When culture does not hold the dyad, when the mother is alienated from her culture or when cultural transmission has broken down, then the infant-mother dyad is in trouble" (Muller 1996, 189). But what is the function of culture in promoting the normal development of the child in the mother-infant dyad? Again, according to Muller: "[T]he presence in the mother's life of sociocultural frameworks... contextualize[s] and delimit[s] the role of the child in her life and is usually highlighted by the presence of the father, who sets limits on the grandiose totalization of desire" (Ibid., 148; Ver Eecke 1997, 116-7). In the language we have been using, we can summarize Muller's views as confirming that the symbolic does not perform its function separate from the imaginary, but rather with it, and in such a way that both are operative at the same time. The failure of the symbolic (failure of the paternal metaphor) in the schizophrenic should then most likely be understood as the failure of the symbolic due to an already existing failure of the imaginary.

II. Developments in Schreber Scholarship

A number of important new studies have appeared on Schreber, whose *Memoirs* both Lacan and De Waelhens use to develop their theory of schizophrenia (Israëls; Allison, de Oliveira et al.; de Oliveira; Niederland; Schatzman; Lothane; Devreese; and Devreese et al.). I cannot review all of the new scholarship, so I will instead restrict myself to discussing work that develops ideas presented in De Waelhens' book *Schizophrenia*.(28) In the first section, I will use new historical research about Schreber to reconfirm or even strengthen the arguments for De Waelhens' explanation—following Lacan—for schizophrenia. In the second section, I will use new theoretical claims about Schreber's basic problem in order to show that the suggestion by De Waelhens that both the maternal and the paternal function are defective in the schizophrenic can now be developed into a theory with clear implications for the therapy of schizophrenics.

A. New historical research on Schreber

First, recent historical research disputes the claim of the Niederland-Schatzman thesis which states that father Schreber, through his educational practices, his authoritarianism, and even his sadism, made his son, Judge Schreber, crazy. Indeed, the research by Han Israëls and even more so that of Zvi Lothane shows that the women (his mother, his aunt, his wife) in Judge Schreber's life also played an important and not always positive role (Lothane 1998, 13; Lothane 1992, 443, 446, 450). Furthermore, Lothane argues that Schreber developed too great an attachment to both his mother and his father and that the latter was a deficient figure due to his illness during most of Judge

Schreber's youth (Lothane 1992, 446). Lothane's conclusion is precisely the theoretical explanation suggested by De Waelhens for schizophrenia: it is neither the mother nor the father who can be called the cause, but *rather the way the child uses the structural relationship* between the father and the mother (This book Chapter Five, Section VII).

Second, Lothane's historical research provides evidence for what was but a postulated fact in Lacan's theory. Indeed, Lothane points out that Paul Flechsig would as a rule accept patients only if they could be cured—or were expected to show significant improvement—within six months. Judge Schreber's improvement from his first mental breakdown occurred within that period. However, it became clear to Judge Schreber that he would not meet that deadline during his second mental illness. Judge Schreber seems also to have discovered the complicity of his doctor (and his own wife) with the authorities to deprive him of his judgeship (Schreber saw an advertisement for his job in a newspaper). It was then that the hallucinatory-delusional phase of his illness began (Lothane 1992, 433). At that point, Flechsig's image changed from that of a successful healer, to whom the Schreber family was grateful, into that of a doctor who did not care for his patients and conspired with legal authorities to deprive Schreber of his job and his freedom (he was put under tutelage and sent to a state asylum). Such a change in the perception of an important (male) figure is precisely what Lacan's theory postulates. Lacan speculates on the possibility of such a change in perception of Flechsig by Schreber (Lacan 1977, 220-1). Lothane provides the proof that such a change actually occurred (Lothane 1992, 433, 457-8; Ver Eecke 1995, 475 ff.).

B. New theoretical claims about Schreber's basic problem

In a significant article for *Psychosis and Sexual Identity* (Allison et al.), an anthology about Schreber, William Richardson uses some of Lacan's texts to explicitly claim a deeper interconnection between the symbolic and the imaginary than De Waelhens claimed. Thus Richardson writes: "If this is how the Symbolic, Imaginary and Real are differentiated, how are they related? They are absolutely linked. The Symbolic never functions without the consort of the Imaginary, the Imaginary never without orientation toward eventual symbolization-neither without conjunction of the Real that their task is to bring to representation. So closely are they intertwined that Lacan speaks of them as a knot—composed of three circles so intertwined that if one is broken the whole knot falls apart" (Richardson 1988, 22). Richardson interprets the speaking of the infant (particularly the infant speaking about the mother as in Freud's "fort-da" analysis) as introducing a distance between mother and child. That distance created by speech or language is made possible by "the law of language (the symbolic order), the Law which is the Law of the Father" (Ibid.,

23). If the child can successfully talk about or signify the mother, then primal repression has occurred in the form of the child distancing itself from the mother. If such talk or signifying does not occur, then the law of language, which is the Law of the Father, fails. Failure of the Law of the Father is called foreclosure of the Name-of-the-Father. This expression seems, according to Richardson's reading to indicate that there is a close connection (if not an identity) between language and the function of the father (Ibid., 23-24). For Richardson, the close connection between the imaginary and the symbolic is expressed in this way: "The first relationship between mother and child is a dyadic one, completely on the imaginary level. But when the infant begins to talk, the dyadic tie with the mother ruptures and he starts to relate to her by means of language" (Ibid., 22).

I agree with Richardson that the symbolic is present in the life of the child prior to the Oedipus complex. It is an original contribution of Richardson's article to demonstrate that the symbolic is present in the speech of the child. However, in my opinion, the act of speaking by the child is not the same as the paternal metaphor. First, even though the possibility of speaking and signifying by the child is conditioned on some kind of presence of the paternal function, it remains a fact that the paternal presence is much more interiorized in the Oedipus complex than in the act of speaking exemplified by Freud's grandchild (Ver Eecke 1984, 78 ff.). If one accepts my position, one can understand why children must be more than three years old and must be in the classic Oedipal position, before they are able to understand ordinary metaphors such as "you are a pig," whereas they can start using language, in the way that Freud's grandchild did, from around one-and-a-half-years old. Second, speech performed within the dyadic relation accomplishes other things than those achieved by speech performed within the paternal metaphor.

But what different things are accomplished if speech is performed in these two different circumstances? We find a hint in the perceptive observation by Jozef Corveleyn about the speech of Judge Schreber. Corveleyn observes that in his *Memoirs* Judge Schreber did not succeed in making himself "a co-human who speaks as equal to equal. Instead his book is there to demonstrate his exceptional place among humans. He is not one of them. He is beyond all of them" (Corveleyn 1998, 204). In an article by Antoine Vergote we find an explanation as to why Judge Schreber was not able to overcome his grandiosity. Vergote's explanation also provides the positive definition of schizophrenia which complements Lacan's negative definition (failure of the paternal metaphor). For Vergote, Schreber's central problem was his experiencing sensual pleasure as destructive (Vergote 1998, 234). He therefore situates Schreber's main problem and also the origin of psychosis in general in the autoerotic period of the subject, at which point the future psychotic has not been able to well integrate his or her bodily sensations into a more or less harmoniously constructed libidinal body (Ibid., 237). Rather, the body is excluded from the ego and the ego is created from cultural ideals that flatter the subject's narcissism: manly honor, respect for the order of the world, respect for God, concern for God, and self-control. Very perceptively, Vergote observes that in his brilliant *Memoirs*, Schreber fails to use one form of language: metaphors. For that to be possible, one must possess and be able to mix two chains of signifiers belonging to two different orders (God is a light for the mind; you are a chicken). However, the exclusion of the libidinal body from his or her ego deprives the psychotic of a second ontological aspect capable of being the source of a second series of signifiers which are needed in order to produce metaphors (Ibid., 242). Examples of metaphors borrowed from the bodily dimension are: my heart is heavy, my heart bleeds, my soul is stained.

In answering the question as to why a psychotic excludes the body from his or her imaginary ego, Vergote provides a further proof for my dual epistemology. Indeed, Vergote gives psychic, psychosomatic, and biological facts as possible causes for the psychotic's inability or refusal to construct a libidinal body as an integral part of his or her ego: sensations providing too much pleasure or not enough satisfaction, too many terrifying experiences, a broken rhythm of different experiences and a neurobiological deficit in the "gate screening the excitations" (Ibid., 237). Unfortunate coincidences, too, might be contributing causes of schizophrenia. Recall the example of the family physician who explained to the boy that he had "bad nerves" and that nerves are like worms under the skin. The boy, who with his siblings experienced the very ugly divorce of his parents, knew about worms from fishing: when they dried they burst. When the boy compulsively wetted his hands and face, went into a rage when forced to stop this practice, and talked about worms under his skin, he was diagnosed as psychotic. He had taken literally the metaphorical explanation of nerves as worms (Karon & VandenBos, 159-61). In another case, the coincidence which broke the happy coadaptation between mother and child which is required for a satisfactory imaginary creation of a body image, was the fact that the mother decided to stop breast feeding at four weeks and the child happened to be allergic to the formula milk given as a substitute. The mother interpreted the unhappiness and cries of the child as capriciousness. She ignored them until two months later when the pediatrician diagnosed the allergic reaction. "After the formula was changed, the baby calmed down considerably. But by now he was no longer placid and happy as he had originally been; he was anxious-looking, whined a lot" (Pao, 148-9; Pao defends explicitly the dual epistemological view in Pao, Chapter 11).

Thus, the development of Schreber scholarship—as it pushes for a positive definition of schizophrenia—explicitly introduces the idea that there is a failure of the imaginary (imaginary construction of a libidinal body) as well as of the symbolic. As a consequence, one can expect that successful treatment of schizophrenia will have to deal with the failure of both the imaginary and the symbolic. The suggestion by Vergote about the failures in the imaginary in Schreber case provides me with the necessary theoretical element for explaining at an even deeper level those successful interventions in the treatment of schizophrenics that were discussed before.

Gisela Pankow, a neuropsychiatrist teaching at Bonn University and a practicing psychoanalyst in Paris, describes some remarkable successes in treating schizophrenics (Pankow 1969, 72, 135-6, 176-7, 204). Pankow confirms my dual epistemological approach in understanding schizophrenia inasmuch as she explicitly affirms that her psychoanalytically informed approach in treating schizophrenics does not imply that the cause of mental illness is [exclusively] psychic (Ibid., 29). She also states that the use of medication can help psychotherapy (Ibid., 25).

Pankow's originality consists in explicitly locating the problem of schizophrenia in a defective body image and in developing techniques to restore the body image (Ibid., 206, 278, 286, 291). The body image of the schizophrenic is defective in at least two ways. First, the schizophrenic experiences the body as broken and consisting of parts that have no connection with the body as a whole (Ibid., 23). Second, the schizophrenic's body does not function as an envelope, a contour, or a limit (Ibid., 28). Furthermore, the method of giving content to the body, of giving it a meaning, and of relating that body to other people is defective. It is, as it were, a dead body, not inhabited by acknowledged desires (Ibid., 23-4, 30).

Pankow presents several techniques to help repair the body image of schizophrenics. Her first technique consists in helping the patient to experience and accept his or her body as a limit. She accepts the suggestions of Fromm-Reichman and Sechehaye that it is helpful to give schizophrenics bodily care such as bathing them, giving them a massage, or wrapping them. Pankow, however, considers this care helpful, however, for other reasons than those of most authors. Schizophrenics need not be given what they were deprived of in their childhood, rather they need to be given opportunities for bodily sensations—tactile and other—that limit their magical world and promote the recognition of the limits of their body (Ibid., 24).(29) Letting the patients have bodily sensations lets them experience a limit and thus imposes a retreat on the psychotic process (Ibid., 25, 278).

For her part, Pankow invites patients to model something for her in clay. The major challenge for the patients—so Pankow writes—is to touch the clay (Ibid., 27). Touching the clay establishes a kind of limit. In a second phase, Pankow asks questions about the clay model—say, a shoe. If the patient still has a sense that his or her clay model models something in the world, Pankow asks a question like: "To whom could this shoe belong?" If the patient is not any more capable of seeing the connection between his or her clay model and the world, Pankow asks a question like: "If you were this shoe, what could you do with my body?" The purpose of these questions is to promote the recognition of any unconscious desires with reference to the patient's own body or the body of the therapist.(30) The patient's recognition of his or her desires is achieved by a detour: i.e., through the formation of dynamic structuring phantasms (Ibid., 28, 277, 287). Work with the phantasm is work on the borderline of the imaginary and the symbolic or, better, it is work aimed at repairing the body image (the imaginary) by means of imaginary products (phantasms of the patients) that are given their symbolic efficacy through the words of the therapist.

Pankow's work with phantasms can be illustrated by her intervention with a catatonic patient who had cut her right arm. The patient had been hospitalized and given a sleeping cure and three insulin treatments. During the time of the persecution of Jews in Europe, her father had hidden the fact that her deceased mother was Jewish. In order to prevent his daughter from marrying—which could have exposed her Jewish lineage—he had sex with her for years. Seeing a bandage on the patient's right arm, Pankow asked if she was left handed? The patient answered, "Yes, but I asked myself which was the more precious hand. I had to sacrifice that hand for my father.... I suffer much. Why did I deserve that? Am I that bad? (Silence). The hand had to disappear." (Ibid., 290-1). In this nonsense, Pankow discovered the patient's phantasm which expressed a connection between herself and a dissociated body part and made possible the communication of an unspeakable desire in which she had been involved. Pankow then said to the patient "that she had given her father the hand which he had given her in matrimony. Her father now created with her hand his second marriage and she had her marriage with her husband. For the first time in her therapy she smiled and said to me [Pankow], 'Is it that serious, what I did at eighteen [the incest]?'"(Ibid., 291). The intervention had been preceded by detailed work in which Pankow tried to let the patient understand that she had been a non-Jew during the day and a Jew at night. Since the father had declared her a non-Jew, she could experience herself completely as a non-Jew. At night, the rejected Jewish part could play the role of the Jewish mother so that she could have intercourse with her father (Ibid., 290). Pankow's final comment is that once a rejected body part has been psychically reunited with the body, the patient can assume his or her history (Ibid., 291).

Muller invites his patients to draw or to paint their horrifying experience and to bring the drawing or the painting to his office. He explains that such an exercise presents the patient with an object that is "limited, differentiated from its surroundings, *subject to the constraints of its materiality as a medium* [emphasis mine], and it [the created object] rests in itself with an emerging coherence. Its sensuous qualities are held by its form, however rudimentary it may be. In these ways it presents possibilities for the patients' evolving experience, possibilities for differentiation and coherence that are not being controlled by the therapist but are determined by the specific medium. In this way the patient is enabled to delimit narcissistic grandiosity" (Muller 1999, 9). Thus, work with matter is credited with the ability to let the psychotic curtail his or her grandiosity. To turn this around: curtailing grandiosity by means of imaginary work on matter makes the objective world, in some way, again available to the ego. Such an ego then has access once again, however minimally, to a second world (matter, the body, objectivity) with the result that a second chain of signifiers becomes available. In some cases, the psychotic is able to create a constructive metaphor and the therapist only has to *hear* the metaphor. This was the case with the patient dealing with his fear of committing suicide by first painting on his bedsheet, then hanging his painted sheet on the wall, and reporting to his psychologist: "I hanged my painting instead of myself" (Muller 1999, 12).

In other cases the patient does not create the metaphor. He or she only creates the imaginary gesture that *allows* for a metaphoric interpretation. The task of the therapist is then not so much to hear the metaphor spoken by the patient, but rather to provide the proper metaphor. This was the case with the patient who forgot his pipe and the therapist said to the patient, "You forgot your pipe. You did not break it [you did not commit suicide]. You had a choice" (Gaudillière 1998) . That this was not an empty play with words but a metaphor ready to be heard by the patient is proven by the fact that the suicidal ideas of this patient disappeared after the exchange (Ibid.). The above examples provide practical, and sometimes spectacular, illustrations for the theoretical claim that the symbolic (metaphors, limitations, prohibitions) should be introduced as an extension of prior imaginary work. A successful metaphor, just as a prohibition that is accepted, depends upon prior imaginary work.

The idea that effective treatment of schizophrenia needs to start with work at the imaginary level in order to implement improvements at the symbolic level was derived both from developments in Lacan and Schreber scholarship. That idea is elevated into a program at the *Groupe Interdisiplinaire Freudien de Recherches et Interventions Cliniques et Culturelles* (GIFRIC) in Québec that works with psychotics. Willy Apollon writes that the two tasks for treating psychotics in their Center is to reconstruct the patients' body image (work at the imaginary level) and social relations (work at the symbolic level) (Apollon et al., 19, 79, 92-97, 102-108). Reconstructing the social relations includes helping the patients to discover an interest in creative work meaningful to others (Bélanger & Riou, 200-202), to trust in the word of another (Apollon et al., 105), and also to assume their sexuality as it involves them potentially in the desires of others, and in motherhood or paternity (Ibid., 102).(31)

Coming back to the major thesis of this chapter, it is important to note that GIFRIC's psychoanalytic orientation is infused with an explicit dual epistemology: in addition to psychotherapy, GIFRIC also gives an important function to medication. The physician must try to limit the effects of psychosis on the organism. He or she must make it possible for the patient to rest and sleep so that psychotherapeutic work can be performed (Apollon, 95). The dual epistemology present at GIFRIC encourages the physician to take into account whether the patient struggles against the medication or overinvests in it (a family member was helped by that particular drug; the name of the drug resonates emotionally with the patient). In the first case, more medication will be needed, whereas in the latter case, less will be needed than is necessary for patients who are emotionally neutral to the medication (Turmel, 164-68). In order to minimize the level of medication needed in order to be effective, the team will discuss and consult with the patient about the medication, thereby trying to maximize the psychic impact of the medication.

Conclusion

My thesis of a dual epistemological approach to mental illness—in particular to schizophrenia—implies that besides an obvious somatic dimension there is also an autonomous psychic aspect to schizophrenia. Professionals responsible for schizophrenics should, therefore, also pay attention to the psychological dimension of the schizophrenic patient. De Waelhens' part of this book provides a systematic approach for understanding the psychic world of the psychotic, in particular the schizophrenic. That systematic approach can be illuminating to psychiatrists and therapists in two very different areas. First, it is helpful in forensic psychiatry and psychology because it provides the basis for a simple and reliable criterion to argue legally why and when a person should be declared incompetent to write a will or sign an order preventing a medical intervention for him- or herself or for his or her children. The criterion connects the concept of freedom with the role given to a hypothetical third party in a person's conception of truth (This book, Chapter Six, Section IV). Second, it argues that there is a double failure in the psychic structure of the schizophrenic person: a failure in the symbolic (paternal function) and a failure in the imaginary (internalized maternal relations). In turn, this insight can be used to structure psychological services for schizophrenics. Therapy and therapists must be able to relate to the imaginary of the patient in order to promote some healing at that level before the disorder in the symbolic (language, thought) can be repaired. I demonstrated that successful therapists—Lacanians and non-Lacanians alike—did just that, even if they did it with different means, and even if they explained what they were doing in a different vocabulary.

In short, this book provides crucial theoretical help in at least two domains to professionals involved with severely mentally disturbed patients. It establishes a phenomenological criterion for the practice of forensic psychiatry and psychology. Additionally, it supplies a systematic theory of psychosis and schizophrenia which teaches us why the successful treatment of psychosis requires the art of combining interventions at the imaginary level with those at the symbolic (e.g., establishing emotional contact and at the same time either introducing an appropriate distinction, making a sensible limitation acceptable, or doing both).

Postscript

I. On the definition of schizophrenia

Nancy C. Andreasen, a well-known researcher in neurobiology, defines schizophrenia as "a disease of the brain that is expressed clinically as a disease of the mind.... [P]atients have a variety of symptoms and impairments in cognition. Behind this diversity, however, is a final common pathway that defines the illness. For schizophrenia, it is the misregulation of information processing in the brain" (646). This is a very helpful interdisciplinary definition confirming the dual epistemological approach I have defended in my essay. However, I agree with only one third of the definition as formulated.(32)

The one third of Andreasen's definition of schizophrenia that I agree with is the claim that the disease expresses itself clinically as a disease of the mind. This is confirmed by a clinical psychiatrist quoting a patient: "I had no sense of my being as self, that is I wasn't aware that my feelings were related to myself" (Kafka, 26). According to Kafka, "What distinguishes the psychotic individual... is the fact that the person, the self, does not have a privileged position in the object world" (Ibid., 27).

If the disease is understood to express itself clinically as a disease of the mind, then the goal of therapy should be the healing of the mind—in Andreasen,'s formulation—or in restoring a sense of self—in Kafka's formulation. To be a self is to be able to tell some kind of consistent story about one's life. Treatment methods that make that more difficult are problematic. Consider the following testimony of a patient: "I remember waking up after each ECTC electro-convulsive therapy [sic] and finding a little less of my memory remaining. I couldn't remember my friends in high school, my distant or immediate past was less clear to me.... It was supposed to eradicate bad memories, yet the treatment showed no discrimination" (Ibid., 25). The interdisciplinary definition of schizophrenia by Andreasen invites a search for treatment methods with less negative side effects—methods that will treat the clinical symptom itself and also restore a sense of self.

Discontent on the part of schizophrenic patients is not limited to electro-convulsive therapy. Clinicians have also reported such discontent with the use of neuroleptics. Such complaints are documented in several studies (Awad, 743). If the subjective problem of the schizophrenic expresses itself as a problem of the mind or if schizophrenics have a problem with their sense of self, then it would logically follow that they will also need help with these psychic problems. Not to do so is to disregard the definition of schizophrenia proposed by Andreasen and confirmed by Kafka.

The research in this chapter invites me to broaden Andreasen's definition of schizophrenia. Indeed, the clinical expression of the disease is not limited to "impairments in cognition" or "misregulation of information processing" (Andreasen, 646). The clinical expression of the disease also consists of the

schizophrenic's difficulty to include the body—with its sensations and its desires—into one's self-image and the difficulty of relating as a human being—with desires, including sexual ones—to other human beings. These two
problems involve more than cognition. They involve the emotions; they involve moral life; they involve the problem of human re-cognition. Such a
broadened definition of schizophrenia implies that schizophrenics have ended
up with profoundly dysfunctional relations towards their own body, towards
others, and towards language. Such a broadened definition of schizophrenia
also has implications for therapy. Supporting therapy might be very helpful;
however, it cannot be considered adequate since profoundly different relations
towards the body, others, and language need to be developed. Theoretically,
one needs to defend "transforming therapy."

The research presented in this chapter demands that I disagree with the
claim by Andreasen that schizophrenia is "a disease of the brain." That research demonstrates—so I believe—that a psychological cause is as necessary
for the eruption of schizophrenia as a biological cause. I have presented statistical evidence for that claim (Tienari 1992, 163) and psychological mechanisms which causally explain the statistical evidence. The efficacy of the
psychological mechanisms is supported by statistical evidence and by its conceptual explanatory power (communication deviance studies, the Fort study on
proverb identification, Karon's pathogenesis intrafamilial risk variable (Karon
& Widener, 47, 52-3), and studies on expressed emotions).

Stressing the claim that schizophrenia is a disease of the brain as opposed
to stressing that schizophrenia is also (if not primarily) a psychological dysfunction is not a minor matter. It can lead to misinterpretations and then to
mistreatment of the dysfunctions of the schizophrenic. This can be nicely
demonstrated by the work of Louis Sass (Sass 1992; 1994; 1999). Taking a
psychological-philosophical point of view on schizophrenia, Sass points out
that the negative symptoms of schizophrenia are often interpreted by psychiatry as forms of diminished functioning. Instead, so argues Sass, at least some
of the negative symptoms such as alogia are the result of hyperactivity, in
particular hyper-reflexivity.(33) Such hyper-reflexivity then paralyzes normal
human behavior.(34) To make his point, Sass relies, among others, on the
self-description of the French artist and writer Artaud about the difficulty
experienced in performing the simple act of saying "it is cold."

If it is cold I can still say that it is cold, but there are times when I am incapable of saying it: this is a fact, for there is in me something damaged from
the emotional point of view, and if someone asked me why I could not say
it, I would answer that my inner feeling on this slight and neutral point did
not correspond to the three simple little words I would have to pronounce
["it is cold"]. And this lack of correspondence, therefore, between a
physiological sensation and its emotional response in the first place and
next its intellectual response—insofar as it is possible to summarize and

synthesize in general terms this series of swift, almost instantaneous operations which give rise to the truism *it is cold*—this lack of correspondence, since it does not select its subjects or spare me in any way, culminates, as it spreads, in the colossal troubles which correspond perfectly, alas, to the loss of personality (Sontag 1976, 294-5).

Artaud correctly points out in this text that saying "It is cold" is the result of a process consisting of three steps: there is an objective reality which produces a physiological sensation; there is an emotional reaction (burr...); one says that it is cold.

For most people, these three steps occur in a *nice continuum*: first, we are affected by the cold; second, we react bodily to that cold by shivering, that is, we *experience* the cold; third, we describe the experienced situation by saying: "It is cold." The continuum consists in the fact that the "I" that says, "it is cold" is fused with the body that shivers. One could almost say: I am so fused with my body that it says for me: "it's cold" or better, I let myself say, "it is cold."

For Artaud the situation is different. Instead of a continuum between the three steps, those three steps fall apart. Artaud can be physiologically affected by the cold but his emotional reaction to the cold is not "burr..." which would make him say "it is cold." Rather Artaud's emotional reaction is—as Artaud himself claims—some other emotional reaction.

Let us call the "burr..." reaction making me say, "it is cold," X. Let us call Artaud's emotional reaction, which is different, the Y reaction. Artaud's Y reaction consists of two moments:
1. Awareness of the strangeness of the emotional reaction to the cold.
2. Transformation of the expression "it is cold" from a sentence that expresses a meaning (i.e., a signified) to a sentence that consist of brute signifiers "three simple little words I would have to pronounce" (Ibid.).

Artaud himself describes this double dimension of the Y reaction as: there is a "lack of correspondence, therefore, between a physiological sensation and its emotinal response in the first place and next its intellectual response" (Ibid., 295).

While for us, our embodied self makes almost automatically steps two and three in the process of feeling cold, there the embodied self of Artaud creates for Artaud a discontinuum. Still, Artaud is similar enough to us, that he realizes that his embodied self *should do for him* what it does for us. He writes: sometimes "I am incapable of saying it [that it is cold]:... but there are times...[that because] in me something [is] damaged from the emotional point of view,... [there is a] lack of correspondence" (Ibid., 294).

Let us use Husserl's concept of "passive synthesis" for referring to the activity that smoothly combines the three steps, since that combining activity occurs in us almost automatically. It is almost as if it is done for us by our embodied self. After this "passive synthesis" is done for us, we might initiate a philosophical act of reflection and say, "how smoothly did this all happen! How can I distinguish between what happened to me and what I did?"

According to Artaud this "passive synthesis" breaks down in him from time to time. However, he still remains aware that the "passive synthesis" should have occurred. As a consequence, where we need a decision to start the process of reflecting philosophically on what happened, there Artaud has an existential reason to start such a philosophical reflection. Indeed, Artaud senses that result X, which includes a "passive synthesis", should have taken place. However, he feels that Y has taken place and that the Y event or experience is a failure.

Consciousness is non-thematically present to its embodied activity, whether that activity is experienced as a success or as a failure. When the embodied activity succeeds, there is normally no existential reason to thematize the conscious presence to our embodied activity unless one is in a program to improve one's embodied performance (athletics) or unless one is a philosopher. If one's embodied activity fails there is an existential reason to thematize our conscious presence: one then starts to reflect almost naturally.

In the example of Artaud, his situation leads to his inability to say, "it is cold." There is no observable activity where one could expect one. Sass correctly points out that behaviorists mistakenly conclude that in this situation—exemplifying typical schizophrenic behavior—one is in the presence of a negative symptom: diminished activity, diminished speaking (a-logia). Sass perceptively argues that there are all kind of intentional activities that go on behind the failure to say "It is cold." In particular there is hyper-reflectivity. Unfortunately, all the activity does not lead to the normal single "passive synthesis" X.

As argued in the main body of the chapter, for De Waelhens, following Lacan, the essence of schizophrenia is a radical failure in the constitution of the subject. Lacan himself pointed to the radical failure of the function of language in the schizophrenic because of the failure of the paternal metaphor. As a consequence everyday words loose there metaphorical meaning and are reduced to their literal dimension.

Post-lacanians, building upon Lacan, argue that in schizophrenia there is also a profound disturbance in the relation to the own body. This is called a disturbance in the imaginary. The mirror stage function has failed. We know that the child jubilates at about 6 months of age in front of the mirror. That joy is interpreted as indicating that the child recognizes itself as a totality, whereas before, it experienced itself in body parts. It now knows itself to be the object of love by the other and can now also love itself. The mirror stage demands that the child inhabit both its external form, and its proprioceptive interiority and furthermore that it makes a synthesis between the two. By means of that synthesis it is ready to translate inner feelings into actions in the external world. The child prepares itself for "passive syntheses." In schizophrenia, the basis for "passive synthesis," the mirror stage failed.

Let me apply the insights of the two previous paragraphs to the testimony of Artaud on his inability to say that it is cold. Artaud himself reports two failures. First, there is the strangeness of emotional reaction to cold which makes it unavailable for translation into words for people in the world. Lacanians would call this a failure of the imaginary, a failure of embodiment. Second, there is the fact that the expression "It is cold" is reduced to its materiality, its literalness:" three simple words I would have to pronounce." This is a failure in the symbolic.

Pointing to the psychological cause of schizophrenia helps to explain better and more correctly some schizophrenic symptoms (the negative symptoms) by putting them in a broader framework such as their defective relations towards their own bodies, towards language, and towards others. It also explains why the combination of psychosocial treatments with somatic ones has demonstrable additive and supplementary effects(35) with schizophrenics and why the beneficial effects of psychosocial treatments have durability (Mojtabai et al., 569, 574, 576, 580-82, 584).

Psychoanalytically informed therapy, in general, is aware that patients have a defective relation towards their own bodies, towards language, and towards others. De Waelhens, informed by Lacan and contemporary philosophy, teaches us that a defective relation to language is the crucial defect of the schizophrenics. I argue that accepting a psychological cause for schizophrenia demands that one gives an important place to psychoanalytically informed therapy in the treatment of schizophrenics.

To the objection that the psychic regression demanded by classic psychoanalysis is too painful, one can reply that the successful therapeutic interventions reported in this chapter do not obey the rules of classic psychoanalysis. These reported interventions actually violate several of the rules of classic psychoanalysis.(36) They are therapeutic techniques adapted to the needs of schizophrenics but inspired by psychoanalysis. These therapeutic techniques have in common that they take the subjective position of the patient so seriously that they use it as the starting point for treatment (Castoriadis-Aulagnier, 219-220).

Because of the argument that schizophrenics end up with profoundly defective relations to their own body, to language, and to others, psychoanalytically inspired therapies should regain importance in the treatment of schizophrenics. These therapies will become more important the more one pays attention to the subjective complaints of schizophrenic patients and the more one addresses the question of the quality of life for those patients, not just the containment of their symptoms.

II. On the treatment of choice for schizophrenics

The arguments in this chapter also demand that I disagree with two recommendations of the Patient Outcomes Research Team (PORT) schizophrenia treatment study. Both recommendations are based on level C evidence, meaning the weakest level of evidence on which recommendations are made in the study. Level C evidence is defined as: "Recommendation based primarily on expert opinion, with minimal research-based evidence, but significant clinical experience" (Lehman & Steinwachs, 2). The first recommendation relevant to this essay is Recommendation 22: "Individual and group psychotherapies adhering to a psychodynamic model (defined as therapies that use interpretation of unconscious material and focus on transference and regression) should *not* be used in the treatment of persons with schizophrenia" (Ibid., 7). The authors give the following rationale for the Recommendation: "This risk [using regression and psychotic transference], combined with the high cost and lack of evidence of any benefit, argues strongly against the use of psychoanalytic therapy" (Ibid., 7-8). The second recommendation relevant to this essay is Recommendation 26: "Family therapies based on the premise that family dysfunction is the etiology of the patient's schizophrenic disorder should *not* be used" (Ibid., 8). The rationale given by the authors is: "Research has failed to substantiate hypothesized causal links between family dysfunction and the etiology of schizophrenia.... The presumption that family interaction causes schizophrenia... has led to serious disruption in clinical/family trust without any evidence of therapeutic effectiveness" (Ibid., 8).

Before discussing the two Recommendations in detail, I want to point to two aspects of the Recommendations. First, the authors of the Recommendations rightly hope that their work will be useful. They hope that "the Treatment Recommendations [will] stimulate close examination of practices at both the aggregate and at the individual patient levels to ensure that treatments are offered in the most effective manner" (Ibid., 9). Second, the authors are proud to mention their requirement that the Treatment "[R]ecommendations be based on substantial scientific evidence" (Ibid., 1). They confess that their approach has unintended consequences such as the fact that their Recommendations "are silent about or may appear to understate the importance of other aspects of treatment that have not been evaluated adequately. Therefore, there are many more recommendations about pharmacotherapies than about psychosocial treatments. This does not mean that psychosocial treatments are less important than medications, but reflects the fact that we know much less about which psychosocial treatments are helpful" (Ibid., 1-2).

The authors make four recommendations about psychological treatments. Two recommend family psychosocial interventions, first, for families with high levels of "expressed emotions" and then, second, for other families as well (Recommendations 24 and 25) (Ibid., 8). The two other recommendations are the two negative Recommendations quoted above. If these Recommendations are followed then I do not see how psychoanalysis can have a function in the treatment of schizophrenics or how family interventions which use any model that attributes some etiological role to family relations can be practiced.

I believe that Recommendation 22 and 26 are unfortunate recommendations. For recommendations with level C evidence, that is with minimal research-based evidence, the Recommendations are formulated in very absolute terms: "should *not* be used"(Ibid., 8, 9). The rationale, too, is formulated in absolute terms: "lack of evidence of any benefit" or "[r]esearch had failed to substantiate hypothesized causal links" (Ibid., 8).

Let us take first Recommendation 22 against the use of psychoanalysis. In all research and practices that I have studied, I have not encountered one case where classical psychoanalysis was used. All treatment of severely mentally disturbed patients which was psychoanalytically inspired therapy violated several rules of classical psychoanalysis. There are several moving reports of healing resulting from a non-classical psychoanalytic approach. There is also statistical evidence of the efficacy and cost effectiveness of such psychoanalytically inspired treatment approaches to schizophrenia and psychoses (Karon & VandenBos, 382-453; Apollon et al.). The PORT Recommendations are silent about the difference between classical and non-classical psychoanalytic approaches and seem to condemn them all indiscriminately. But even when one overlooks the difference between classical and non-classical psychoanalysis, the PORT Recommendations' facts are disputed by a meta-analytic review compiled by Ramin Mojtabai and his colleagues of 141 sources reporting on 106 individual studies. That study concludes that adding psychosocial treatments for schizophrenics to somatic ones produces an improvement effect of .35 on the Cohen scale. The authors write that such a size effect "implies that a typical patient in the experimental treatment group was better off than 65 percent of the control patients" (Mojtabai et al., 576). These effects proved durable (Ibid., 580). Comparing the efficacy of different psychosocial approaches, the authors conclude that there is no statistically significant difference between the different approaches, with the exception of group therapy which has a lower size effect (Ibid., 579-80). They explicitly state that "therapies based on various psychodynamic principles were not significantly less effective than verbal treatments based on other theoretical rationales.(37) Thus, our review provides no evidence that psychodynamic therapies are harmful" (Ibid., 583). The Mojtabai study thus flatly contradicts the research basis for PORT Recommendation 22 against psychodynamic treatment of schizophrenics.

Let us now turn to Recommendation 26. An attempt to avoid accusations and the imposition of guilt on family members of schizophrenics is laudable. Accusing or imposing guilt is not therapeutically effective. However, the rationale given for the recommendation is false. The claim that "[r]esearch has failed to substantiate hypothesized causal links between family dysfunction and the etiology of schizophrenia" (Lehman et al., 8) is contradicted by

Tienari's Finnish study, by communication deviance studies, the Fort study on proverb identification, Karon's pathogenesis intrafamilial risk variable (Karon 1994, 47, 52-3), and many other studies surveyed in this chapter (Part One, I, B, 1,a/). In this chapter, I also pointed to a mechanism by which family dysfunction can cause maladaptation and ultimately illness. That mechanism is defective attachment to the mother figure. That attachment can become defective for reasons that are frequently independent of the mother: there can be psychosocial factors related to the father, there can be factors outside the family (painful operations without anesthesia), there can be genetic defects in the brain, and so fort (Part One, I, B, 1, b/). Helping families to adapt to the tragedy of having to deal with a schizophrenic family member includes advising change. Advice about change need not be coupled with accusation even if the past relations have possibly played a contributing factor. Understanding and correcting defective relations is to be promoted. Let us recall that one study demonstrated how communication deviance in adoptive families was very harmful for genetic high-risk adoptees and how the absence of such communication deviance was surprisingly helpful for them. Even if the study does not consider communication deviance as the (sole) causal factor in schizophrenia, still it is in some sense the final contributing factor and its absence the decisive saving grace for avoiding schizophrenia in those children (Wahlberg et al., 355). Let us recall also another study which found that no genetic high-risk adoptee became schizophrenic in a psychologically healthy adoptive family (Tienari 1992, 162-3, 168). Recommendation 26 should therefore be reformulated in order to keep its constructive contribution without contradicting scientific research.

III. Palle Villemoes' ego-structuring psychotherapy(38)

Palle Villemoes, a psychiatrist in Sweden and Denmark, developed a treatment plan for schizophrenics based on De Waelhens' philosophical presentation of Lacan's theory (Chapters II to VII of this book). Villemoes is able to train psychiatric nurses, and claims to be able to treat schizophrenics in one to two years. The treatment plan has three phases. The first phase has as its goal to help the schizophrenic to idealize the therapist and thus to create a bond. The second phase has as its purpose to let the patient develop historical narratives. The third phase has as its purpose to end the therapy without a sense of loss from the point of view of the patient.

Villemoes makes a number of assumptions about the patient and the ideal role of the therapist. Villemoes asserts, as De Waelhens does, that the schizophrenic is not a dialogue partner. He therefore recommends that the treatment should not be face to face. Rather the patient should sit next to the therapist, three feet apart. The therapist should not use personal pronouns. Pronouns isolate and put the patient on the spot (E-mail, June 24, 2000, p.2). The therapist should not ask any direct questions. That too puts the patient on the spot. In Lacanian language, any question is making a demand upon the patient. Other theoreticians could point out that therapists must be experienced by the schizophrenic as giving, since he is fixated at or regressed to the oral stage. If questions need to be asked, one can say something like: "I wonder, if...?" Do not gainsay the patient (Ibid.). The purpose of the first phase is to promote bonding and to overcome autism, not to create separation which would be experienced as rejection.

According to Villemoes the therapist must positively do three things. He must give the patient one explanation, and one only, when asked about the reason for any of the therapeutic arrangements (time, length, frequency, sitting arrangement). That explanation is: "because it has been so told to me" or something similar (Ibid., p.1-2). The second task of the therapist during this first phase is for the therapist to describe sceneries to the patient in which the patient is the center. His sceneries should start with descriptions of the consultation room. Later it can be the hall to the consultation room, the bedroom of the patient, other rooms that he frequents—all rooms not directly present to the senses of the patient. The descriptions should use language as a structuring function. The therapist should use genitives, prepositions, conjunctions—even adverbs, adjectives, and subjunctives (ex: the legs of the table and of the two chairs in front of us are shorter than the height of the wall) (Ibid., p.3). Villemoes warns that this is a challenging task for the therapist. The therapist should therefore think beforehand about what themes he will talk. He should expect to do most or all of the talking. The third task of the therapist is to present a specific attitude towards questions by the patient. The therapist should not answer the questions, but admit the legitimacy of the questions (Ibid., p.3).

The Lacanian explanation for the first task of the therapist, as I see it, is that the therapist must present him- or herself as a finite subject, a subject submitted to a law, or as Lacan calls it, a "barred subject." The idea of a third is introduced from the beginning of the therapy just as the idea of the finitude of the therapist. This technique corresponds, at least partially, to the recommendation by Bertram Karon that the therapist must introduce very early in the therapy that the patient—just as the therapist—can make mistakes and that this is good, because only people who do not do anything new make no mistakes.

The Lacanian explanation for the second task of the therapist, in this first phase, is that there is a basic deficiency with the relation between the schizophrenic and language. Following Freud, I would stress that the schizophrenic develops an overinvestment of words and an underinvestment in the things themselves. As a consequence I would have thought that a good technique would be to let the patient relate words to things, or even to help the patient invest in the things by letting the patient feel, touch, smell and taste things.

110

Villemoes takes a totally different approach. He encourages the therapist to introduce language as a structuring instrument capable of structuring the experienced environment. According to De Waelhens, language allows human beings to take distance from the things, from the world, such that a human being can experience the world. Without language, human beings seem to be glued to the things in the world and thus cannot experience them.

Villemoes reports that after a while the patient starts seeing the environment as the therapist sees it (the patient starts to identify with the therapist or with his voice). The patient will then react and make small comments. This indicates that the patient has become somewhat of an agent. The patient accepts the structuring of objects around the patient as done by the therapist. In his reactions and his comments the patient shows that he accepts the structuring role provided by the therapist. The patient does not yet actively structure his environment, but he accepts the structuring result provided him by the therapist. The acceptance of the structuring role of the patient identifying with the speech of the therapist prepares the patient to become even more of an agent when he is introduced to narratives in the second phase.

Villemoes warns that the therapist should not focus upon people. If people are brought up by the patient, it is best to focus on work, cars, or holiday habits of people.

The third positive task of the therapist is to admit the legitimacy of the questions of the patient, but not to answer them. This attitude promotes the advent of the symbolic in two ways. It encourages the patient to develop agency by encouraging wonder about the world. It also presents the therapist as someone who either does not know or as someone who encourages and tolerates wonder in the patient.

When the patient starts to assume the function of agency offered him by the therapist's attitude and his description of sceneries by structured language, the patient will reciprocate by idealization of the therapist. Signs of idealization are: "The patient arrives by his own and in time. He sits down in the waiting room. He smiles and arises quickly when the therapist invites him in. He looks at the therapist and seeks eye contact. He becomes ingratiating. He uses good-bye gestures when leaving. He combs his hair and arranges his clothing. He becomes sensitive to alterations in the room. He agrees with the therapist in everything. He uses phrases of the therapist on leaving" (Ibid., p. 3). Villemoes argues that the patient has made the therapist a fetish. From Freud we know that a fetish is that object that permits a patient to organize and to act in his world as a desiring subject.

When the patient calls the therapist to ask that the session takes place today rather than tomorrow or two days later, Villemoes argues that the patient develops erotization toward the therapist. Villemoes argues that erotization makes it more difficult to make the next step in the therapy.

The second phase of the treatment has as its goal to develop historical narratives. This will require a higher form of agency than was reached in the first phase. Villemoes recommends that this phase be initiated at the appropriate time by an act of delegation by the therapist. The therapist takes of his watch before the session and tells the patient that he is from now on responsible for keeping time and thus for ending the session. This delegation of responsibility guarantees that the patient will from then on have the last word in every session. That delegation guarantees the autonomy of the patient and anticipates what Lacan calls the advent of the paternal metaphor (Ibid.).

In order to prepare for the development of historical narratives, the therapist must shift from actual sceneries to historical ones, while still focusing on factual matters such as the patient's primary school, its location, and its structure. By moving to the past tense, the construction of the sceneries is not anymore a description of immediate sense impressions. The reconstruction of the past sceneries must again be done by the structure of language: adverbs, adjectives, prepositions, subjunctives and conjunctives. This work is hard for the patient. Slowly and with the shared interest of the therapist a picture with sufficient detail can be reconstructed, which in turn has an effect: it creates fascination with what is lacking. It generates, as it were, blind spots about which the patient develops curiosity.

The work of reconstructing matters of the past creates several signs of growing agency in the patient. The signs come in sequence. Villemoes reports the following sequence. First, the patient starts making *subtle and coordinated movements* which indicate that a functioning image of the body is taking hold of the patient (Ibid., p. 4). Later, the patient shows *signs of inspiration*. One thought (linguistically formulated) brings up another and the patient shows signs of delight in these thought combinations. Still later, the patient starts *reflecting on facts* as if he seems concerned with *truth*: "my brother was born in 1976–or was it 1977? No I think it was 1976" (Ibid.). Still later the patient makes associations: "that reminds me of...; speaking of that ..." (Ibid.). Combining signifiers allows the creation of new meanings. Next comes the *modulation of speech* and *increased body language*. Prosody, modulation of speech, and body language are efforts to empower the signifier so as to help the creation of the signifieds. This in turn leads the patient to show an *interest in his environment* (Ibid., p.4-5). The patient asks the therapist if he should close the door when leaving the office. He wonders if there used not to hang another picture on the wall. Villemoes interprets these signs as evidence that the patient is structuring, by means of language, the objects around him into a world *for him*. The patient is no longer an object among objects. He is the structuring center, even more, he is the structuring agent.

Next the patient develops the possibility of *empathy*. Before, sympathetic or empathic feelings led to fusion with the other person so much so that many of the symptoms of psychotic patients (or of children–as is well known in child-psychiatry) are symptoms of others. Empathy is the capability to identify with another person without losing one's own identity. As a consequence the patient can put himself in the shoes of others and remain autonomous enough to make observations about the person empathized with (e.g., it must not have been easy for my mother to look after so many children (Ibid., p.5)). Empathy prepares the patient for the next step in which *people start to appear in the memories* of the patient. Whereas before people seldom emerged in the patient's memories, now they emerge as centers of opinions. Schoolmates have names and characteristics. Family members are described as having a life of their own. Villemoes attributes this to the increasing structuring role that language starts to play in his patients. In accord with Lacanian theory it is not amazing that Villemoes mentions as the next step in the process that language creates in his patients enough of a *split that self-reflection becomes possible.* Indeed, as Villemoes himself points out, self-reflection requires that the person is not identical to himself. He must be able to look at himself from outside of himself. Two forms of self-reflection (historical and contemporary) are observable, which allow Villemoes to postulate two forms of split in his patients. A historical self-reflection—I used to listen to my parents in every matter, nowadays I seldom do—implies a non-coincidence of the self with the self over time. A contemporary self-reflection—I am not a shoplifter—implies the awareness of an ideal and its opposite as possible identities and the emerging awareness of the person's own freedom in choosing to be one or the other (Ibid.).

Symbolic identification (I am not a shoplifter) leads to the next step because the patient is now identifying or refusing to identify with a word, with a signifier. Symbolic identification puts the patient in a historical context. To not be a shoplifter means that yesterday, last year, four years ago, I had the opportunity to steal; and, even if my friend did it, I—the patient—did not do it. The sceneries are replaced by beginning narratives. Also symbolic identification is quite different than imaginary identification. Mentally ill patients who claim to be Napoleon, Caesar, or Christ do not feel obliged to conquer Moscow, cross the Rubicon or preach to the masses. Symbolic identification, though, imposes obligations. When those obligations have historically only been half fulfilled—or have not been fulfilled at all—then the symbolic identification is defective or has failed completely. The telling of their poor and failed symbolic identifications makes the patients sad. Their past traumas becomes now—*nachträglich*—painful. Villemoes considers the sadness around the construction of historical narratives guided by themes of symbolic identifications a sign that *castration* takes place (Ibid.., 6).

At this point Villemoes believes that the patient is able to accept the *dialectic demands of language as discourse.* When he speaks, the patient—like human beings normally do—*look* at their interlocutor. The patient thereby signals that he understands that the value of his message depends upon a decision of another, and he is now willing to participate in negotiations with others for the creation of meaning (Ibid., 6).

From now on, Villemoes considers the patient's ego as structured and points to three signs of such structuring. First, the future becomes part of the present in that the future is not just a series of possibilities, but rather a requirement that the present needs to be structured such that a future becomes possible. *The future begins today by the planning required to achieve the anticipated future.* Second, all the possibilities open in the present cannot be realized. *Priorities need to be established following the dictates of anticipation which needs already to be planned today.* Third, whereas before other people were divided between idols, foes and all the others, there the patient now starts to develop a much *more nuanced view of people* (Ibid., 6-7).

Villemoes now starts the third and last phase of the therapy. The agency of the patient has been increased by the collaboration between patient and therapist. The therapist provided structuring forms of language and the patient accepted first passively and then actively by means of identification and idealization the help of the therapist. For the patient to become not just an agency but a semi-*autonomous* agency, the idealization of the therapist must be broken. Otherwise the patient will be tied for ever to the therapist as an authoritative father figure. The process towards ending the idealization of the therapist starts by a new act of delegation of power to the patient (Ibid., p.7). The therapist says something like: "Therapy cannot go on forever." Normally the patient agrees. The therapist then enjoins the patient to chose a date for the last session. Putting the calendar in front of both, the therapist asks the patient to choose a date–say, between the 4th of May (about a month from the present date) and the 30th of June. The patient is encouraged to think it over. Normally, the patient chooses a date somewhere in the middle. From then on, it is the task of the therapist to give the power he received by identification and idealization back to the patient (Ibid.). The therapist can do so by taking less initiatives, and by using less his knowledge and professional insight in the sessions so that the patient can start taking over more and more (Ibid.). The challenge is for the therapist to master his own narcissism, so as to be able to be a disappointment to his patient in order that the patient can leave the therapist without feeling a loss. The felt loss should only be the therapist's. If that is the case then the Name-of-the-Father is correctly located in the structure of the patient and not in the power of the therapist (Ibid.). When that is not the case, then the patient calls back and asks to have an appointment. Villemoes recommends giving the appointment to discuss the problem. In the session the therapist should listen carefully and answer something like: "About that problem, I do not know too much," so that the patient is given back the power he had invested in the therapist.

Villemoes makes an overall remark about his therapy. He argues that no effort is made to understand the symptoms of the patient. Effort at understanding the symptoms of the patient are attempts to integrate the world of the patient into the world of the therapist. The effort should be on letting language structure the patient and thereby promote agency in the patient (Ibid.).

Several evaluative studies have been done of the ego structuring method pioneered by Villemoes. First, there are two TIPS scientific reports of the

114

psychology department at the University of Umeå. TIPS report nr. 49 by Annika Stencrantz and Britt Marie Malmgren is a description of the ego structuring therapeutic process of the first four young psychotics treated in the therapeutic community of Norrgården in Härnösand. The ego structuring therapy followed a therapeutic community treatment. The authors used the detailed notes of the therapists and of the supervisors to discover the different signs of emerging ego structure in the patients. Not one of the three therapists had done ego structuring therapy beforehand. The actual progress is compared with the theoretical model for each of the patients. The length of the therapy was 1 year, 2 month; 1 y, 3 m; 1 y, 2 m; the fourth case needed two ego structuring therapies for a total of 2 y,10 m (Stencrantz & Malmgren, 14). In TIPS report nr. 50, by Annika Stencrantz, a number of tests prescribed by the Strupp and Hardy model are reported. Two of the four patients showed marked improvement according to the following measures: 1. Diagnosis, personality assessment and mental health (Table 2); 2. Symptom SCL-90, self image and object image SASB (Table 3); 3. Social function, living, work/occupation (Table 4); 4. Relationships (Table 5); 5. Medication (Table 6), where two improved patients are said to be no longer on medication. Stencrantz finishes this study by comparing the patients at Härnösand with those of another therapeutic community in Sweden. In the other therapeutic community 264 to 900 hours of therapy was given while in Härnösand 46 to 150 sessions were given and the results were markedly better in the latter (Stencrantz, 33-34). Villemoes remarks in a letter to the author (WVE) that at the beginning he had not understood yet the necessity of letting the patients pass through what he calls "castration" and his therapists were under training and not yet experienced. Still, he declared himself happy with the results.

Second, there is the study by Gunny Bertilson and Eskil Berggren which gives a quality assessment of the first 46 patients receiving ego structuring therapy at the psychiatry department in Skellefteå. One patient could not be found; one underwent a new therapy; five refused to participate in the study. The therapy took between 30 and 100 sessions with two sessions a week thus lasting between 6 months and two years. The mental illness had become evident between the age of 5 and 50 years. Many were thus chronic patients and many were hard to help with other methods (Bertilson & Berggren, Data part, p. 1). Thirty eight percent were borderline patients and 62% were psychotic (Ibid., 2).

Using medical reports and personal interviews the authors provide the following statistics using five categories: Clear improvement; Improvement, but less; No change, not clear improvement; worse; much worse. For subjective experience of the effects of the therapy the results are: 20, 12, 6, 1. For subjective experience of changes after the therapy: 19, 18, 2. For changes in symptoms: 17, 17, 5. For social capacity and ability to say no to surroundings: 11, 21, 6 and one unknown. For quality of life, company and friends: 15, 14, 10. For quality of life, leisure, hobbies: 12, 18, 8. For quality of life, work, and studies: 10, 14, 15. For medication: 10, 13, 16. For sick-listing and disability pension: 7, 6, 25,1. For ambition for future, energy: 16, 15, 8 (Ibid., 7-9).

To give a rough total picture of the qualitative evaluation of improvement I added the numbers for clear improvement for all tests (35.1%); for improvement but less (38%); for no change, not clear improvement (27%). For the categories of "clear improvement" and "improvement, but less" we thus have jointly 73%. This was considered a good result for the length of therapy and considering that the patients were chronic ones.

Villemoes concluded from this study that the therapists could use more training; that some patients should start a second therapy; and that support for the relatives was very much needed. In an e-mail Villemoes specified that this study taught him that relatives need support particularly at the moment that the patient becomes more independent, for instance, when the patient moves independently to an apartment.

Third, there are the two studies by Bengt Göran Aronsson and by Bo Edenius. Aronsson's study is TIPS report nr. 51 of the psychology department and Edenius' book is his published dissertation for the department of psychiatry, both at Umeå University in Sweden. The two publications study about 24 patients at Norrgården therapeutic community who started their ego structuring therapy between 1986 and 1992 (and ended it in or before 1992) (Aronsson, 16). The patients had received prior treatment and had been given up by classical psychiatry and were expected to become chronic, on medication and receiving a disability pension (Letter by Villemoes). Aronsson did the psychological evalutions. Edenius added a detailed description of the therapeutic method and its theoretical basis. Edenius also provided an English summary of the description of the therapy, the theory underlying it and the evaluation of the results of the method pioneered by Villemoes. Of the twenty four patients thirteen interrupted their treatment. Eight did so in the beginning of the treatment because either they or their parents did not accept the treatment. Five interrupted the treatment in a later phase because of social conflicts resulting from a pregnancy Aronsson, 14). The final pool thus consisted of eleven patients–ten diagnosed as psychotics, mostly schizophrenics and one diagnosed as personality disorder with drug abuse. The patients were retrospectively evaluated in 1992 (1 to 4 years after patients were discharged) and 1996 (5 to 8 years after discharge) (Edenius, 174). The evaluation used interviews of patients, a questionnaire for the staff, DSM/III/R, medical reports, the Strauss-Carpenter scale and a questionnaire about quality of life. In 1992 50% of the patients were not anymore diagnosed as psychotic. Medication was diminished 50% and two patients were without medication (Edenius, 175). The cost per patient changed from 350,000 Swedish Crowns the year before the treatment to 30,000 Crowns in 1996 (Aronsson, 21; Edenius, 176). The social capacity as measured by the Straus-Carpenter scale went from an average of 2.8 before the treatment to 11.6 in 1996—out of a maximum of 16—giving an

116

average improvement of 8.8 (Aronsson, 26; Edenius, 142). The average quality of life index moved from 3.3 (1992) to 3,6 (1996) compared to 3,4 for a control group consisting of employees of the institution. The employees of the institution were mentally healthy people, from the same social class, but unemployed except for their acceptance in the institution (Aronsson, 27; Edenius, 141). Individually, by 1996, six patient experienced clear progress. The development of one was in 1996 stunted compared with 1992. Three patients had become worse and one had committed suicide (Edenius, 175). One puzzling fact in this group was that of the eleven patients who continued the treatment eight were women and three men. One important theoretical point is that the ego structuring method does not so much concentrate upon the person of the patient as on the signs of restructuring occurring in the patient.

NOTES

(1) In later studies Tienari and his colleagues try to articulate that interaction (Wahlberg, et al., 1997, 24-25).

(2) For two survey articles taking the same position, see Diamond 1997; Gottesman 1993.

(3) Functional psychosis is defined as bipolar psychosis and spectrum psychosis, the latter consisting of DSM-III-R schizophrenia, schizophreniform psychosis, and delusional disorder (Tienari 1992, 162).

(4) Eleven index and eight control families were not yet rated at the time of publication (Ibid., 163).

(5) These results are consistent with the hypothesis that the environment is an important contributing factor in bringing about schizophrenia. However favorable to the nurture hypothesis, the results overstate the importance of the nature argument for two reasons. First, the index group includes children who lived with their biological schizophrenic mother up to age four. Thus any influence of the environment up to the time of the separation from the biological mother was considered a genetic influence. In an e-mail, Tienari provided the following statistics: separation from biological mother occurred at birth in 50.2% of the cases, before one year of age (total or cumulative) in 84.1%, before two years in 95.8%, and before three years in 98.6% of the cases. Final placement to an adoptive family took place before one year in 46.8 % of the cases, before two years in 75.6% of the cases, and before three years in 87.9% of the cases.

Second, the study by Myhrman et al., commented upon later in this chapter, found that children from unwanted pregnancies had a statistically significant higher incidence of schizophrenia between 16 and 18 years of age than children of wanted and wanted-but-mistimed pregnancies. Thus, studying children who were adopted at birth, would still overstate the nature thesis, as all psychological influences during pregnancy are counted as influences of nature which would be an incorrect conclusion, according to the Myhrman study.

Another way of looking at the results of the Finnish adoption study is to point out that the environment can have beneficial effects even after age two. This idea suggests that the influence of the mother-child interaction during the first year might not be so decisive as implied by the schizophrenogenic-mother thesis. Family communication or what Lacan calls the paternal or symbolic function might also be important. This latter claim is an important thesis of De Waelhens.

(6) Two had died, 5 had moved abroad, 5 were adopted by a relative, 5 had a biological mother who was diagnosed as not having a functional psychosis that number was first 7 but 2 were re-diagnosed and included in the sample, and one did not have the adoption confirmed (Tienari, e-mail).

(7) Twenty five adoptive families refused interviews. As 159 of the 179 index families were interviewed, it follows that 20 index families and four control families refused interviews (Tienari 1992, 160-1).

(8) The percentages of pregnancies are given as percentages of the total population instead of percentages of pregnancies where the attitude towards the pregnancy is known, as was done in the article.

(9) For a case see: Silver 1992b, 116.

(10) Lacan's theory attributes schizophrenic breakdowns to a cause and an occasion. The cause is a deficiency in early psychic development whereby the person develops an impaired relation to language. Lacan refers to that deficiency as foreclosure of the name-of-the-father. The occasion for a schizophrenic breakdown in Lacan's theory is the emotional stress resulting from encountering a person who becomes in the life of the pre-psychotic an "A-Father." Lacan gives as possible examples of an "A-Father": the husband's face for the woman who has just given birth; the confessor for the penitent who confessed his sins; or the young man's father for the girl in love who is introduced to her fiancé's family (Lacan 1977, 217). Laplanche, a student of Lacan argued that Schiller played the role of an "A-Father" for Hölderlin (Laplanche 1969).

(11) Can be found in Chapter Two, Section 1 of this book.

(12) For a review and extensive summary of Blatt and Ford's *Therapeutic Change. An Object Relations Perspective*, see Gabbard.

(13) Aulagnier herself, in a publication later than the one used by De Waelhens, insists on the active role of the schizophrenics in the formation of their illness and thus by implication points to the contribution of the child in the failure of its psychological development. She writes: "This surplus [in meaning creation by the schizophrenic] is sufficient to criticize the different theories, which, in the name of the desire of the mother, of social oppression, or of double bind, intend to reduce psychosis, and more specifically schizophrenia, to an imposed passive response which was formed by the desire, the discourse or the craziness of others" (Castoriadis-Aulagnier 1981, 220).

(14) Recall the recent Finnish study which reported that the cumulative incidence of schizophrenia between 16 and 28 years of age was more than double for children of unwanted pregnancies as compared with children of wanted ones, including wanted but mistimed ones (Myhrman et al., 637).

(15) Even though the mother has a privileged role in allowing the child to accept the pain and displeasure of its own body, Aulagnier stresses in her later works that it is also necessary for the child to experience that it is the fruit of the desire of the parental couple and that it can give pleasure to the parents. If the parents hate each other, or if the child is told that the parents did not want children, or that they contemplated an abortion, then the child has great difficulty not interpreting the displeasures and the pain of the body as caused by the other, thought by the child to be omnipotent anyway (Castoridoris-Aulagnier 1981, 228-9, 232-4, 236-9).

(16) For a confirmation of many elements of this report see two case studies in Karon and VandenBos, 329-353.

(17) Aulagnier, in a work later than the one used by De Waelhens, gives us the example of Madame B. who unconsciously refuses to acknowledge the sexual origin of children.

Indeed, B... believes that the sperm of a male plays no role in the creation of the child. The sperm only incites the productive apparatus of the mother. B... also believes that in each intercourse the woman incorporates part of the man's substance. Consequently, men die earlier than women and loose their hair (Castoridoris-Aulagnier 1981, 256). In that context, Aulagnier does not analyze the impact of the mother's unconscious upon her children. She only analyzes the mother herself.

(18) The later Lacan connects law with the introduction of language (Fink 1996; Muller & Richardson 1982, 9ff).

(19) Searles's claims are so similar to De Waelhens'and Lacan's dialectic way of thinking that the preeceding text could have been written by them.

(20) For a definition of the three technical Lacanian concepts of the Imaginary, the Symbolic, and the Real, see Evans or Laplanche and Pontalis (1973).

(21) In at least two places Lacan invokes Melanie Klein's ideas to make the connection between the ego as body image and that body ego being a container of feelings (Muller 1996, 50, 138; Lacan 1977, 15, 20).

(22) See Lacan's comments on Melanie Klein's techniques in his Seminar I, 80-88; also Strauss 62.

(23) In the language of Charles Peirce, one can make a distinction between a mirroring move that is iconic or indexical (Muller 1996, index). Gaudillière here provides indexical mirroring: I/you; here/there; now/tomorrow. An example of an iconic mirroring would be: to want to kill is reasonable, but to actually kill sounds stupid to me (Karon & VandenBos, 198).

(24) A-L Silver, from Chestnut-Lodge, Rockville, Maryland has a similar arrangement for telephone calls (discussed later in this chapter); for an example in which a therapist stresses almost exclusively the importance of imaginary reassurance when giving his telephone number to his patients, see Karon and VandenBos (211).

Many aspects need to be considered in deciding whether or not to give a telephone number to schizophrenic patients. The overwhelming reason for doing so is provided by Karon and VandenBos (211) when they write that schizophrenics are confronted with such degrees of anxiety that they need to be encouraged to call when they need to. Without the help of other persons, schizophrenics cannot manage their life. Having the telephone number of their therapist and having been encouraged to call when in need provides such patients with a permanent anchor.

Borrowing from Gaudillière's example of calling his patient from Alaska, it might be possible to provide even more help to schizophrenics in crisis situations. The therapist might decide to call the schizophrenic at preset times simply to announce when the next call will come (depending on the intensity of the treatment, that could be every day the therapist does not see the patient; it could be twice a week or even once a week for patients with less intensive therapy). Such calls would provide through a mirroring move a regular anchor for the patient. In Peirce's terms, it would provide an index for the patient. The patient thereby becomes semiotically something even if he or she does not thereby become a full subject.

Providing one's telephone number to patients and encouraging them to use it, if they need it, is for the therapist to place him- or herself within the logic of the imaginary demands of patients. It is very possible that patients start calling the therapist too much. At this point, the problem is to put limits to those calls. Even if giving the telephone number is accompanied with an admonition not to call after, say 11:00 PM, in order not to disturb the therapist, abuses may occur.

Setting limits for schizophrenics is a delicate task. Setting limits can be ineffective and can even provoke rage. If done artfully setting limits is therapeutic. Artfully setting limits involves, first, presenting the prohibition as an appeal for help from the patient so that the therapist can continue to help the patient. The limit is thereby anchored within an imaginary mirroring: I ask you to help me so that I can better help you. Artfully setting limits involves, second, that the therapist present him- or herself as having limits as well, I cannot help you the next day if I have not been able to sleep, and once awakened I do not easily fall asleep again. With such an intervention, the therapist presents limit setting as a helpful way to deal with acknowledged shortcomings between human beings.

(25) For a confirmation of the hidden but massive presence of the prospect of death in one psychotic speech, see Rosenbaum and Sonne, 71, 79. For a more general argument see Searles 1965, 489, 495.

(26) Using Peirce's terminology, as applied by Muller (Muller 1996, 141), one could say that Karon by his "mirroring moves" aims at generating an iconic response in his patient: he thinks it is stupid, so I too think it is stupid. Mentally ill persons mostly do not think that they are stupid. They often feel that they are bad. They are therefore likely to respond to a mirroring move based on the idea that something is stupid and are likely to reject a mirroring move based on the idea that something is bad.

(27) The texts by Benedetti are translated by WVE.

(28) This book is reprinted as chapters II-VII in this volume.

(29) Fromm-Reichmann gives a similar argument in order to explain the therapeutic effects of dancing (69-71).

(30) For a theoretical explanation as to why offering the body of the therapist as an object of imagination for the patient might be helpful, see: Rosenbaum and Sonne, 89, 96, 103.

(31) For a theoretical claim of the interconnection between difficulties with language, social relations, and sexuality, see Samuels 1993, 31.

(32) I am not here debating the question of the heterogeneity or subtyping of schizophrenia. For that question, see Tienari and Wynne.

(33) Among the negative symptoms are besides alogia (poverty of speech), affective flattening, avolition, apathy, anhedonia, anergia and inattentiveness (Sass 1999, 1).

(34) Pointedly, Sass links "hyperreflexivity" to another characteristic of schizophrenics: "altered ipseity," i.e., a change in self-awareness (Sass 1999, 3).

(35) Medication only often improves the positive symptoms, whereas psychosocial treatments improve also the negative symptoms (Mojtabai et al., 583, 584).

(36) Thus a well-known therapist of schizophrenics, Benedetti, writes: "My thesis here is that the classic psychoanalytic concept of analysis of resistance must be combined with a therapeutic attitude which is its dialectical opposite: the attitude of over-inclusion of the image of the therapist in the system of resistance (1995, 365; trans. by WVE).

(37) The study also writes that the analysis does not "suggest that psychodynamic treatments are superior to other interventions" (Mojtabai et al. , 583). In order to prove that psychodynamic treatments are potentially superior one would have to distinguish between different psychodynamic treatments and maybe even between skilled and unskilled psychodynamic therapists. The hypothesis is that psychodynamic therapy is based on a more complex theory and makes more excessive demands upon its therapists than other psychosocial therapies. The potential superiority of psychodynamic treatment may be lost because the theory is not quite adequate or because the individual therapist is not skillful enough. A hint that this is a promising way of thinking would be if there is a greater variation in the size effect between different psychodynamic therapies than between other psychosocial ones, or if there is greater variation in outcomes between indi-

vidual psychodynamic therapists than between other types of therapists.

(38) Palle Villemoes obtained his M.D. at the University of Copenhague (1963). He was head of the department of psychiatry at Sundsvall (1976-86). He was supervisor and lecturer in psychotherapy at Umeå University (1978-1995). He is head of the unit of psychotherapy at Härnösand since 1988. Two of Villemoes' books relate directly to his treatment method of schizophrenics: Hur jaget struktureras (How the ego becomes structured). Härnösand: Internet, 1989. Jagstrukturerande psykoterapi. Senare rön (On egostructuring psychotherapy-New experiences)1989-94. Internet, 1994. At the Umeå University, four TIPS scientific reports appeared from the Department of Applied Psychology, two by Bengt-Göran Aronsson (1994 and 1999) and two by Annika Stencrantz (1997 and 1998). At the same University there also appeared one medical dissertation by Bo Edenius (1999). Finally, there is also the study by Gunny Bertilsson and Eskil Berggren about the first 46 patients using an ego structuring therapy at the department of psychiatry in Skellefteå.

Chapter Two*

SOME CLASSIC PSYCHIATRIC CONCEPTIONS OF SCHIZOPHRENIA

De Waelhens

I. Kraepelin, Emil (1865-1927)[1]

Even today the majority of psychiatric conceptions of schizophrenia, at least in German publications, are dependent upon the original formulations by Bleuler and Kraepelin.(1)

Actually, their contribution itself is bound up with several decisive options and hypotheses of psychiatry of the second half of the 19th Century. Kraepelin seems to have deplored the fact that psychiatry was forced by circumstances to confine itself for the most part to a description of the psychological or behavioral aspect of mental illness, since the organic aspect was inaccessible to it. This way of speaking supposes a parallelism between mind and body in appearance only; in reality, it is a causal theory. Kraepelin, like all of his contemporaries and many subsequent thinkers, was convinced that organic alterations of the mind "caused" mental illness. Hence, we should expect from scientific progress the construction of a term by term correspondence between the psychic and the organic. In his opinion, the most serviceable model for the derivation of such parallel terminology between the two areas seemed to be general paralysis. He was well aware that, in regard to schizophrenia, the entire task of establishing such terminological rapport lay ahead, but he scarcely doubted that it would be accomplished. He anticipated this accomplishment by advancing an hypothesis of biochemical self-intoxication connected with the development—today we would say hormonal development—of sexuality. This, in his opinion, was responsible for the deterioration of the cortical cells.

This way of thinking, which was generally accepted for a long time, and of which Kraepelin is not the extreme example, for from time to time he expressed some reservations, involves inevitable consequences which must be

---

* Chapters II to VII and the Conclusion are written by A. De Waelhens and translated by W. Ver Eecke. References and clarifying notes written by the author, A. De Waelhens, appear as endnotes. Clarifying notes provided by the translator, W. Ver Eecke, appear in footnotes.

[1] By Kraepelin, the following works are available in English translation: *Dementia Praecox and Paraphrenia*, Huntington, Krieger, 1971; *General Paresis*, trans. by J.W. Moore, Johnson Repr. in *Lectures on Clinical Psychiatry*, Hafner, 1968; *Manic-Depressive Insanity and Paranoia*, trans. by R. Mary Barclay, New York, Arno, 1975.

clearly comprehended. In the first place, a clinical description will attempt less—if it does so at all—to bring to light the global *meaning* and *significative structure* of the totality of a case of pathological behavior than to discover a number of particular alterations. In such a procedure it will be a question of tying behavioral abnormalities and deficiencies together into clusters. Each such cluster is determined by certain statistical regularities, and is viewed as characteristic of a specific illness. Moreover, this sort of procedure is stimulated as much by the hope of demonstrating in the future the causal derivation—which is much easier to imagine in the perspective of behavior analyzed into a multitude of isolated functions and sub-functions—as by a psychology which had espoused an atomistic view of behavior. In this regard, one should be aware that certain attacks leveled by psychiatrists against faculty-psychology were coupled with a clinical practice which in fact postulated that very psychology. From this point of view, the substitution of the concept of syndrome for that of nosographic entity constituted only apparent progress.

Given these conditions, it is no wonder that Kraepelin's analyses of schizophrenia have retained a great deal of their prestige. As long as the horizon of the problematic remains as I have just described it—and the psychiatrist's medical training is surely not going to help him change it—Kraepelin's description is *de facto* unsurpassable. In effect, concepts such as hebephrenia, catatonic stupor, and paranoia are operational ones which are to a great extent quite valuable. These, together with everything which Kraepelin taught concerning their relationships, their eventual mutations, their common aspects or their divergencies and the possible developments which may be expected, remain just as verifiable.

There was, however, a weak point in Kraepelin's system which provided the starting-point for Bleuler's reaction. This weak point is located in other areas of the problematic, but, of its nature, it weakened the usefulness of this psychiatric theory for medical practice. Indeed, Kraepelin was always embarrassed by having to draw a distinction between paranoia and schizophrenia, especially schizophrenia of the paranoic type. We shall have occasion to see that psychoanalysis has a theoretical way of maintaining this distinction. Such a theory is lacking in Kraepelin's thought and (let us stress this) there is a reason for it. He extricates himself from this difficulty by defining schizophrenia as not only an incurable illness, but also one which necessarily progressively worsens. He is telling us, in effect, that a diagnostic and a prognostic which have any value presuppose that one can fall back upon an observation of the course of the illness. If the illness doesn't grow more severe, or if its development doesn't always result in irreversible defects, then one speaks of paranoia; if the opposite is true, one speaks of schizophrenia. The paranoiac's condition remains stable; the schizophrenic's worsens. Having admitted this, Kraepelin's clinical objectivity is indeed obliged to concede, with further detriment to his logical rigor, that one sees from time to time—since one encounters almost everything in schizophrenia—a stabilization of the process of schizophrenic deterioration, or even an apparent reversal and improvement. However, he did not have the nerve to say, in the words of a great Dutch teacher whose lectures I have occasionally attended: "this only proves that the apparent schizophrenic was not a true schizophrenic."

* * *

It doesn't enter into my subject matter, and much less into my competence to offer any opinion on the research done relative to the anatomical-physiological or biochemical foundations of psychosis in general and schizophrenia in particular. Nevertheless, we must show that, whatever success these studies may have in realizing the hopes of Kraepelin and many others for the achievement of their ideal of a term for term correspondence between the organic and the psychic—something which would, moreover, seem to us to be impossible for the same reason as above, i. e., the bankruptcy of the *problematic*—this would not change a thing as far as we are concerned. Our own effort aims at laying the foundation for a *comprehension* of the structure of psychosis, and, if possible, for an understanding of the different forms of psychosis. We shall focus on schizophrenia, chosen for evident reasons as the proto-type of psychotic behavior. This study is being done in order to further the aims of philosophical anthropology. What is insanity, and what is its significance in and for human destiny? How and why does it originate? In reflecting on questions of this sort—we don't intend to do more—it is not at all difficult to see that the "causalist" or "parallelist" perspective—again, whatever may be its legitimacy or fruitfulness in other areas—is condemned to an absolute sterility, of which Kraepelin's work, be it ever so useful and solid, is a perfect example. Such a method gives and can *give no insight* into the above questions. It postulates the legitimacy of a connection which is in itself incomprehensible, in order to organize the data by means of it in a fatal way. For no constellation of factors discoverable in the universe as this latter is defined by the methods of natural science can succeed in giving or even less in creating the meaning of human behavior and discourse. Similar methods can lead only to the formulation of rules for the change and transformation of these factors, and hence, to the prediction of the creation of new constellations, an achievement which is bound to mean a great advance for science, since it is precisely such a task which science sets for itself. The problem is that the elements of behavior and discourse are not—except when they are misconceived—such factors, but rather are components of a significant whole by means of which their author—even if we don't understand exactly what this word means either in general or in a particular instance—situates himself *vis-à-vis* his own existence, the world, and other men. It is only through this that he can succeed or fail to locate himself *vis-à-vis* his body and that of others, *vis-à-vis* love, birth, and death; through this process he receives his identity and his name.

There is no need to show that, in response to these questions, Kraepelin's work not only has made no contribution but also infallibly obliterates them in as much as it forecloses the possibility of their being asked.

For it is inevitable that every attempt to derive behavioral characteristics from certain injuries or organic deficiencies results before long in the decomposition of such behavior into an alphabet of symptoms or abnormalities, since this procedure provides the causal approach with its sole chance of apparent success. It is—it would seem—comprehensible to affirm that a certain type of injury might be the origin of a lapse of memory, and that another might be responsible for certain problems with the power of association. Such a procedure might succeed in explaining how an educated person can no longer remember the name of the capital of Italy, and confuse the geography of Europe to the extent of thinking that Switzerland borders on the Soviet Union. But this genre of explanation collapses when one explores the patient's total behavior, and if one must thus render a second fact which occurred at the same time compatible with the first—namely, that the patient in question gave the exact location of Manchester on the map of England. Such a theory must explain this without resorting to the sham extrication of supposing that the patient had spent some time in Great Britain while never having visited Switzerland. In fact, the opposite was true. At the level of memory alone, or of association, or of all the other faculties or functions considered in isolation, our problem is insolvable and only leads to false questions. But if one locates it where it should be, that is to say, on the level of meaning, which these lapses and misconceptions have for the actual and "real" experience of the patient, "causalism" is put to rout. This is what is really shown by the example of general paresis, which Kraepelin took as the ideal model for the fruitfulness of causalism.

If, in effect, one is able to *comprehend* the causal inference which connects the inability of a patient to pronounce the adjective "anticonstitutional" without stuttering to organic alterations caused by spirochetes, it is nevertheless much less clear how one can hold such damage responsible for delirious speech. And it does not seem comprehensible at all how these microbes, by attacking cerebral tissue, should account for the fact that a particular delirium should necessarily be a delirium of megalomania rather than one of persecution, of jealousy, or of pettiness. We need not go further.

For a true comprehension of psychopathological phenomena cannot but originate in a method which is almost exactly the opposite of the above. One should attempt to consider, from the perspective of the discourse and behavior of the patient, the meaning and structure of the modifications which occur in his rapport with himself, others, and the world; one should furthermore, attempt to describe a significant type of those modifications which would be proper to each "illness" and would define it. This method in no way implies that the manifestations and symptoms in which such a structure is concretized should be identical in each patient. This means, for example, that the presence or absence of "mannerisms," "inconsistencies," "stereotypes" or "neologisms" does not constitute a necessary or decisive criterion on a particular nosographic entity. But, up until now, psychiatric theory and practice is in general committed to the reverse procedure. The majority of nosographic types are worked out using groupings of symptoms whose connection is furnished by a higher or lower degree of statistical invariance (the importance of each symptom being a function of the degree of invariance), but never, or rarely, by the global meaning of a structure. This can be clearly seen through the example of the four symptoms cited above, taken (with others, of course) as typical of a schizophrenic profile. Yet one does not clearly perceive the significant relationships which unite them. Moreover, in the spirit of their authors, they are all only make-shift, provisional hypotheses until each profile is able to be connected to that which would explain it—anatomical injuries or biochemical deficiencies. But, we must insist, even if this ideal be realized, and it is far from being accomplished, our comprehension of mental illness in general or of each type in particular would not have advanced a single step because of it.

II. Bleuler, Eugen (1857-1939)[2]

One cannot doubt that Bleuler—even if his work lacks the practical significance of Kraepelin's, even if it remains incapable of situating and limiting the legitimate value of anatomical—physiological "explanations," even if it lacks the conceptual apparatus necessary to accomplish its ambitions (which set it in opposition to the spirit of its age)—felt the insufficiency of such a method. Bleuler refused to locate on one level the cluster of symptoms which were customarily judged to be typical of simple schizophrenia or its catatonic, hebephrenic, or paranoid variations. The important distinction between primary symptoms, where the pathological process inscribes or expresses itself directly, and secondary symptoms, not directly revelatory of that process, is a first step on the way to true comprehension.(2) Secondary symptoms are induced by the primary one either directly or by the reaction which the pre-psychopathic personality or the "complexes" of the patient have to them. Therefore, these secondary symptoms vary to a great extent with each case. It is rather insignificant in this perspective, that the notion of a "complex"—which Bleuler frequently employs and believes he has borrowed from Freud—is used by him in a sense radically different from that of Freud, if only because of the static quality of Bleulerian thought. The essential point is that Bleuler's psychiatric thought attempts to acclimate a more

---

[2] By Bleuler, the following works are available in English translation: *Dementia Praecox; or the Group* of *Schizophrenias,* trans. by Joseph Zinkin, Foreword by Nolan D.C. Lewis, N.Y., International U.P., [1950], 548p.; *Textbook of Psychiatry,* Authorized English Edition by A.A. Brill, N.Y., Macmillan, 1924, XV11 + 635 p.; *Theory of Schizophrenic Negativism,* trans. by William A. White, Johnson Repr.

structural conception and comprehension of illness, the inverse of the tendencies of his contemporaries. Perhaps it is therefore of secondary importance to report that the immediate benefits of this shift of emphasis proved rather meager because of the limits imposed by the anthropological horizon in which his work is situated.

For, after all, the symptoms called primary (or at least those which belong to this category without any doubt) are limited to two. Furthermore, both are deformed by being referred to the associationistic psychology in terms of which they are described.(3) This reference is surely in contradiction with the major tendency of Bleuler's thought, but it is almost inevitable—moreover, one sees that this is also the case to some extent with Freud—since the psychology of that age offered no other basis or points of reference.

The first of these symptoms is the *Assoziationslockerung* 'the disturbance of the process of association,' by which one should understand a radical disturbance of the power of association. Associations, or rather, the terms associated, lose their logical affinities. This problem is different from that which is described as the "flight of ideas" found in the manic. This latter appears as an acceleration of the process of association due to a confluence of perceptions, ideas, and memories which the sick person is no longer able to control. Certain intermediary terms are telescoped or omitted, so that the patient's speech abounds in incoherences and nonsense. However, the problem is not the associative process itself; it continues to function according to ordinary laws. Put simply, its products are confused because speech cannot succeed in "following" the multitude of associations which occur in the consciousness of the sick person. On the contrary, the *Assoziationslockerung* registers connections which none of the ordinary principles of association are able to justify. It is therefore, as the German term suggests, a question of a deficiency in the associative connection itself. Hence, that which Bleuler meant, while using the terminology of his time which saw in the "association" the motor-force of conscious thought, is nothing other than a global modification of the patient's presence to the world.(4) It is from this starting-point that one should interpret the secondary manifestations.

The second primary symptom—at least, most probably a primary one, for Bleuler expressed some doubt in regard to its primitiveness—is constituted by the category *Benommenheitszustände* 'state of sluggishness,' that is, the state of sluggishness or inertia in which the sick person remains fixated in spite of the efforts which he attempts to make to collect his thoughts and to coordinate his actions toward an end, or particular course of action, which he continues to completely fail to attain. In Bleuler's view, this condition is only partially of psychic origin, but, to the extent that it is, it is directly related to the fundamental disorder. We understand it today as the incapacity (or the reduced capacity) of the patient to inhabit the world or his own body. In regard to any further primary symptoms mentioned by Bleuler, they have to do with the organic repercussions of the illness, and are therefore less interesting for us.

We have spoken of the way in which Bleuler explained secondary symptoms. We note in this regard his manifest tendency to reduce as far as possible such symptoms to the accentuation and exaggeration of phenomena which in themselves are not pathological. He did not even renounce this tactic in explaining catatonic stupor, citing an incident involving Newton, who, during an entire day remained immobile, seated on the edge of his bed and holding a sock which he was about to slip on when he was seized by the reflections which continued to absorb him all day long. In regard to schizophrenic "mannerism," Bleuler affirmed its similarity to the affectation proper to someone who tries to feign a distinction or a feeling which in reality he doesn't have. One understands then, that Bleuler, though he is far from renouncing the organic approach—he even remarked that only an organic explanation, if it should succeed in establishing itself, would prove completely satisfying—maintained nevertheless that one cannot exclude as untenable the hypothesis of a psychogenetic origin of mental illness, even if he did not personally rally to it.

One will without doubt be forced to admit that Bleuler's positive theses scarcely justify the fame which his work has acquired. But, in spite of its imperfections and at times its poverty, Bleuler's book gave rise to an exigency which it is impossible to renounce, even if it remains unfulfilled to this day, i.e., the demand for a *comprehension* of the nosographic profiles which can go beyond the statistical descriptions of syndromes in order to locate them in a global meaning which concerns the very being of a human person.

III. Minkowski, Eugene (1885-1972)[3]

Minkowski, a student of Bleuler, but also strongly influenced by Bergson, attempted, like his teacher, to comprehend the ensemble of problems characteristic of schizophrenia by beginning with the primary process. But, beyond the fact that he takes the notion of primary symptom in a more restricted and rigorous sense than Bleuler had, it is not the dislocation of the associative bond or the disturbance of logical thought which constitutes for him its essence; this role is attributed to the loss or rupture of vital contact with reality. This substitution, which clearly reveals Bergson's influence on Minkowski, involves important methodological consequences. For if Minkowski remains faithful to Kraepelin's and Bleuler's division of non-organic psychoses into two groups(5)—on the one side, the diverse forms of schizophrenia (to which

---

[3] By Minkowski, the following work is available in English translation: *Lived Time: Phenomenological and Psychopathological Studies,* trans. by Nancy Metzel, Evanston, Northwestern U.P., 1970. For more bibliographical references, see Spiegelberg, Herbert, *Phenomenology in Psychology and Psychiatry, p.* 391-92. In the same work one finds an excellent presentation of Minkowski's thought: p. 233-247.

one can add paranoia), and on the other, manic-depressive psychosis—he is concerned with the attitude of the patient in regard to his environment, and, correlatively with the way in which the psychiatrist "resonates" this attitude—that which is involved in causing the absence or interruption in us of the famous "Praecox-Gefühl," he promotes these concerns to the level of differential concepts. Without denying their practical import, one is nevertheless forced to recognize that they will not advance the theoretical elaboration of structures which might be typical of this or that behavior by a single step. The way in which Minkowski proceeds at times does nothing at all to take away this impression of relative failure. He tells us, and indeed not without reason, that if one considers the patient's affectivity, will, and intelligence in *isolation,* one is not forced to recognize *in every case* the disintegration of *each* of the faculties. On the contrary, a diagnosis of schizophrenia will become inevitable if one should establish "that the injury concerns not simply this or that function, but rather their cohesion, their harmonious interplay as a totality."(6) In brief, these functions have lost all their dynamism, and the coordination which they derive in ordinary circumstances from their being rooted in the capacity of having vital contact with reality. Here is the source of the "geometric character" of schizophrenic thought and behavior, on account of which deliriums and all the manifestations of "rich" autism would appear to be not effects of the illness, but the confused remainders, deformed and altered but for the time being not destroyed, of thoughts, feelings and will—acts formerly issued from a vital participation in existence. We have here a conception whose descriptive exactitude conceals theoretical positions difficult to defend. There is, in effect, little sense in raising questions about the insular functioning of "faculties," for the condemnation of such a method does not authorize one to substitute for a defunct faculty-psychology the normative notion of participation in and vital contact with reality. Such a notion presupposes, if it attempts to go beyond the intuitive level, a series of theses which a problematic dealing with psychosis would have the burden of establishing. If philosophical or phenomenological reflection is concerned today with psychosis, it is precisely because it expects from its study a clarification, perhaps decisive, of what should be understood by the experience of reality, effective participation in it, and vital contact with it. In this regard, one cannot contest the superiority of the Freudian and Lacanian theses concerning the structure and liquidation of the Oedipal complex, foreclosure, and the mirror-stage. In our opinion, the relative weakness of Minkowski's point of view is further aggravated by the rapprochement with Kretschmer's characterology which he attempts to outline. According to this latter conception, there would be some sort of continuity between a certain character-type or *normal* temperament, a type of character corresponding to it but *abnormal,* and finally, a mental illness properly speaking, resulting from the further deterioration of this abnormality. Thus, one would have, in approaching schizophrenia, the (normal) *schizothyme* character, the (abnormal) *schizoid* character, and finally, schizophrenia as a psychosis. In regard to

130

manic-depressive madness, the progression would be from the (normal) *cyclothymic* character, to the (abnormal) cycloid temperament, to mania or melancholy (or their alternation.)

In terms of this conception, schizophrenia would only be able to occur in those individuals endowed with a schizoid temperament, which would play the role of a predisposing constitution. It would thus be a question of an unknown process which, now and then, would graft itself onto a schizoid temperament (and only onto it), causing it to veer towards the clinical profile which psychiatry describes as schizophrenia.

This theory scarcely clarifies our comprehension of psychosis. On the contrary, it adds new difficulties to the problem which our study attempts to solve. First of all, it is in no way proven that schizophrenia strikes *only* those individuals of schizoid character. In the second place, the theory invests a certain *descriptive psychological* profile (the schizoid temperament, or, in the other direction, the cycloid temperament) with a *real* function: that which is normally claimed for the notion of constitution, itself an equivocal concept. Furthermore, Kretschmer's and Minkowski's views clarify nothing in regard to the process whereby psychosis is initiated or started, i.e., the nature of such a process, its action and its development. All this, it seems to us, is to combine or rather to confound in a most unfortunate way a psychology built on intuition rather than on the apperception of structures, with hybrid concepts like that of constitution whose meaning is not rigorously formalizable. Furthermore, there is added to the above a process, to all appearances organic, charged with the explanation of the pathological changes of a behavior whose meaning is only able to be reconstructed by interpretation and hermeneutics. One sees accumulated here, as if by design, most of the confusions, imprecisions and obscurities which prevent classical psychiatry from attaining to the level of perfection at which knowledge becomes capable of questioning its own proper foundations.

IV. Berze, Josef (1866- ?)

The idea that schizophrenia is to be *comprehended* also inspired Berze's work. He wished to isolate the *Grundstörung*, 'fundamental disorder,' that is, that which characterizes the process of schizophrenia as such. This fundamental disorder, which does not correspond to Bleuler's primary symptom, must be distinguished from the phenomena of deterioration. For, contrary to what Bleuler believed, the primary process is never directly ascertainable. It must be *inferred* from the ensemble of symptoms which can be read. It gives us the relations which hold between such symptoms, or, as we say today—although the term is not employed explicitly in Berze's book—it gives us their *meaning*. This induction is difficult since, for that matter, the perceptible symptoms in a particular case do not depend exclusively on the primary process. In effect, symptoms ordinarily are observed only after having undergone a certain development which causes them to interact, and hence, to modify each other; moreover, they are appropriated by the patient's personality and are partially directed by it; they are influenced by a more or less advanced process of deterioration. One can appreciate, therefore, without this fact compromising the real and conceptual unity of the illness, the fact that symptoms develop in appreciably differing ways from one case to another. These considerations confirm that the "fundamental disorder," as Berze understands it, concerns the very meaning of schizophrenia, and not merely one or several invariant elements of a clinical profile. This does not rule out, furthermore, the possibility that, in the spirit of Berze, the fundamental disorder might be of an organic nature, although presently unknown to us. It is his intention to study the fundamental disorder on the psychological and phenomenological level—this being understood not as a descriptive task, but one of interpretation.

Moreover, Berze does not reject Bleuler's distinction between primary and secondary symptoms. The first are characterized by their irreducibility to any other symptom, and are therefore able to pass for direct effects or expressions of the fundamental disorder. However, Berze disputes the list of primary symptoms given by Bleuler; in particular, he argues against the importance accorded to the disturbance of the associative linkage, offering the pertinent observation that the prominence accorded to this symptom is a function of the weight given to the theses of associationistic psychology. It is however only fair to add that Bleuler's language is more associationistic than his thought implies, for the symptom which he intends by the *Zerfahrenheit*, 'befuddlement,' of associations in fact transcends to a great extent the associationist problematic.

But what then is the fundamental disorder in Berze's view? It concerns, he tells us, *thought*. But this must be understood in the broadest sense, as designating the totality of that which makes experience possible in all that is characteristic of a human subject. In fact, one will see that it is a question of what we call today being-in-the-world, or comportment (in the sense that this term is understood, for example, by Merleau-Ponty.)

No intellectual or practical activity is realizable without a certain "schematic anticipation" of it, without a certain project, we would say. Then, it is necessary to develop, order, and structure this schema. If one attempts to analyze it more precisely, one sees that it is necessary to distinguish within it 1) the givens—the object—on which reflection or work has to take place; 2) the project to be accomplished, that is, the direction in which work on the object is to proceed; and 3) the way in which it is appropriate to present and to verbalize that which has been thought in regard to the objects under consideration and the projects which they suggest.

The fundamental disorder bears upon the ability to project this anticipative schema; it affects each of the modes of elaboration which we have just described in a way that tends to crescendo: the second modality is always more affected than the first, and the third still more so. To the extent that the disorder is slight, one will be able to notice an alteration only in the third phase. On the contrary, in serious cases, one will no longer be able to ascertain either what the object in question is, or what the subject proposes to do, or what he might wish to communicate to us about his projects.

It would be evidently superficial to pretend to reduce these deficiencies to a simple problem of attention; this would be to fall back into the pitfalls in which associationism ensnares itself. For, first of all, what is it that attention could aim at *beyond* the activities just studied? Furthermore, how can one do justice to the fact that such subjects are still capable of being aware of their own incoherence and inefficiency and do not fail to complain of that which is happening in them even in spite of their efforts at attention?

If one is going to consider all of this from a point of view more directly pertinent, one will ascertain that, where thought which is called normal attempts to proceed by linking its objects by means of logical connections and by submitting its results to the testing of experience, such concerns become all the more strange and indifferent to the schizophrenic the more gravely he is affected: his thought is completely satisfied by engaging in a game in which he is the only player.(7) The importance of this remark is to show that, for Berze, the fundamental disorder of schizophrenia is the problem of the actual exercise of thought. The materials for and the means of a functionally correct thinking process remain intact, even to the most advanced stages of the illness, and nothing appears to prevent in principle such functioning from being resumed entirely, tomorrow or later.(8) Berze here misses the point by indicting an actual insufficiency of the personality and the ego's thought processes which prevents the integration and direction of its own behavior. In fact it is not a matter of deficient thought processes but rather of the subject's inability to use them. And, for our part, we would say that it is perhaps even more a matter of a lack of "realization." The subject no longer "realizes" that which the situation calls on him to do. It is a quite remarkable fact that, in the early stages of the illness, the behavioral deformations are sudden, change a great deal, and do not cover all the dimensions of the subject's personality. It is this which Bleuler expressed in his celebrated concept *Spaltung*, 'personality split.' Again, this is why it is always practically impossible to predict the tasks which a particular schizophrenic will or will not be capable of, and why it is impossible also to expect that the failures or successes of today will repeat themselves tomorrow. It is this which radically differentiates the schizophrenic, be he the most severe, from the mentally retarded, in whom the level of performance is at the same time predictable and constant.

* * *

However valuable and interesting these considerations may be, they are marred by the following double deficit. First of all, they don't succeed, or scarcely succeed in tying together the diverse components of the notion of schizophrenia into an intelligible and structural unity from a plurality of phenomena, symptoms, and processes. Certain authors, for example Wyrsch, are so convinced by this failure that they will practically deny the possibility of describing a schizophrenic mode of existence in the way that is done in the case of mania or melancholy. But this is precisely the question which must be asked. One should begin by recognizing that, on the level of clinical practice, the schizophrenic profile has limited value. One must indeed admit that the profiles sketched of schizophrenia are not always verified, at least not to the extent to which the profiles of mania and melancholy are. But the same type of existence doesn't necessarily express itself in identical behavior-patterns, especially if these behavior-patterns are described on the level of their component elements rather than that of their global meaning. It is quite possible, for example, that stupor and agitation are different manifestations of the same fundamental pathology. A proof of this is the case of melancholy, which remains melancholy whether its manifestation be stupor or anxiety. But, in the case of melancholy, as opposed to that of schizophrenia, the prevalence of the global meaning is so readily apparent that it can absorb or explain behavioral alteration between stupor and agitation.

Yet, few authors would be disposed to expunge the term schizophrenia from their vocabulary; hence, beyond the diversities which they stigmatize, they retain or at least feel a common meaning. But what might it be?

As for a second reproach which we mentioned, it too must be seen in light of the remarks just made. The traits spoken of by the authors as characteristic of schizophrenia are almost exclusively negative, in the sense that they consist in so many failures or lacks vis-à-vis normal functions and processes.[4] But if everything which distinguishes the sick person from the normal one reduces itself to negative differences, one evidently cannot hope to comprehend the meaning of schizophrenic existence itself, even if this meaning were real. From this point of view, the Freudian understanding of delirium marks a considerable step forward over those about which we were just speaking, and others too, since it understands delirium as an attempt to reinvest in reality, and hence as a step towards "the cure," rather than as a simple aberration resulting from the "loss" of that reality. But this advantage is centered around a more profound breakthrough yet, which is nothing other than the Freudian theory of narcissism. We will see that this, augmented by the later acquisitions of psychoanalytic thought—and these are, especially on the subject of psychosis, considerable—possibly furnishes us with a clue leading to a unified comprehension of schizophrenia, and that without either contradicting or glossing over the diversity of clinical manifestations.

---

[4] At least, one exception would be Bleuler, and his description of the secondary symptoms. Those symptoms are seen to be exaggerations of phenomena that can be observed in everyday life.

V. Binswanger, Ludwig (1881-1966)[5]

One can only hesitate, therefore, to follow Binswanger when he tells us that the problem of schizophrenia should be centered on the problem of delirium, and that this—one will see why—finds its privileged expression in the delirium of persecution. Moreover, Binswanger's thesis clashes with the observation, however banal, that the prognosis—all things being equal—is always less dismal for a case of the paranoic type—and all the more when it is acute and sudden, than for that of a non-delirium hebephrenic which invariably has an insidious and torpid development. This being said, it is important to stress that an interpretation in the style of Binswanger's *Dasein-analysis* will evidently be more easy and more fruitful when it is applied to a case of paranoia. But this is no justification for this author's theory on the rapport of delirium and schizophrenia.

Binswanger maintains that schizophrenia can be understood through a series of notions referring to existential attitudes. Furthermore, he attempts to demonstrate the unity of these notions as they apply to schizophrenia. The first deals with the coherence and evidence of the natural world. These are disrupted in the sense that the sick person can no longer consent to simply let things be what they are and to interact with one another as they always do. The sick person wishes that they would be other than they are, but, unlike the revolutionary, he is not capable of effecting their change. For, to do that, it would be necessary first to allow them to be what they are. So he plunges into some arbitrary *Diktaten,* 'orders,' whose inanity, always more or less apparent, aggravates his suffering. But, above all, this capricious *(eigenartig)* way of relating to things engenders an experience which is more and more distorted and empty, less and less able to supply the springboard for a genuine project. According to Binswanger—and this remark is quite significant for us—these lacunae in the comprehension of the manifest meaning of things would already be discernible in the infancy of the future schizophrenic. But, at the same time the sick person feels the loss of the consistency of the past and he attempts to retrieve it by corrections and imaginary overcomings of the lacks of the present. These activities result in the aggravation of these lacks, and hence in the increase of his nostalgia.

A second dimension of schizophrenic experience is that everything is arbitrarily seen in terms of the radical alternatives of either victory and salvation,

---

[5] By Binswanger the following works are available in English translation: *Being-in-the-world; selected papers of Ludwig Binswanger,* trans. and with a critical intro. by Jacob Needleman, N.Y., Basic Books, 1963, IX +364p. *Ideas of the Dream from the Greeks to the Present,* N.Y., Spring Publ., 1974. For more bibliographical information, see: Spiegelberg, Herbert, *Phenomenology in Psychology and Psychiatry, p.* 370-372. In the same work one finds an excellent presentation of Binswanger's thought: p. 193-232.

or defeat and impotence. The inconsistency of experience develops toward the rigidity of an "either-or," which itself leads to the formation of ideals which lack reality because of their excessiveness and their otherworldliness *(verstiegene Idealbildung)* in which the subject shuts himself up and locks himself in, more and more. He does so because, should he renounce them, he would find himself delivered into the hands of an insupportable agony, that of the defeat which would place him in the hands of his persecutors.

Whence, according to Binswanger, comes a third dimension of schizophrenic existence: camouflage *(Deckung)* which the subject has to construct again and again, in the fashion of Sisyphus. He does so without interruption or without success. His purpose is to disguise the intolerable aspect of the alternative by trying to hold on to the realm of his ideals.

There follows a final phase, which one meets in fact in all the cases described by Binswanger: the moment of abandonment, of dislocation, of catastrophe. The patient ceases to struggle any longer against confinement in an asylum and against suicide; he permits his conduct to be dictated by the signs which things emit for his sake. He is no longer able to maintain himself in the common world, and it is here that the decisive meaning which delirium has for *Dasein-analysis* becomes apparent. Indeed, delirium is interpreted by Binswanger as the most profound and serious capitulation of the subject; it is that which makes him renounce his power of decision vis-à-vis himself, which dispossesses him in every respect of his own life and experience. The subject hands his power over to foreign powers and instances, of which he becomes the play-thing and the victim. Instead of rending himself between irreconcilable oppositions, his experience becomes a non-problematic one, from which all self-correction is excluded. Such an existence becomes entirely dominated by the delirious theme, the proliferation of which will soon engulf and submerge everything.

Binswanger thinks that the analysis of the diverse modalities of this capitulation will permit him to differentiate the diverse pathological modes of being-in-the-world, which authors since Freud and Bleuler designate by the unique name *autism,* and in which these authors and Binswanger himself see a central symptom of schizophrenia.(9)

Even if one admires the finesse and richness of the descriptions by which he supports these theoretical views, it is difficult to be satisfied with them.

Firstly, it is certain that the schema presented by Binswanger does not apply to all the profiles which clinical work presents as schizophrenic. Among other things—but we shall not pause to discuss the problems involved—certain psychiatrists have disputed whether this diagnostic is valuable for the very cases offered by Binswanger. We repeat: the problem of delirium does not lead to the core of schizophrenia since all schizophrenics are not delirious, and the majority of authors are also in agreement in admitting that it is indeed the delirious schizophrenics, and especially the acutely delirious ones, for whom future prospects are least pessimistic. This argues for Freud against Binswanger. Moreover, even on the phenomenological level, it is not extremely exact to describe delirium as a capitulation. For it is *also,* even on this level, a discourse which attempts to reestablish communication.(10)

Finally, even if one admits the theoretical views of Binswanger, one cannot deny that they leave the central questions entirely unanswered. Why does the coherence of the world cease to prevail in this particular subject? Why and how is the collapse of this coherence related to the incapacity to allow things to be what they are? One cannot fail to be aware of the Heideggerian overtones of the formula. Binswanger has too fine an understanding of the work of the thinker of Freiburg not to have known this or not to have intentionally sought it. For, in the Heideggerian perspective, anxiety is already sufficient to ruin all possibility of letting things be, so that one is not able to speak of an anxiety which would be provoked by the collapse of familiarity with the world and the incapacity to allow things to be what they are. For Heidegger, anxiety is not a response to the destruction of our usual being-in-the-world; it is the experience itself of this collapse, of the incapacity to let be that which is. Assuredly, we must be careful not to confuse the anxiety described by the philosopher with that which the psychotic feels. But one can no longer say that this is simply a pathological phenomenon. Rather, one will say that the modifications and alterations of structure which constitute the sickness itself—and which it is necessary to try to understand—pose a situation from which arises not fear or unsureness, but a real form of anxiety which, if one wants to interpret it, leads finally back to the meaning explicitated by Heidegger, even if this ultimate meaning is not discernible to the one who experiences it.

Hence, one has to invert the terms of Binswanger's description and not maintain that the loss of familiarity with the world, the power to dwell in it while accepting it as it is, is the origin or cause of anxiety. The concept cause goes beyond the letter of Binswanger's texts. It is necessary to broaden our critique. For, finally, if *Dasein-analysis* renounces in principle all explanation, we are not forbidden nor are we dispensed from making an effort to grasp that which begins and controls schizophrenia. We cannot allow ourselves to remain locked within the alternatives which allow us only to choose between an existential analysis which is merely descriptive and a causal organicism which in no way would have anthropological import.

VI. Szondi, Leopold (1893-1986)[6]

Having come abreast of the properly Freudian theories, we would wish to say a word about a conception of schizophrenia quite different from those which we have just treated—and which properly speaking is not even a psychiatric one. We are alluding to the ideas of Szondi. For Szondi, the usage of this term—and of the other psychiatric concepts which he employs—does not in any way imply a reference to mental pathology or the way in which psychiatry understands its own vocabulary. The creator of *Schicksalsanalysis,* 'analysis of destiny,' in effect, only conceives pathology as the ensemble of deviations—individually or collectively—of the factors which together constitute the structure of the unconscious. Thus, Szondi distinguishes eight fundamental instinctual factors, which are arranged in four groups of two each. Each of these factors is susceptible to quantitative deviations more or less severe in either the positive or the negative sense. If a great number of factors are altered, or if these alterations can no longer be balanced by the action of other factors, the subject's conduct veers toward the abnormal, and beyond minuscule anomalies, gives way to the various profiles or syndromes which the science of psychiatry describes.

The theses which we have just recounted suffice already to entail some important consequences; notably, that there is not, for Szondi, any mental illness in the strict sense of the word since one passes by simple quantitative modifications (negative or positive) from normality to any psychosis, all the intermediary states being able to be encountered, in principle, in reality. And there is this further consequence—that the state which one calls mental illness or pathological conduct is able to be stimulated or inhibited to a great extent by the social, familial and professional milieu, etc, of the sick person, depending on whether or not he finds in this milieu a socially valuable or at least inoffensive outlet for his instinctual surpluses or deficiencies.

As has been said, the rubrics under which Szondi arranges his factors and his groupings are borrowed from psychiatric vocabulary, but he intends in no way to imply by this that these instincts may be pathological of their nature; much the opposite. That such psychiatric terms serve to designate such instincts signifies only that, for Szondi, the corresponding pathological profile ought to be connected to the quantitative alterations of the instinct of the same name.

And even this is not rigorously exact since, in reality, an identifiable pathological profile would only make its appearance following upon the combined alteration of *many* instinctual factors; the factor which gives its name to

---

[6] Concerning the work of Szondi, there is a short English book available: Painton, Max B.: A *Clinical validation of the Szoni test,* Bern, Huber, 1973, 83 p. A good German introduction of the work of Szondi is: Schneider, E., *Der Szondi-Versuch,* Bern, Huber, 1952, 80p.

the corresponding profile is only responsible for that profile in as much as it is its principle cause. For our purposes it is interesting to reflect on that which Szondi, in the context of what has been said, understands by schizophrenia—not without insisting once again on the remarks which have just been made, which, should they be forgotten, would lead immediately to grave misunderstandings.

The vector which is named 'schizophrenia' (also called the *ego-vector*, for reasons which we shall see) combines and opposes in dialectical fashion two antagonistic and mutually complementary instinctual possibilities: the 'k' factor of the catatonic state, and the 'p' factor, the paranoic factor. These factors, essential moments for the constitution of the ego, which has for its function the arbitration of the conflicts between the other instinctual groupings, have a function which is comparable to that of the diastole and the systole in the cardiac rhythm. The diastolic factor (p) tends to dilate the ego until it is equal to the universe, the totality of that which is. It is this factor which, considered in the state of isolation (a state, evidently, fictive and abstract) empowers the ego to *be* everything, while as we shall see, the antagonistic and complementary 'k' factor concerns *having*. But the ego is able to be everything under two opposing modalities: that of *inflation* (p+) and that of *projection* (p-); in inflation, it attempts to be, by itself, all that exists. One sees without the need of explanation how an uncontrolled development of this instinct is able to veer towards delirium and the paranoic psychosis. In regard to projection (p-), it creates the tendency to see in the other, in every other, only one's own self. Hence, it is a question again, but in an inverse fashion, of an equality and a correspondence *in being* between the ego and the universe. The instinct expressed by the 'p-' factor can be called, in its excess form, the origin of paranoia, if one admits, with Freud, that projection onto the other of that which is in one's self is, in effect, one of the major resorts of that mental illness.[11]

The systolic movement, for which the 'k' factor is responsible, is constituted by the drive to have everything, to possess everything. The positive dimension of this factor (k +) attempts to realize this complete possession of the world by its incorporation, by *introjection*. One will understand the reason for the name which Szondi gives it by considering the intermediary notion of (rich) autism. The autistic person, who carries the universe within himself, is able to be completely disinterested in that which one calls the outside world and others, since these would not be able to offer him anything which he did not already have. In regard to the opposing mode (k-), it attempts to reject everything outside the ego. In order for the ego to be able to expel everything and to empty itself of everything, it would have to possess everything. Szondi terms this instinct *negation*, which, if pathologically increased and dominant, becomes negativism. Autism and negativism are indeed the traits which dominate in catatonic schizophrenia.

There is, to be sure, no need to insist on the fundamental importance of these two drives and of their four modes. Their equilibrium defines a perfectly integrated ego which, because of the equal development of all its possibilities, is prepared to exercise its function as arbitrator between reality and desire, between the other conflicting instincts. Incidentally, that which Szondi terms the *vector of schizophrenia,* the joining of the 'k' and 'p' factors, testifies that, for him, this psychosis—in which he sees psychosis par excellence—is to be conceived of as a disorder or a disintegration of the ego. This is true whether it be the result of a considerable over or under-development of one of these factors. Such a development would radically change the relation of the subject to being and to having. But, in what sense can these alterations be interpreted as corresponding to clinical descriptions of schizophrenia? We have spoken a bit about this apropos the symptoms or isolated traits which are fundamental to schizophrenia, such as autism and negativism. But this is but a mere first approach to the real question. One cannot, in effect, be content to discover certain traits—even though they be extremely important, as in the present instance, which would be recognized as being common to both instinctual alterations and the clinical profiles. The true objective should be to comprehend what it is about the former which allow them to constitute the global meaning of the latter. Should one think that Szondi has completely succeeded in showing this? An affirmative response supposes that one accepts the location of the kernel generative of psychosis, or at least, a good part of it, in the unconscious instincts of the ego. But this is a thesis difficult to defend, without bringing considerable modifications to it, as happens with the Freudian conception of narcissism. Of course, there is no schizophrenia without some grave disturbances of the ego, which, moreover, are already less perceptible in many paranoias. But it still remains a question whether an ego, in which the instinctual mechanisms of inflation, projection, introjection and negation would function in an exaggerated or insufficient fashion, would result in the manifestation of a behavior which would allow us at the same time to recognize and comprehend the meaning of the profiles which the clinic lists under the rubric of schizophrenia or paranoia (we will explicitate the difference between these terms further on; they are terms often confused in certain texts about which we are going to have to speak). For us, the response will tend to be, in the final analysis, negative; notably because, within the horizon of Szondi's problematic, there is no or scarcely any place for the structuring dimension of language.

And there is in his system not much more room for the role, no less structuring, that the positing and liquidation of the Oedipal complex ought to play both for the constitution of subjectivity and for the subject's access to a full and complete experience of the real. For we will have the occasion to see that the problem of language, like that of the Oedipus, is decisive for the comprehension of schizophrenia.

We have already stated several times that the properly Freudian conception of the unconscious offers, for the comprehension of psychosis, a contribution with some considerable advantages, especially if one interprets it in the light of Jacques Lacan's work, whose contribution here is, if it be possible, more important still than in some other areas of psychoanalytic theory. It is to this that we are now going to turn our attention.

We do so not, however, without having stated one last time the impasse which both theories of the Kraepelin-Bleuler type, which one may perhaps label causal, as well as conceptions diametrically opposed to them, such as Binswanger's, have reached. It is precisely the absence of all reference to a *constitutive* unconscious, in the one as well as in the other, which limited the import of their acquisitions.

From this point of view, as we have just seen, the work of Szondi already signifies, for our study, a considerable progress.

NOTES

(1)   While the term 'schizophrenia' was coined by Bleuler, the psychosis which it designates is that which Kraepelin describe by the name 'dementia precox.' Bleuler opposed this expression as inappropriate, because schizophrenia does not necessarily nor even ordinarily develop as far as dementia (according to Kraepelin, 25% of the cases do, but this figure is even less today), and because it is not always premature (precox). Morever, the expression has the defect of suggesting a connection with senile dementia, which is totally different from the psychosis in question.

(2)   Bleuler lists the well-known schizophrenic *Sperrungen*, 'barriers, blocks,' which many authors would tend to consider as primary symptoms, as examples of the symptoms imputed to these "complexes." Likewise, he lists certain at least of the *Spaltungen*, 'splits,' that is, the difference in behavioral quality which manifests itself among the different dimensions of the behavior of schizophrenics.

(3)   The study of primary symptoms in Bleuler's book takes up exactly two and a half pages of the 394 which comprise it.

(4)   It is this which he half-explicitly recognized when, for example, he writes: "Nevertheless, it is not without significance that, in the case of no other psychosis (other than schizophrenia) are the Ego and its position in the world, thought, and feeling so violently altered." *Gruppe der Schizophrenien*, 1911, p. 316.

(5)   By this is meant all the psychoses whose organic substratum is unknown to this day. In such a case, one can either opt for the inexistence of this organic substratum or believe, with the immense majority of authors, that the failure to discover it is only the result of ignorance which is more or less provisional. We have already said that none of these opinions solves the problem of the meaning of psychosis.

(6)   *La Schizophrénie*, first ed. p. 79-80.

(7)   It is clear that one cannot be content with such a conception of autistic thought, even though the description which it offers is formally exact.

(8)   "Knowing as such, the conditions of experience are 'intact' and 'potentially' capable of functioning." J. Berze, *Psychologie der Schizophrenie*, Berlin, 1929, p. 44.

(9)   We have seen above that such is not exactly Bleuler's thesis.

(10) We are not saying that it is *only* this, nor that the delirious discourse has as its subject the "I" of the first person pronoun, even if this is the word which appears in such discourse.

(11) Let us note that Szondi speaks of a reaction of original projection (factor p) which would not be paranoiac but paranoid. Indeed, to be everything, when the ego does not yet exist, is to equal the self with something outside of the self to which nothing internally is opposed. This is not a projection of the ego, but an inflation without ego. Szondi terms this inflation without ego: *participation*.

Chapter Three

THE ACCESSION TO LANGUAGE AND PRIMAL REPRESSION.
THEIR FAILURE IN SCHIZOPHRENIA

De Waelhens

I. Language and experience

The accession to speech can be explained in Hegelian terms as the passage which guides immediacy to mediation.[1] One finds a concrete illustration in the famous example found in *Beyond the Pleasure Principle*,(1) where Freud describes the child who throws and retrieves his toys again and again while crying *Fort*, 'away,' and *Da*, 'there,' to indicate their disappearance or their return. Although this observation has given rise to much commentary, we would like to focus on it once more! In this observation we witness the creation of a metaphor, which in turn is subsumed by a second metaphor. Indeed the child signifies the successive presence and absence of the mother's body by the appearance and disappearance of his toys and then the absence and presence of these toys by the words *Fort* and *Da*. To interpret this phenome-

---

[1] At the beginning of the *Phenomenology of the Mind (p. 149-160),* Hegel presents a view of the world which takes what is *immediately present* to be the truth. Hegel argues that such a world is very poor: it must be limited to what is *here* and *now*. What is absent has in this view no validity. This view cannot even explain or explore the richness of what is present in the *here* and *now*. Indeed, in order to explain what is present, one needs language. And language is a mediation between the object and the subject. Thus Hegel accepts the following thesis: in order to unfold the richness of the world one needs *mediation* between the self and the world. The *Phenomenology of the Mind* can be understood as an analysis of such a mediation and the proof that the richness of one's world depends upon the sophistication of the mediation that one has. The first mediation that Hegel presents is that of language. Words provide a tool to cut the real into pieces such that I can perceive objects.

It is clear that the Hegelian mediation is different from Freud's child game. However, one thing is similar in the approach of both: there is no reality for man if he does not dispose of mediation. Hegel's abstract way of formulating this insight will be to stress the function of *negativity* for the purpose of having access to the real (Thus he will say that the sceptic does not see the relativity of his own scepticism. *Phenomenology, p. 137*). Freud's way of formulating this insight will be to stress the need for primal repression. Otherwise, one has schizophrenia. One's unconscious desires appear in a delirium and replace the real. Thus, Judge Schreber will think that he feels his male body is changing into a female body, and that these changes become noticeable and can be observed by anybody. (Schreber, *Memoirs of my Nervous Illness, p. 207.*)

non we have to distinguish and articulate the diverse dimensions of the child's behavior.

There is first of all, as was stated in the first sentence of this chapter, the renunciation of the immediate and the entrance into mediation. This latter element is disclosed as inseparable from the constitution of symbolism. Second, there is the access to negativity. At each step, the loss of the object provides the motive for the further development of the game. Freud notes, furthermore, that the stage of throwing and concealing the object seems to arouse in the little fellow a more intense pleasure than its return, since, as everybody has been able to observe a hundred times, the game is frequently limited to the staging of the first phase. This can no doubt be understood—but one would be absolutely wrong to hold to this single interpretation—as the liberation of a desire for vengeance, (which is repressed in the real) against the infidelity of the absent mother. "Go away, I don't need you, I don't want to see you any more." In fact, it is surely more exact, and of a much greater significance, to read in this disappearance which the child instigates, the anxiety of death. This anxiety is surmounted in the gesture which symbolically expresses and reproduces it.(2)

Anxiety and death are both recognized and conquered in the symbolic and active reproduction of the traumatic event. However, it is also true that the game remains tied to the death instinct since the subject breaks away from his anxiety only by offering death new pledges(3)—the obligations of which he could withdraw from afterwards. One must therefore draw attention to a third moment in the interpretation of this game, even if this moment has sometimes been contested: that of the acquisition and establishment of a certain domination over the real, of the exercise of a certain mastery.(4) Caught in the horrors of a birth and a death which hasn't stopped renewing itself and which is imposed on him by the disappearance of the mother, the subject hereafter proves capable of moving in his own experience instead of being "glued" to it like an insect on a lamp. This will allow the child to *situate* his experience as much as to *live* it, to give it meaning as much as to be it. The child hereby enters (although in a very modest way) the typical human level of what is meant by the word 'experience.'[2] After the period where attachment and fragmentation

---

[2] The word 'experience' is used in recent philosophical tradition in two totally different ways. The Kantian and neo-Kantian tradition labels experience the encounter of a subject with the things. (e.g., Kant, *Critique of pure Reason, p. 162;* Wagner, *Philosophie und Reflexion,* § 11. p. 87-91). The Hegelian tradition labels experience the encounter of the subject with his own view of the world. Nice persons often expect that other people will be nice to them as long as one is nice oneself. Being robbed when one is a store owner, or facing a revolt in the class when one is a teacher, are events which question the validity of this view of the world. When one is forced to change the world view by which one guides one's life, one has made an experience in the Hegelian sense. The event which caused the change in guideline is an experience in the Kantian or neo-Kantian sense (Hegel, *Phenomenology, p. 144, 148.* See also:

constantly alternate, the child begins to experience a *reality* which is there (or which is not there) *in front of* the "subject"(5) and which will soon be appropriated *by* him because he begins to signify it. This process of signification is illustrated by the unambiguous jubilation and provocative stubbornness of the little player. "The moment when the desire becomes humanized is also that when the infant is born into language."(6)

However, the accession to language is also the beginning of *reality*. The subjective operation also lays the foundations for a true object. The ability to name confers a double, yet relative, autonomy: that of the subject who stands at a distance from his own ordeal but also that of the realm of the real—the object, in philosophical language—which presents itself or disappears, which the subject pursues or which he turns away from, without the object stopping, for all that, to remain real. Moreover, linking and uniting both, there is a *world*[3] which appears, in the precise sense that the phenomenological movement gives to this term. It manifests itself in the effort of insertion which is brought about by the infant in order to engage himself in the system of concrete discourse of his surroundings through reproducing more or less approximately in his *Fort!* and in his *Da!* the words he hears."(7)

Clearly then, this involves the founding and the progressive development of a certain mediating distance, which establishes, by language itself, the dialectic of presence and absence, where there were previously catastrophic successions. (The idea of *succession* corresponds only to a qualification brought *post factum*, when language has already intervened).

This distance, therefore breaks away from and frees the subject from the immediacy of the experience while preserving the experience itself. This is done, however, without completely and irrevocably destroying the immediate.[4]

Heidegger's essay on *Hegel's Concept of Experience*. Heidegger, *Holzwege, p. 105-192).* English language uses the word 'experience' in both senses. Thus, one can hear American parents say that it is beneficial that their children go overseas, since they will encounter many *new experiences.* They also say that it is beneficial because it provides them with a *new experience:* they start seeing the situation at home somewhat differently. The expression: 'many new experiences' uses the term in the Kantian sense. The expression 'a new experience' uses the term in its double meaning. With his toys, the child can make experiences both about the world and about himself. The same doll must at one time play the role of the mother, and at another time the role of the child.

[3] For phenomenology, the concept 'world' does not mean the physical universe nor the totality of things. The phenomenological usage of the term 'world' is closer to the usage made of it in the expression: 'the world of Shakespeare.'

[4] In Hegel's philosophy, such a process is called: *Aufhebung*, 'sublation.' In psychoanalytic literature this problem is touched upon in the discussion of "Transitional object:" Winnicott, D.W. "Transitional Objects and Transitional Phenomena," in *International Journal of Psychoanalysis*, (XXXIV), 1953.

This distance, in fact, neither equals nor coincides with a pure dismissal of immediacy. If, by the word, something is made present in its absence, the word itself, or any sign which could be substituted for it, must be immediately present but also, if one dares say, absent from its presence. If the word could only be itself, confined in the opacity of its matter and confused with it, it would cease to be a signifier and would obstruct our access to the signified,[5] it would no longer be a word and would no longer speak to us.

II. Repression of Immediacy and Primal Repression

The preceding is but a modest beginning for the understanding of the problematic of the unconscious. It has at least marked the place where the unconscious can arise. For as soon as one has admitted that to become a subject one must leave oneself without simply losing oneself (this is what Heidegger alludes to, on another plane, with the notion of existence)[6] the idea of the unconscious is possible. This is, of course, not enough to specify its content and structure.

It is perhaps not too daring here to attempt a comparison with certain Freudian texts.

One knows the discussions—although sometimes confused—which are raised with respect to the interpretation of what Freud called primal or original repression *(Ur-verdrängung).*[7] It is true that these texts themselves, whose importance the author rightly underlined, are few and hardly clear. We will begin therefore by recalling the elements which are not subject to dispute.

---

[5] Indeed, the crucial moment for the emergence of language in a child is his capability to understand that something (a finger) points to something else (the chair). As long as the child keeps staring at the point of the finger, the finger is what it is; it is not a *signifier of.*

[6] The word game often used by existentialists is that human existence is *ex-(s)istere,* i.e., in order to be (sistere), one has to go outside one self.

[7] For a presentation of the different elements involved in Freud's concept of primal repression, see Laplanche and Pontalis: *The Language of Psychoanalysis,* under the index word: primal repression, p. 333-335. For an interpretation which uses the Lacanian concept of metaphor see: Laplanche and Leclaire: "The Unconscious: A Psychoanalytic Study," *Yale French Studies,* 1972, p. 155. It is important to get a clear idea of the Freudian text, the Lacanian interpretation and the ultimate philosophical nature of the problem itself. It is nothing less than the body-mind relationship as psychoanalysis is confronted with it by speculating about the constitution of the first signifier, the first element of the unconscious, the first psychic element, the first connection between instinct (or drive) and the psychic. This same problem reemerges in the concept of "representative." Furthermore, it has important connections with the problem of "fixation." For a good selection of articles about the philosophical debate about body and mind, see: C.V. Borst (ed.), *The Mind-Brain Identity Theory.*

Primal repression, which is placed by Freud at the origin of any repression, remains, notwithstanding its importance, but a hypothetical process which he infers or postulates as a result of its supposed effects. Primal repression concerns the first representative of the instinct in consciousness; the effect, of this primal repression, once it has taken place, is ineradicable in the sense that no analysis will succeed in bringing back the repressed content to consciousness; analysis will only be able to reveal its "offspring," that is to say the secondary representatives[8] (they are this time really presentations) which were repressed by attraction because of their kinship with the content which underwent the primal repression. Serious, if not unsolvable problems arise concerning the content and the nature of that which was "conscious" and which falls victim to primal repression. Indeed, no direct proof can be given of the fact that something "has been conscious" and of what it was that one was "conscious" of, before the primal repression. Nevertheless, the *Urverdrängung*, 'primal repression,' is a crucial event since its relative absence or failure is held by Freud to be responsible for psychosis (and not merely for neurosis).

"The *origin* of the unconscious should be sought in the process which introduces the subject to the symbolic universe."(8) This assertion of Laplanche and Leclaire seems to present our point of view rather well, but also emphasizes the risks and the importance of the primal repression. One will wonder therefore if what Freud alluded to with the name of *Urverdrängung* is not equivalent to this renunciation of the immediate which I already showed is linked to the initial moment of the establishment of language. This hypothesis, which I will try to defend, has great advantages for the understanding of the Freudian doctrine and for the integration of various recent theoretical advances which we will soon have to discuss.

What could in fact be, this first, this original representative of the instinct in consciousness? We know that it was once conscious, although since the primal repression occurred it has become forever inaccessible for this same consciousness. However, it is not destroyed or without consequences (i.e., traces). Could this not be our engagement in the immediate; or the push by beings, who are essentially incomplete, towards the fullness of Being and hence towards fulfillment.[9] Indeed the original immediate presence is precisely what offers itself falsely as fulfilling the incompleteness or the lack.[10] It

---

[8]   The problem of the nature of these representations and of representation in general is a crucial philosophical problem. A very aggressive usage has been made of the problems involved with this concept by M. Tort in his article: "De l'Interprétation ou la Machine Herméneutique." (Temps Modernes, 1966, p. 1461-1493, 1629-1652). This article is a sharp attack on the whole philosophical enterprise of P. Ricoeur, particularly his philosophical usage of psychoanalysis in *Freud and Philosophy*.

[9]   De Waelhens is here using Heideggerian language to prepare his own position.

[10]   With this theme, psychoanalysis revives an idea that is part of the history of philosophy. It is the idea of the essential incompleteness of the human person, and his psy-

is clear that the future subject would cling and attach himself in the almost physical sense of these words to such an object, because it promises him the return—but how precarious—to the lost fusion.[11] The immediate, which must be renounced, is this state of consciousness in which the child is absorbed by and dangerously attracted to the other, who in turn is not experienced as another but as the self.

One can indeed see that displacement and metaphor which are essential for language establish distance from this immediate in an irrevocable way. Language achieves this distance by means of an intermediate phase where an imaginary object is used. It is the need for such an object which makes this intermediate phase a deficient form of language as is shown in Freud's analysis of the bobbin.

In a sense, one can say about the linguistic phase in a human being's development that it cannot be undone: one cannot *unlearn* how to speak, even though language can become de-structured as in the aphasic. On the other hand, this immediate is not simply obliterated: one is never completely liberated from it.[12] This immediate is our real prehistory, of which we find evidence, only in mythic form, encountered and created when history is already begun.

chological sufferings. This theme was indeed dominant in stoicism (Freud chose personally a stoic solution to this problem). It was also dominant in Augustine (idea of *cor inquietum* "the restless heart'). Psychoanalysis is capable of describing the distortions that the human person is willing to go through to avoid facing his own incompleteness. As a theory, psychoanalysis transforms human incompleteness into a fundamental theoretical concept. Psychoanalysis is, however, methodologically unable to interpret the ultimate meaning of this phenomenon or to suggest a solution for it. These tasks are to be performed by philosophy. In his book, *Freud and Philosophy,* Ricoeur delineates the legitimate domain of psychoanalysis in the same way. He then personally goes on to argue philosophically against a stoic interpretation and for the possibility of a Christian interpretation. The value of psychoanalysis in this area is the fact that it can provide through its case descriptions and its *psychoanalytic* case analysis an objective and standardized testimony to the depth of the emotional dissatisfactions of human beings with their own incompleteness.

[11] This sentence makes use of two words which have a technical meaning in psychoanalysis. '*Object*' is in psychoanalytic terminology any person or any thing to which affects are projected. The first object is normally the mother. Psychoanalytic theory postulates that the relation between mother and child is special in the sense that the child must psychologically establish its independence from the mother. Thus it is postulated that the original way in which the child experiences its relation to its mother is not that of separation but of *fusion.* See also: Laplanche and Pontalis, *The Language,* under the index word: object, p. 273-276.

[12] The permanent influences of the original immediate, i.e., the "lost object" expresses itself in the influence exercised by this "lost object" upon all further object choices, particularly friends and marriage partners. See Laplanche and Pontalis, *The Language,* under the index word: Object-Choice: p. 277. Freud, G.W.; V, p. 123ff; VIII, p. 80; XI, p. 442; XIV, p. 345; X, p. 154-58; XIII p. 260; S.E., I, p. XXIII; VII, p. 222n.; XI, p. 181n; XIV, p. 87-90, 100-101; XVI, p. 426-27; XXI, p. 23-24: XIX, p, 246n.2.

However, we wish to understand still more. Freud tells us that the absence or the insufficiency of primal repression is responsible, in all or in part, for psychosis.[13] We have to reflect on this observation. For, finally, if we arrive at a better understanding of the nature of this failure, its reasons, and its victims, we will be more informed about the phenomenon of primal repression itself. But this poses a multitude of questions which we must now approach.

III. Failure of Primal Repression

In what, therefore, consists the failure or ineffective achievement of this primal repression? Let us guard, at the outset, against a certain risk of confusion. One is familiar with the famous formula, stated to be sure in summary fashion, but which is nevertheless not simply to be rejected: the neurotic represses the unconscious; the psychotic represses the real.(9) It is obvious that it is not the same mechanism of repression which is at work in both. Indeed, repression can only be defined as a function of that which represses and that which is repressed. Moreover, we know that the German terms employed by Freud to designate the two repressions are different—at least from 1915 on (the date which Freud published his study of the *Wolfman*). He entitles the repression at work in neurosis *Verdrängung*, whereas he speaks of the mechanism characteristic of psychosis as *Verwerfung*,(10) a term which J. Lacan proposes to translate into French as *forclusion,* foreclosure.

In addition, we have just seen that, for Freud, psychosis has as its total or

---

13 The author hereby summarizes the thought of Freud with a clarity that is not present in the texts of Freud. What we find in Freud's texts are the following statements:

1) Repression described as "after-pressure," preceded by another event called fixation. (S.E. XII, p. 67.)

2) The concept 'primal repression' is related explicitly to the concept of 'fixation' (S.E., XIV, p. 168.)

3) The force responsible for primal repression is called 'anticathexis.' (S.E. XIV, p. 181.)

4) The kind of repression at work in psychosis has little in common with the kind of repression at work in neurosis (S.E., XIV, p. 203).

5) The defense of psychosis consists in 'repudiating' an intolerable representation and the affect that it produces. (S.E., 111, p. 58). The term 'repudiating' is used in connection with 'castration.' (S.E., XVII, p. 85).

If we accept that psychosis is related to the repudiation of castration; if we accept that castration is the representation that results from the primal repression; then it is possible to state that *for Freud psychosis is related to a failure of primal repression.* This latter statement is not in Freud's texts. However, such a statement does justice to the many remarks Freud made about this problem. The justification for interpreting Freud's many remarks in the above synthetic proposition can be found in Laplanche and Pontalis, *The Language of Psychoanalysis,* under the index words: primal repression (p. 333ff) and foreclosure (p. 166ff).

partial point of origin the failure or insufficient accomplishment of the *Urver-drängung* or primal repression, which therefore should not be confused with either of the two above mentioned "repressions," although it has something to do with foreclosure, which would be somehow the opposite of it.

Finally, and we have already partly explained this, these diverse processes are closely connected with the access to the realm of the imaginary and of the symbolic, which must themselves be distinguished.[14] Since primal repression seems to coincide with the renunciation of immediate reality, let us begin by asking ourselves, what can be held responsible for the failure of this renunciation, or, to put it positively, what is needed to achieve it.

Human beings, of all the higher animals, are probably the ones whose birth is most premature. The consequences of this fact are as immense as they are ineradicable. Our immaturity at birth signals, to begin with, the possible confusion (in the sense of identification) of birth with death and death with birth. It allows birth, by the radical maladjustment which it inaugurates, by the abrupt rupture which it engenders in the equilibrium between the organism and its environment, to be the first existential trauma, with the result that, *nachträglich,* 'after-the-fact,' death is longed for and desired as a birth. This immaturity entails the fact that our original and inescapable lot is dependence, in the sense of parasitism. All later autonomy must be wrested from this state and, in a certain sense, in opposition to it and even in opposition to the "self," since every separation or severance will have, from then on, some taste of being forsaken and abandoned, of being a repetition of the trauma of birth, against which the "self" rebels. Moreover, it is this immaturity which is responsible for the new "being's" discovery of itself as projected, as "thrown" into existence without or before his being able to experience himself as a definite and articulate unity, as "this person." One cannot say of the individual what Marx thought about humanity: that it only poses for itself those problems

---

[14]   For a definition of *imaginary* and *symbolic,* see Laplanche and Pontalis, *Language, p.* 210, 439-461. It is crucial to check also the index word: mirror-stage, p. 250-252. Lafon, Robert: *Vocabulaire de Psychopédagogie et de Psychiatrie de l'enfant p.* 308-309; p. 567-68. One finds an essay on these two concepts in: Wilden, A., *The Language of the Self, p.* 159-185; 249-284. For a philosophical application of these concepts: W. Ver Eecke: "Symbol as a philosophical concept" in *International Journal of Symbology,* 1975, p. 20-30. One has understood these two Lacanian concepts if one can make sense out of the following Lacanian thesis. The absence of the symbolic is the absence of the real, because the imaginary will replace the symbolic. Indeed, it is typical for the imaginary that it cannot signify the real, because it will be treated as a part of the real. An example of the imaginary replacing the real and thus creating an "imaginary real" is discussed by the author (A.D.W.) in this book (Ch. V, n. 21). One can find the essence of the two articles by Wilden in the "Note and Glossary on Lacanian terminology" under the above mentioned concepts in the translated works of M. Mannoni: *The Backward Child and his Mother, p.* 223; or *The Child, his "Illness," and the Others,* p. 270.

which it is able to solve. Initially, and for a long time, the contrary is true: the problems with which the individual is confronted are manifestly beyond his means.(11)

It is our very nature to be close to things.[15] The philosopher will say that we are from the outset of and in the real. This we are even to such an extent that at the outset, reality cannot reveal itself *as reality* to the subject who experiences it. There is indeed *no awareness* of the real in the infant since there is no *subject* which can be aware. And awareness requires a form of distancing which nothing as of yet guarantees. This can be put in another way by saying that lack and need are certainly real, but nothing permits them to appear as they really are. The structure of the dual union and of its vicissitudes is essentially opaque to itself, because it is devoid of all mediating negativity. This could also be expressed by stating that the pseudo-subject in question has not, as of yet, acceded to the level of desire.[16] Its life remains a prisoner of a

---

[15] This theme of the closeness of a human being's nature to nature itself is presented in philosophy in two ways. The first way is the attempt to point to the emergence of the typical human dimension in nature with the appearance of desire (Hegel, *Phenomenology of Mind, p. 225;* or more generally the whole passage on "Self--Consciousness"). There is an instructive difference on this point between Hegel and one of his most influential commentators in the 20th century: Kojève. Indeed, for Hegel, the master and the slave make both *jointly* an experience about human nature (*Ibid*, p. 232-33). For Kojève the experience made by the master and the slave are pure social experiences, i.e., experiences about the class struggle. (Kojève, *Introduction, p. 11-34*). This divergence between Hegel and Kojève interestingly enough mirrors the divergence between Freud and the neo-Freudians. Where Freud locates the human psychological traumas in biological origins (economic point of view: quantities of energy), there the neo-Freudian locate the origin of human psychological traumas in the social relations of human beings. If one stresses the closeness of a human being's nature to nature itself, then human tragedy will unavoidably occur. If one stresses the social origin of human tragedy, (Kojève, neo-Freudians) then one can hope to eliminate human tragedies by the creation of social utopias (The Marxian classless society or the Marcusian pan-eroticism). A second way in which philosophy is touching upon the theme of a human being's closeness to nature is the treatment of a person as a body. The real problem arises because the body is a thing among things, but it is not a corpse and thus not purely a thing. This problem has been central in phenomenological and existential thought. One finds a condensed review of the position of different philosophers on this problem in De Waelhens' introduction to Merleau-Ponty's book: *The Structure of Behavior.* One should also read the excellent chapter "Le Corps, chose ou acces aux choses" in De Waelhens' book *"La Philosophie et les expériences naturelles,"* p. 59-70.

[16] As De Waelhens will explain in the next page, the concept of desire is part of a triad: need, demand, desire. No one concept can be understood without an understanding of its function in the triad. One finds a short but dense statement about this triad in M. Mannoni, *The Backward Child*, p. 226-27 or *The Child*, p. 273-74. One finds a longer essay in J. Wilden, *The Language of the Self, p. 185-204*. For a relation between Lacan's concept of desire and Freud's concept of wish, *see* Laplanche and Pontalis, *The*

greedy and complacent demand which does not transcend itself. But let us distinguish more carefully between need and demand. Need refers to a state of psychological tension (thirst, for example) which originates in a physiological disequilibrium (dehydration). Need disappears as soon as an adequate compensation (a drink) has reestablished the equilibrium of the organism. It can reappear as soon as the equilibrium becomes disturbed once again. The "craving" does not survive the extinction of the need. Either one does not find the adequate object—a fact which signifies, in the envisioned situation, that one does *not receive* it—and dies for want of it; or, the needed object is given and one ceases to be in a state of need. Demand, on the contrary, attempts to eliminate the fundamental incompleteness of the human condition through the reestablishment of the original symbiosis. It is clear that such a reestablishment is impossible, except on the level of phantasy or delirium (and even that is not completely successful), and that no particular object can make good the lack which in fact constitutes our being.[17] From this point on, there is a choice between two possibilities. Either the subject does not renounce the quest to repeat the original state, and attempts to go from partial object to partial object without finding satisfaction in any of them, since, in fact, the satisfaction sought after is illusory, and each of the objects which, in turn, he yearns for is a mirage. Or, on the contrary, he consents to live as a being who lacks. Such a way of living is marked by negativity since the various partial objects will then be for him so many possible signifiers of his desire to be recognized by the Other's desire. Thus, it is the renouncement of total fulfillment which breaks the vicious circle of demand and its illusions to raise that demand to the level of desire.[18] We shall have to determine under what con-

---

Language, p. 482-83.

[17] For the theme of *Lack* see note: p. 76.?

[18] The idea that the wish for total fulfillment leads to a vicious circle is a key insight in psychoanalysis. It is however already present in other authors. It is dramatically present in the passage of the "Law of the Heart and the Frenzy of Self Conceit" in Hegel, *Phenomenology,* p. 390-400. This passage shows that it is unavoidable that general resistance develops against a reform, if a reformer insists that the reform be executed in its purity. This will be the case even if the reformer has the general well-being of all honestly in mind. Such a reform leaves no room for the general well-being *as it is perceived by others.*

The same idea is also present in another passage of Hegel's Phenomenology: "The Beautiful Soul," p. 642-679. This passage shows that moral choice is not a choice between good and bad, but between baskets which are a mixture of good and bad. Good for a human being is thus never the pure good, but always a mixture of good and bad. Thus the morally acting person is necessarily guilty and is therefore always in need of forgiveness. The transition from the wish for the ideal moral good towards the insight that guilt and forgiving are essential is parallel to the transition in psychoanalysis from demand to desire. In both one has to give up an impossible ideal. In both a transition to a more refined (and also frustrating) solution is suggested.

ditions this occurs, and at what price.

The future subject can effectively extricate himself from the alternatives of the dual union wherein he is caught,[19] and succeed in an attempt to transcend it, only if he can *also* situate himself at a *place other* than that where he is held captive. This was the case for the child with the spool of thread. He situated himself on a level other than that on which he underwent the throes of his drama. For this to occur it is first of all necessary but not sufficient that some help be offered to the infant. Such help might be absent. We will have to study if and how the absence of such help contributes to the genesis of psychosis.

The availability of this help, at the moment it is needed, implies that it be available even before it is in actual fact required. There is no paradox here. Psychoanalysts, anthropologists, and philosophers are unanimous in recognizing that real history of a being begins even before it is born. "Every subject comes to be in a familial myth: this myth, whose importance is demonstrated to us, if need be, by the place which it has in the primordial phantasy,(12) assigns to a person, in regard to the tragi-comedy which is his life, a role which determines in advance his interaction with his fellow actors."(13) Therefore, the fact that the subject is not called to assume his own existence as a simple "biological accident" has as its counterpart the insertion of the subject into a determinate chain of signifiers. It is here that appears that first and terrible paradox: the future subject, in order to avoid being an alienated being, must recognize "his origin as alienating by definition."(14)[20] In fact, that prenatal history, in which the first possible signifiers of the subject's life are constituted, is not limited to merely allowing the subject to situate himself in the interparental discourse. This prenatal history also confronts the subject with the most archaic relations that either of the parents maintain towards their own desire. And there is no need at all to invoke Melanie Klein to understand that this is particularly true in the case of the mother. Her rapport with her own body, and especially her body in the state of pregnancy, will prove to be fundamental.[21] For the bond between mother and child is established at the very

---

[19] For instructive examples of overpowering dual unions between mother and child, see M. Mannoni, *The Backward Child,* particularly Ch. IV: "The Fantasy Relationship of the Child to the Mother."

[20] The idea that the child has to assert himself into the symbols presented by the culture, through his parents, is clearly formulated in Hegel's analysis of the family. Hegel analyses the family in the passage on Greece in the *Phenomenology*: "The ethical world," p. 464-482. The alienating dimension of this situation was quite obvious to Hegel. He wrote that in order to become independent the children would have to separate themselves "from the source whence they came—a separation in which the spring gets exhausted," p. 475.

[21] For a report on empirical research about the imaginary relation of the pregnant woman to her own body and to the future child, see: Jessner, Lucie: "On Becoming a Mother," and Jessner, Lucie, Weigert, Edith, Foy, James C.: "The Development of Parental Attitudes during Pregnancy."

moment of conception. From this moment on, if things occur, as we say, "normally," the future mother attributes to her child an "imaginary body" completely distinct from that which the foetus really is (physiologically). This "imaginary body" serves as a correlative, a support, an "object" of the mother's desire. Among other things, it will constitute a protection for the mother against "the danger of experiencing childbirth as a loss,"(15) as the loss of a part of her own body, or as a threat, pure and simple, against her life. There is no doubt that the mother makes a considerable libidinal investment in this "imaginary body" which she ascribes to her child. There is danger that this investment includes or releases the most archaic layers of repression of the mother's personality. Correlative, and this is perhaps still more important for us, this "imaginary body" through which one will constantly "address" the child in its being with-the-mother, serves to give the subject that point of reference outside of himself of which we were speaking a while ago, which will permit him to see himself as "other" than that state of coenesthesia, which is experienced in an immanence at times anxious and at times complacent. And it is at this point that an entrance into the realm of metaphor and the symbolic is afforded him. It is the first step towards the disengagement which will be offered by the primal repression. "This first signifier, which comes to veil the primordial absence of meaning, is the origin of the imaginary. This latter includes everything which is of the order of representing an object, in as much as it is an object of desire and a support for speech."(16) Even before the separation of the two beings has taken place in the real, the infant already exists as a being and as an other, opening the way for a possible play of identifications and recognitions, first, on the part of the mother, and then for both the mother and the child.

But what happens if the mother does not accomplish this "work of giving birth" (in the sense that Freud speaks of the "work of mourning")? And why would she not accomplish it? And what does it mean to say that she does not?

In this regard, Mme Aulagnier, who inspired this section, answers by attempting to describe and understand a certain type of woman in whom the literature dealing with schizophrenia is showing more and more interest: the mothers of psychotics. Indeed, much work has been done on this subject, especially by the Americans and the Dutch.[22] If we have chosen to center our reflection around Mme. Aulagnier's work, it is because she situates herself far beyond a simply empirical framework (statistical, psychological, characte-

---

[22]   Some crucial publications on this subject are: Mischler, *E.S.* and Waxler, *N.E., Interaction in Families: An Experimental Study of Family Processes and Schizophrenia,* New York, Wiley, 1968. Lidz, T., Fleck, S., and Cornelison, A., *Schizophrenia and the Family,* New York, International University Press, 1966. Alanen, Y.O., et al., *The Family in the Pathogenesis of Schizophrenic and Neurotic Disorders,* Acta Psychiat. Scand., 42 (Supplement 189). 1966. Alanen, Y.O., *The Mothers of Schizophrenic Patients,* Acta Psychiat. Scand., 33 (supplement 126), 1958.

riological and social studies, etc.) and locates herself in a climate of reflection which is both psychoanalytic, in Lacan's sense, and philosophical (if she would be willing to accept this latter characterization). Such a point of view is, to a great extent, the same as that of our work.

The mother of the psychotic is not, as familiar language puts it, "a woman who lays down the law," or, in psychoanalytic terms, a phallic woman. She is, we learn, a woman who is herself the law. This is infinitely different than the first characterization. A woman who wants to lay down the law for herself and for everyone, if possible, in no way contests the existence of a law nor the indissoluble connection between the right to promulgate it and possession of the signifier that represents this right. Simply, she refuses to recognize herself as deprived of that signifier, and, identifying herself with the man, she unconsciously imagines herself endowed with it (hence, the frequent preference which she displays to collect and accumulate for herself symbols of it.) Thus, she arrogates to herself the right to enter into rivalry with the man in order to impose on him her own law. This is not done, however, to contest the legitimacy of that law. It is useless to say more, since it is common experience that such a woman is little inclined to accept the inobservance on the part of others of any social etiquette which is more or less symbolic of the law in question here. It is different with the mothers of psychotics. These women neither recognize nor comprehend the law as such. That which replaces the law—for themselves and for the others upon whom they attempt to impose it—is their own caprice. Mme. Aulagnier's apt analogy is a perfect example of what we mean: "They neither accepted the rules of the game nor, which is worse, understood them: one could say that the only game they understood is 'solitaire,' a game without partners and without stakes, except perhaps at the level of an autistic omnipotence.

The cards which are normally only symbolic instruments through which a game can be played between myself and others, a game in which the very fact of cheating means that I understand the rules, become in this case an end in themselves. One no longer needs to know, in order to play, that the King is higher than the Queen, nor that the established order determines the value: to play such "solitaire" there is no need to understand the symbolic value of the signs—the signs by themselves suffice, and one can, in each instance, make a new law. It is a law which has no need of any symbolic support, and which only depends on the arbitrary choice of the one who plays. It is a law which, in the last analysis, is nothing else than the proof or sign of the fundamental absence of law in the arena in which these subjects locate themselves.[23] I am not

---

[23] This is probably an overstatement which could be corrected as follows: The view of pregnancy as a "simple physiological happening" is also a product of the imagination. It may even be an imaginary defense. This view of pregnancy, however, does not prepare the woman psychologically for the following traumatic event: the child at birth will leave her body.

speaking of psychotics, but of their mothers."(17)

One can easily see that such a disturbance, in the mind of the mother—which one would better call a perversion—can have grave and pathological consequences for the future subject. For, precisely, this ahistoricity renders the maternal figure(18) incapable of inserting her future child in any symbolic order. This will become apparent in the manner in which such a mother speaks of her pregnant body. She will view it as a simple physiological happening in which the embryo is considered as the cause or stimulator of organic activity. One can establish without difficulty that the dimension which is thoroughly lacking in such a view is precisely that of the "imaginary body." The women in question are those for whom pregnancy is closest to being accepted in its pure reality as a process of organic development. One such patient who, being accused by her mother-in-law of being a bad mother because she did not knit clothes for the future baby, found the reproach absurd, because one cannot reasonably knit clothes for an unknown body. "This type of woman is the only one who has a relationship with the real child, in as much as it is an embryo."(19)

It is likewise that there will be no room for the libidinal investment of the child's body, distinct from the mother, and that the foetus—under such circumstances, this is the appropriate term—will be taken as an internal object, good or bad, whose expulsion will be thoroughly resented as a loss or injury, or as a purgation or *restitutio ad integrum.* In fact, there will be no transference of the mother's narcissism into the child, but rather a higher investment of the mother's own body (by the increased attention and interest—positive or negative—which will be accorded her, and by the higher evaluation of herself because of what the mother will consider her "creative power" etc.). This phenomenon more than any other is indicative of the mother's incapacity to construct a corporeal signifier.

It is evident that this must result in a "massive castration" of the future subject. In particular—and we must emphasize this, since, as we will see later on, the father precisely represents, in the Oedipal triangle, the term which is the generator of the law and of distance—"everything which, in his body (the body of the child) refers to the paternal contribution is denied and annulled. Most significantly, all that can serve as a reminder that he is the fruit of a sexual union is denied. (e.g., that as a sexual being he is also the son of the father). The foreclosure of the name-of-the-father has here its point of origin."(20) And how might it be otherwise? The integration of the future subject into any symbolic order whatever is correlative to his insertion into the relationship of the mother to the Other;[24] there, where the symbolization is deficient, the reference to the

---

[24] Thus, the symbolic World, is a necessary condition for the imaginary work of the pregnant mother. The mother must accept her own finitude in order to be able to create the imaginary independence of her child. Also, the mother herself must relate positively to another in order to be able to create an imaginary independence for the

Other—through which the child locates himself *vis-à-vis* the father—must be even more deficient, and the interparental discourse can only sink to the level of a soliloquy—happy, sad, or indifferent—of the mother with herself.

In fact, the partner which is co-intended through the libidinal auto-investment of the mother will not be the "imaginary body" of the child, which does not exist for her, but rather its real (or pseudo-real body) that is, "the physical collection of muscles which takes its substance from her body (the mother's) for whom it means the confirmation of her being the sole creator of the child,"(21) of her omnipotence to make a human being. There is no need of extensive clinical experience to comprehend the extent of the damage which such a state of affairs can reach when the mother has herself inseminated artificially by an unknown father "to have a child." The child will henceforth be reduced to "remaining the witness of the excellence and omnipotence of the maternal function."(22) From this point onward, the danger of only seeing one path open to the child becomes more precise: he sinks to the level of being the *"support and means of the demand, and of the total refusal of desire."*(23) The child will have no other existence than to serve to persuade the mother and others that his mother is the perfect creator, a fact illustrated by this simple and magnificent appendage of herself which is constituted by the chubby-cheeked youngster whom she goes on stuffing full—sometimes even to death (if such a death should some day be the only way for the child to achieve the right to say "no" to her who created him.) There can be no question of the ex-embryo, now annexed by the mother, ever attaining access to negativity and to desire, an attainment which would immediately contest the maternal myth of plenitude, verified by her having the abundance to indefinitely feed the child. How could this new being—for indeed, this is the point we want to make—discover that signifier of himself through which he might situate himself outside of his coenesthesia? We would like to add that the state of total dependence of a human being at the time of his birth certainly does nothing to diminish the most archaic wishes of the mother for omnipotence—wishes which have already been stimulated by the purely narcissistic experience of her pregnancy.[25]

Therefore, there is little or no possibility of the future "subject's" positing any "other" beyond his chaotic immanence, an other which would serve as a signifier of the unity which he still has to achieve. He will neither be able[26]

---

future new reality: her baby.

[25] Against the dangerous solutions to which a mother might be reduced by her totally dependent child, or by the experience of pregnancy, there is only a symbolic defense, i.e., the awareness of the functions of the third.

[26] In "The look, the body, and the other," I argue that the future child should theoretically be able to appropriate his own body as a unity, but that he later will become aware of the alienating dimension of this enterprise. He therefore would tend to give up this achievement because of its dangers. De Waelhens seems to imply that the fu-

nor dare to enter into desire or assume it, inasmuch as this desire is also the desire of desire, that is to say, the desire to be recognized by the "other." How can one situate or locate oneself in relation to one's own situation, if that situation is reduced to being a simple lack which awaits a total completion which will fulfill and definitively extinguish it?

This is all the more impossible since "before being a divided body, the child is a body composed of pieces. Inasmuch as it is such a fragmented body it can remain a sign of the maternal law; although separated spacially from the mother, it remains indissolubly bound to her at the functional level."(24)

The truth and importance of these interpretive remarks are overwhelmingly confirmed by everything that one can attempt to demonstrate and understand about schizophrenic language and behavior.

One will find an important illustration of such a confirmation in what authors have to say about the reactions of the schizophrenic to his mirror image. We will return later on to the central significance and the multiple consequences of the mirror stage, as it has been described and interpreted by J. Lacan. Nevertheless, it is comprehensible right now that, if the recognition of one's mirror image precipitates the formulation of a unified imaginary self, this is only possible if the subject, in referring to himself, possesses a signifier which is not confused with its coenesthetic immanence. For it is precisely the lack of such a signifier which will reveal to us the attitude of the schizophrenic towards his body-image.

That which normally initiates the process of identification with one's self-image, as well as the consequences of this identification, is the *"Process whereby the child looks to the person who takes care of him for his approval"* (Lacan). It is by means of being recognized by an Other that the subject attains his self-image.[27] It is because the Other has, from the outset, recognized the child as identical with this 'imaginary body' which really antedates him that the child is able to recognize his ideal Ego in the mirror-image. It is because the mirror ego is already an object of desire, since it has a priori been invested with the maternal libido, that the subject transforms it into an ideal Ego (the object of primary narcissism[28]). The variations which this ideal Ego

ture schizophrenic would never succeed in unifying his body experience.

[27] For Lacan, the other can relate at two levels to the ego. In the imaginary level he does this as alter *ego*. The origin of this relation is the mirror stage. Lacan will use a small 'a' for this kind of other. In the symbolic order, the Other is the place from where the question about his existence is put to the ego. Lacan uses a capital 'A' for this kind of Other. Thus there is in the Lacanian texts a technical difference between *other* and *Other*. For some references to texts of Lacan, see Wilden, *The Language of the Self,* n. 49, p. 106-108.

[28] For empirical studies about the importance of the maternal libido for the child, see Spitz, R., *The First Year of Life.* For an attempt to relate the empirical information of Spitz, with the theoretical speculations of Lacan see W. Ver Eecke: "Vers une philosophie de la psychose"; "The look, the body, and the other."

will undergo in the case of the neurotic are diverse, but it is certain that the identification of the mirror self with the ideal Ego is just as valid in the case of the neurotic as for what we consider to be the normal person."(25)

Things are naturally very different in the case of the schizophrenic. As he does not possess any signifier of himself which is distinct from his coenesthesia, his image appears to him as what indeed it is at a certain level of reality:[29] a combination of flesh, bones, and organs, and "something which comes from the eyes" as an emission (comparable to other emissions of the body—sweat, urine, feces etc.) and strikes the surface of the mirror. Assuredly, we do not contend that every schizophrenic, looking at himself in the mirror, is incapable of using language about himself which the "normal" person will employ in similar circumstances. But it is a language which he imitates and repeats. It is not necessary to probe schizophrenic language very long to discover that what the patient really believes himself to be is indeed this physiological assemblage.(26)

What he sees is the physiological body which the original other has given him. "It is this which, in his history, has replaced the 'imaginary body:' it is his body as it is really seen by the Other—an assemblage of muscles held together, maintained and connected by the arms which enfolded him or by the clothing which contained him: that which appears in the mirror is himself plus the Other."(27) We are dealing with a body "inexorably emasculated, because it has never been recognized as an autonomous subject who desires."(28) In the place where the "normal" person discovers in the mirror the image of the ideal Ego given for him to identify with, the psychotic can see only the "place of castration" to which he is riveted, and which he can only flee.[30] In fact, the mirror sanctions for the psychotic the irrevocable foreclosure of *"every possibility and every path towards self-identification."*(29)[31] If, in the case of the

---

[29] One can find a nice illustration of such a pathological relation to the body in the case of the Wolf man, known as the nasal injury. Gardiner, Muriel (ed.), *The Wolf-Man*. See index, under word: nasal injury.

[30] A. De Waelhens mentions in the French text, in a parenthesis, that he will return later to the dialectic relations which take place when the Ego identifies with the ideal ego. He already points out that these relations are both gratifying and frustrating.

[31] It might be illuminating to recall the philosophical positions of Sartre and Hegel on the problem of intersubjectivity. For Sartre, real intersubjectivity is not possible because he takes the look—not desires or emotions—as the privileged form of intersubjective relations. In such a relation, Sartre argues that the one who looks reaches subjectivity; the one who is looked at is, however, reduced to objectivity.

For Hegel, real subjectivity requires intersubjectivity. Indeed, to be a subject is to be desire looking for recognition from another. By concentrating upon recognition and desire, Hegel can allow for real intersubjectivity.

The problem with the psychotic is that he has lacked a certain quality in his early emotional environment which prevents him from reaching full subjectivity. The group of Lacan has concentrated mainly on the quality of the emotional life of the mother.

normal person, the mirror-self, which is an "Other Me," functions as a bridge between the self and the Other which is not me, this mediation will be absolutely lacking in the case of the schizophrenic, with all the ruinous consequences which follow. If the expression were not self-contradictory, one would say that the schizophrenic is only present to himself as a void to be perpetually filled, and which never is. This state of affairs will have, among other things, the result that the partial object will not be able to be recognized as a possible vehicle for desire. Hence, we can once again verify the fact that subject, object, ego and other articulate the diverse moments of a unique dialectic which is of such a kind that any alteration of one of these moments will necessarily entail a correlative alteration of all the others. From this point on, the partial object does not get beyond the simple level of demand (in the example which we will read: "I need a fork") without libidinal investment. In this case, "the subject perceives the partial object in the dimension of its brute physical reality... he collides with it and recognizes it as a blind man would."(30) Or else the subject does take a certain significative import from the object, but, as that meaning can only receive its place in a global system of signifiers, a system founded upon desire, our subject will fail to organize this signifier in rapport with others and will fail to combine them into a perception which views reality from a distance as a totality and as an "*Umwille*" of himself, to use Heidegger's excellent expression. This failure appears, in the example which we will consider, in the statement "a fork is something which causes pain." It is to this failure that the surprising language of one of Piera Aulagnier's patients testifies: "You see, for me a fork is either something made of wood and of steel, and it is the way the others use it that enables me to understand what it's for; or else, sometimes, it is just something which pricks, which pierces; but then the word 'fork' no longer has the same meaning for me which it has for others."(31)

This example will appear more important as we achieve a better comprehension of the meaning and significance which the mirror-image normally has. What precisely does it signify? In order to comprehend this, we will have to first make reference to the author who has most insisted on the decisive contribution which it makes to the construction of the self.

It is known that recognition of the mirror image occurs at a time of life (about the sixth month) in which the child remains almost entirely at the

The emotional qualities of the father seem for this group to be relevant only in so far as they influence the mother's emotional life. (See studies of Aulagnier and Mannoni). For an ongoing report on empirical studies of the emotional family environment of schizophrenics, see the annual review by Cancro: The *Schizophrenic Syndrome*. For further elaborations on the relation between Sartre's view on the alienating dimension of intersubjectivity and the schizophrenic's alienation see: W. Ver Eecke, "The look, the body, and the other."

mercy of "its motor deficiency and dependence upon breast-feeding."(32)[32] At this stage of development, every experience of the self in so far as it is a corporeal unity which is real and identifiable remains beyond the subject's grasp. He cannot, if one dare say it, experience himself as a unity from the inside. But now that unity is suddenly *offered* to him, in archetypic fashion, as an imaginary Gestalt of himself.[33] (The word *imaginary* is here employed in the double sense which refers, on the one hand, to the order of the image, and on the other, to the fictional or the unreal). Hence, the mirror image provides for everyone the first experience of himself as *a definite unity and totality,* and furnishes this in the form of a revelation. The "joyful behavior" which always accompanies it is, to be sure, the "manifestation of a libidinal dynamism which remained problematic up until now."(33) This event is the foundation of the objectification and unity of the self.[34] It is produced prior (although only slightly so) to the experience of objectification and unity which occurs in the dialectics of identification with an other. It is prior also to something that occurs even later, i.e., the progressive elaboration of the ego, by means of language, towards a universalizable subject, as it appears and is constituted by the usage of the first personal pronoun. The fact that such an immense gain should be originally granted to us in the form of a visual lure will, nevertheless, not be without consequences which are both frightening and decisive. First of all, there is the fact that the child, at the moment in which he discovers for the first time his appearance and his cohesiveness as a subject, can also apply to himself the famous words of Rimbaud: "I am another." The revela-

---

[32]   The crucial publications of Lacan concerning this problem are: "Le stade du miroir comme formateur de la fonction du Je" and "Propos sur la causalité psychique" in *Ecrits, p.* 93-100, 151-193. In psychology of child development, there is R.A. Spitz's concept of "eight-months-anxiety," which is richly documented with empirical descriptions *(The First Year of life*, p. 150-167). In my own work *(Saying 'No')* I try to relate the theory of Lacan's mirror stage to the observations of Spitz connected with the "eight-months-anxiety."

[33]   Lacan refers to two pieces of research that are extraordinarily fascinating. These pieces of research prove that *seeing* has physiological or anatomical consequences: "Visual stimulation and ovulation in pigeons" by L. Harrison Matthews and "Contribution á l'étude physiologique du criquet pèlérin et du déterminisme des phénomènes grègaires" by R. Chauvin.

[34]   This problematic dominates the child's life from the second half of the first year until roughly one and a half years. Joyful behavior can be noticed certainly from about six months. At eight months, the child is afraid of seeing and being seen by strangers and is thus aware of the alienating dimension of the look. The emotional relation with familiar persons is thus quite important for a non-alienating relation with the own body. At age one and a half years, the child starts saying "no." This 'no-saying' is the assumption of autonomy, and can thus be interpreted as the moment whereby the assumption of one's own image has been satisfactorily mastered. These theses are worked out in my *Saying 'No.'* They are partially presented in "Vers une philosophie de la psychose" and "The look, the body, and the other."

tion which is constitutive of the self is bound to a dimension which is intrinsically suicidal for the subject,[35] just as the myth of Narcissus has proclaimed it to our culture from time immemorial (But according to this myth, the lethal notion of the image of the self has yet other roots, which we will soon have to uncover). The initial experience of the self is thus also, and at the same time, the discovery of the self's otherness, an otherness rooted in creation of the self.[36] To be sure, such mirror otherness is not yet the experience of the other as fully real and authentically other. This comes about at a later and distinct moment of the subject's development and experience. As we will see later, a regression to or an unconscious fixation at the level of an experience of otherness which is purely mirror-otherness is the fundamental mechanism in which paranoia is rooted.

All that has been said is far from exhausting the significance attributed to the mirror-image. Its essential meaning lies perhaps in the fact that the revelation of the self, because it is inaugurated in the perceptual order, entangles the ego in all the pitfalls of objectifying alienation, or, if you prefer, of alienating objectification.

There will be—from the moment at which the subject begins the task of giving significance to his life, a task which will encompass his whole existence—the temptation and great danger that he will evade the task and deceive himself, that he will replace it with another which, like Sisyphus', is both secure and futile, and which would consist in the attempt to absolutely identify with his mirror image, an identification which would define his life forever and irrevocably "such that he is something for all eternity." Thus, in his imagination he would be irrevocably either this or that. Now it is precisely this radical impossibility of total convergence with the ideal image of one's self (of which the mirror-image is the foundation) which will serve to unleash the subject's aggressivity against this very image, because the subject will feel deceived at not being able to alienate himself there for good. Similarly, Narcissus drowned himself in pursuit of his impossible dream.[37]

---

[35] The suicidal tendencies are related to the fact that the mirror-image constitutes a preliminary but ultimately false pattern for the self. This self must relate to the real other, not just to an image it wants to mold itself after. Lacan calls the latter attempt *imaginary,* the other attempt he calls *symbolic.*

For a specific reference in Lacan, see Wilden, The *Language of the Self,* p. 12: the passage on aggressivity. Lacan also mentions another form of suicide, i.e., that situation in which a person renounces to face further renouncements. Such a form of suicide is giving up the task of confronting human frustration. This often leads to passive or unconscious suicides (Lacan, "La Famille," p. 8.40-8).

[36] Although the other is constitutive of the self in Freud and Lacan, one should keep in mind that for them, the self is not purely a social self as it has become with the neo-Freudians, inspired as they were by George H. Mead.

[37] This sentence is a short translation of a longer sentence in French which repeats the ideas of the previous sentence, but this time explicit reference is made to the case of

Psychoanalytic experience in all its aspects is there to teach us that the original mirror-image always plays the role of the substrate of the ideal ego, of which it is not only the principle signifier, but in some fashion the reality itself, although in the fashion of a temptation, a lure. This is why it merits the title 'imago' (in the specifically psychoanalytic sense of the term) prior to its being, for the self, "the source of secondary identifications."(34) It is, to employ a particularly apt phrase of Lacan's, "my statue."

However, the mirror-image has no prospective effects at all, if one understands by this effects which contribute to the further development of subjectivity. Still, there are certain retrospective, or "after the fact" consequences. We envision by this latter term everything which Freud designated by the term *nachträglich* in regard to other phenomena as well as this one. The authors of *The Language of Psycho-Analysis* define this term as designating everything which constitutes *"experiences, impressions, mnemic traces which are re-evaluated later on in function of new experiences, or through the access to another level of development. They can then be viewed as conferring, at the same time, a new meaning and a psychic efficacy."*(35)

Freud offers this example among others: a young child who is a noncomprehending witness to a sexual scene whose real meaning he cannot perceive. This experience will acquire a traumatic import only later on, if, having arrived at sexual maturity, the subject chances to observe a scene analogous to the first, which allows him to reinterpret it and to give it its true meaning with all the consequences which this entails for him. Hence it can be concluded that "the revaluation after the fact is precipitated by subsequent events and situations, or by organic maturation which serves to allow the subject to understand a new type of meaning, and thereby to rework his prior experiences."(36)

We can apply this to the mirror-image. Its recognition transforms "after the fact" the "subject's" prior experience into that of being the experience of a body which is divided, fragmented, whose anachronistic actuality is (for us) one of the most certain characteristics of schizophrenia, where there are "phantasies of dismemberment, of dislocation of the body. (Among those, the phantasies concerning castration receive their symbolic meaning only in the context of a particular complex"(37) [Oedipus complex. W.V.E.] which also influences prior structures "after the fact"). The body "then appears in the form of disjoined members, or of organs pictured in separation, fortified and armed for a kind of intestinal conflict, as they have been captured forever in the work of the painter and visionary Jerome Bosch.(38)[38]

Narcissus. The sentence in French is: "C'est alors que Narcissus en vient à se noyer, dans l'attente contradictoire ou de détruire cette image en la pénétrant ou de ne laisser subsister qu'elle en faisant disparaître celui qui aurait à l'égaler."

[38] There is a motion picture available and a sound slide set. The motion picture is entitled *Garden of Earthy Delights* (New York, the University at large/Chelsea House Publishers). The sound slide set is in French and Flemish and distributed by Arsonor (n. 9).

We will return to all of this shortly when we have to speak of the coenesthetic image of corporeal unity. Prior to this, we must still clarify some aspects of the mirror-image in as far as it prepares for the "turn from the mirror I to the social I," together with the consequences which this turn will set in motion, especially for the nature of knowledge.

In effect, the experience of the mirror-image creates the existence of a couple even if only an imaginary one. In this couple, the ego and its other are indefinitely reciprocal and reversible. The subject seeks to find his identity in the image, but this identity with himself is, in some fashion, his other. Inversely, the "I" which he takes on in the image qualifies as "other" the eye and the coenesthesia which see it. This couple is narcissistic in the sense that interest in the other (my image) is essentially carried and nourished by the interest that the one who sees it has in himself, nourished for himself. The one who sees, sees *himself*. I see myself, but it is this seeing which allows (will allow) me to say "I." Moreover, and most importantly, the other in this couple is privileged since it will serve as the norm, the *imago,* of that which I must become... in order to be.

The modalities through which the imaginary couple develop (through which it appears that the sameness and otherness are inextricably bound up with one another in the creation of the ego), explain the principle traits which originally characterize such a couple. These traits are narcissism, transitivity, and aggressiveness. In effect, the libidinal investment of the mirror-figure only occurs because the figure which is mirrored is my own. This investment is originally made on the self, and is therefore narcissistic.(39) Secondly, everything which characterizes one member of the couple calls forth identical characteristics in the other. Hence, between the members of the couple there is a radical transitivism; this will be the origin of the phenomenon of projection in the strict sense.(40) Finally, the desire to wipe out all difference between the members of the couple, and the impossibility of accomplishing it, engender a destructive aggressivity that, on whichever member of the couple it is set loose, will always be self-destructive.

It is evident therefore, that if, as is normal, a non-imaginary relationship between myself and a real other is achieved, this development will have its source in my connection with the mirror-figure, and this new relationship itself will tend to manifest all the characteristics originally belonging to the mirror-couple. If it happens that the non-imaginary couple turns out to be nothing other than a transference from the mirror couple, these traits will remain attached to it. As we have already said: the paranoic is one for whom every relation to otherness is structurally a reproduction of the mirror-couple. Thus, the description of paranoia which psychiatric literature sketches for us is comprehensible. And this is especially true of the surprising alliance which it traces, under the heading of projection, between stenicity, jealousy, homosexuality (which is not necessarily overt) and the unshakable conviction of acting in absolute evidence which is typical for a manichean world. It is for this reason, moreover, that all paranoiacs manifest a predilection for choosing as an object of hate and persecution (which they pretend to undergo, but, in fact, which they carry on) that perfect symbol of the mirror-other, the neighbor. Mrs. T. complains of being the butt of the evil behavior of a neighbor who, through pure spite, "steals" her husband. Her husband daily takes the 5: 00 A.M. train. In reality, the patient assures us, he only leaves on the 6:00 A.M. train and secretly spends an hour in the company of her pretended rival. Can she verify these facts? Not exactly. At 5: 00 A.M. the husband actually leaves home in the direction of the train station, but she "feels" that he pretends to go there, and that he uses the cover of darkness to come back and pay a visit to his girl-friend. What proof does she have? All kinds of proof, and especially this: while once looking through her neighbor's window (something which she did practically all the time) she noticed, at ten o'clock, the neighbor's corset which "still lay" on the kitchen table. When one responds that this in no way proves that this piece of clothing was already there five hours earlier, nor even less that the housewife is interested in her husband, she, smiling with pity, answers in a superior air: "How naive you are! It's easy to see that you don't know women very well!" One could employ here the transmutations which Freud used in Schreber's case, and translate "She hates me" by an original "I love her." For it soon becomes clear that the woman's continual observation of her neighbor is only a pretext allowing her to be occupied with the woman and to continually spy upon her in order to surprise her in her private affairs. As for the injuries which the patient claims to suffer, and which, in fact, she inflicts upon herself, they disguise, under the cover of hate, an unconscious love.

We must, at this point, raise the problem of the third person, the witness and guarantor of discourse. If I attempt to know and to speak the truth, I must constantly try to state only that which an other—who is any Other whatsoever—would say were he in my place. A proof or a thesis—no matter what the proposition be—that would *only* be true for me would be *ipso facto* false.[39] However, as I know that the meaning of things is not there but must be created, and as I am aware that I do not know everything there is to know, I have no doubt that the coincidence of what I say with what a third party says is a goal rather than a de facto achievement. Even approaching that goal requires a precarious struggle which is long and difficult, in which any success is only very partial and continually threatened by the static character of my attempt at expression. But things are quite different with the paranoiac. He acts as if he coincides de facto, by right, and by definition with the position of the third as

---

[39] Linguistic philosophy encounters this problem when they discuss the impossibility of private languages. The necessity of language to be public excludes propositions whose truth or falsity can in principle only be verified by me. For an instructive survey of the problems involved in this area, see: Edwards, Paul (ed.): *The Encyclopedia of Philosophy, Vol. 6, p.* 458ff.

witness and guarantor. The paranoiac occupies this position as one would a throne, by a privilege which is as inalienable as it is natural. As it used to be said of the Holy Office, he is the "definer" of truth. The meaning of things, of myself, and of the world is not *constituted* by the effort of human beings. This meaning is simply there, given as a painting or, to put it more exactly (since to understand a picture in this way is not at all to comprehend the painting) like the multiplication table in a student's textbook. It is only necessary to read out loud, for the others, that which one sees—and one sees everything—in order that the *truth* be *spoken*. The fact that feminine underwear is sitting on a kitchen table at ten o'clock has a clear and certain meaning, as evident as 2 + 2 = 4. It is inscribed in the picture of the world, even in the stars. One who does not see it can only be naive, or, more likely, an evildoer who practices injustice, lying and vice.

How could one not recognize in this eternal "view" of the meaning of things and of the world, from which all indetermination, all ambiguity, and especially, all transcendence has been banished, a type of experience which brings us directly back to the mirror-image? Let us go further yet: by looking at this world as a geometrician sees his figures, the paranoiac sees himself there and locates himself in it as an object, an object perhaps more important than the others, to be sure, but whose meaning is just as clear and translucid as that of all other objects.(41) Kierkegaard asked who can call himself a Christian. The paranoiac can without hesitation, name all Christians one by one, and especially can name the entire immense number of heretics. His discourse is only discourse in appearance (as is also true for the schizophrenic, only in a different way). In effect, the "I" which he utters is not a true "I," since it is supposed to coincide absolutely with the mirror-picture. Such an "I," of necessity, cannot be an instance of a real "I," even if this, as was explained, be its hope and ambition. The paranoiac realizes an alienation which, because of uncertainties experienced by the normal or pseudo-normal person, will for these latter never be more than a continually disappointed hope. The full and complete objectification of the "I" is only an absurd chimera, a negation of the condition itself of being a subject: it is supported only by its pseudo-realization in the mirror image. Moreover, the subject is so little susceptible to an exhaustive objectification that some will argue from this fact that there is no "I" at all.[40]

This leads to our recognizing yet another consequence. We have just shown that, for the paranoiac, both himself and all other subjects are subject-

---

[40] This position is typical for the Humean tradition. In contemporary philosophy, this position has been defended by Schlick and is known as the "no ownership theory" (i.e., in the expression "I am in pain" there is only a state of pain, but no person to whom the pain could be ascribed, in short no owner of the pain). This Humean position and its contemporary version have been attacked by P.F. Strawson (Individuals), and by Derek Parfit ("Personal Identity").

objects. For, it is evidently more easy to pass from one such self to another, than to discover a path from the "I" to the "You" or from the "You" to the "I," a fact that is totally beneficial for projection.

IV. The Sibling or the Incarnated Mirror-Image

Hence, there is no doubt that "the tendency through which the subject restores his lost self-unity is at the heart of the problem of consciousness. This tendency is the source of energy for his mental development, a *development whose structure is determined by the predominance of visual functions.*"(42) It is the original unity of an objectifiable "I," constituted and discovered in the mirror image, which installs in the visible realm the paradigmatic norm for every object. Objectivity becomes in its turn the norm of all knowledge and truth. The primacy of *theorein,* 'to look at,' in cognition serves to canonize this primacy.[41] Nevertheless, we know that reference to a third person, of which we have already spoken above, is also an essential constituent of truth. How are we to comprehend this reference, and where should it be situated?

In this regard, we will try to know what will transform an experience of the other which is visual and narrowly narcissistic to one, no longer imaginary but real, of a relationship between *ego* and *alter ego.* This will happen with the entry into the Oedipal Complex and its correct resolution. Nevertheless, between the "mirror other" and the later other which will be called a full object [in the psychoanalytic meaning of the expression. W. V. E.] there is an intermediate and transitional "other" which is germane to the problem of the third person. This "other" appears in the person of the sibling (or of one who can play a corresponding role in the development of the subject), *a fortiori* if the sibling happens to be a twin. Let us add that, in the sense in which we are understanding the term here, all siblings are to some extent twins, just as, for the child, everyone his own age is, to some extent, a sibling. The sibling is the first "equal" (or the second, if one wants to count his mirror-double) who resembles him infinitely closer than all those whom he can call "his equals." It is he who par excellence provides a counterpole to the mirror experience, one which tends to lead one from a mere lure to reality. The sibling is the *incarnate* visual image. The relationship among siblings clearly exhibits characteristics which have been described as constitutive of the mirror image.

But this sibling will sooner or later be experienced as an intruder. The mirror-image however, does not include the concept of intrusion. Contrary to the sibling, it is welcomed, despite the dangers which it can portend and which it necessarily brings. The friend, and the sibling himself, can, for a time, remain the inverse reflection of the subject because of the visual mime

---

[41] J. Derrida is one philosopher who maintains that Western philosophy exaggerates the primacy of the look.

which the subject projects onto them. But this state of affairs cannot continue. At some moment "discord interrupts the mirror-satisfaction."(43) We know, for example, that the intervention of the mother figure, necessarily and no matter what she may wish, tends to destroy or compromise the symmetry or reciprocity between the subject and his mirror-sibling. And it is precisely on this maternal figure that the subject's original affectivity is invested, in such a way that she does not even, properly speaking, constitute a separate person. Whatever she might do, the mother introduces difference and disparity between the siblings. The double then changes into an intruder, a rival. He becomes a "third who substitutes the rivalry of a triangular situation for the affective confusion and thorough-going ambiguity."(44) It is thus that the dual relationship and the mirror-double becomes structured for the first time into a triangle productive of the Other. However, let us note that the other encountered here is in no way that complete and distant other which is the paternal and legislative third, which will result from the Oedipal conflict. The sibling or fraternal third is an intruder without right; he is a *de facto* disturber. The father, on the contrary, forbids in absolute fashion that which he retains for himself; he exercises a right. The father substitutes the realm of law, of prohibition, and the bestowal of the name for a realm of jungle rivalry, more or less well pacified by the mother, and, in fact, never really pacified. It is the confrontation with this father which will truly constitute the identity of the subject, an identity which, up till this point, is not yet reached. But in the meanwhile, the fraternal third, the rival and alter ego (alter ego which the father is not, save in the measure to which he enjoys the privilege to which the subject aspires, but which he will be forced to renounce) exercises his intrusion as a challenge to the subject. This intrusion, in effect, gives its victim what Lacan calls an "alternative." The fate of the subject, and moreover, the responsibility of experiencing the reality will depend on this alternative. For indeed the subject will attempt to retrieve the "maternal object and will cling to a refusal of the real and the destruction of the other." Such indeed is the meaning of the regressions, which are at times spectacular and which classically occur in an older child at the birth of a younger sibling. "Indeed, having been confronted with another being he relates to it as to an object with which he can communicate, since competition implies not just rivalry but accord as well; but, at the same time, he recognizes in him the other with whom he enters into competition or contract; in brief, he discovers otherness and the socialized object at the same time. Thus also here, human jealousy is different from rivalry in service of survival. Indeed, human jealousy creates its object instead of just discovering it. Human jealousy thus appears as the archetype of all social feelings.(45) This means that, in accepting the ordeal of competition and struggle, the subject makes a first step towards the abandoning and surpassing of the simple dual union, since he recognizes himself here as supplanted, at least in a partial and provisionary fashion. That necessity "leads him to an

168

other object," other than that which had been for him, up until now, his only object and with which at the same time he felt united. From the time at which the subject measures himself against this new object, communication begins with this new object. From then on siblings form, together with the maternal figure, if not a society, at least its outlines.

However, and it is easy to understand this, "the familial group, reduced to the mother and the siblings, sketches out a complex in which reality tends to remain imaginary or completely abstract."(46) It is "imaginary" and "abstract" because only the Oedipus complex and its *Aufhebung*, 'solution,' will fully situate the subject, and consequently introduce him into a truly symbolic society, characterized by the law. It is this which will make the subject ready to take a place in the real, and gives him the ability to deal with it. Such would be, without doubt, the essential structural meaning which the mirror experience has for the constitution of subjectivity.

Before undertaking the study of the decisive moment of the constitution of the subject, we must further clarify another aspect of what was just said.

V. The Lived Body Schema

Actually, the mirror image, although it is indeed the basis of bodily unity, is not the only thing which contributes to the experience of that unity. It is a fact that the unity of our body is not something which is solely *seen;* it is also interiorily *felt.*

Psychologists and phenomenologists have been telling us for a long time that the unitary space internal to our bodies presents some very special characteristics. For example, the objects which are contained or located within the contours of a particular space appear *external* to each other; they are juxtaposed and do not comprise an internal reciprocal reference; they border on each other without internal relationship. The pipe is in or next to the ashtray, which itself is located on the table. Things are not exactly the same if this space is our body. It has a typical unity. Its elements, our members, for instance, are not simply related as *parts outside of parts,* but constantly refer to each other. Therefore, it is not sufficient to say that the interior of the body is always and normally experienced as a *Gestalt;* it must be added that we are dealing with a *Gestalt* in which each element "represents" in some fashion all the others. The proof of this is that, at every moment, the condition of any member of my body "informs" me immediately about the condition of any other member.(47)

That unity, however, is *imaginary;* but it is also an experienced, felt unity. By this latter trait, bodily unity differentiates itself from the mirror image. The mirror-image manifests and designates itself as being me, but without having a *felt* unity with myself. This is the reason why fusion *with* it or *in* it is a *tendency* and not an accomplished fact. We have already tried to comprehend

169

both the elements involved in such an attempted fusion, and the difficulties which it entails.

As for the experienced schema of corporeal unity, one can consider it as an anticipation and a preparation for the more properly symbolic order to which it will lead. If, in effect, each part of the body is felt as being one with any other, that identification, nevertheless, is posed in a *certain fashion only*. We are here at some sort of half-way point between identity and the rapport of metaphor. The internal reference of which we are speaking is therefore not reducible either to a relation of self to itself, nor to the relationship which the child makes between the spool of thread and the mother's body. The imaginary corporeal unity will only be able to ultimately lead the subject to the symbolic order if the identification among the body's members is an identification by reference (one member referring to another) and not a real identity. For it is very significant to note that psychotics—for whom the failure, either total or partial, of the primary repression results in an inaccession or a disturbed accession to the properly linguistic order, due to their confusion of the *signifier* with the *signified*—will display, in some fashion, an analogous disturbance of the corporeal schema (in regard to its structure). This problem can manifest itself in one of two ways. Either certain elements of the schema will be excluded or sundered from it, as in the case of the patient who, while not at all blind, pretended to be struck blind because she viewed her eyes, projected out into the visual field, as that which prevented her from seeing anything other. Or it may happen that the identification by reference is experienced, consciously or unconsciously, as a real identity pure and simple. For example, one may experience all of the openings of the body as one and the same cavity, understood *mainly* in terms of the mouth. Such was the case with the telephone operator who used only one verb, "snoepen," 'to savor,'(48) to designate, totally indifferently, eating, smoking, sexual relations, and defecation.

That which this fragmentation, or failure to articulate the corporeal image, signifies is once again the lack of that which, for want of a better expression, we have called "the third position vis-à-vis the self," or "the other place." The correct formation of the bodily image is inseparable from a development beyond the coenesthesia; to make reference is not the same as to feel. But that development will only occur if the coenesthesia is already seen as other than the self which is also its negative. Only this negativity permits and fosters the coming and going of the *movement* of identification, without which there is no correct corporeal schema, since, where the movement is lacking, the identification congeals into a real and reified identity, as it no longer succeeds in surmounting the original fragmentation. But, then, the subsequent passage from the image to metaphor, to the symbolic, and to language is also blocked. Every path between total identity, and the plurality of parts outside of parts becomes foreclosed. In this sense, the discourse of the patients dealt with above does not differ from the relation of other schizophrenics to their mirror image. They manifest in paradigmatic fashion an absence of all "transcendence" (and, by this, of all distance) of the situation, without which, the constitution of a symbolic reference becomes illusory and impossible.

NOTES

(1) Freud, S.E., XVIII, p. 14-17.

(2) Furthermore, Freud says that in general children have a tendency to actively reproduce in games the important events that they underwent in reality. This is all the more so when it concerns unpleasant events such as, for example, a medical examination.

(3) Everybody knows that it is precisely in his study of the compulsion to repeat that Freud introduced and justified for the first time the existence of a death instinct. (In: *Beyond the Pleasure Principle*, S.E., XVIII).

(4) Freud says that one could talk in this connection about a *Bemächtigungstrieb*, 'instinct to master.' (S.E., XVIII, p. 16.) For a translation in different languages, see Laplanche and Pontalis: *The Language of Psychoanalysis*, p. 217.

(5) The quotation marks mean to indicate that we encounter here only the beginnings of subjectivity.

(6) J. Lacan, *Écrits*, p. 319. (In the English translation *Ecrits. A Selection*, abbreviated as E: p. 103.)

(7) *Écrits*, p. 319. (E: p. 103.)

(8) J. Laplanche et S. Leclaire, "L' inconscient: une Etude Psychanalytique," in *L 'inconscient* (Colloque de Bonneval), Henry Ey, Ed. Paris, 1966, p. 121.

(9) Laplanche and Pontalis allude to this thesis in their *Vocabulaire de la Psychanalyse* in which they write, in the article on Psychosis: "Whereas, in neurosis, the ego, compliant with the demands of reality (and of superego), represses instinctual demands, in psychosis, there occurs a complete rupture between the ego and reality, which leaves the ego under the control of the id," p. 358. (*The Language of Psychoanalysis*, p. 372).

(10) The term appears in the 'Wolf Man,' G.W. XII, p. 111. The English translation of this term in the Standard Edition is: 'condemning judgement' (S.E. XVII, p. 80). It is noteworthy that this work is subsequent to the study of the memoirs of President Schreber. On the other hand, Laplanche and Pontalis remark that (*Vocabulaire de la Psychoanlyse*, p. 165) the Freudian terminology is fluid in this regard: "One can establish, in limiting himself to the terminological point of view, that the usage of the term *Verwerfung* does not always have the connotation 'foreclosure,' and, inversely, some other Freudian terms designate that which Lacan attempts to establish." (*The Language of Psychoanalysis*, p. 167).

(11) Lacan, following Freud, has forcefully insisted on these theses throughout his article in the *Encyclopédie française* on "La Famille." (vol. 8, article 40.)

(12) It seems to us—but we will return to it further on—that this fundamental phantasy is exactly the first offspring of the representation of the original repression. It is the first signifier, yet completely imaginary, through which the "subject" sees in the unconscious to which that signifier has gravitated, that which is immediately renounced and is irretrievable. Nevertheless, this most archaic signifier will be able to be brought to consciousness.

(13) P. Aulagnier-Spairani, "Remarques sur la structure psychotique," in *La Psychoanalyse* (8) (1964), p. 48. Lacan gives great emphasis to the same idea: "Man is, prior to

his birth and after his death, caught up in a symbolic chain whose links were founded before history," *Écrits*, p. 468.

(14) *Op cit.*, p. 48.

(15) *Op cit., p. 50.*

(16) P. Aulagnier-Spairani, *op. cit.*, p. 51.

(17) P. Aulagnier-Spairani, *op. cit.*, p. 52.

(18) It is clear, in effect, that the capacity to lead a life which is fully and really historical supposes recognition of the law. Simone de Beauvoir once wrote a story about a unique individual who was immortal, entitled *Tous les hommes sont mortels*. The main character, presently our contemporary, but already several centuries old, was denuded of all historicity, because he was removed from all irrevocability. No event of his life could be branded irrevocable, since that event would always be susceptible of being cancelled by a contrary one. Was he an emperor or a slave, learned or ignorant, misanthrope or philanthropist, lover, or misogynist? How could one tell, for everything was always being indefinitely redone, and since he had eternally before him not only his own future, but the entire future. Exempted from the law of death, he was also removed from existence. It is like the player who would know that he were capable of indefinitely doubling the bid; he would be exonerated from the risk of playing, but, by that very fact, would be incapable of playing. This same law—that of the absence of law—applies to the women of whom we are speaking, and entails for them the same sanction. Only, they do not even understand this—for such comprehension entails a knowledge of the law—they do not know that their existence is pure inexistence.

(19) P. Aulagnier-Spairani, *op. cit.*, p. 54.

(20) *Op. cit.*, pp. 54-5. On the foreclosure of the name-of-the-father, cf. below.

(21) P. Aulagnier-Spairani, *op. cit.*, p. 55.

(22) *Idem.*

(23) *Idem.*

(24) P. Aulagnier-Spairani, *op. cit.*, p. 55-6.

(25) P. Aulagnier-Spairani, *op. cit.*, p. 56.

(26) One could make an analogous remark—we will return to this—with regard to the use of personal pronouns in language. There are plenty of occasions on which the schizophrenic appears to employ "I," "you," "he," etc., correctly. In reality, his comprehension of these terms (of these "shifters," or according to Benveniste's translation, these "*indicateurs*, 'indicators'") is greatly disturbed.

(27) P. Aulagnier-Spairani, *op. cit.*, p. 56.

(28) *Op. cit.*, p. 57.

(29) *Op. cit.*, p. 57.

(30) *Op. cit.*, p. 58.

(31) *Idem.*

(32) J. Lacan, *Écrits*, p. 94.

(33) *Idem.* An author such as Melanie Klein would situate the manifestation of this libidinal dynamism even earlier yet, without connecting that manifestation to the experience of unity, which cannot occur earlier.

(34) J. Lacan, *op. cit.*, p. 94.

(35) Laplanche and Pontalis, *Vocabulaire de Psychanalyse*, p. 33. (*The Language of Psychoanalysis*, p. 111).

(36) Laplanche and Pontalis, *Vocabulaire de Psychanalyse*, p. 34. (*The Language of Psychoanalysis*, p. 112b.).

(37) J. Lacan. Article on "La Famille" in the *Encyclopédie française*. Vol., 8, Art. 40.

(38) J. Lacan, *Écrits*, p. 97 (E: p. 4).

(39) Psychoanalysts speak of a primary and a secondary narcissism. Even though there is no absolute agreement about the usage of these expressions, it is rather generally admitted that primary narcissism would concern all libidinal investment prior to the investment of an object *in the full sense of the word.* (Therefore, since the investment of the object in the full sense only appears at the Oedipal stage, all pre-Oedipal investment is primary narcissism.) Secondary narcissism would be that in which the subject, after having invested an object, recalls that investment not in order to reinvest the freed libido in another object (as is the case for one who changes his love partner or love object) but in order to reinvest it in himself. It is this which seems to occur in every psychosis. Freud has described the mechanism whereby it occurs, especially in the instance of melancholy. Therefore, mirror-narcissism would be, in principle, a form of primary narcissism, but it would be secondary narcissism in paranoia, if it be admitted that the paranoiac was not always paranoid, a fact which appears evident to many. (See in this regard, Laplanche and Pontalis, *Vocabulaire*, p. 263; *The Language*, p. 137.)

(40) The term 'projection' does not belong specifically to psychoanalysis, and, in any case, it is widely used outside it. We are taking the concept in its most narrowly psychoanalytic sense, as defined in Laplanche and Pontalis' definition: "*the operation through which the subject expels from himself and locates in another—be it a person or a thing—qualities, desires, etc., even 'objects,' which he denies or refuses to see in himself. We are dealing here with a defense quite archaic in origin, which one finds operative especially in paranoia but also in 'normal' modes of thought such as superstition.*" *Vocabulaire*, p. 344. (*The Language*, p. 349).

(41) This relation of imaginary objectivation with itself has been analyzed with much insight by P. Demoulin in his book, *Névrose et Psychose*, (Paris-Louvain 1967) p. 120 ff.

(42) J. Lacan, *"La Famille,"* in *L'Encyclopédie française*, Vol. 8, Art. 40-10. We italicized. [ADW].

(43) *Idem.*

(44) *Idem.*

(45) *Idem.*

(46) *Idem.*

(47) Cf. in this regard, Merleau-Ponty, *The Phenomenology of Perception*, p. 144.

(48) One could translate *snoepen* by *to savor* if one only wanted tot take into consideration that it is a question of a familiar term which only properly applies to delicacies.

Chapter Four

THE STRUCTURAL ROLE OF THE OEDIPUS COMPLEX. ABSENCE OF THE OEDIPAL TRIANGLE IN PSYCHOSIS

De Waelhens

I. The Psychotic and the Oedipus Complex.
A Case Study: The Electrician of Rotterdam

We must now approach the problem from a new point of view. The language creates for a "subject" the necessary opening towards another which will allow him to take this other as an object but without confusing himself with him or losing himself in that confusion. This establishment of language coincides at the affective level with what psychoanalysis calls the libidinal investment of the body of another. This investment will therefore be different from the anterior phases of evolution of this same libido. Indeed of these phases one could not say that they were either auto- or hetero-erotic, in the strict sense of these terms, since there could not yet have been either *autos,* 'self,' or *heteros,* 'other.' But since it is customary, we will call these early phases of the libido auto-erotic in the following precise sense that even if, in fact and *quoad nos,* they were aimed at another, they would remain *quoad se* (if I dare say) in a stage prior to all differentiation between self and other.(1)

So this first *true* object usually tends to coincide with the object that nature, as well as his own prehistory, proposed to the "subject" as original and still undifferentiated term of libidinal investment. It is indeed the mother who will be this privileged *other.*

At this point we have to consider what psychoanalysis calls the Oedipus complex. The decisive point is not, despite what is sometimes said, that the mother becomes an object of love. The essential points, on the contrary are: first, that the structural and constituting relations, which permit the subject to correctly accede to the Oedipal relations, be accurately posed. Second, the liquidation of the Oedipal relation should be without any aftereffects except those inscribed within that structure itself. (This defines the favorable limit case). It must now be evident that a subject for whom the unconscious image of one's own body remains confused and fragmented, who furthermore has not acceded to the order of the symbolic–of which the Oedipus will be the ridge–and who, finally, has not bypassed the purely specular relation between the self and others, that such a subject will not be able to enter into a correct Oedipus, nor a fortiori, be able to surmount it. Where guiding marks which authorize and impose, for example, the correct usage of personal pronouns, are not established, all object love, in the psychoanalytic sense of the expression, is simply impossible. One must not be deluded by certain appearances. It is readily affirmed, in fact, that the psychotic is characterized among other things, by his incapacity to accede to the Oedipus complex, whereas the neurotic is never able to free himself from it. Let us leave aside for the moment the problem of neurosis and ask ourselves how one must understand the thesis relative to the psychotic. For, generally speaking, it would be misleading to say that one does not find in the psychotic those elements from which the Oedipus complex is constructed. How, then, can we uphold, with the psychoanalytic tradition, the thesis that the psychotic is excluded from the Oedipus complex?

We may better comprehend the scope of this discussion in the light of an example. The patient in question is an electrician from Rotterdam currently confined to the University of Utrecht Clinic as a diagnosed schizophrenic. He is a man in his thirties, of towering height, whose troubles seemingly began at about the age of 19 years following a traffic accident in which he was driving a truck which collided with another vehicle at an intersection. The patient himself was uninjured, but his younger brother, who had been sitting at his side, was ejected from the truck and killed instantly. The patient then started to develop depressive guilt feelings which grew progressively more intense and were then transformed into diverse delusions.

For about ten years the patient alternated between sojourns at the clinic and normal social life, but these periods in society became shorter and rarer. At the time of our meeting, he had not left the asylum for almost two years, except for a few leaves of absence.

Two delusions dominate the life of the patient. The first has to do with traffic accidents. The rules of right of way and the general traffic code reached such a high degree of perfection in his delusion that any accidents were virtually impossible. The patient spends all his time and his walks to the town "refuting" the account of supposed accidents which he reads in the local papers. He compares the various accounts reported by various newspapers and investigates the accident himself on the scene. The incoherences or contradictions which he discovers force him to conclude that no such accident took place and that the story was a fable. These fables are spread by the "neurologists" in order to practice all sorts of amputations and mutilations that go as far as decapitations on the supposedly injured persons. However, the patient is not absolutely sure that these operations are real; they may have wax dolls as their victims and it is possible that the "neurologists" are only trying to intimidate people. When he is not investigating, H. meditates on traffic laws or teaches them to other patients.

The second delusion concerns filiation. His "legal" father is not his real father. He feels that his name is but a borrowed one and he wants to find his real father. However, he dedicates most of his investigations to problems of traffic circulation rather than to his problems of filiation. He knows he is a descendant of Saint Anthony of Padua and of Pasteur. In fact, a miracle would

176

be necessary for him to find his real father. His view of impregnation is such as to make it impossible, short of prodigious chance or miracle, for anyone to know who engendered him. Spermatozoa constantly escape from the organism of all males and circulate by billions in the air, bombarding women without interruption and without them being aware of it. From time to time a woman is properly hit by one of these spermatozoa and she becomes pregnant. Under these conditions, spotting the father would be pure luck. It would probably be more fruitful to count on divine revelation which happens once in a while, but H. will certainly not be favored by this since this revelation can only befall (and still only through the intervention of the queen of the Low Lands) the "Dutch Fundamentalists" *(Oernederlanders)*. There are very few of these people and H. is not among them for at least two reasons. First of all, the "Dutch Fundamentalists" are necessarily "reformed" *(hervormd)*, which cannot be the case of a descendant of St. Anthony and Pasteur and who would thus necessarily be Catholic.(2) Secondly, the "Dutch Fundamentalists" must be free from mental problems. Now H. readily concedes, although with embarrassment, that he does not fulfill this second condition either.

Let us try to interpret a few traits of this delusion with the help of the patient's accounts.

To start with we will demonstrate a narrow link between the theme of traffic regulations and that of filiation. It is obvious that the non-existence of traffic accidents is destined to exonerate the patient from the culpability he feels for his brother's death, a death which at one time had been hoped for and now was obtained. But this traffic accident masks another one, also wished for and imaginarily obtained, for which the guilt must also be erased. Let us remember that the misfortunes of Oedipus have as their origin a traffic accident provoked by the non-observance of the rules of right of way. The patient defends himself against Oedipal guilt by the affirmation that all transgressions of the prohibitions posed by the rule or the law relative to rights of way are impossible. He cannot, however, eliminate the menace of castration: this is not symbolic but imaginarily real. Nevertheless, the menace, which is hardly consciously admitted, is already repressed; we must believe or may think that the "neurologists" only castrate wax dolls for the purpose of intimidation. Besides, "Catholics" are not "reformed."

That the Oedipal desire, under its twofold dimension of love for the mother and of murder of the father, is present here is clearly demonstrated by the delusion concerning filiation. But, the foreclosure of the father appears openly in the patient's myth of conception. But this myth has still another meaning. For the patient not only desired his mother, he also wished–according to a frequently manifested phantasy of schizophrenics–to beget himself with his own mother and thereby to become his own father.[1] This signifies that if the

---

[1] It is worthwhile to draw attention to the fact that the questions of the origin of the self as a consciousness is a problem to which people have given many solutions. One kind

father is found, his incest would become evident. However, he protects himself from such a discovery by a "theory" of conception which renders his father practically impossible to find except by miracle or divine revelation which we know will never happen to him. But, at this moment, H. runs the risk of becoming a foundling. This is corrected by his distant parentage to St. Antoine and Pasteur thanks to the superb confusion of the signifier and the signified,[2] combined with an imaginary return of the signifier into the real, as

of solution is the thought that a person has a soul which is permanent: this soul is thought to exist after the life-time of the self. This gave rise to certain rites as in the case with the Kikju women of Kenya or the Konyak Nagas of Assam. The first worshiped a tree of dead souls in order to have children. The last one performed rituals with skulls in order to have a child of the desired sex. Another form of our first kind of solution to the question of the origin of the self is the belief that gives meaning to head-hunting. The human soul is supposed to *be* or to *reside* in a body part: the heart, the skull or most often the head. As a theory of human beings, the thought of the permanence of the soul is known in the West as metempsychosis (Orpheus, Plato, and Neoplatonism). In India it is known as transmigration of the soul. A second kind of solution is the thought that person as consciousness is the cause of himself. Sartre's position is a nice example of this solution. Sartre uses the expression: "to be its own foundation" *(Being and Nothingness,* p. 109-110, 693*).* The frequently manifested phantasy of schizophrenics–that he begets himself with his own mother and thereby becomes his own father–can thus be understood as an attempt to deal with the very puzzling problem of the origin of the self. One might reject as absurd the answer of the schizophrenic, but one cannot reject the question to which it is supposedly an answer. (A useful survey of the problem of metempsychosis and head-hunting can be found in the *Encyclopedia Britannia 1967,* Vol. 11 and 15).

2 The confusion of signifier and signified leads in the theory of Lacan to the creation of the *imaginary real.* This confusion occurs because of the loss of the symbolic or metaphorical power of the patient. In order for language to be used properly, a person must master the metaphorical dimension: he must be able to understand that something (a word such as 'table') stands for something else (the object: table). Furthermore, language has the peculiar possibility of using some words in a metaphorical dimension of the second degree. Thus one can use the word "chicken" to refer to an object (metaphorical dimension of the first degree). One can use this same word 'chicken' to refer to a peculiar characteristic of a person (cowardice). Such a use of the word 'chicken' is called in linguistics: metaphorical use of the word. Within our context, such a metaphorically used word is really metaphorical in the second degree. It is a word that refers to an animal in order to point to an aspect of a person's character. A confusion of signifier and signified is based on the loss of the second degree metaphor. It finds its origin in the fact that the signified is for some reason unacceptable and is thus repressed. There remains then a signifier with which the subject identifies unconsciously as if it were a signified. For instance, the patient would make noises similar to those of a chicken rather than accept that he is a coward.

Signifier   Signified

'chicken' ——————————→ (M_1)animal ——————————→(M_2)aspect of man's character

Imaginary Real or Confusion
of Signifier and Signified

shown in the fable presented by Leclaire to illustrate the mechanism of fore-closure.(3)

In fact, the spermatozoa are confused with microbes. And we know that Pasteur is the "father of microbes," since he discovered them. Our patient is thus a descendant of Pasteur. As for St. Anthony of Padua, tradition invokes him as a guardian, as the "father" of all lost objects who enables us to find them again. St. Anthony is therefore also his ancestor.(4) As for the theme of the Queen of the Low Lands, we will understand it by listening closely to what the patient literally says. He tells us that only a few rare persons who are com-pletely "reformed," can obtain the revelation of their origin from God. But, isn't it true, in fact, that only those who have accepted reformation,(5) which is brought about by the symbolic castration imposed by the father, can be given the knowledge of their father's name and be recognized by him. They are the real nobility of the Low Lands,(6) the *Oernederlanders*. Since H. cer-tainly did not accede to this symbolic castration–his delusion states that he is not reformed–there is no possibility that God would consent to such a revela-tion for him. But who are those that God, the absolute Father, would favor with such a message, which, in effect, is a message of authentification? It will be those whom the Queen of the Low Lands will designate by her interven-tion. Let us note here a curious inversion. Psychoanalytic theory holds that the child renounces being the phallus of the mother[3] as soon as the intervention of

---

Lacan calls the unconscious identification with the signifier, the creation of an imagi-nary real. He thereby means to convey that something which is symbolic (the signi-fied of the signifier 'chicken,' i.e., cowardice) is repressed *and replaced* by something which takes place in the real (making noises like a chicken), but which has its origins in the imagination of the patient as *it is guided by the signifier* of the repressed signi-fied. Thus, in the example of De Waelhens, one has a metaphor of the second order: Pasteur is the *father* of microbes (he discovered them), or St. Antony is the *Father of* lost objects (he was the Saint to which Catholics prayed when they wanted help in re-covering a lost object). The patient of De Waelhens does not accept the second order metaphor. Instead, he treats Pasteur and St. Antony as a non-metaphorical father (This is similar to the non-metaphorical use of 'chicken'). The imaginary real symptom of De Waelhens' patient is that he considers himself to be a Catholic because his imagi-nary fathers are Catholics. In *fact,* however, he was a Calvinist. (See notes 2, 3, 13, 14 of Ch. IV and note 21 of Ch V for further explanations or examples).

[3] This is particularly the case of Lacan and his school. But Lacan claims that he is redis-covering the real Freud. Lacan goes back to Freud's analysis of "little Hans" to support his own thesis. (Freud, S.E. Vol. X). For the relation between Lacan and Freud, see Wilden. *The Language of the Self, p.* 186ff. For the validity of the Lacan-Freud thesis about the phallus see the study on the phallic symbol by Vanggaard, Thorkil: *Phallos: A Symbol and its History in the Male World* or Scott, George R.: *Phallic Worship.* For a critical study of the use of the phallic theme in Lacan, see Bär, Eugen: *Semiotic Ap-proaches to Psychotherapy* and "Understanding Lacan" in *Psychoanalysis and Contem-porary Science,* Vol. 3, p. 473-544. See also: Gear et al.: *Sémiologie psychoanalytique.*

the Father distances him from her and in addition upholds the prohibition that the Law proscribes concerning his relation to her. But, one must add, the child will not accept this law and will not accede to the name-of-the-Father unless the mother appears attentive and respectful to the father's word, which she will sanctify (or debase) by her own attitude towards him (the father). "The father is only present in the form of the law which is shown in his words. The validity of these words, and thus of the Law, depends upon the degree to which they are acknowledged by the mother. If the father's position is called into question, the child remains subjugated by his mother."(7) In this case the subject remains foreclosed to the "paternal metaphor" and this is exactly what H. tells us about himself. H. is dependent upon the symbiotic union with his mother to such a degree that he projects the initiative for the typical paternal act of recognition upon her (the Queen of the Low Lands). At the same time he adds that he is personally excluded from this initiative and from this recognition.

II. The Elements of the Oedipus Complex

We are attending here to what could be stated about all psychotics of the schizophrenic type: if the delusion shows the presence of most of the material elements which contribute to the formation of the Oedipal relations, the elements are present in such a way that they cannot possibly lead to a correct position of the Oedipus complex so that the latter cannot fulfill to any degree *the constitutive and structuring role of subjectivity* which in the case of the normal person it is its function to fulfill. Furthermore, there can be no question of its liquidation. All this is impossible because of the simple fact that H. never acceded to what one has come to call, following Lacan, the "paternal metaphor." To accede to this "paternal metaphor" means to be able to substitute the name-of-the-Father for the desire of *being* the phallus of the mother. It therefore remains perfectly correct to uphold the thesis that the schizophrenic did not *truly* enter into the Oedipus complex since the opposite sexed parent, to whom the libidinal investment is directed, is not present to a sufficient degree to create the Oedipal scene. Indeed, the parent of the opposite sex does not appear for the schizophrenic as another differentiated from the "self" of the subject, another upon whom the prohibition resulting from the paternal promulgation of the law will fall. The pseudo-subject remains, in his being, identified with the phallus of the mother and could therefore not be another for her, nor she another for him. For such is the meaning of the delusion: to be one's own father with one's own mother.

The establishment of the Oedipus complex failed because the structural moments preceding it (moments which we have tried to elucidate in the above pages) were in themselves failures. The actual investment by the schizophrenic of the opposite sexed parent is thus but an object-relation in appearance. In fact, it remains absolutely narcissistic and pre-oedipal.

But, then, what is the real Oedipus complex or rather–since our purpose is not just to repeat the psychoanalytic theory–how does this complex help us, philosophers, understand the constitutive moments of the structure of subjectivity?

The Oedipus complex places the child before the dual experience of disappointment and prohibition. In reality this disappointment, which is caused by the loved-object itself, is not the first disappointment that "reality" imposes upon desire. In one sense disappointment, as Lacan has remarked in his article in the *Encyclopédie française*,[4] begins with the birth of the subject. The weaning, the intrusion of the third person, and the Oedipal dissatisfaction only recapture and reactivate that first disappointment. But each time the frustration inherent in the disappointment transforms the subject and deepens his experience of the otherness of others. The typical result of the Oedipal disappointment is not to place the subject before an unavoidable destiny but for him to learn that love is radically dependent on its object[5] because this object *can* always escape, if he (she) loves someone else. Furthermore, in the case of the Oedipus complex the loved object *has to* love someone else besides the child, because of the presence of a third: the paternal figure, which thus becomes the privileged representative of the interdiction, of distance, and of the Law. Once again, what counts here is not the specific anecdotal events that are more or less real and which can be discovered in normal cases by an analysis of the unconscious. On the contrary, what is important is the constitutive role played by these dialectical and structuring moments of the Oedipus complex for the subject and his experience of reality.

The decisive contribution of the Oedipus complex is to insert the subject into the Law. In exchange for the renouncement which is imposed upon him and to which, come what may, he must comply, the subject receives the name of the father, which will also be his name.(8) And so he finds himself forever *situated* in the succession of generations–and that with a certainty as radical for himself as for others.[6] This also symbolizes a transcendence of "natural

---

4   "La Famille." No English translation is available of this important article. One can find a summary of its main theoretical points in: W. Ver Eecke: "Freedom, Self-Reflection and Intersubjectivity," p. 236ff.

5   What the child learns about love in the Oedipal situation is that love is negativity. Indeed, a love relation is a double relationship. i.e., my love of the other and the other's love of me. The other's love for me is dependent upon the freedom of the other. This other *can* or could refuse or withdraw his love. It is precisely this possibility of negativity that the child comes to realize and hopefully accept in the Oedipus complex. Indeed, the child learns that the mother *also* relates to the father. Thus the mother has not as her only function to relate to the child.

6   In the history of philosophy, there is at least one philosopher who is aware of the crucial function of the name: L. Wittgenstein: *On Certainty,* 569-572; 576-579; 642;

existence." In such an existence, one's appearance is determined only by the chance of copulation. This in turn would make it impossible to discover one's origin and thus to be located in the succession of generations. The symbolic pact which seals the renouncement of Oedipal love withdraws me from the swarming and profuse disorder of biological nature in order to complete my identity in the patronym which I carry. This name precisely situates me, both for myself and for others, giving me the right, from the place which I occupy, to desire and to engender. This pact similarly consecrates my entry into negativity: for I have full and complete identity only in assuming a name *which is not exclusively my own*. The name of the foundling, of which he is the sole possessor, is not *really* a name. Thus the name which is the mark and the marrow of all identity is inextricably intertwined with negativity. This is a first meaning of symbolic castration. But castration can also be explained otherwise, using psychoanalytic language (or at least a certain psychoanalytic language). Castration transforms the child who thinks of himself as *being* the phallus of the mother in order to constitute him as a subject who now *has* a phallus or who can receive one.[7] The importance of this symbolic castration can be seen in the fact that Lévi-Strauss holds that the prohibition of incest defines the transition from nature to culture. It can just as well be said that this prohibition–if at least we understand it broadly enough to include all the connotations just exposed–founds the accession to subjectivity and all of its correlates: the true other and full and complete reality. This is also confirmed by Lacan.(9) The Oedipus complex lends to the object "a certain emotional depth,"(10) by the separation imposed upon the subject and the loved object. This object will, from then on, be able to be recognized as real in the full sense of the word, i.e., as autonomous relative to our own drives. At the same time this love object can now inspire respect in us. All these aspects were foreign to

660. In anthropology, Lévi-Strauss gives a crucial function to names for the purpose of regulating what he calls the exchange of women. *(The Elementary Structure of Kinship)*. For a broad survey of this question, see Fox, Robin: *Kinship and Marriage*. In American literature there is a novel in which a great concern is expressed about 'the name': Conrad's *Lord Jim.*

[7] The usage made of the concepts of "having" and "being" in psychoanalytic theory is different from the usage made of these same concepts by the French existentialist philosopher Gabriel Marcel. In psychoanalytic theory, the two concepts refer to the way one experiences one's own body or a body-part. The concept "being one's body or body-part" stresses the fact that the relation between the self and the body-part is *contingent*. Gabriel Marcel uses the concept "to have" in order to indicate the relation of possession between a person and an object. He uses the concept "to be" to indicate the typical form of human existence, i.e., that a subject is only through a respectful and loving relation with another. (For a misinterpretation of this Marcelian concept, see Merleau-Ponty: *Phenomenology of Perception, p.* 174, n. 1*)*. Benveniste, an eminent French linguist, wrote an excellent and illuminating article on the linguistic difference between "being" and "having": " 'Être'et 'avoir' dans leurs fonctions linguistiques" in *Problèmes de linguistique générale, p.* 187-207.

the preoedipal relations.

Let us insist again on the fact that the above must be understood neither as anecdotal history nor as psychology in the ordinary sense. We tried to show the structural moments of the formation of subjectivity. The problem of knowing what concrete repercussions these moments could have had in the affective history of this particular person and how they marked his history, these are problems for psychoanalytic practice and do not concern us. Similarly we need not ask ourselves how these articulations of structure can be translated into terms of genetic psychology. Let us not forget that, for Freud, "the idea of the Oedipus Complex is born from a reflection upon phantasy."(11)[8] What gives the Oedipal problem unity, is neither an undecomposable instinctive force (Freud denied its existence and substituted a theory of instinctual conflicts for it) nor a psychology of sentiments such as love or hate, for what is in question in these sentiments are the positions which the subject can occupy towards other subjects. The necessity of recognizing oneself in the word, prevents the subject from absolutely identifying himself with his ways of being. It recreates in him the possibility of differentiation. It is in this perspective that one must understand the concepts of identification and the choice of the object; they define the constitutive modes of the relation which sets itself up between the subject and an other in what we call 'the expression of a desire.'(12)

III. The Unconscious and the Primacy of the Signifier

This long voyage brings us back to our point of departure: the problem of the unconscious. Does the reflexion upon a few theses and a few psychoanalytic concepts furnish us with the material to outline an answer? Can one comprehend the status of the unconscious? How can one articulate this comprehension? It is perhaps worth the trouble to examine our results, even if they remain well below our expectations.

First, the unconscious is made up of drives in the Freudian sense of the word. These are situated at the junction between the organic and the psychic; they consequently have no meaning in themselves and that is why they can, as such, neither be nor become conscious. We can say that their existence is inferred from behavior, if we understand by behavior all that phenomenology alludes to by this term (which includes, specifically, the discourse). The her-

---

[8] Indeed, Freud discovered the Oedipus complex as a universal structure of the human person, when he was forced to abandon his theory of seduction as the cause of neurosis. Freud, then discovered the function of sexuality in children and of phantasms in the aetiology of neuroses. These changes occurred in 1897 and found their culmination in the publication of *Three Essays on Theory of Sexuality*. For references see *Standard Edition*, Vol. III, p. 160, 262; Vol VII, p. 128.

meneutic of normal and pathological behavior allows us to refer to those drives with the Freudian terminology of *Eros* and *Thanatos.*[9] Because a human person is essentially a being who creates meaning, these drives will be supplied with "psychic representatives" which will give them, so to speak, a face. These may be conscious, but are not necessarily so, because some of them might be or have to be repressed. The representatives and their successive offspring are articulated between themselves as a language. We will try to lay out, at least in broad outline, the possible destinies of these representatives. As for the question of knowing if the drives are translated exactly by their psychic representatives, it is a question without pertinence since the passage of the drive to its first representative is also the passage from the absence of sense or non-sense towards meaning. And, moreover, the problem of the exact translation of an expression can only be significant in the context of two constituted linguistic systems.[10]

The constitution of the fundamental psychic representatives, of their derivatives, and of the derivatives of the derivatives, is precisely what determines the elementary material for the future psychic history of the subject. Psychoanalysis is perhaps able to reproduce it (even this may not necessarily be its goal) by annulling the gaps, the blanks and the substitutions of terms that were provoked by the intervention of repression. This history has little or nothing to do with what one can call, not without some abuse of language, the objective reality of events encountered by the same subject. This is so be-

---

[9] For an excellent book-length treatment on these two crucial concepts in Freudian theory, see: Jean Laplanche: *Vie et Mort en Psychoanalyse.* For shorter studies see. H.W. Loewald, "On Motivation and Instinct Theory;" J.H. Smith, Ping-Nie Pao, N.A. Schweig: "On the Concept of Aggression;" W. Ver Eecke "Myth and Reality in Psychoanalysis."

[10] Freud used the words *Repräsentanz* or *Repräsentant,* 'representive,' and *Vorstellung,* 'presentation.' The two concepts are used in two different contexts. The first concept, translated in English as a 'representative,' is used in a context where the problem raised by De Waelhens is appropriate. This first concept also raises the problem of the relation between body and mind; it arises when one asks how the drives relate to their psychic representatives. Freud's position is that this relation is not one of parallelism nor of causalism. Laplanche and Pontalis propose the following reading of Freud's view of the problem: the drives relate to their representatives as the mandator to his delegate. Typical for such a relationship is that the delegate gets his mandate from the mandator, but can enter by himself a system of relationships that have their own laws. (Laplanche and Pontalis: *The Language,* under the index word 'representative' p. 203, 223, 364). Such a view is compatible with the thesis of De Waelhens that the question of whether the psychic representatives are the exact translation of the drives is a false question. The second concept, translated in English as 'presentation,' is used by Freud to distinguish and oppose a psychic context and the affect that is invested in it. Freud maintains that the two can be separated and then start their own history of transformation and/or distortion. This concept does not directly raise the problem of the relation between the body and soul.

cause, as we have seen, the original "representatives are created at an evolutionary stage where the perception of and the libidinal relationship with an object remain absolutely below a level at which we could talk about a reality or a real subject and even less about any kind of notion of truth. It is in the creation of this web or of this framework that the primacy of the signifier over the signified becomes evident. The literality of the signifier and the principles of combination which govern their possible constellations have priority over the requirements of the signified and that both for the mutations of old forms as well as for the arranging of new forms. This is true to such a degree that we can say that the signified is led instead of leading.

This is illustrated by the dream where the problem of the death of the dreamer is hidden under the guise of a free visit to the cellars of a wine merchant whose name signifies in Dutch "of the end." Besides, it so happened that this wine merchant was also a highly celebrated European soccer player during the dreamer's youth. Among other talents, he possessed the one of "transforming" a "penalty" into a goal, to the point of only having missed one in his entire career. And this career was prematurely terminated following a quadruple fracture of the leg provoked deliberately, in exceptionally brutal conditions, by a vindictive adversary. Let us add that the player belonged to a team which had chosen as the color for its uniform the color of mourning, or more exactly half mourning. This color was chosen because at the time of the founding of the team, the principal owner was actually mourning.

Great psychoanalytic knowledge is not necessary to understand that the signifiers present in the dream evoke most of the fundamental questions about life as psychoanalysis elaborates them. This evocation centers around the theme of death, represented by the image of a free visit to "the cellars of the end." This latter image itself also hides multiple meanings.

Thus the "set" of the above described signifiers could not have been inferred. They were given by the real world in the arrangement in which they were found there. But in the dream these signifiers themselves succeed in interrelating in a particular way the problems of death, of desire and of castration.(13)

The laws of these combinations have been presented by Freud as a result of his research on the dream and were named *condensation* and *displacement* by him. J. Lacan related these concepts to the work of linguists and called them *metaphor* and *metonomy*. The relative autonomy of the signifier vis-à-vis the signified, leads one even to admit the existence of an order of the signifier closed in upon itself.[11] The effects of this order are originally or even forever

---

[11] This is another way of expressing Lacan's thesis that there is a primacy of the signifier over the signified, and that it is thus imperative to study the signifiers, their connections, and their distortions in order to understand the symptoms of the patients. Through this thesis, Lacan wants to ground Freud's consistent practice of paying close attention to words and word games (See Freud's interpretation of dreams, of jokes and

unknown to the subject. But this order contributes to the articulation of the unconscious and appears periodically and abruptly in the manifestations of the unconscious, as, for example, in the rebus of the dream or the spoonerisms of the lapsus. And for those who know how to read them, these manifestations of the unconscious are very meaningful. Witness the radio announcer, who having to describe the floral decorations of a church choir where a royal marriage was to be celebrated, announces to his listeners that he is going to describe the "choral defloration."

The psychoanalytic investigation has as its goal to discover the key-signifiers which for each of us elaborate and organize the unconscious. This unconscious is made up of these signifiers, of their derivatives and of the derivatives of these derivatives in their infinite possible combinations and ramifications. These key-signifiers produce in their allusive literality those differences and those nodal points by means of which the original distance of the primal repression has been created. However, the attempt to abolish this gap through an ineffaceable phantasy which seeks to fulfill it is the immediate response to this situation. This phantasy is the initial term of an endless offspring of substitutes, more and more unrecognizable but where one can find–if one knows how to listen and read–the mark of the original seal.(14) These substitutes serve as terms of libidinal investment, as well as hieroglyphic inscriptions referring to the lost object.

The ultimate frame of all unconscious is made, if one dares to say so, of phantasmatic traces which have as their purpose to restore first in an imaginary and then in a symbolic mode (yet the passage to symbolization may fail) the lost fullness which is a result of the dehiscence and incisions which came to mark the subject as a consequence of his retreat from the immediate or the defection of this immediacy.[12] An important paradox of this state of affairs can certainly be found in the fact that the creation of a substitute object is exactly that which also makes definitive the dismissal of the lost object, which it is supposed to safeguard. This paradox brings to mind, under a new form, a similar paradox which we have spoken of with regard to language. We said before that the identity conquered and established in the "I," because it can only take place through the mediation of the universal, is also that which forever prevents direct access to subjectivity. Even though this subjectivity is not accessible, we are continuously informed about it in the discourse of the first person.

That this is, in effect, the role and the scope reserved for the key-signifiers; and for the object that these signifiers designate and even give birth to can be clearly demonstrated by a certain psychotic discourse, where the "key-signifiers" disappear after they have hardly surfaced. These signifiers are mo-

---

[12] slips of tongue). For striking illustrations, see footnotes 13 and 14 of this chapter.
The classical psychoanalytic expression for "retreat from the immediate" or "the defection of this immediacy" is: object loss.

bile, floating, erring, ungraspable because of their incessant intertwining. They are pseudo-rivets from a chaotic pseudo-universe. This is so because they did not arise from the chasm of a retreat. The immediate which they attempt to mask is always there. The key signifiers are only apparently part of the *discourse*.(15)

This is why one can maintain that the "before" of the primal repression is actually our prehistory, but a prehistory for which no other subsequent or retro-active history is possible. Our real history only begins with the radical negation of this prehistory; such a negation renders inaccessible that which it negates. That is why it will again be necessary to recognize that, in a certain way, the psychotic has never emerged from this prehistory (we will return to this later).

The articulation of the unconscious concerns at the same time, the desire, its object, the reality of the subject, and even all that the subject has said to himself about these matters. The Oedipal desire–which is the first to deserve the name of *object*-relationship in the full sense of the word–forms the driving force as well as the center of this movement of articulations. However, both these desires and the knowledge about them are subjected to repression, although this time it is a secondary form of repression as Freud explained it. But according to whether or not the subject succeeds in maintaining these secondary repressions, and according to whether he succeeds to a greater or lesser degree in replacing the repressed by the diverse formations which Freud describes under the name of "super-ego" and ideal ego, there will surge from these first representatives of the impulses an off-spring and substitutes more acceptable to the ego and which can become satisfactory guides for libidinal investments.

And so the subject displays and carries within him a hidden language which is himself as much as it is not himself. Psychoanalysis has always given itself the task of deciphering this hidden language. It has forged for itself the proper methods needed to succeed at this task. For it is clear that a subject trying to live by the image of himself (of which he is the prisoner and which he searches to impose upon others so that the other in turn will authenticate it) cannot conceal this hidden language which is the void and the negative of himself. The subject will then be referred to his true text or image as soon as he is able to listen.

NOTES

(1) Some authors distinguish auto-erotism into two phases: the auto-erotic phase proper and the narcissistic phase. The first would refer to investments made prior to the acquisition of the mirror-image. These investments would thus be carried onto a dismembered body, i.e., a part of the body. The second phase concerns libidinal investments projected onto a unitary *image* of the body. This can only occur after the ac-

quisition of the mirror-image. Certain texts of Freud make allusion to this distinction. See to this effect the still unpublished work of Thomas Ewens: *Essay on the ground of an interrogation: the theme of schizophrenia in Freud.* Ch. II, 5.

(2)   In view of our interpretation, it is not without interest to note that H. is in fact a member of the Reformed Church, and, in reality, he never abandoned his Calvinist faith. He is 'Catholic' in *as much as* he is a descendant of St. Anthony and Pasteur.

(3)   "I have attempted... to illustrate this concept (foreclosure) by the story of two happy companions' holiday night on the town. The foreclosed element was constituted there by a drunken and nocturnal encounter with a pair of swallows (traffic policemen) who were obliged to forcibly conduct them home.

It was evidently not possible, for either of them, to recollect that scene, lost in the fog of alcohol; some bruises, and the fact of being home were the only traces of an event which at first escaped their memory.

But the striking thing about this story was that, several months later, one of the revellers abruptly evidenced an ornithological delirium in which there appeared not only the swallows but all sorts of birds.

Thus, it is that there surfaced in the imaginary and hallucinatory reality of the delirium, the pair of birds which had constituted the center of a nonintegrated experience, *as the banished "signifier," the repressed symbol, independent of its imaginary correlations.* According to Lacan's formula, one can say that *what had been rejected from the symbolic order*–in this case the signifier '*swallow*' which was nevertheless known to the subject–reappeared, in the course of the delirium, *in the real*, or at least in a mode of deliriously experiencing the real. Such a real, however, is evidently imaginary and is deprived of any truly symbolic dimension." Translated from S. Leclaire, "A propos de l'épisode psychotique que présente l'homme aux loups," in La Psychoanalyse, p. 6, p. 97.)

(4)   St. Anthony of Padua and Pasteur represent here that which Lacan calls an "A-Father" (*Un-Père*). See below.

(5)   The word *hervorming* is a literal translation of the English word reformation. In the Dutch *hervorming*, just as in the English term, the etymological meaning is quite apparent.

(6)   *Low-Countries* is a literal translation of Nederland(en). The double-meaning perceptible in English is exactly equivalent to the Dutch.

(7)   J. Lacan, *Les formations de l'inconscient. Séminaires de l'année* 1957-58 (typewritten). Also, *Écrits*, p. 579 (E: p.218): "But what I do wish to insist on is that we should concern ourselves not only with the way in which the mother accommodates herself to the person of the father, but also with the way she takes his speech, the word (*mot*), let us say, of his authority, in other words, of the place that she reserves for the Name-of-the-Father in the promulgation of the law."

(8)   This interpretation of the Oedipus-complex finds no difficulty in the fact that not every civilization bestows the father's name on his offspring. The important thing is that the name is always conferred on the basis of a symbolic system, and that this system stamps personal identity with the characteristic of negativity; at the same time, this system of conferring a name, whatever it might be in a particular civilization, is equivalent to an interdict issued against the possession of the Oedipal object and its substitutes. Such substitutes could be, in certain civilizations quite numerous, although in our own they don't extend further than marriage with one's sister. The fact that the Pharaohs were exempted from this interdict precisely underscored their divine nature.

(9) "It (the Oedipal Complex) contributes to the construction of reality." cf. the article in *L'Encyclopédie française*, 8' 40-13.

(10) *Ibid.*, p. 13.

(11) Marie-Cécile and Edmond Ortigues, *L'Oedipe africain*, p. 64.

(12) Marie-Cécile and Edmond Ortigues, *L'Oedipe africain*, p. 67-8.

(13) Another example, taken from the clinical work of Mme. Dolto, is that of twin sisters (*soeurs jumelles*) who suddenly became mute, oblivious to their surroundings. A long investigation revealed that the illness began the day after their father, upon discovering an old pair of opera glasses at the bottom of a drawer, had exclaimed: "throw the glasses (*les jumelles*) in the garbage!" One can find some other decisive examples of the primacy of the signifier over the signified in the analysis which Serge Leclaire made of certain dreams of his patient Philip and of Freud himself. Unfortunately, these examples are too lengthy to be reproduced here. cf. S. Leclaire, *Psychanalyser*, chapters I, II and V.

(14) Such as the roman numeral "V," in which Freud's genius was able to discover a significant key to understanding the case of the 'Wolfman.' This signifier stood for, and at the same time literally was the position of the mother at the time of the patient's perception of the primordial scene. This signifier also stood for the time of day at which this perception took place, at which time the patient's mood would deteriorate every day. This "V" further signifies the dream of the five wolves, as well as his fear of butterflies whose wings were spread in the "V" position, butterflies striped and colored like Grouscha's dress (the small housemaid whom the patient attacked when, while scrubbing the floor on her knees, her legs spread, she reproduced for him the image of the mother in the primordial scene.) Going beyond the dream of the wolves (Wolf), one discovers the presence of the same signifier in the excessive importance which a series of persons, (whose only common trait was that they were named "Wolf"), had for the future patient. [The first letter of Wolf is double "V." In German 'W' and 'V' are very similar phonemes. W.V.E.] And finally, there is the extraordinary dream of the wasp (*Espe*), in which the patient, whose initials were S.P. (*Espe*) punishes himself by the signifier which denotes for *him* the original deception. ['W' or double 'V' W.V.E.] We quote here the Freudian text S.E., XVII, p. 94. [W.V.E.]: " 'I had a dream,' he said, 'of a man tearing off the wings of an *Espe!*' '*Espe?*' I asked: ' what do you mean by that?'– 'You know: that insect with yellow stripes on its body, that stings.' This would be an illusion to Grouscha, the striped yellow pear (which represented, as did the butterfly, Grouscha (the maid) herself a substitute for his mother–as were all the women whom he observed in a squatting position, and towards whom he developed an irresistible attraction) (the text between the brackets is ours) [A.D.W.]–I could now put him straight: 'So what you mean is a *Wespe*? (Wasp)–'Is it called a *Wespe*? I really thought it was called an *Espe*.' (Like so many other people, he used his difficulties with a foreign language as a screen for symptomatic acts) [He was Russian A.D.W.] 'But Espe, why, that's myself, S.P. (Which were his initials)' [In Austria 'Espe' and 'S.P.' would be pronounced exactly alike. Note of S.E.]. The *Espe* was of course a mutilated *Wespe*. The dream said clearly that he was avenging himself on Grouscha for her threat of castration." It referred to Grouscha's threat of castration uttered following the patient's attempted assault at the time of the floor-scrubbing scene.

(15) S. Leclaire makes the same assertion: "However, the importance of the question of the determination or fixation of the elements constitutive of such an unconscious will be more readily apparent if, going beyond the boundaries of the study of neurosis, one

takes into consideration that which the study of psychosis, and, more specifically, the study of schizophrenia reveals; one finds, in effect in these cases an ensemble literally composed of the same elements as the unconscious of the neurotic, but in which no term provides balance or context, or in which, to put it more simply, nothing assures order; in fact, this phenomenon corresponds to the absence of the unconscious. Hence, in the case of the schizophrenic, one finds oneself confronted with a ghostly script in which each element either refers indiscriminately to the totality of the other ghostly signs, or is exclusively related to one of them which seems to play the role of its sexual compliment. However, one could recognize in the analysis nothing which really deserved to be called a sign. The materiality of each sign, manipulated by the schizophrenic, seems in effect doubly stripped of all bodily reference. It seems, in the last analysis, to be nothing more than a shadow of a sign–that is to say, one whose materiality refers to the materiality of all signifiers." S. Leclaire, *Psychanalyser*, p. 124-25.

Chapter Five

PSYCHOANALYTIC INTERPRETATION OF PSYCHOSIS.
THE PATERNAL METAPHOR AND FORECLOSURE

De Waelhens

I. Paranoia (Schreber)

The fundamental texts found at the origin of Freud's ideas on psychosis (or, as Freud sometimes refers to it, *of narcissistic neuroses,* a name which commonly designates without further distinction schizophrenia, paraphrenia, and paranoia) are the study of the recollections of *President Schreber (1911)* and his *Introduction to Narcissism (1914).*

In Freud's opinion, the Schreber case can be presented at least upon an initial analysis as a paranoia(1) linked with either the genesis or the resurgence of homosexual desires.[1]

For reasons which Freud himself attempts to clarify, but which find their fullest elucidation in the article of J. Lacan on the same subject,(2) this paranoia develops afterwards into an erotico-religious delirium. Freud links these desires to what he calls the narcissistic stage during the evolution of the *libido.* In the course of this stage, originally auto-erotic, the *libido* evolves progressively toward an object-choice. However, before directing itself toward a completely different object (i.e., of a different sex) the libido undergoes an intermediary stage wherein it chooses an object more like itself, that is to say, of the same sex. Every fixation or regression to this phase, a regression which operated in Schreber's case, will be responsible for an overt or latent homosexuality which will be permanent if the phase in question has never been overcome, or for a homosexual drive if there is a regression.(3)   The subject can defend himself from this fixation or this regression by responding, for instance, in a delirium of the paranoid type. Therein is the classical connection that psychoanalysis has established between paranoia and homosexuality. One also knows that homosexual tendencies are not simply annihilated when the libido reaches the heterosexual stage, but also that, sublimated, they are at the origin of most social attitudes and feelings.[2]

---

[1]   Freud states this thesis unequivocally in G.W. VIII, p. 280, S.E. XII, p. 45.

[2]   Freud uses this idea to analyse group formation, particularly in the army and the church. (S.E. XVIII, p. 102-103). Lacan defends a similar thesis through a detour, i.e., the jealousy, typical of the mirror-stage, is according to Lacan the basis of all social feelings. This mirror-stage, however, represents an emotional development that is a-sexual. Thus the ego does not yet relate to a heterosexual other. Within the developmental framework of Lacan, one can call pre-heterosexual attitudes homosexual ones. (" La famille" p. 8.40-10/11).

191

But how does paranoia constitute a defense against these tendencies? Of what does this defense consist?

Freud remarks–and the statement is of importance–that "the principal known forms of paranoia can always be traced to the various forms of contradicting a proposition such as 'I (a man) love him (a man);' moreover, they exhaust every possibility of expressing that contradiction."(4) In this manner, one may distinguish three main types of paranoid deliriums: the delirium of persecution, which contradicts the verb of the proposition (I don't love him, I hate him, because he persecutes me); the erotomanic delirium, which contests the object of the proposition (I don't love him, I love *her,* because she loves me); and the delirium of jealousy, which grasps the subject of the same proposition (I don't love him, it is she who loves him).(5)

The delirium of persecution reverses love to hate. He hates me since he persecutes me; thus I am justified in hating him. One may ask why the hate does not express itself directly but rather demands the roundabout path of the other. The answer is that what we have here is a fundamental mechanism of paranoia known as *projection.* The feeling of hatred felt with regard to the loved object is projected outside of the subject and returns to the subject from without in the form of a persecuting hatred which in turn justifies the subject's own hatred. Thus Flechsig, the old doctor to whom Schreber is quite attached, "hates Schreber and persecutes him: he strives to kill his soul and to unite with God to transform him into a woman," which justifies the unatonable hatred that Schreber feels for him. The mechanism of projection and of the subsequent content upon the self are particularly evident when one considers the bonds of affection which exist between the two men and the kind of persecution claimed. But, in fact, these mechanisms are easily noticed in every delirium of persecution because the persecutor is invariably a person loved at another time, or a representative of that person.

The erotomanic delirium changes the sex of the object. "It is not him I love, it is *her.*" What evolves, through the mechanism of projection, is that "manifestly, she loves me; so I can love her." This interpretation is justified by a double reasoning found in every erotomanic delirium. It is initially that, in every erotomania, the object takes the initiative. Before loving, the subject suddenly perceives through numerous and obvious signs that he is loved by this person, so that he then undertakes a love with a most absurd passion. And it is then that the object is always linked in one way or another to some other person whom the patient holds in great interest. For example, one perceives oneself as loved by the wife of a friend. Or perhaps a woman feels loved by her parish priest, giving her the occasion to incessantly encounter the priest's sister in order to discuss her problem of love. Another woman is loved by a male colleague and seeks the advice of their boss, a woman who knows both of them.(6)

The delirium of jealousy substitutes for the subject of the proposition a subject of the opposite sex: "It is not I who loves him, it is she who loves him." Or, if the patient is a woman, "it is not I who likes women; it is my husband, or my boyfriend, who likes women." The jealous patient suspects his or her mate of loving whomever he himself, or she, is tempted to love. Here there is no need for reversal since, from the start, the process is supposed to evolve in the other: it is the other who loves the third party. This interpretation is based on certain peculiarities, difficult to explain otherwise, which are traceable in every delirious jealousy. Most particularly the jealous person always appears more concerned about the behavior and personality of the rival than he appears about the foul play of the unfaithful one. Frequently, the rival is quite attractive and endowed with such cunning as to render him practically irresistible, such that the jealous person spends his time incessantly trying to decipher all of the rival's suspected plans. Yet this suspicion of every instant is also a way of rendering him present at every moment.

There is yet another way of contradicting the proposition in consideration, and that is to deny it totally, purely and simply: "I do not love anyone." But, as Freud tells us, surely it is necessary that the libido cathect itself somewhere; thus the proposition in fact is changed to mean that the libido is cathected on myself and that "I love no one but myself." Thus the delirium of grandeur is merely a sexual overestimation of oneself, and it falls on the same pattern of generally overestimating the love object, just as in the delirium of jealousy it is the rival who is overestimated. Furthermore, since as we shall see that, according to Freud, psychosis is always characterized by a more or less important reflux of the libido flowing back upon the subject himself, it is not surprising that there are more or less large traces of delirium of grandeur in most psychoses of the paranoid or schizophrenic types. It is quite evident in the case of Schreber who at once succeeds all by himself in keeping God in check by turning the object of his sensual pleasure into the person of God, and at the same time producing a new humanity through the deeds of the former.

Let us examine more closely, however, the mechanism of the formation of symptoms and the kind of repression to which they are bound, since homosexual desire, as obvious as it appears to us, is, at least in Schreber's case, never recognized. It is not probable, in fact, that the two coincide, since the repression aims at wiping out, whereas the objective symptoms–such is Freud's constant doctrine–try in a more or less disguised way, to satisfy the repressed.

As has already been shown, at the heart of the formation of symptoms is the mechanism of *projection*. A certain "lived" interiority is impressed with the forbidden; rejected from without, it undergoes a certain deformation and, in that form, it is admitted to consciousness. The clearest case is that of persecution, where the love that one has towards the other is transformed into a hatred that the other shows toward you. Let us note with Freud that this projection is not equally important in all types of delirium, and further that the mechanism of projection does not belong to the domain of paranoia or even to that of pathology in general. This finding interrupted Freud's investigations,

193

which were then aimed at specifically studying the problem of paranoid regression.

Freud states at the outset that every repression (understanding the word here in its broadest sense) appears in three phases or elements: (A) the fixation, (B) the repression, properly speaking, and (C) (if the case in question is pathological, i.e., if the repression has failed) the return of the repressed.

(A) The fixation. This results from the fact that, for reasons to be determined, an impulse or a composite of impulses has not followed the process of development of the libido with the rest of the organism, finding itself immobilized or *fixated* at an infantile stage of development. In relation to the later and more complex organizations of the libido, this immobilized sector is bypassed and made unconscious, finding itself in a situation equivalent to that which would result from a positive repression. These regions, solidified and provisionally drowned out of consciousness, will acquire great importance in the case where, for some reason, the less archaic structures, more developed, but also more fragile, come to face a crisis and indeed may collapse.

(B) The repression, properly speaking, or the inhibition of access to consciousness and to its acts is carried out by the superior demands of consciousness and of the self (Freud uses both expressions; at that time he does not yet distinguish the various unconscious repressive demands). With respect to psychical expectations rendered unacceptable by these demands, or even with regard to impulses which are underdeveloped and subject to fixation, Freud notes that repression will be more easily realizable as the elements to be repressed become more and more closely connected to already repressed elements, implying an attractive action on the part of the repressed unconscious. The dynamic involved here operates in a double sense: it tries to clear the way for an outlet towards consciousness, and at the same time it aims at draining towards itself that which is not yet unconscious.

(C) The return of the repressed, when the repression has not been sufficient. Freud insists that "this irruption is born at the point where the fixation took place and [that] it implies a regression of the libido to that precise point."(7)

There exist, of course, as many possible points of fixation (and as many "failures" of libidinal development) as there are phases or distinct stages in this development. One can imagine that the modalities of repression, as well as those of the return of the repressed, will have their character determined according to the point of fixation in question and the correlative regression. Let us remark here that Freud, without saying so, delineated the plan of a systematic diversification of "mental diseases" without, however, this plan having since been fully realized. He adds, but does not explain further, that it would without doubt be chimerical to expect that one could explain all the particularities in a given clinical chart by the development of the libido alone. This is in no way a retraction, but rather it is the discovery at the outset that no psychoanalytic investigation, however thorough, can ever be exhaustive, and further that there are *secondary* effects of the disease which are no longer directly dependent on the origins but rather are induced by the primary effects or by other factors, such as the premorbid personality, for example.

The application of the notions described above to the case of Schreber allow Freud to note some new points in his interpretation of psychosis. Freud remarks, as much on the basis of medical accounts as of recollections of Schreber himself, that at the initial acute phase of the disease, the patient experiences a feeling of being present at the end of the world. The living beings (humans and animals), appear to him as mere shadows, and he himself is the only survivor in a petrified and devastated world. But at other times, the transformation of the real seems to encompass himself above all: he feels himself dead, his body decomposes; he even reads in a newspaper the announcement of his own death. Then he verifies that the dead person is his shadow or his double, from which he had separated himself. Afterwards, all these delirious ideas disappear in order to give way to others. It is then that his progressive transformation into a woman begins, accompanied first by a divine persecution and subsequently by a divine alliance. The only link between the two groups of deliriums is the malevolence and the persecution of Flechsig, responsible for the cosmic catastrophes as well as for the killing of Schreber's soul and the divine persecutions which started upon his instigations. It is not until the moment of Schreber's success in turning the divine persecution into an alliance (in every sense of the word) that Flechsig finally finds an adversary of his statute.

It is banal to notice, in one form or another, a *Weltuntergangserlebnis*(8) at the time of the initial acute stages of paranoid schizophrenia or "paranoia," as Freud would say. But Freud gives here, for the first time, an analytical explanation. This discoloring, this downfall is nothing but the experience, in the real, of the withdrawal of the libidinal object cathexes by the patient, a withdrawal characteristic of the "narcissistic psychosis:" the cathexes removed from the object are now linked with the self. With regard to the death of the patient and the decomposition of his body, they express the profound shock felt by the rupture and the failure of the affective links with the world. My indifference, the absence of feelings that is present in me, can only mean that I am dead. This disaster, which underscores many delirious hypochondriac impressions (which otherwise have a different meaning which shall be discussed later) can be quickly overcome since, while the subject completely abandons his objective cathexes, he gathers all his libido unto himself, which eventually leads him to overestimate himself in the same manner in which, as a rule, love "objects" are overestimated. This self-overestimation is present in Schreber's case under the guise of a divine alliance and of a redemptive action for the benefit of humanity.

More difficult to conquer is the *sinking into* the nothingness of human beings and things. For this purpose, Freud adds a new building block to his structure, a new dimension to his conception of delirium. If, in fact, the delirium can and ought to be understood as a manifestation of the subject's unconscious and proportionately less disguised as one has to do with a more regressive psychosis): if it is also, as every symptom, a way of fulfilling masochistic and self-punishing wishes (and proportionately less disguised, again, as one encounters a more archaic fixation from which it arose)–then the delirium possesses still another function, one which Freud reveals to us in his commentary on Schreber. Indeed, the delirium is *also* and essentially an attempt to restore the world, an effort to reconstruct a common scene where people and objects can be rebuilt and then cathected. The delirium, then, far from being the mere confirmation of the disease, is already the beginning of a recovery. This point of view should not be paradoxical except to those who have never had the occasion to compare a grave hebephrenic without delirium and a paranoid schizophrenic, even in his acute phase, with regard to their possibility of interpersonal relations (their being-for-others). But let us cite Freud's own text, with apologies for its length.

"The paranoiac rebuilds the universe.... . That which we grasp in the morbid production, in the formation of the delirium, is in fact an attempt to recover a reconstruction of his world. Its success, after the catastrophe, is more or less great; it is never total. Nevertheless, the ill patient has reconquered a rapport with people and things in the world, and often his feelings are very intense, although they can be hostile in situations where they were previously sympathetic and affectionate. Thus we can say that the proper process of repression consists in the fact that the libido detaches itself from people or things previously loved. The process is carried out in silence, and since we have no knowledge of it, we are forced to infer it from the processes which follow it. That which most attracts our attention is the process of recovery, which cancels the repression and attaches the libido to the objects or people from which it had been detached. In paranoia this is accomplished through the mechanism of projection. It is not accurate to say that the feeling was repressed from within and then projected to the outside; one should say rather... that what has been abolished within returns from without."(9)

The interpretation presented here invites an essential question to which, in 1912, Freud gives only a hesitant answer: to what extent does the explanation of the objective investments and their relation to the self supply us with the key to understand not only paranoia, but also every psychosis, such that the expression "narcissistic psychosis" which Freud volunteers would become a tautology? Or having admitted this, one has to find on this common basis an element to differentiate schizophrenia from paranoia, since Freud here more clearly than before thinks that the two concepts cannot be confused. The answer is that if there is narcissism in both we can nevertheless say that schizophrenia is characterized by "another localization of the predisposing fixation and by another mechanism of the return of the repressed."(10)

What are they, then? Freud already addressed himself to the second point

196

and thinks that in the case of schizophrenia the return of the repressed and the attempt to restore the world are not quite accomplished through projection, but rather through a "hallucinatory agitation." The content of the latter is made up by the "residues, to which the ill patients cling convulsively, of the objective investments of the past."(11) One may reply that it is far from certain that every schizophrenia shows this hallucinatory agitation, or that the contrary may be the case. Freud would respond without a doubt and quite correctly that schizophrenics who are neither delirious nor hallucinatory–extending here to delirium the interpretation which Freud gives of the hallucinatory agitation– are precisely those for whom prognosis is the most grim, because the absence of delirium shows that the narcissistic retreat has not at all been combated. These are the patients for whom the "repression" reigns massively, since any attempt at re-cathecting has not occurred. However, this explanation would require a further elaboration of the role and functions of the symptoms. Clearly, one may not reduce every delirium to an attempt to grasp the lost reality again in order to combat the autistic repression. That which also appears in every delirium, and preferentially so, is a fictional realization of desires, unconscious to the normal state, and which, far from being able to restore an effective link with reality, are to the contrary essentially *realitätswidrig,* 'contrary to reality.' Let us imagine a young woman who reproaches herself for having ruined her parents' marriage and for having pushed her father to the massacre of her brothers and sisters. This is a very ambiguous situation. Without doubt, this particular delirium reestablishes something "real", i.e., "my father loves me more than he loves my mother and he loves me to the point of eliminating all who may cause me jealousy." But this "real" is precisely that which reality fiercely requires to be repressed. Where, then, is the compromise proper to the symptom? The answer becomes clear in the case of Schreber. The persecution which Flechsig exerts on the person of Schreber (in the opinion of Schreber) reestablishes a certain "real" and at the same time it allows the old love a certain satisfaction (although a simulated satisfaction) since the love has returned as hate for the persecutor. It seems that there is no such thing in the case of Marie-Thérèse, to which we have just alluded. Her delirium expressed without the least disguise an eruption of desires and ghostly images, normally unconscious, to the point that her consciousness is totally submerged and devastated. How is one to restore the "real" since *all that is there is* an explosion of the instincts? I must add that only a few days after Marie-Thérèse told us the above story she fell into a state of catatonic stupor which, in other times, may have put her life in danger. Through a return to a delirious reality, Schreber defends himself against an autistic repression, which guards him–so Freud tells us–from an outburst of homosexual impulses. The President thus would conquer a position of relative equilibrium: he surmounts (not with total success, granted, but that is not important here) the autism by creating in the "real" a disguised and acceptable satisfaction of his homosexual desires. In both a very great and very relative both a very great and very relative sense, one may say that he is on the way to "recovery." And so said Freud. No such midpoint appears in the case of Marie-Thérèse, who goes from a totally subjugated "me" to a totally empty "me." One could describe her case, with Minkowski and others, by saying that she has undergone the transformation from a rich autism to a poor autism. What she actually manifested is a defense *against* the delirium, and not the delirium as a defense.

Thus one must conclude that, at this point in the thought of Freud, the classification and distinction of the various functions of delirium (or of hallucinations) are left uncertain and obscure.

Let us come now to the other question, which we have left suspended, concerning the point of fixation of schizophrenic psychosis. Freud approaches it by remarking–and this after Kraepelin is hardly contested–that the prognosis of such psychosis is much less favorable than that of paranoia. As a general rule, the repression remains victorious in the end and is in most cases even totally victorious. Autism is never overcome and regression goes beyond that narcissistic stage which is called the mirror-stage and where, in the opinion of psychoanalysts, paranoia originates. This indicates that the flaw where the predisposition towards schizophrenia becomes fixated is situated even prior to the period of the mirror-stage–or more specifically at "that part of the beginning of primitive evolution which goes from auto-eroticism to the love of an object."(12) That allows us to understand why in such a regression, or in his eventual recovery of the future or past, the schizophrenic goes through a paranoid stage where one can then observe a clinical picture with the traits of both affections. In fact this is what happens in Schreber's case, justifying the hesitations in the diagnosis of which I have spoken earlier.(13)

II. Freud's Study about Narcissism

Before going on to the study of Lacan concerning the book on Schreber and its Freudian commentary, a study which will throw a decisive light on problems which are not resolved by Freud, it would appear preferable to stop at the texts which Freud, after his study of Schreber, devotes to an exposition of the psychoanalytic theory of psychosis. In this context we have already stated that the article on narcissism (1914) merits a privileged place.

A first point is immediately called to our attention. The narcissism peculiar to psychosis–the retreat to the ego of the objective investments–must be "conceived as a secondary state which is itself constructed on the basis of a primary narcissism (a fact which has been hidden by multiple factors).(14) This strongly suggests that the original narcissism was never completely abolished, and *that in any case* the objective investments represent only a part of the global quantity of libido to be invested, varying according to circumstances. "Fundamentally, the investment of the 'ego' persists."(15) In other words, psychosis can be described, in a certain sense, not so much as an accident as the intensive reestablishment (and perhaps exclusively so), of an order which never was quite absent. There are thus ego instincts directed towards the self which can and do turn away from the ego (although never completely) but nevertheless can return to it at some other moment. One even observes certain non-pathological phenomena of this retrieval of the objective investments: mourning, dreams and organic diseases are obvious examples. The bereaved, the sleeper and the ill person concentrate upon themselves an interest previously accorded to the outside world and which they now refuse to give to it. (This condition, though, is temporary if the sleeper awakes, if the ill person recovers, or if the mourning itself is not pathological). Freud even ventures a further hypothesis. The normal evolution which forces the individual to break away from his original narcissism and forces him to love another object is set in motion by nothing other than the accumulation of libido in the 'ego' which creates there a state of painfully excessive pressure.[3] One knows that for Freud every tension is necessarily painful and calls for no less forceful an effort to suppress it: these are absolute and general psychic laws. This state of excess pressure in the 'ego' is liberated while discharging part of this libido into the external world, to the object. The same principle helps us to understand that the massive return to the self of abandoned objective investments results in the constantly painful bodily perception of the lived body which the psychiatrist calls hypochondria.(16) A first attempt to overcome this is the delirium of grandeur, and we have seen how both break loose in Schreber's consciousness. To summarize, the typically paraphrenic or paranoid delirium would be a more successful effort to recover, since it expels from the ego, towards fictitious and imaginary pseudo-objects, all the excess libido which had become stagnant and which, without this measure, would become intolerable.

These views are not necessarily incompatible with those developed by Freud in his commentary on Schreber, but they differ from them rather substantially, since what was seen there to be a defense mechanism, or a form of repression, is seen here not only as an original situation but a permanent one, which at certain moments becomes indeed the dominant and even exclusive aspect. But when it comes to the reason which explains this reversal in the proportions of object-libido and libido directed to the ego, we must return to what has been said about it in the study of Schreber.

---

[3]   Freud here makes quantities of energy responsible for a change in psychological attitude. The attempt of A. De Waelhens is to reinterpret Freud's insights into a framework of meaning. It is clear that Freud's usage of the language of energy is contrary to De Waelhens' general re-interpretative effort. Ricoeur on the contrary defends this Freudian point of view in *Freud and Philosophy,* 69ff; 472ff. De Waelhens himself questioned the validity of such a position ("'La force du language et le language de la force"). A. Vergote in turn questions De Waelhens' "idealistic" position in this regard in: "Raisons de la déraison."

But "frequently–if not most often–the libido of the paraphrenic is detached only partially from the objects, which is what allows us to distinguish within the spectrum of his affliction three distinct groups of manifestations: 1) those which respond to a conservation of the normal state or of the neurosis,(17) (residual manifestations); 2) those of the morbid process (that is to say, the detachment of the libido from the objects: the delirium of grandeur, the hypochondria, the destruction of affect and all regressions); 3) those which respond to the restoration, which attaches anew the libido to the objects, in the form of a hysteria (dementia praecox, paraphrenia in the proper sense) or in the form of obsessional neurosis (paranoia). These most recent cathexes of the libido occur at a different level and under different conditions than the original investment."(18)

Thus, a concrete picture of psychosis ordinarily manifests three dimensions. First of all, if the autism is not complete (and that it certainly cannot be), it follows that some previous investments are preserved. Schreber explains that, in spite of his gradual transformation into a woman,(19) and his divine alliance, he nevertheless still feels what he felt before for his own wife. One also knows that after his release from the clinic he tended to his family's juridical affairs and was able to solve them with an intact legal knowledge. Secondly, the manifestations of the acute phase may remain after its disappearance. While writing his memoirs, Schreber tells us that he believed in his own death and in that of all the other men. He no longer actually thinks that, *but* he is no less sure that Flechsig "murdered his soul" and also that the men of today are not quite like those of before. They are not dead, (as he had thought wrongly before) but they are nevertheless reduced to mere shadows of men, to *flüchtig hingemachte Männer,* 'fleeting-improvised-men.'

Finally come the deliriums which attempt to restore reality. In Schreber's case these include his actual convictions: his gradual sex change, his relations (in every sense of the word) with God, his role in the future of humanity. We even have a curious combination of types (1) and (3), (i.e., his relation to Flechsig). In the preface to his book, Schreber draws a distinction between, on the one hand, the eminent professor Flechsig, of whom he is a respectful patient and whom he apologizes for attacking, and on the other hand, the monster Flechsig who wished to deliver him to prostitution and who has killed his soul and trapped God into becoming an accomplice in his satanic plans–nevertheless here Schreber has been victorious when understood that the universal order required that he should become the spouse of God.

In the text cited above, there is a last point which deserves our attention. Freud distinguishes between the mechanisms of restitution, which fall under dementia praecox and paraphrenia on the one hand, and those which are characteristic of paranoia on the other. The first would in his opinion approximate hysteria; the second, obsessional neurosis. The relation is not explained, but it is clarified if we note that somatic conversion and identification are typical of hysteria, just as displacement is typical of obsessional neurosis. In the first case, the appearance of delirium is marked above all by the somatic conversion (is this not itself the definition of hypochondria?) and by identifications (with God, with the Virgin, with Napoleon); in the second case, by displacement (of the communists, the Jews, the freemasons, the Jesuits, the inhabitants of Brussels, etc.) where projection is but one mechanism, and not the only one as we have seen from the change in subject, verb, and compliment, which Freud exposes in his study of Schreber.

There are three kinds of symptoms present in Schreber's case, which again explains that the diagnosis of his case is uncertain. Indeed, Freud gives successively or simultaneously the following different diagnoses of Schreber: dementia praecox, schizophrenia, paraphrenia or paranoia. To reconcile these facts, one must recall another thesis of Freud concerning the possible transitions of paranoia to schizophrenia in the ascending phase, and of schizophrenia to paranoia in the descending phase. There seems to be little doubt, either from the information from the doctors or from the descriptions of his own memories, that Schreber was schizophrenic at the time of his internment. The crisis which motivated the latter has, in fact, all the markings of a schizophrenic "push." On the contrary, however, at the time when Schreber composed his book and shared with us his theories and convictions, as they were formed after the catastrophic stage, he appears to manifest more of a paranoid picture. In reality, one recognizes the symptoms of both psychoses. He lacks neither the delirious somatic conversions (for example, he becomes a woman and he himself verifies the progress of this transformation), nor the identifications (for example, to the spouse of God), nor, on the other hand, the projections (for example, all his feelings concerning Flechsig).

III. Other relevant Studies by Freud

A. *The Unconscious*

Freud's later texts concerning psychosis provide some very interesting additions to the ideas presented in the previous sections. In his article on the unconscious, Freud notes explicitly (G.W.X., p. 295) that the inability of the schizophrenic for transference–and thus the impossibility of his undergoing analysis–argue in favor of the thesis of narcissism and the destruction of the objective investments or cathexes. In general, this point may be applied to all the characteristic traits of autism.

Freud also assures us, without giving an explanation, that in the case of the schizophrenic one will notice the explicit appearance at the conscious level of ghostly images and other elements which, in the case of neurosis remain at the unconscious level and thus would not be accessible in the course of analysis. This can be used as a justification of the following formula which is so often used: the neurotic represses(20) the unconscious; the psychotic represses the real. At first glance it appears to be difficult to relate this formula to the idea of a narcissistic investment of the "ego." Nevertheless, if it is true that the repression operates under the pressure of the real and that the narcissistic investment diminishes this pressure, it is understandable that the barriers which oppose the emergence of the unconscious into consciousness come to fall. But it is no less important to notice that these ghostly images are transported to the real, in a more stable and more permanent way than is the case in the pseudo-reality of a dream.[4] There is a difference between Schreber's dreaming, prior to the manifestation of his disease, that it would be pleasant to be a woman, and his experience of this transformation which he believes to be verifiable by others, during the actual manifestation of his disease.

Freud also studies certain alterations of language which are considered typical for schizophrenia and which we have already treated from a different perspective. He notes that the construction of phrases shows a disorganization which renders them absurd. This disorganization can be described as a confusion of signifier and signified.

In this context, Freud cites the example of a patient who was brought to the clinic following a bad quarrel with her fiancé. She complains of troubles in her eyes, that her eyes are "crooked," and demands that they be straightened. She explains that the whole matter is related to the fact that her boyfriend is a beautiful talker, a hypocrite who "twists the eyes of people."(21)

There is an obvious confusion here between the meaning of an expression and the image which expresses it, i.e., the signifier. These elements, the signifiers, are grasped by themselves and replaced in the real. The fiancé "twists" the eyes of the patient, just as the night prowler in Leclaire's fable who–having been beaten up by policemen flics–pretends to have been attacked by real birds. But one must also notice that the patient complains of not seeing well, of having eyes that are not hers, of seeing the world through someone else's eyes–the hypochondriac phase of an acute schizophrenia. The world, which is not emotionally cathected, appears to him to have different colors, more faded, less clear. And the libido which returns to the ego is accumulated and finally discharged–after transformation–into an illness (i.e., the delirious ocular lesions).

To this example Freud adds an explanatory and "topological" comment which merits mention here, although it might create some confusion.

The thesis which explains schizophrenia as a disinvestment of objects and a reinvestment of the "ego" needs a corrective. One must distinguish, in the conscious system, the representation of the object and the word which designates that object. If the investment of the first disappears, that of the second

---

[4] The difference is between a dream and a phantasy which one knows to be a dream or a phantasy, and a product of imagination, which the patient experiences as being part of the real. Within Lacan's terminology this latter phenomenon is called the *imaginary real*.

remains. The patient no longer understands the symbolic expression "to throw dust in someone's eyes" but judges herself blinded by the dust. Freud assumes that as a general rule the conscious representation encompasses *both* the representation of the thing *and* the representation of the word, whereas the unconscious understands *only* the representation of the thing. Normally, the role of the *preconscious* insofar as there is nothing to be repressed, would be to initiate the communication between the representation of an object and that of its name, while transmitting to the latter the affective investment of the former. Neurotic repression consists of a prohibition of this transmission by blocking the possibility of a connection. To be sure, the object remains invested in the unconscious, but this investment does not pass over to its *verbal* representation. The neurotic "knows" perfectly all the names of the objects invested and repressed by him, but he *is not aware* of the libidinal charge attached in the unconscious to the object designated by those names.

It seems, then, quite clear–and the conclusion is of the highest importance for us–that what we call *repression* with regard to psychosis must be an entirely different mechanism, since in psychosis, repression succeeds in withdrawing the unconscious investment in the object itself, while investment of its verbal representation remains and is even augmented. These remarks prepare us for Lacan's thesis about psychotic "foreclosure," which is indeed anticipated by Freud's remarks concerning "Verwerfung" in the case of the Wolf man.

In Freud's opinion one may think that (and this is not incompatible with the previous discussion) one finds in psychosis an over-investment of the verbal representation, which constitutes the attempt at recovery by the psychotic and which is manifested, as we have seen, in delirium. The signifier is situated in the real and overinvested and by the same token this signifier is excluded from the unconscious and the libidinal energy which was attached to the signified is withdrawn and returned to the "ego." A part of this energy is then displaced onto the word. The patient looks for a reinvestment of the things and, to bring this about, begins by reinvesting the words, but without any longer being able to pass from the words to the things.

B. The Loss of Reality in Neurosis and Psychosis

A short article written by Freud between 1920 and 1924 furnishes some clarifications on other points. One could present the distinction of neurosis and psychosis by saying that if the neurotic represses the unconscious or the id under the pressure of reality and on behalf of the latter, the psychotic does the opposite. Under the influence of the "id" the psychotic retrieves his investments of the reality to attach them to himself and thus, in a certain way, represses this reality.

Apparently these formulas do not exactly coincide with the ones under which we have been operating. There is, however, no contradiction among them. That which compels the patient to escape reality is not directly the power of the unconscious but rather, as we have seen in Schreber's case, the danger which the real represents by virtue of the uncontrollable investments given to it by the unconscious. The defense consists then of a divestment of the real, while returning these libidinal charges to the "ego." That first movement is followed by a second development: that which tries to return to a cathesis of the real, but, as we have explained, in a delirious or hallucinatory way.

But this new formula is susceptible to another objection. Indeed, the neurotic also escapes reality, but in his own way, which is not the way used by the psychotic. No doubt he does not feel at ease in this reality *because* he became neurotic.

This is all true. But let us note that to escape reality is not at all to *deny* it. The neurotic tries to escape that part of reality whose exigencies he can no longer face. But in behaving in this manner, he in fact recognizes reality.

If the repression has been undertaken, it is under the rule and pressure of the real. If repression obtains its goal–total confinement to the unconscious of the unacceptable impulses and their psychic representation–no neurosis appears. Every time, however, that the repression fails, more or less, a partial and disguised return of the repressed will follow. The unconscious will compensate itself by the creation of the symptom, which constitutes a formation created specifically to give satisfaction to the unconscious. The satisfaction, however, is hidden and is done in such a compromised fashion as to elude the repressive forces while at the same time respecting them. It does not matter that very often, sooner or later, a new repressive action will attack the symptom, which only aggravates the conflict between the recognized exigencies of reality and the subject's incapacity to yield to them without reserve. Thus, a new displacement of the symptom follows with an aggravation of the conflict. The subject has no other recourse but to attempt to remain as distant as possible from the area of conflict, as little Hans, who does not leave the paternal home so as to be sure to encounter neither horse nor car. This escape has nothing to do with the repudiation or the foreclosure proper to the delirium, and the neurotic resents it both as a protection and as an unbearable limitation of his existence.

This leads Freud to affirm that which we have stated above: the delirium, if it is an attempt to restore reality, *is not only* that. The pseudo-reality which it creates and invests is not reducible to a mere attempt to overcome autism, it is also destined to satisfy the unconscious; we have verified this claim in Schreber's case, for example, in his transformation into a woman or in his immortality. What remains of the "ego" then rebels and defends itself against this dimension of the delirium through various defense mechanisms: disguise, return of the feelings, diverse deformations such as (a) the idea that the transformation into a woman is willed by God and will take place only through the centuries, and (b) that the homosexual love for Flechsig takes the form of the most atrocious hate. Or again, as in nightmares, where anguish and terror accompany hallucinations and ghostly images. This is the case of Marie-Thérèse who feels pain and horror when she tells about her having ruined her parents' marriage and of her having "seen" (or "heard") her father murdering all her brothers and sisters.

IV. Lacan's Study of the Case of Schreber: General Point of View

Thus far we have presented the various elements of the Freudian doctrine of psychosis. As decisive as these elements are for an understanding of psychosis, they nevertheless lack an essential link. Freud suspected this link but did not succeed in grasping it. Thanks to this link, the set of elements can be ordered in the best structure proposed up to now. It is to the authoritative work of Lacan that we owe this decisive step forward. We will attempt to understand and to interpret this progress by referring to his study on Schreber, entitled *On a Question Preliminary to Any Possible Treatment of Psychosis.*(22) The text originated in a seminar given at St. Anne in 1955-1956.

Of course, one can only agree with Lacan when he states that before psychoanalysis there was no comprehension at all of what the psychotic phenomenon *was,* however admirable and refined certain clinical descriptions were (especially French), or however clear and useful certain attempts were (especially German) in isolating various distinguishable entities.

The reason for this failure is epistemological and even, if one dares to say it, philosophical. The 19th century never questioned–and here the most skeptical empiricism joins the most frankly speculative idealism that the unity of the perceived object is constituted by the perceiving subject. Empiricism was convinced that this unity was achieved by way of associations. Idealism was convinced that this unity was the result of some form of constitution *(Setzung).* In the 19th century it was thought that this function of unification belonged to the perceiver alone and remained unchanged, whatever "alterations in identity"(23) may otherwise have taken place in the perceiving subject. In psychosis these changes are as serious as they are evident. It follows inevitably from this view that in order to explain the perceptual abnormalities of the psychotic (hallucinations, "voices," false recognitions, etc.), one was forced to describe them as perturbations in the *sense-data.* For example, visual hallucination consists in seeing an object as present (similar in its structure to all other objects), while the sense data which compose it are, in fact, *not present.* The essential point is thus missed by both empiricists and idealists, i.e., the question of whether or not the pathological *perceptum is* generated or worked out by a *"percipiens"* who operates in the same fashion as the *percipiens* of so-called normal or common perceptions.(24) Although Lacan does not say so, this question is asked today and is intelligible because the phenomenological mode of thought has familiarized us with what it calls the correlativity of no-esis and noema. To a different type of object, there corresponds a different way of apprehending this object.

Against the common conception which we have just criticized, we may put forth the fact, by no means pathological, that "the act of hearing is not the same if it applies itself to" the modulations and rhythms of the heard voice, i.e., to the sonorous and musical qualities of the word or if, on the other hand, "it refers to the coherence of the verbal chain. In this latter case one is atten-tive to the determination of each element of the discourse in reference to the total discourse as well as to the possibility of a change in meaning of the sen-tence by the metaphorical usage of words."(25)

But, then, what will be the peculiar characteristics of the *percipiens* of a pathological *perceptum?* In the category of voices, the first peculiarity is that the subject cannot evade the captivating power of suggestion which emanates from these voices. Unlike all other voices, the hallucinatory voice is an ine-luctable one. The subject cannot attempt to escape its fascination except by displacing it. But this move does not change the basic characteristic of such a voice. The subject will state, for example, that the "voice" may not express the thought or the intention of the one who emits it. But, then, surely he must think that this voice is controlled by someone else. Another example is when this voice appears to make only insignificant or soothing remarks. In this case the subject will tell us that, in reality, these remarks must be taken as very precise allusions to the most frightening and unpleasant truths.

Not less surprising will be the attitude of the *percipiens* toward himself. Indeed, it happens that the patient produces certain partially formed phonetic movements. This sensible *hulei* (material) thus murmured as a subtraction (signifier) for what the psychotic intended to communicate (signified) is, in fact, unrelated to the signifying chain (signifier) which should have been pro-nounced. However, these "phonetic movements" are immediately identified as a "voice," a voice which will be heard for a time corresponding to the duration of the real message. Finally, if it is a question of a dialogue between "voices," the *percipiens* has an ambivalent role, since he must "pose, at the same time, as the voice (the subject) who speaks and as the voice (the subject) who listens before replying." Furthermore, the dual role itself is susceptible to redoubling.

The fact that this "subject" is ambivalent is clearly shown by Lacan in the example which he cites. A patient complained that, at the turn of a corridor in the building where she lived, she was called a "sow" by a co-tenant who was of no importance to her. In reply to the question of Lacan, when he asked her what words could have been "uttered" in her at the instant preceding the en-counter, she admitted "having murmured the following words upon seeing the man: 'I have just come from the butcher.' But according to the patient those words should not have offended the man."(26)

But toward whom were these inoffensive words directed, and what "I" expressed itself in them? Regarding the first question, the patient was confused and admitted it. However, there was a context to all this. The patient was the daughter of a mother with whom she formed a delirious pair. At the instigation of her mother, who wished to live with her, she had just left her husband and had broken off relations with all of her in-laws, because they proposed "cutting her in pieces." Needless to say, this justified the mother's having always disapproved of this marriage and of her having predicted its dangers.

The patient eventually recognized the allusive character of her own words, but without successfully deciding whether the allusion was addressed to any of the co-tenants or to her absent mother. Her recognition was tantamount to a fundamental linguistic thesis, the importance of which, in matters of psychosis, cannot be overestimated, i.e., the "I," as subject of any phrase and in keeping with its function of *shifter*–that is to say, as a potential indicator without its own content–designates a concrete bearer only insofar as all of the points of reference are given in the discourse. But here these references were not given–and they are almost never given in psychosis, for reasons which we will discuss later–since the allusion remained an oscillating one. Who speaks and of what does she speak, when she thinks and murmurs, "I have just come from the butcher." This is the whole question. "I am not a June bug" a patient suddenly cried to me one day, while flinging her cup of coffee at my head. This occurred at the very moment when we were having the most peaceful and "reasonable" chat in the world about our common love of cats. Clearly, this phrase and this gesture were not really addressed to her actual interlocutor and the "I" who pronounced it was not the one whom the file identified as "Monique J., born in Tirlemont in 19... and daughter of. . . ."

But in the case of Lacan's patient, the uncertainty regarding the allusion was resolved. All doubt as to the "I" who had muttered "I have just come from the butcher" was resolved. This occurred when, after a pause following the murmuring of the allusive phrase, she thought that she was actually (i.e., by someone in the real) called "sow." This apposition was too brutal, "too full of invective to follow isochronically the allusive oscillation."[5] The patient understood that she was the "I" and that she was a sow. "This is how speech has come to realize the aim behind her hallucination. At the point where the unspeakable object is thrown back (rejected) into the real, a word is heard. Because this word gives a name to that which cannot be named, it cannot be the result of the intention of the subject. This word is therefore detached "from her (the patient) through the empty pause before the reply."(27) The phantasm of being cut in pieces dwells and wanders about in her and is itself an echo of the secret, unspeakable and unconscious sentiment of having to be torn apart and devoured by her mother. It makes itself concrete and relevant to her in the form of an insult, realized in hallucinatory fashion in the signifier "sow," just

---

[5]   Lacan, *Écrits*, p. 535.

as it had previously become materialized and objective in the delirious accusation that her in-laws were plotting to cut her into pieces, because they could not tolerate "this worthless city woman." Although Lacan does not say this, one may suspect that the threat came more specifically from her mother-in-law, whom she opportunely substituted for her own mother. Clearly, "the function of ir-realization is not all there is to the symbol."(28) Rather–we would be tempted to add–this function of ir-realization in psychosis appears as such only *quoad nos* (for us). In fact, for our patient, the signifier "sow"–a symbol for us–plays a role altogether different from that of a pure symbol. It serves to throw back into the imaginary real, in the form of a pseudo-speech by an other, an unspeakable signified, which thus finds itself ejected from her own unconscious: the phantasm of being devoured by her own mother, which serves, in turn, as a signifier for the phantasm of a cut-up body. It was not a symbol for the patient but rather a transference into the imaginary-real. Let us compare our case to one which is so often cited; the case of the child who plays the game of throwing and retrieving a spool of thread. The child thus expels from himself the pangs of anxiety, also unspeakable, which are linked to the alternations of presence and absence of the mother's body. This is accomplished by means of identifying the missing body with the reality of the spool of thread, which is not missing–or rather, the absences of the spool of thread are produced *in order* to be overcome. Hence, on first sight, one will say that, in the case of the patient, the threat of being violated by her mother is transformed into an identical threat coming from someone else, unrelated to her and against whom the defense could appear to be easier. But the differences between the two cases are considerable. If, for the child, the spool is a signifier of the mother's body, it does not cease, for all that, to be what it was: a spool. The spool *signifies* the body of the mother but is not confused with it. Whereas, for the patient, if her being cut up in pieces by the co-tenant or by her in-laws, is the signifier of a signified which is unknown to her (i.e., her violation by the mother and the dismemberment of her own body), it is also, *as signifier* an element of the real, which identifies her in-laws and co-tenant purely and simply with what they are not and never have been: murderous butchers. The spool enters into the real, not as the mother's body, but as signifier of the latter. It is and remains a spool of thread, with the added dimension of being a *signifier of...* . In contrast, the enemies of the patient are not signifiers of murder but murderers. Moreover, the second metaphor, that of the *Fort-Da,* which is derived from the spool and which inaugurates the order of the truly symbolic, is absent in the case of the patient. No word expresses the cutting up as its *other,* whereas the *Fort-Da* expresses the absence and presence of the spool while at the same time referring beyond itself.(29)

It is precisely to this ambiguity of the imaginary, produced by the destructuration of the symbolic order with which the imaginary is linked, that the subject adheres. Thus the *percipiens* engages in duplicity, in that he is, *at the same time,* the famous normal perceiver, definer of the real, and this archaic, divided subject, who only seizes himself in the other, an other represented in our example by the imaginary butchers.

These ideas will receive their full articulation in a reconsideration of the Freudian presentation of the Schreber case.

This reconsideration begins, as Lacan likes to do it, with an examination of the relationship of the subject to the signifier.

Whoever attempts to investigate Schreber's "voices" will immediately note that they include two distinct types of phenomena. These types correspond to what linguists call *message phenomena* and *code phenomena.* The former have a content; the latter state the rules of linguistic organization in the former. The divine, fundamental language *(Ursprache),* which is different from the German of ordinary human beings,(30) is only utilized for code messages which "inform the subject of the forms and usages which constitute the neo-code."(31) One should recognize here those messages which linguists call *"autonyms,* inasmuch as it is the signifier itself (and not what it signifies) which is the object of the communication."(32) But the strange thing is that, in turn, these messages are *realized, reified* and supposed to coincide with beings. Hence, in this case too, the signifier is thrown back into the imaginary real.

In regard to message phenomena properly speaking, they also have their peculiarities. They stop halfway, as it were, since they consist in incomplete or uncompleted phrases, which the patient *must* complete. This is an obligation which, if not carried out, would immediately result in great damage to the patient, even his annihilation. The test is not at all like that of the riddle of the Sphinx; its real difficulty is not in finding the answer but in withstanding, while continuing to play the game, the positively offensive stupidity and banality of the divine half-phrases. Let us give three examples chosen by Lacan.
1. "Now, I shall"... /resign myself to being stupid.
2. "You were to"... /be exposed(33) as denying God, as given to voluptuous excesses, etc.
3. "I shall"... / have to think about that first.

Obviously, one will note the resemblance of all this to the previously cited example of Lacan's patient at St. Anne. The major difference between the two is in the way projection is executed. In the opinion of the patient at St. Anne the word "sow" was supposedly said directly by the other. Schreber, however, reports that he himself was forced by an other to say what, according to the working of the mechanism of projection, can only be said by another. But in the case of Schreber, just as in the case of Lacan's patient, the words spoken do nothing more than to ambiguously situate the patient as speaker. Indeed, the literally divine phrases stop "at the point where the group of words which one could call index-terms ends–index-terms being either those words designated by their function as *shifters* (in accordance with the definition of the term employed above) or precisely the terms in the code which indicate the position of the subject on the basis of the message itself."(34) In contrast, the content of the messages is left to the infallible divination of Schreber himself.

Lacan takes advantage of this to emphasize "the predominance of the function of the signifier, " since the "voices" properly speaking–and which use the fundamental language–are exclusively using "speech consisting of messages regarding the code, and of messages reduced to those parts of speech which really announce a message."(35)

This is without doubt, but what should we conclude from it? First, in the explanation of psychosis, and particularly of Schreber's psychosis, one cannot, by any means, be satisfied (as Freud was not, if one reads him carefully) with describing mechanisms by which the patient projects out of himself certain unconscious impulses (in the case of Schreber, masturbation and homosexuality), in order to defend himself from and accommodate himself to them. It is also misleading to see the hallucinatory phantasmagoria of the psychotic simply as a curtain interposed by the *percipiens* between the unconscious tendency and its real stimulant.(36) Such an explanation on the part of the theoretician would not be sufficient, for applying the concept of projection to Schreber's case is almost an abuse of the word. Furthermore, the psychotic aspect of the impulses involved in this case, or for that matter in any other case can only be understood by analyzing *the modification which these impulses have undergone as a result of the alteration in the subject, of moments and complexes regarded by Freud as constitutive of every human psyche:* "namely, the equivalence of the imaginary function of the phallus in both sexes as maintained by Freud... the castration complex found to be a normative phase in the subjects assumption of his own sexuality, the myth of the murder of the father which is rendered necessary by the constitutive presence of the Oedipus complex in every personal history; and, *last but not least... , the* ambiguity which love-life creates by re-initiating the search for a unique [object but on the model of the lost object (W.V.E.)]."(37) Now it is precisely the nature of the alteration of these structuring moments which creates problems in psychosis; and it is this alteration which explains the emergence–either masked or unmasked, in the case of Schreber or of any other psychotic–of masturbatory and homosexual tendencies. It is not the emergence of these tendencies, even less the defense mechanism against them, which can explain psychosis.(38)

Our task, if possible, will therefore consist of investigating and determining this *other* theater ("*eine andere Schauplatz,*" writes Freud). This theater is different from the *stage* occupied by the *percipiens;* but it is here that the drama of psychosis actually takes place. We know already that this Other, this Elsewhere, has the structure of discourse, that it is, to use Lacan's phrase so often quoted, "structured like a language." Again following the thought of the same author, we will add that, in this language, the subject finds his existence called into question, perhaps without knowing it, even though he himself gives expression to this questioning by asking: "What am I?" This question concerns "his sex, (that he is a man or a woman) and the contingency of his existence (that he might not have been). These two aspects of the question have a mysterious dimension which is evoked by the symbols of procreation and death."(39) Furthermore, "this calling into question extends from him (the subject) to his intra mundane relationship with objects and even to the existence of the world, insofar as not only its order, but even its mere existence can be called into question."(40)

"Serving as supports of this structure, we find the three signifiers by which the Other can be identified in the Oedipus complex. They suffice to symbolize the meanings related to sexual reproduction. They do so by signifying both the relation of love and of procreation."(41)

Let us understand by this that whenever a subject questions his own existence, he will always tend–by the most diverse vicissitudes possible, some of which (we will understand why) will be generators of psychosis–to traverse the necessary path of a triadic and triangular relationship, in which we first find the fruit of "sexual reproduction." This triad is made up of the existent whose identity is called into question; the mother, as signifier of the love relation; and finally the father, as signifier of procreation.

But the movement of these signifiers aims at a fourth term, absent from the literal system just described, and which is none other than *the subject as he will define himself and be defined by the relationship of the signifiers*. This subject *is* not and never *will be* anything in himself, in the way that one says of the table that it is round. In particular, he will not coincide with his own signifier as it appears in the Oedipal triangle, despite the temptations to do so. He is perpetually that which is signified and that which is to be signified by himself. That is to say, he is the empty square on a game board which permits the opponent to make his moves. Or better said, he is the one who, as in bridge, only enters "the game of signifiers under the guise of the dead, but becomes the true subject insofar as this game of signifiers makes him such."(42) This living being "the offspring"–is the result of a sexual relationship of his parents. The dialectic of the relations between the signifiers will take hold of "this child," son or daughter of... and of... in order to throw him on the path of a becoming-subject. On this path he must never equate himself with some collection of attributes, qualities, or determinations, which could define him exhaustively; nor will he ever be able to do so, except in an illusory fashion and to his great detriment. The child who exists becomes a subject by trying to be the identity which constitutes itself by the distance between the signifiers; however, he will never fully succeed.

For these signifiers are not at all inert. Each of them, as well as their constellation, is shaped "by the whole history (imaginary or not) of the rise of other realities" which the signifiers represent "in the contemporaneity of the subject."(43) However, the arrangement of these signifiers at the apexes of the triangular figure and in the dialectic cannot be isolated from the unfolding of another triad. These two triads unfold simultaneously in the child who will become a subject. Moreover, there is a link which connects the components of the fundamental signifiers just mentioned to the elements which constitute this second triad. This second triad unites "the three agencies: (ideal) ego, reality, superego, which Freud created in his second topography."(44)

Let us explain briefly the three terms introduced here. We will understand their scope somewhat once we have recognized that the Oedipal scheme, by the very fact that it begins, entails the establishment or, to be quite exact, the transformation of another system of "agencies," the oldest origins of which precede the Oedipus complex. Indeed, how could the subject place himself in the Oedipal situation, if not by situating himself, at the same time, relative to the *reality,* which obstructs the satisfaction of the Oedipal desire. And how could the subject force himself to accept the real, if he were not also under the dependence of those coercive and repressive forces–which the theory designates by the term superego–and to which the paternal chastisements will contribute by transforming the structure of these repressive forces. Finally, these two agencies would be as vain as they would be superfluous, if their function and effect were not to contain and limit–and thereby also, in some measure, determine–an *ideal ego,* a vestige of and an heir to the original and imaginary narcissistic omnipotence, transferred for a moment to the victorious father, who is an enemy but also a model. Let us reiterate, since an omission would be extremely serious: the first outlines or the first antecedents of these agencies are older than their Oedipal equivalents. But they have been modified and restructured by the Oedipal relations–without, however, the archaic versions being totally effaced. Moreover, these archaic versions are sometimes capable of reappearing, but not without producing grave damage. In any event, one can easily understand that these agencies have a considerable effect in the constellation and in the reciprocal differentiation of the basic signifiers.

Regarding the subject, one can say that even if he remains destined for the place of the dead, by this not *being this* or *being that,* he will still be led and precisely by his own nothingness, to assume, in his real existence and in earnest, the roles and figures which the constellation of signifiers has drawn for and presented to him. In order to succeed, vis-à-vis himself and others, he has at his disposal certain imaginary prototypes, of which the incarnate reproductions are both innumerable and faintly modified with respect to the primary image. The subject will distribute these prototypes in such a way as to "cover homologically the symbolic triad."(45)

V. Lacan's Study of the Case of Schreber: New Theoretical Contribution

It is at this point that Lacan brings in a new element which will be decisive for the meaning, the development and the success of his interpretation of the Schreber case, and more generally also be decisive for the understanding of what constitutes the nucleus of schizophrenia, the psychosis par excellence.

We can find this new element in our very prehistory, where it is inscribed and where it can therefore be discovered.

Lacan has drawn attention to this new element since the time he wrote his article on *"La famille"* for the *Encyclopédie française*. He shows how the various renunciations (such as birth, weaning, alienation through the mirror image, intrusion, the Oedipus complex, and castration) which are successively imposed on the human being are, at the same time, both reactivations and reminders of each other, although at each stage they must structure themselves at a higher, richer, and wider level of integration. However, the condition for this structuring is the correct resolution of each of the previous crises. In other words, the correct liquidation of one phase is the condition for the proper positioning of the terms of the next phase. From this perspective, the death instinct can be defined as the omnipresent temptation not to face the test, to let oneself go, to slip into death in some fashion and, if one dares to say it, thus to renounce the implacable necessity of renunciation.[6]

According to these views, it becomes understandable and mandatory that every constellation and, in particular, the Oedipal constellation (which summarizes, transforms and enriches all of them) have some place or root from which it plunges into the preceding ones. The Oedipus complex is built particularly upon the mirror image, which immediately precedes it. More precisely, the base line upon which the Oedipal triangle will be built and will rest is none other than the duality of the mirror image itself. This will allow the Oedipus complex to develop its typical symbolic relations. In turn, the polarity which constitutes the mirror image will have, as homologue, the earlier and by this time outmoded mother-child relationship. But we can also consider these processes in a progressive, rather than regressive order: the mother-child relationship transcends itself by being reactivated in the polarity between the (ideal) ego of the mirror image and the fragmented and coenesthetic body which, in facing the mirror image, unifies itself in it and through it. But this transcendence of the original human couple of nurse and nursling is *also* a reactivation of it. In its turn, the specular dyad lays the foundation on which the Oedipal triangle will unfold. This unfolding will include the passage from the imaginary to the symbolic.

This is what we may learn from the study of Schreber, in an extremely obscure passage which the above commentary will perhaps render less difficult. Thus, in order that the dialectic of signifiers be set in motion–a dialectic to which the subject owes the identity that he gives himself–it is necessary that "the polar relationship whereby the mirror image is connected, as a unifier, to the set of imaginary elements known as the fragmented body, furnish a couple which is not only prepared, by a natural suitability in terms of development

---

[6]   Lacan mentions as examples: anorexia nervosa, certain toxicomanias, and certain gastric neuroses. He gives as proof the fact that in analysis these patients indicated that they hoped to restore the image of the mother by abandoning themselves to death. Lacan, "La famille," p. 8.40-8.

and structure, to serve as a homologue of the symbolic Mother-Child relationship. The imaginary couple of the mirror stage... finds itself called upon to provide the imaginary triangle with a base, upon which the symbolic relation can in some fashion be built."(46)

At present, it is necessary for us to determine what failure in the construction of this edifice is responsible for psychosis.

At each of the stages and changes which we have just recalled, a gap appears which, in some way, the subject attempts to fill. The first, and the most original gap, is created by birth itself, because a human being's birth occurs when his body is still very immature. The "subject" first attempts to overcome this gap through the maternal embrace, which constitutes the dual union. The deceptions which he necessarily encounters in this union–no matter how warm and earnest it may in fact be–become deeper and more irritating in the weaning, which starts almost immediately after birth. The subject partially surmounts this experience of birth and this threat of weaning in the mirror image. For this image offers to the fragmented and separated subject an imaginary unity through which he overcomes his dislocation. But this is accomplished at the price of opening up a new abyss: the ego of the mirror image, although *the same is* also an *other,* with whom any coincidence is impossible, indeed would even be deadly, if the subject were to persist in attempting to achieve it. Finally, we have previously shown that the liquidation of the Oedipus complex generates, through the imposition of the law, a new renunciation and a new distance, even more painful, if that is possible, than the preceding ones. But this renunciation and this distance are certainly more fruitful, since they assure the subject of his true and entire identity. This identity is correlative to the installation of the subject in what we may now call the *real;* at the same time it gives him the right, temporarily postponed, to love and to procreate in his own turn, under the sanction of the law, even though this law is first experienced in its prohibitive dimension.

But what is it that, each time and up until the moment when everything in the Oedipus complex is reversed, motivates the subject to fill up, at all costs, the gaps which he has successively traversed and which separate him either from fusion with the mother, or later, from coinciding with the mirror image? This motivation comes from his own identification with "the phallic image. It should be noted that the revelation of the function of the phallus is not the least scandalous of the Freudian discoveries."(47) What does this mean?

It means that the subject cannot abandon himself to or be swallowed up in the lack *that he is.* He will therefore imagine himself as being that which fills up all lack, and particularly the lack of the mother, that is to say, the phallus. *To be* that which annuls the lack of the mother protects the subject from all abandonment, from all separation from his mother, to the point of making abandonment or separation (imaginarily) impossible. This is what the psychoanalytical language means when it speaks of the child as the [phallus] of the mother.

214

However, it is all too clear that such an identification, no matter how advantageous at the start, must eventually be surmounted, under penalty of the most radical failure. For how else could that which fills up all lack succeed in recognizing itself as subject of lack, a lack which is the only entry into negativity and desire? For, as long as he remains in the position just described, the subject cannot accede to either negativity or desire, since desire is recognition of lack and an appeal to the other to be recognized by him as subject of this lack. The problem, then, is to know where this mutation and this reversal can take place, and how, when, and in what manner the subject will give up *being the phallus,* to become subject of desire. Here again the Oedipus complex is found to be the fundamental axis, since it is in it that the decisive reversal takes place. The experience of the Oedipus complex, of disappointment, of the imposition of the law–all this reveals to the subject that what complements or fulfills the lack of the mother, is not himself as phallus of his mother, but the father. Such is the famous "metaphor of the name-of-the-father," in which the name-of-the-father is substituted for the subject who imagined that he could fill up this lack. Lacan presents this metaphor in its most formal aspect as follows:(48)[7]

$$\frac{\text{"Name-of-the-Father}}{\text{Desire of the mother}} \cdot \frac{\text{Desire of the mother}}{\text{Signified to the subject}} \longrightarrow$$

$$\text{name-of-the-Father} \left(\frac{A}{\text{Phallus}} \right)$$

Let us comment briefly on this somewhat enigmatic formula. The desire of the mother has as its real signifier, the name-of-the-father, as bearer of the phallus. But this is what, at the same time, the subject does not know and which will be signified to him when he takes the desire of the mother as signifier of his own "desire." This discovery signifies for him that the phallus is in the Other.

The consequence of this metaphor, a consequence which we will not examine at the moment, will be that the subject–dislodged from the position he occupied in identifying himself in imagination with the phallus of the mother

---

[7] Mathematically the formula should be: $\dfrac{a}{b} \cdot \dfrac{b}{c} = a\left(\dfrac{1}{c}\right)$

The formula used by Lacan is however: $\dfrac{a}{b} \cdot \dfrac{b}{c} = a\left(\dfrac{d}{f}\right)$

This requires that $1/c = d/f$, or that what is "signified to the subject" ($=c$) is the same as "that the Phallus is in the other, written by Lacan as capital a. i.e., 'A' " ($=d/f$).

215

and forced to submit to the law—will henceforth be able to *have* or to receive a phallus, instead of *being* the phallus.[8] Notice, however, that the subject, by ceasing to confuse himself with the object of his "imaginary desire," accedes to real desire, in accordance with the order prescribed by the law.

But at this point in our account a question imposes itself. What happens when the metaphor of the name-of-the-father is not achieved or fails (whatever the reasons are for this failure, which we know can be traced to each one of the authors of the drama separately, or on the contrary, to several of them, indeed to all of them)? That is to say, what happens when the Oedipus complex is not correctly structured and the subject remains blocked in his first position as the imaginary maternal phallus? In this case, psychosis occurs.

How and why does this occur? "Let us now try to conceive of a situation for the subject in which the appeal to the Name-of-the-Father corresponds, not to the absence of the real father (for this absence is compatible with the presence of the signifier) but the absence of the signifier itself."(49)

In ordinary life, it is not unusual for a subject to lack a signifier; this is the case when the signifier is *repressed* in the unconscious of the subject. But we know that it can then be found again indirectly or negatively in the signified of the subject, in the form of a symptom, a lapsus, a slip, or in some disguise or offshoot, and thus be susceptible to discovery by analysis.

But this is not the case in psychosis; things happen differently if this signifier is not repressed, and hence buried in the unconscious, but rather *foreclosed* and rejected from it. In this case, we have something corresponding to the *verworfen* in Freudian terminology.(50)

"At the place in the structure where the Name-of-the-Father is invoked (we will see how), there can thus emerge in the Other [the unconscious] a *hole,* pure and simple, which, due to the absence of the metaphorical effect, will induce a corresponding hole where the phallic signification should take place."(51)

This means, therefore, that the symbolic significance of the phallus and the phallus as symbol are from now on excluded from the unconscious of the subject, where nothing will ever be able to make them appear.

However, as we know, and as the definition of Laplanche and Pontalis cited in the footnote reminds us, this signifier, inaccessible to the subject, is not, for all that, purely and simply annihilated. It reappears in the real, but in the mode of an hallucination. Freud gives us the *prime* example in his account of the 'Wolf man.' The 'Wolf man' foreclosed symbolic castration, but its signifier surges back into reality in the form of an hallucination: one day, when the child is playing with a pocketknife on the bark of a tree, he "sees" that, by mistake, he has cut off his finger, which is only hanging onto the hand by a piece of skin. Terrified, he stops for a moment to look at his hand. Having

---

[8]   Italics are mine (W.V.E.).

regained courage, he finds out that his finger is not the least bit hurt. An analogous mishap will occur many years later when Freud transferred the continuation of the analysis to Mrs. Ruth McBrunswick: the patient "sees" that the acne from which he suffers has eaten away his nose to the point where his nose has disappeared and been transformed into a gaping hole. He knows that he is mutilated forever. But this time the episode lasts for several weeks, during which, disheartened and delirious, he refuses to leave his apartment.(52)

Let us try to understand how the same mechanisms are put into play in Schreber's madness.

There is a gap which opens itself up in Schreber's imaginary world, in response "to the absence of the symbolic metaphor".... This gap in turn "could only find its dissolution in the accomplishment of the *Entmannung*, 'emasculation.'"(53) According to the same process, the 'Wolf man' sees the disappearance, through mutilation, of his finger or his nose.

Since he did not find the paternal metaphor in its place[9] and was consequently unable to accept symbolic castration, the *Senatsprasident*, 'Presiding judge,' was led to bring this signifier back into the hallucinated real and indeed into the most appropriate place. He will "see" his body subjected to a progressive emasculation. As we know, the horror of "recognizing" this transformation will develop during the course of the illness to such a degree that he finally resigns himself to the will of God, decides that this will must conform to a certain order of the universe, and consents to divine intercourse, since the latter should assure the redemption of the world and of human beings. However, this union is delayed for several centuries, indeed until the end of historical time, when the transformation of Schreber into a woman will have been completed.

---

[9] Let us remember that for Judge Schreber an important disappointment occurred: he realised that he would have no children. If we may use a spatial metaphor, Judge Schreber had located himself in his own eyes in relation to others and in relation to the world through an ideal ego, i.e., that of himself as a father. The disappointment that Judge Schreber mentions in his *Memoirs*, means that Schreber is dislocated from the position he took in his own eyes. The problem arising for Schreber is how he can represent this experience of dislocation. There are symbolic forms to express this dislocation from one's ideal ego, i.e., "fate has struck me" or "why always me?" It is Lacan's thesis that because the symbolic order is not available to Schreber, he is forced to express this dislocation, this deprivation of his ideal ego, by way of an *imaginary real* castration: his emasculation. Imaginary desires for some form of castration in schizophrenia have been noticed by other psychiatrists. Sullivan writes of a patient who returns from a laryngologist to whom Sullivan had referred him because of his continuous complaints about his throat. The patient had been shown pictures and had been convinced that his throat was all right. Upon return, the patient said to Sullivan: "Look, Doctor, I don't care . . . about what ails my throat; I want something cut out." *(The Interpersonal Theory of Psychiatry,* p. 363). The difference in this example between Sullivan and Lacan is that the first has the intuition to see and describe a striking symptom of schizophrenia, whereas the latter is giving a theory why such a symptom can and should be part of the schizophrenic syndrome.

This presentation of the delirium places the main focus on the hallucinatory resurgence of the foreclosed signifier of castration; and we understand at the same time why Lacan–perhaps in contrast to Freud, and certainly in contrast to other authors–refuses to consider the homosexual impulse of the libido as primary. According to this alternative interpretation, homosexual impulses would have submerged Schreber and made him sink into psychosis.(54)

But all the above still does not explain everything. In particular, the emasculation *(Entmannung) is* not identical with the transformation into a woman (V*erweiblichung)* into which it extends. How is one to understand this transformation? Lacan is careful not to ascribe it (although one would be tempted to do so) to a mechanism of defense, i.e., to a compensation for the loss of virility.

We will understand this linkage better if we go back a little. Indeed, we know that, before acceding to the Oedipus complex, i.e., before knowing the law of the father and the symbolic castration imposed by it, the child does not experience real desire properly speaking; indeed, in order to escape from his own lack, he constitutes himself as that which fills the lack of the mother. And since the mother symbolizes and signifies this lack through the absence of a phallus, it is precisely this phallus that the child will have to be and will be imaginarily. From the moment the signifier of castration is foreclosed, the only solution for Schreber is precisely to regress to this situation, which is nothing other than that of the dual union.

For Schreber, the failure of this regression will entail consequences which are as catastrophic as those which would have marked its success. Schreber will be forced to dissolve this regressive relation beginning at the point where this identification expresses itself, i.e., the ideal ego of the subject. Indeed, because of the subject's identification with the phallus, the ideal ego is related to the mother in the same way that it is related to his own mirror image. This image in turn has become a simple doublet of the primordial object.

The proof that things have taken this direction is found in Schreber's very utterances, although he is not aware of the meaning of what he says. As Lacan notes, "Remarkably enough, it is in his mother's apartment, where he has taken refuge, that the subject has his first attack of anxiety confusion accompanied by an attempted suicide."(55)

There is just one possible solution left: "Without doubt the divination of the unconscious warned the subject very early that, if he is not able to be the phallus which the mother lacks, he can at least be the woman that men lack."(56)

Unfortunately, this project is not any more practicable than that of being the phallus of the mother. The refusal of symbolic castration is universal; it is not less valid for the others than it is for himself. The "fleeting-improvised-men" that all males have become in the course of the cosmic catastrophe that Schreber tells us about are just as deprived of the primary signifier as he is. These men are incapable of making use of the primary signifier for themselves and are thus also not able to use it for his benefit!

We are approaching the crucial point. According to Schreber's memoirs, it occurs two years after the beginning of the illness, when the subject finds that the divine *Versöhnung*, 'reconciliation,' has been offered to him. The ordinary meaning of this German word includes the ideas of sacrifice, expiation and reconciliation, and God invites Schreber to participate in these.

Now it is this *Versöhnung* which will permit the restoration of the structure of the imaginary, which could not be achieved–and we know for what reasons–either in a regression toward the dual union or in a feminization of the patient with respect to and for the use of other men. However, from then on, thanks to the connection established between the feminization of the patient and the promise of divine marriage, a means is discovered whereby a certain restructuring of the imaginary plan and a certain restructuring of the symbolic plan can be reestablished and brought into communication with each other.

As to the first level (the imaginary), Schreber attempts to coincide and identify himself with his mirror image. This mirror image shows him a Schreber who is transforming himself into a woman. The sight of this image brings him, according to his own words, a full and entire gratification. However, this coincidence with his mirror image will take place only when the metamorphosis has been fully achieved (at the time he wrote his book, the metamorphosis is limited to the bust only). The completion of feminization will also be the sign for the union with the divinity. The completion of this feminization and this union with the divinity is supposed to occur only several centuries later, maybe even only at the end of time. This latter has the advantage of reconciling the salvation of what remains of the subject's present ego (his masculinity)(57) with the preservation of the erotic gratification which he experiences in being and becoming a woman while contemplating himself in the mirror.

This hallucination also opens up the possibility of some restitution of the symbolic structure. Normally, this structure is created in the Oedipus complex by means of a triangular constellation; at the apexes of the triangle are the ideal ego, (a), the primordial object or the mother (b), and, finally, the father (c). The name-of-the-father has in fact come to be substituted for, and has taken the place previously occupied by, the phallus of the subject, when he was guarantor and mediator of the dual union and when he filled up the lack of the mother. For Schreber, due to his rejection of symbolic castration, the father and the name-of-the-father are foreclosed, so that at the apex which is reserved for them, a gap opens up and the triangle collapses. Nevertheless, this gap tends to fill itself up by the return of the foreclosed signifier, from the unconscious into the hallucinatory real, in accordance with the mechanisms described above. It appears here under the form of the Schreberian God, in whom it is not difficult to recognize an ironic caricature of the *paterfamilias* as one sees him at the age of four. As far as the ideal ego is concerned, it affirms itself in the omnipotent word by which the unfortunate Schreber, "thinking" continuously, day and night, without respite or repose, manages to hold God at bay and to save himself from annihilation."(58) Finally, the primordial object, which is normally the mother, is here symbolized by the creature which God "drops," abandons. What Schreber loves and wants to save is the persecuted creature, destined to shame and nothingness, which he keeps alive by his own word, insofar as he does not cease to respond to the divine challenge. In fact, the ideal ego and the primordial object also tend to coincide, to collapse into one another. Since the triangle is being truncated, the two remaining sides tend to coincide in one line and finally in one point. This tends to happen because these sides are only separated from each other by a void. To the degree to which he is capable of pronouncing, at each instant, the word which maintains him in being, against God, Schreber thereby completely salvages that abandoned creature that he was and which is also his only object of love.

But while conserving the same pseudo-triangular scheme, one can also read this hallucination in another way. By unifying himself with the primordial object, Schreber identifies himself with his mother; he does so in order to become the spouse of his father, as symbolized by the hallucinatory God of his delirium, with whom, one day, he will unite himself but at the end of time, since the consummation of this union will also signify for Schreber the loss of what is left of his present ego, which is to disappear in the femininity of a divine wife.

VI. The Eruption of Psychosis and the Concept of "A-Father"

Let us summarize, one last time, the principal features of this interpretation which we consider to be essential.

It is in "the foreclosure of the Name-of-the-Father at the place of the Other, and in the failure of the paternal metaphor, that we designate the lack which gives psychosis its essential condition and hence the structure which separates it from neurosis."(59) Or, in other words, "In order for psychosis to be set in motion, it is necessary for the Name-of-the-Father to be verworfen, "foreclosed,' i.e., that it has never reached the place of the Other, and cannot be invoked there in symbolic opposition to the subject."(60)

Let us understand that if it is the foreclosure of the paternal signifier, rejected from the unconscious, which makes psychosis possible and virtually constitutes it, this psychosis will not, however, become manifest or active until the time when this signifier reappears in hallucinatory form in the real. Let us recall the fable of Leclaire: the forgetting–in the manner of foreclosure, of the roughing-up by the police-swallows– will not become, for the victims, a psychotic delirium until the moment when one of them says that he is attacked by the birds; in contrast, his companion remains a virtual psychotic, awaiting the possible time when he will encounter, in his turn, in the real, some hallucinated signifier of the *verworfen* content.[10]

But from where will this signifier, confused with its signified, rise up? And how will it arise precisely, where it must be and where it has never been, i.e., at the place of the father in the symbolic triangle? "By means of nothing other than a real father, although not at all necessarily the father of the subject, which is to say by A-father."(61) This A-father rises up in the real at the moment when some personage of paternal mien imposes himself "in third position"(62) in the field of any one of the eroticized relations between the subject and his object, indeed also between the ideal and real. He appears "to a woman who has just given birth as the figure of her husband, or to the penitent confessing her fault as the person of the confessor, or to the young girl in love as the 'father of the young man.' In all these cases one will always find him and one will find him more easily if one looks to romantic situations in the literal sense of the word."(63) At this moment, "a cascade of modifications (delirious) of the signifier is set in motion, from which the growing disaster of the domination of the imaginary proceeds, until a level is attained in which signifier and signified stabilize themselves in the delirious metaphor."(64) Indeed, as we have shown, there is no doubt that the Schreberian cosmo-theology, through successive "modifications," finally resulted in a position of equilibrium. And if we may say so, this equilibrium safeguarded all the interests involved, to such an extent that Lacan refers to it, as a mathematician might, as an "elegant solution."(65)

Is it possible to find, in what we know of Schreber's biography, the crucial points corresponding to the theoretical terms discussed above? This will not be too difficult. Who, then, is this "A-father" responsible for having engendered the Schreberian God in this resolute atheist–as Schreber calls himself? Evidently, it is the position occupied, in the real, by Professor Flechsig. His science, upon which the fate of Schreber depends, has had Schreber's respect for a long time:(66) his intellectual prestige, his devotion, the old and affectionate friendship that his client has for him, all this places him justifiably in this role. But what makes this old and stable situation veer toward catastrophe? And in what eroticized field does the university psychiatrist take up the position of third person? This is also known to us with quasi-certainty: at the time which immediately preceded the outbreak of her husband's attack of schizophrenia, Mrs. Schreber had reached the period of her life which, for Schreber, definitely ruled out any hope of his ever being a father himself. The fading away of this hope writes Schreber, was the most painful experience in his life. At the moment when a breach was created between the real subject and the ideal subject which Schreber had wished to be, "A-father," Flechsig, came to fill it.

At this point, Flechsig can only render manifest the prior foreclosure of Schreber's father. Indeed, the delirium discloses to us very clearly the modali-

---

[10]   See note 3 of Chapter IV.

ties of this foreclosure. If Schreber's father has never been the symbolic father who established and safeguards the law for his son, it is because this father, like the one of the 'Wolf man,' blended, for his son, with the primordial object of the dual union–the object which is forever lost. Schreber also tells us about this aspect, with all desirable clarity, although unconsciously, when he explains that God had "dropped" *(liegen lassen)* his creature. The father, foreclosed from his paternity, becomes like the original object and is as such found back through the promise of divine nuptials.

It is all this that Flechsig, "A-father," causes to arise, in hallucinatory fashion, in the imaginary real. The rest, namely, the hatred and the accusations against the professor, the cosmo-theology, the redemption of humanity by means of the divine intercourse, are only "modifications" of the signifier, destined to render acceptable that which could never be acceptable to an atheistic and rigorously presiding judge. This unacceptable fact is simply that Schreber has not assumed the position of a rival of his father but has chosen him as an object of love, which is equivalent to the foreclosure of his paternity. When the doctor was substituted for Schreber's father–who has never played the role of father–then it becomes possible for this wish to appear in the real. In order to mark this wish, love was turned into hate, Flechsig was replaced by God and Schreber became the divine spouse.

In his beautiful book on *Hölderlin et la Question du Père*, Laplanche, making use of numerous references to passages from Lacan which we have been commenting on here, describes a similar process in the pathological evolution of the illustrious poet. We know that the poet lost his father at the age of two and that his mother, soon remarried, became a widow again when the young Hölderlin reached his ninth year. In the case of Hölderlin also, the name-of-the-father is foreclosed, because having never truly accepted his stepfather, he was excluded by his mother from all access to his true father. The mother refused him any mediation which could have led him to the dead father. The "A-father" manifests himself, much later, in the person of Schiller.(67) Schiller took over as protector, guide, and counselor of the young poet, by whom he was passionately admired. But Schiller also found himself to be the close acquaintance and the most intimate friend of a household where Hölderlin was tutor and lover both of the mother and of the governess of his pupil. Thus, to all of the roles he was already filling vis-à-vis Hölderlin, Schiller added that of judge. This conjunction caused Hölderlin to set in motion a series of delirious attitudes toward Schiller, which signaled the beginning of his schizophrenic evolution (Ver Eecke 1995).

VII. The Relative Role of the Mother and Father in Psychosis

What we just have explained constitutes the essential contributions of psychoanalytic theory to our understanding of schizophrenia. There is no need to underline its importance, since it is self-evident. We would only like to insist on the fact that this interpretation by no means contradicts what we have affirmed in the first part of our book. In the first part, we explained the role that the mother can play, during the phase of the dual union, in the outbreak of schizophrenia.

As we said earlier, the child cannot be brought to renounce being the phallus of the mother, cannot recognize himself as being a lack, unless he is offered and presented some "elsewhere" besides his coenesthesia, some signifier of himself. Such a self-signifier can make him capable of seeing himself from the very place where he is not. Referring to the works of Mme. Aulagnier, we have explained that this "elsewhere" is created by the insertion of the child into a chain of signifiers, as worked out by the inter-parental discourse, and by the mother's own discourse. Before birth, the child has found a place in the chain of signifiers, and once he is born, demands will be made upon him in accordance with it. When the time comes, it will be on the basis of this chain that he will be able to question himself, if only to challenge his own place. It is also as a function of this place that the mother endows the child with an "imagined body" which, from the very moment of conception, distinguishes him from the human embryo which he in fact is. Thus he is placed *ab initio* as the Other of the mother, and in addition, as the Other of his physiological reality: a being for himself, always already distinct from the mother and not the fortuitous product of her intercourse, a being who will soon separate himself from her more or less completely.

If this process of imagination and libidinal investment fails to occur, the path of the future child runs the risk of being definitively blocked. In this case, he does not possess any other signifier of himself than the one of his chaotic immanence; hence, any identification of himself with himself will always be prevented, beginning with that of his mirror image. Happy or unhappy, without hope of going beyond it, he remains fixed in the role of annex to the mother's body.

As explained before, such will be the case if the mother is a law unto herself. "For the subjects of whom I speak, i.e., the mothers of psychotics, things are of an altogether different order: the rules of the game have never been accepted, or, what is more serious, understood; one could say that the only game they know is 'solitaire,' a game without partners and without stakes, except those that confirm an autistic omnipotence."(68) And further on, "If, clinically, they (the mother of psychotics) are not psychotics, if their defenses permit them a kind of superficial adaptation to the real, it is nevertheless true that we find that their lives are always very a-historic (i.e., they are poorly inserted into, if not excluded from, the order of the law). Moreover, it is possible and probable that, in these cases, the child may be the factor which sets an abrupt breakdown of the defenses in motion (this would explain why in these mothers the perversion towards the law is concretized precisely in their relationship with their children). However, at the same time, the child will also be that which permits these mothers to fill up the gap in the defense mechanism, by making the body of the child into a fortification which receives and holds back any irruption of poorly dammed-up repression."(69)

But are not these theses, to which we continue to adhere, more or less directly opposed to the Lacanian thesis which we have just developed? Indeed, in this latter thesis the foreclosure of the name-of-the-father is regarded as the structural factor which is responsible for the possibility of schizophrenia. Let us formulate the contradiction in the clearest possible terms. Could we not be reproached for having located the origin of psychosis both in the child's relationship to the mother, and in his relationship to the father?

It seems to us that the difficulty is purely an apparent one and that our position will be strengthened rather than weakened by discussing this difficulty. Indeed, it will become clear that our two theses are not conflicting, but are rather complementary.

If the mother cannot give up being absolutely and completely fulfilled by the child, how will the child be able to accede to the law of the father? If the dual union takes on the form of a circle which is totally and definitively closed, where will there be room for the paternal metaphor? In this case, the third term of the mother-child relationship is and will remain the child as phallus of the mother, for him as well as for her. To borrow for a moment the language of Melanie Klein, how will the child ever be able to discover the paternal penis in the body of the mother, if he himself is this penis? If this child is nothing but an ornament or fuel for the narcissistic omnipotence of the mother, how will he succeed in situating himself in relation to the father?

Conversely, if the father is the caricatural personage so energetically ridiculed by Lacan when he describes Schreber's father for us,(70) how will the mother transform the nonexistent into a presence, and how will this nonexistent be able to impose himself as the guardian and the guarantor of the law?[11] And how can this nonexistence avoid stimulating the narcissism of the mother and child dyad?

To be sure, nothing in these matters is fatal; hence nothing is absolutely predictable either. No set of circumstances ever *necessarily* entails the estab-

[11]   This passage raises a theoretical issue. The book of Schatzman: *Soul Murder,* particularly some of its illustrations (p. 45, 47, 48, 50) suggest that Schreber's father might not have been "in-existent" for his children. On the contrary he might have been "brutally" present. Lacan's theory has a tendency to reduce the role of the father to that of a statue that the mother must respect. This respect, she must communicate to the children, who then are capable of accepting the "name-of-the-father." The thesis I would like to defend with reference to the book by Schatzman, about the Schreber family, is that the acceptance of the "name-of-the-father" depends not only on the respect shown by the mother for the figure of the father, but also on the *father's presence to his children.* Furthermore, the respect of the mother for the figure of the father is not solely a function of the emotional maturity of the mother, it is also dependent on *who that father* shows himself to be (Ver Eecke 1993).

lishment of *such* a structure, if only because circumstances and structure are situated on different planes. Also, the objectively knowable circumstances carry relatively little weight, since they have to pass through the imagination of the subjects involved, a place which can be the locus of their symbolic transformation, and indeed always is to a greater or lesser extent. But if, in one sense, everything is perhaps possible, it is not true that everything is also equally probable. In the cases described, it is probable that the failures in each of the terms in the constellations induced and reinforced each other. Why would the woman who is a stranger to the law ally herself with someone who is able to personify it? Why would a man who cannot fully be the subject of his own desire ally himself with a woman who wishes to fully be the object of it? The paths then are open... .

One more comment. What has been said about the mother who is a stranger to the law still remains ambiguous on at least one point. For this "alienation" admits of a double possibility. Indeed, it is possible that the child be included in the narcissism of the mother, to the point of its being everything for her, just as it is also possible that the child be totally excluded from this narcissism and therefore be worthless for this narcissistic mother. No matter how concretely these hypotheses differ and in how many respects, from our point of view, they prove to be equivalent. In neither of the two cases will there appear for the subject this offer of an "elsewhere" for his real body; and we have shown that this offer alone can open up a path to the dialectic of recognition.

NOTES

(1)   As we have just said, Freud uses various terms to describe Schreber's psychosis; the term "paranoia" is the most frequently used one. But this term is not quite appropriate. In our opinion, Schreber, as it will become clear from Lacan's commentary, is a paranoid schizophrenic. Furthermore it is necessary to distinguish between the Schreber described in the memoirs and the Schreber who wrote them. The first appears as a typical schizophrenic. But the second, who seeks to convince the judges and the public of his mental integrity while recognizing that he has been ill and while correcting partially–very partially, in fact–his old delirium, appears to be a paranoiac. We shall open this question after we have examined the elements of Freud's solution.

(2)   Lacan, "D'une question préliminaire à tout traitement possible de la psychose" in *Écrits*, pp. 531-584 (E: p. 179-225). Lacan disputes [*op. cit.* p. 567 (E: p. 208)], the absolute primacy of homosexual desires in the evolution of Schreber's paranoia. As we shall see, this is probably the correct approach. But this reversal is only a function of a general theory of psychosis which Freud did not possess at the time of his commentary on the Schreber case. In addition, the elements which decisively justify this reversal are furnished only by Lacan himself and can only be extrapolated from Freud.

(3)   Freud, S.E., XII, p. 61.

(4)   Freud, S.E., XII, p. 63. The situation is identical if the subject is a woman, except of course for the appropriate change in the gender of the pronouns. The proposition which

has to be contradicted then becomes: "I (a female), I love her (another female)."

(5) Freud, S.E., XII, p. 64.

(6) There is another indication of homosexuality in the patient's choice of love object. This is often the case in females, whose paranoia often takes the form of erotomania. The love object is normally someone from whom one would not ordinarily fear a proper sexual exigency, e.g., priest, doctor, lawyer, or an unlikely and inaccessible personage (in the case of the patient, studied in Lacan's thesis, it is the prince of Wales). On this matter see F. Perrier, *L'Erotomanie*, in the collective volume: Piera Aulagnier-Spairani et al., *Le Désir et la perversion*, p. 132. Also in that study we found this other remark: "In our opinion, pure erotomania is a-typical of the female passions. In the male it appears normally only as a partial syndrome in a clinical picture where paranoia, debility, or psychopathological disequilibrium, pose more problems than the erotomania. This latter shows more regularity than the other in that clinical picture." *Op. Cit.*, p. 131.

(7) Freud, S.E., XII, p. 68.

(8) For Example: "Things have lost all their glitter." "The light from the sun gradually weakens and soon all will be night and eternal cold." "Nobody has a job. Unemployment is universal. Mankind can only seek refuge in asylums," etc., etc.

(9) Freud, S.E. XII, p. 71. The text tells us then that psychotic repression consists in divesting the libidinal cathexes of objects or of the world under the action of the initiating event. This divestiture occurs because the libidinal cathexes consisted of partial or forbidden impulses to which the subject was affixed. The path for the regression, which follows the divestiture, is dictated by the impulses which formed the original cathexis. The second movement of psychotic repression, the only one that is directly perceptible, is the attempt of the subject to reinvest the world or fictitious, delirious objects, which could save him from both mutism and the danger related to the satisfaction of forbidden instincts. In the first interpretation–which will be considerably modified later on–it is the unconscious homosexual feelings of Schreber for Flechsig, which are abruptly but unconsciously stimulated by the fact that the Schreber family becomes absolutely certain that they will never have children which sets in motion the entire process.

(10) Freud, S.E., XII, p. 76.

(11) Freud, S.E., XII, p. 77. It is clear that this explanation makes it impossible to consider Schreber a pure paranoiac since, undoubtedly, this "hallucinatory agitation" exists in his case. Further on we shall see how Freud overcomes this difficulty.

(12) Freud, S.E., XII, p. 77.

(13) Thus we must conclude that, according to Freud, certain schizophrenics can undergo a paranoid phase (both when the regression occurs or is overcome) but that, inversely, paranoiacs will not manifest properly schizophrenic symptoms, except for the withdrawal of object-investments which Freud believes is common to both psychoses. This is because the failure of the paranoiac is to be located in the narcissistic phase (i.e., in the so-called auto-erotic phase).

(14) Freud, G.W.X., p. 140; S.E. XIV, p. 75.

(15) Freud, G.W.X., p. 141; S.E. XIV, p. 75.

(16) One can find a confirmation of the Freudian thesis by noting that one almost never observes a psychotic crisis of acute nature without hypochondriac symptoms which are most often never massive.

(17) Freud refers to the case where a neurosis precedes the appearance of a psychosis or which serves as a screen prior to the acute phase of the illness.

(18) Freud, G.W.X., p. 153; S.E. XIV, p. 86-87.

(19) The fact that the achievement of this metamorphosis will require several centuries may appear as an attachment to an old "reality." One should also notice the fact that Schreber's memoirs were written to obtain his release and thus to persuade the judges if not of his sanity, at least of the uselessness of keeping him as an intern patient.

(20) We are dealing here with another type of repression, different from the one discovered with regard to narcissism itself, when Freud describes the withdrawal of objective investments as a form of repression.

(21) "Ein Augenverdreher" literally means some one who twists eyes. The expression indicates an individual who has the ability to make himself appear as he is not, because he succeeds in making people turn away their eyes from that to which attention should be paid in order to know him well. A patient would say, in French, that she has dust in her eyes because she is with someone "who throws dust in one's eyes;" [which is a metaphor for the English expressions: "leading one astray" W.V.E.]

(22) *Écrits*, p. 537-538 (E: p. 184-185).

(23) *Écrits*, p. 532 (E: p. 180).

(24) This idea has dominated Lacan's thought from the beginning. Indeed, it appeared in his writings as early as 1932, although in somewhat different words: "Is it not the case that the structure of morbid representations in the psychosis is simply *other* than normal? Blondel . . . has emphasized this fact: the morbid consciousness appears to be of a radically different structure than the normal consciousness. . . ." *De la psychose paranoïaque dans ses rapport avec la personnalité.* Paris, 1932, p. 294.

(25) *Écrits*, p. 532-533 (E: p. 180-181).

(26) *Écrits*, p. 534 (E: p. 181).

(27) *Écrits*, p. 535 (E: p. 183).

(28) *Écrits*, p. 535 (E: p. 183).

(29) The imaginary rebuke "sow" does not disengage the patient from the situation. On the contrary, it makes it concrete and identifies the patient with it. This rebuke, borrowed from the language of the patient, is, in fact, the equivalent of a cry yelled by the patient when the dentist's drill touches a nerve.

(30) Schreber, as we know, compares it to an archaic and vigorous German. [*Memoirs*, p. 13 of original edition. W.V.E.]

(31) *Écrits*, p. 537 (E: p. 184).

(32) *Écrits*, p. 537-538 (E: p. 184).

(33) *Exposed* is a term in the fundamental language, the precise meaning of which may be easily guessed. [In Macalpine and Hunter, this is translated by a word that lacks this second meaning: "represented," *Ibid*, p. 172. W.V.E.]

(34) *Écrits*, p. 540 (E: p. 186).

(35) *Écrits*, p. 540 (E: p. 187).

(36) *Écrits*, p. 542 (E: p. 189).

(37) *Écrits*, p. 543 (E: p. 189).

(38) "Homosexuality, the alleged determinant of paranoia, is really a symptom articulated in its process." *Écrits*, p. 544 (E: p. 190).

(39) *Écrits*, p. 549 (E: p. 194).

(40) *Écrits*, p. 550 (E: p. 194-95).

(41) *Écrits*, p. 551 (E: p. 195-96).

(42) *Écrits*, p. 551 (E: p. 196).

(43) *Écrits*, p. 551. The words between parentheses are ours [A.D.W.] (E: p. 196).

(44) *Écrits*, p. 551 (E: p. 196).

(45) *Écrits*, p. 552 (E: p. 196).

(46) *Écrits*, p. 552 (E: p. 196).

(47) *Écrits*, p. 552 (E: p. 196-97).

(48) *Écrits*, p. 557 (E: p. 200).

(49) *Écrits*, p. 557 (E: p. 200).

(50) This is how Laplanche and Portalis define *foreclosure*: "Term introduced by Jacques Lacan: specific mechanism which would be at the origin of the psychotic phenomenon; it would consist of a primordial rejection of a fundamental 'signifier' from the symbolic universe of the subject (for example: the phallus as signifier of the castration complex). Foreclosure differs from repression in two ways: (1) the foreclosed signifiers are not integrated into the unconscious of the subject; (2) they do not return into the interior, but into the midst of the real, particularly in the hallucinatory phenomenon." *Vocabulaire de la Psychanalyse*, p. 163-164. *The Language of Psychoanalysis*, p. 160. We are leaving aside the question of the relation between Lacan's concept of whether, for Freud, *verworfen* does not have several meanings. On these questions, see the thesis of Mr. Ewens, already cited.

(51) *Écrits*, p. 553 (E: p. 201). The word in italics (underlined) is ours. [A.D.W.] Let us remember that, for Lacan, in this text, the Other designates the unconscious.

(52) One may read about a similar hallucinatory return of the foreclosed signifier in the fable of Leclaire which we have cited.

(53) *Écrits*, p. 564 (E: p. 206).

(54) The existence of this impulse, however, is incontestable, as the ambivalent relationship with Flechsig clearly shows.

(55) *Écrits*, p. 266 (E: p. 207).

(56) *Écrits*, p. 566 (E: p. 207).

(57) Throughout the whole course of his illness, Schreber's "present ego" did not cease, for example, to be that of an affectionate, considerate husband, moved to tears at each of the visits which Mrs. Schreber paid him.

(58) An annihilation sought by God, whom Flechsig has won over to his dark designs. As we have seen, the trap consists of having the divine "voices" utter such extraordinary nonsense that should the wornout Schreber fail to respond to them, even if only for an instant, his immediate destruction would be brought about.

(59) *Écrits*, p. 575 (E: p. 215).

(60) *Écrits*, p. 577 (E: p. 217).

(61) *Écrits*, p. 577 (E: p. 217).

(62) *Écrits*, p. 577 (E: p. 217).

(63) *Écrits*, p. 578 (E: p. 217).

(64) *Écrits*, p. 577 (E: p. 217).

(65) *Écrits*, p. 572 (E: p. 212).

(66) As we know, Flechsig had cared for and "cured" Schreber during the preceding crises. Schreber had remained very grateful and considered him as his savior.

(67) See p. 50 and 57 of the book cited, where two letters from Hölderlin to Schiller leave no doubt in this regard.

68. P. Aulagnier, article cited, p. 52.

69. P. Aulagnier, article cited, p. 52-53.

70. *Écrits*, p. 582 (E: p. 221).

Chapter Six

CONCLUDING REFLECTIONS ON THE PROBLEM OF PSYCHOSIS.
PSYCHOANALYTIC AND EXISTENTIAL CRITERIA OF PSYCHOSIS

De Waelhens

I. The Five Structural Characteristics of Schizophrenia

Having completed both this summary and detailed review of the principal theories and interpretations advanced by psychiatry and psychoanalysis concerning the phenomenon of psychosis, it may be possible to attempt without falling into an unacceptable eclecticism, a brief restatement which will allow us to reassemble and formulate what is relevant to an anthropological perspective such as ours.

Undoubtedly schizophrenia originates in an earlier stratum of personality formation than any other psychosis. It is for this reason that for most people it is the prototype of all psychosis. This does not prevent a rather vague use of the term, for example, in the U.S.A., where it is increasingly becoming simply a synonym for psychosis. Nor does it prevent considerable variations in the choice of both distinguishing criteria and explanatory concepts. We need only mention the names of Kraepelin, Bleuler, and Freud-Lacan to illustrate this remark. Nevertheless, it appears to us that the notion of schizophrenia can be specified more precisely by a set of characteristics which define its very nature. Let us enumerate them and explain how they jointly yield a (pathological) mode of existence.

The order in which these characteristics are presented is largely immaterial, since each one refers to all the others, and transposes them, as it were, into a new dimension. So we may call them *gleichursprünglich*, 'equiprimordial,' not in the temporal sense, but in the sense in which Heidegger uses this adjective to indicate the common origin of elements whose overlapping determines a structure.

We think that it is possible to isolate the following five structural characteristics of schizophrenia:

1) The body-image, to which the patient consciously or unconsciously refers, always appears to be fragmented in some way. This fragmentation is frequently very noticeable, but it can nevertheless be disguised. It will then appear in the subject's unconscious productions where it can be discovered rather easily.

2) At some decisive point in his speech, the subject betrays a confusion be-

tween the signifier and the signified; many of the "neologisms" so widely pointed out in psychiatric literature on schizophrenia originate in this way. This confusion is an indication that the subject has not gained access to the realm of the symbolic.

3) The Oedipal triangle is fundamentally disturbed. The subject, occupying the place of the Ego at the lower point of the triangle, only in imagination, in fact, locates himself at one angle of the upper side from which he ousts the father even though he may replace him in imagination by some famous or phantasized figure. He is inclined to merge and confuse himself with the other parent, the mother, who in principle occupies the opposite angle of the same side. The line is thereby abolished, its two extremities collapse into a single point. The desire of the subject to beget himself with his own mother and thus to be his own father corresponds to this configuration. In short, we are involved here in a pseudo-triangle, which is at the same time entirely pseudo-Oedipal, since the mother intended here is not the Oedipal mother, who is an Other;[1] this is confirmed in the daughter's case, where the configuration is similar although she never has the mother as an Oedipal object (except in the case of an inverted Oedipus, which is a different matter).[2]

4) The subject displays at least a potential bisexuality. More precisely, he fails to locate himself in relation to the difference between the sexes. Without wishing to anticipate the developments which will follow, we can clearly see that this springs directly from what has been shown in the preceding point.

5) The subject identifies birth and death. He speaks of birth as a death, of death as a birth. "I am not yet born," or "I have been dead a thousand years" are, from this point of view, strictly equivalent.(1) In the same way, we can understand the habit Hölderlin assumed, at a certain point in his illness, of dating his letters and writings according to a rule whereby, each January 1st, he would subtract one year from the number he had used to designate the previous year; he started this process from a certain year in the seventeenth century, in which he fictitiously located himself.

---

[1] The Oedipal mother is a mother about whom the child learned, that she has not as her sole function to take care of the child. The child learns this among other ways by seeing that the mother and the father talk to each other, relate to each other, etc. This experience destroys the image the child had of the mother (the imaginary mother,) [written by Lacan as the small a (= *autre* 'other')]. Instead the mother is now situated within the Oedipal rivalry (Oedipal mother), or within the symbolic order, [the symbolic other is written by Lacan as the capital A (= *Autre* 'Other')].

[2] See Freud's essay: "The Ego and the Id," particularly Ch. III. G.W. XIII, p. 256ff (especially p. 260-61); S.E. XIX, p. 28ff (especially p. 32-34).

II. Foreclosure and the Distortion of Language

To begin with, let us underline that all that preceded is in no way opposed to–or incompatible with–the mechanism described by Lacan under the heading of "foreclosure of the name-of-the-father," which we have studied at length above. Actually, our observations only reveal and articulate what takes place for the observer *when there has been a foreclosure of the name-of-the-father;* with good reason, *this latter never appears directly itself.* Foreclosure is the foundation and ultimate meaning of the phenomena described above as constituents of the schizophrenic structure, as registered in the subject's experience, insofar as this is given to us.

Here we will describe the interdependency of these different points while indicating without dwelling on the fact, since it may readily be verified by the reader that all these points appear, without exception, and in an appropriately striking manner, in the exemplary account which President Schreber left us of his own illness. This has a certain bearing on the plausibility of our argument, since the text in question is at the source of some of the most original and profound attempts to give us the key to the phenomenon of schizophrenia.(2)

Foreclosure of the name-of-the-father substitutes for the real Oedipal triangle a bipolar relation, which in turn is reduced to an identity of the polar elements. It confirms the fact that the subject has not gained access to the symbolic realm, even that this realm is inaccessible for him, since the father is its guarantor. Likewise, and as a result, mediation, negativity, and distance remain alien to this subject. Strictly speaking we must go so far as to deny him all correct use of language, since language presupposes these concepts. In fact, writers on the subject all agree in pointing to very serious problems with regard to the language of the schizophrenic. They describe them differently because they approach them in terms of concepts relating to the nature, ends and mechanisms of language which these writers conceive of in almost totally different ways. But throughout these variations in descriptions, however, it is not too hard to find a single central kernel. It corresponds to what we have designated as the confusion of the signifier and the signified. This confusion in fact represents the radical failure of linguistic metaphor.(3) To this is added, in certain cases, the appearance or return of the signifier in the delirious reality of the patient, a return whose mechanism we have tried to understand. The following case, presented by Lacan at the St. Anne Hospital is an example; the patient, although persecuted by a neighbor on the same floor, who stole all his thoughts, had to admit nevertheless that he did not know her at all. His excuses were that the neighbor had been living in the building for only a short time, and that he himself worked at night in a newspaper printing shop and slept during the day. The patient knew only one thing about his neighbor: her name was Madame Maire.[3] The significance of this phenomenon goes beyond

---

[3]   In French "Maire" is pronounced in the same way as *"mère* 'mother.'" The implica-

linguistic behavior in the narrow sense. This is evident in the case of a patient, who, not without ambivalence, accuses her doctor of giving her "burns" on her face every night. When asked if she had been able to see the scars in her mirror, she said "that would be the last straw.[4] Likewise, she explains that her illness dates from the time when her father "unfairly" had her appendix operated on, adding that since then she had always felt that "she was missing something."[5] But she used this expression as it is often used in Belgium, that is in its Dutch meaning, which expresses that one is not in good health, that something is wrong. On another occasion, the same patient established a connection between the beginning of her illness and the setting up of a miniature-golf course in her village, which, moreover, she said she used to visit with delight.[6] The description she gives of the game clearly shows the meaning she attaches to it: the game signified the sexuality of her own body. And the installation of this game in the village where she lived when she was fourteen is unconsciously experienced as the origin of her illness.

The problem, for us, is no longer that of understanding the confusion of signifier and signified, nor whence this confusion originates. The difficulty will rather be to mark the bounds of its havoc and to understand why it does not necessarily pervade and affect all use of language by the schizophrenic. Because it seems, in effect, that in many circumstances, at least certain schizophrenics appear to handle language correctly and use it to communicate an objective truth. It is possible to resolve this problem in two ways. First, it is

tion is that his mother deprived him of the possibility to think in his own right.

[4] This is a nice illustration of an important philosophical thesis that De Waelhens will develop later in the book, i.e., it is typical for a hallucination that the patient refuses to accept logical implications of the content of his hallucination. To accept such implications would be to allow the hallucinations to be subjected to a kind of reality principle. This would make the hallucinations unfit to perform the function they are created to perform: to express unconscious wishes in protest against the law(s) of the real.

[5] This is the reverse of the patient of Sullivan who was not operated upon. He too was discontented. He wanted something cut out from his body. (Sullivan: *The Interpersonal Theory of Psychiatry, p. 363*). The Lacanian theory allows for an interpretation of the discontent of both patients. The patient described by De Waelhens uses an operation "unfairly" permitted by her father as the signifier of her refusal to accept her lack. She indeed accuses her father of making her lack something, since that operation. The patient of Sullivan is struggling with the experience of him lacking something. He wants to express this experience in the real by having something cut out of his body. Both therefore have not succeeded in mastering the lack that they are symbolically. They have not accepted symbolic castration and thus replace it or want to replace it by real castration (operations).

[6] The statement that the setting up of a miniature-golf course is the origin of the illness of the girl can only be understood if we relate it to the manifest refusal of this girl to accept symbolic castration. The miniature golf course is a constant reminder of this unconscious conflict in the girl and can thus very well have triggered the eruption of her problematic.

almost certain that such seemingly adequate use of language is often more apparent than real. In most cases it involves what we would call, using a comparison, a sort of "speech learnt by heart" as opposed to talk really understood in its full meaning. This is the moment to remember Henry Ey's dictum: "the raving man always raves more than you think." Certain banalities or ready-made formulae of current language, although correctly and intentionally recited, communicate, on closer inspection, a meaning which is simply erroneous. The patient of whom I spoke earlier never failed to open a conversation with some remarks, usually relevant, about the weather. Every time we tried to find out the real meaning of her statements, we found that these meteorological phrases concealed a sort of delirious code. For example, "it is hot today" meant "the sun's heat is too strong for me to approach you and shake your hand." And in fact, while saying her "it is very hot today," she seemed transfixed to the threshold, but without explaining her behavior, except in reply to later questioning by me. "The sky is grey this morning" meant: "the sun will never shine as in other times and the end of the world draws near."

So we believe that to the extent, certainly slight but perhaps not nonexistent, that really adequate and correct language persists in the schizophrenic, it proves, as the example of a young child readily convinces us, that it is possible to use language appropriately without understanding it. Furthermore, it shows that for language, as for other forms of so-called social behavior, it is possible to handle with apparent correctness, "constructions" which have survived the catastrophe but whose use no longer corresponds to anything for the person concerned. And if these correctly used constructions still mean something, they mean something totally different than they mean for the normal person.[7]

III. The four remaining structural Characteristics of Schizophrenia

1. The Fragmented Body Image

That all this leads to, or has as its correlate, some fragmented image of the body, conscious or not, more or less readily revealed in the subject's speech or unconscious productions (dreams, drawings, models etc.), will become evident in several ways. In the first place, we agree that the failure to reach the symbolic, and before that, the failure to reach the stage of the mirror-image, holds the subject back at a moment of his formation where he cannot have a unitary image of his body, as we have shown in Chapter III. Lacan provides a proof of this in his celebrated article on the mirror phase, and also in his study on the

---

[7] This is one of the points on which Vergote disagrees in his review of De Waelhens' book: "Raisons de la déraison," p. 784. See also De Waelhens' statement (this book p. 176-77) which seems to support the position of Vergote.

family in *Encyclopédie française.*[8]

But another approach can also be chosen to make sense of what clinical experience has taught us. The constitution of the body-image as a Gestalt presupposes that a very specific reference system be available. Indeed, through this Gestalt, every part of the body is constantly present and represented in every other. If, however, this identity is somehow taken literally by the subject's imagination or perception and if it is thus not seen by him as purely imaginary, then the subject cannot conceive of the identity given to him by the body image as an identity built upon elements that are not identical. The subject will then have an incoherent and fragmented body-image, since certain parts of the body will be apprehended as purely and simply confused with one another (as, for example, all the orifices of the body)–whereas in a different deformation, certain other parts may be excluded or projected into the external world (like the patient who sees her eyes before her and sees only them).(4)

2. The Symbolic Order

In fact, without accession to the level of the symbolic, to the level of metaphor (understood in the broadest sense and not in the restricted sense in which Lacan opposes it to metonymy), that is, without accession to this order, where what must be viewed as the same is simply not completely the same, all elaboration of a unitary body-image is impossible. Without doubt the bobbin is the mother's body for the child, but also–and this is just as essential–it is not identical with it.[9] If they are both simply identical for him, he is delirious. A fortiori this is true for the second case where he mixes up the words *fort,* 'away,' and *da,* 'here,' with what they stand for, i.e., the object as really present or really absent, the mother's body intended through the mediation of the bobbin. Where negation of pure identity does not operate, we fall into the confusion of the signifier and signified, that is, to recall another of our examples, into the persecution by Madame Maire, unconsciously identified with the subject's mother by the concrete materiality of her surname.

The truth is this: accession to the symbolic, the correct constitution of the Oedipal triangle, and the elaboration of a unitary body-image are the parts or interdependent sides of a whole, the articulated moments of a same structure.[10]

---

[8]　The article on the mirror phase is reproduced in *Écrits, p. 93-100.* The relevant passages in the Encyclopedia article are p. 8.40-9/10. For a book length study on the relation between the body image and schizophrenia see: Gisela Pankow: *L'Homme et sa Psychose.*

[9]　Freud, *"Beyond the Pleasure Principle,"* Ch. II in G.W. XIII, 11ff.; S.E. XVIII, 4ff.

[10]　It is not clear if these elements are just interrelated (a thesis which De Waelhens gave proof of) or if they belong to the same level of the constitution of the subject. This last

3. Bisexuality

Our last two points will no longer cause any great concern. Bisexuality, whether actually present or not, is always a real possibility for the schizophrenic, since only the correct position of the Oedipal relation locates the subject irrevocably in relation to the distinction between the sexes. Undoubtedly, it may occur in certain cases that, although the subject knows this distinction, he *denies* it (in perversion). But in such a case the distinction has been constituted and the subject can no longer avoid situating himself relative to it, even if he apparently goes against it in homosexual behavior. It is totally different in the case of the schizophrenic. Prior to the Oedipal position, a subject does not situate himself in a definite way relative to the distinction between the sexes. In the pre-Oedipal period the subject is subordinated to the vicissitudes of the libidinal investments, which are indifferent to the sex of the object or the subject. Moreover, it can be shown without difficulty that pre-Oedipal investments really remain narcissistic. They are directed to an object, to a body whose status does not go beyond that of another-who-is-also-the same, who is not yet specified as a body which *is other because* it is of the other sex. Thus the subject continues to exist in relative indifference to sex. Consequently, it will only be *quoad nos* that his behavior is to be described as homosexual if he is attracted by a partner objectively of the same sex, or as heterosexual, if the partner is objectively of the opposite sex. But this distinction has no relevance *quoad se* and we can therefore call this period one of bisexuality.

4. Confusion of Birth and Death

Let us come to the last point, which presents no great difficulty either: the identity of birth and death. This is a central theme of many myths and legends. It is also rooted in the depths of the unconscious as is attested to by so many phantasies. Finally, this theme has a fairly clear connection with the structure of the schizophrenic psychosis, at least as we will attempt to describe and understand it here. The state of scission, of separation, which initiates biological birth, is precisely that to which the schizophrenic can never consent at any price.[11] For the scission condemns what is thought to fill or blot out the lack

thesis is doubtful, since the formation of a unitary body-image is prior to the constitution of the Oedipal triangle or the accession to the symbolic. It is true that the unitary body-image will allow entrance into the Oedipal triangle or into the symbolic order and that these entrances will solidify the unitary body-image. This, however, does not justify putting the three phenomena at the same level of the constitution of the subject.

[11] The inability of the schizophrenic to consent to the state of separation of biological birth, is but the counterpart of the inability of the mother of the schizophrenic to give

of the mother to the status of a partial object, that is, to a state which is itself one of lack, but without the possibility of being recognized as such lack. Entering such a state is indeed death, the only true death. But, conversely, the path to what we call biological death will be imagined in phantasy as the return to non-scission with the mother's body, that is, to the birth of the subject beyond this death where he now flounders or stagnates.

It may be that this characteristic is neither always apparent nor explicit. However, we believe that its implicit presence can often easily be detected. In Schreber's case it is expressed in the form of his resurrection after the death he has undergone, and again, even more so, in the belief in a terrestrial immortality. It is, moreover, a trait which one finds in many delirious people, and there is no paradox involved in invoking it on behalf of our thesis. Because this would-be perpetuity signifies–as one sees clearly in Schreber himself–the desire for liberation from temporal limitations typical of human life. In ordinary circumstances this is signified by the concept of death. This would-be perpetuity is also nothing other than a continual delirious upholding of the never-broken prenatal fusion. Hatred of death, embodied in the desire for terrestrial immortality, is in reality hatred of birth, just as the desire for perpetual birth reveals itself in reality to be a desire for death.[12]

IV. The Paranoiac

The phenomenon of paranoia and its world are quite different. Indeed, paranoia can be traced back to the level of the mirror phase. At that stage the unity and identity of the body, as also the existence of an other, even of an other rooted in a common world, have already acquired some meaning and relevance–we described these characteristics as typical of the mirror phase. The schizophrenic, on the other hand, has not acquired a true perception of his mirror-image and thus does not have access–or if he has, it is only in a garbled manner–to the experiences which are made possible by the mirror-image.

It is in relation to questions concerning the role of the Other and of the Third as witness that we will take up the problem, and attempt to outline the essentials of the paranoid situation. We will also try to differentiate it from the schizophrenic as well as from the non-psychotic.

It has been reiterated often enough that every word involves an appeal to the Other. Even if I strive to interpret a dream by myself, and if, to return to

---

meaning to giving birth. Both lack the distance created by the acceptance of some signifier to signify the event of birth.

[12] In a delirious way, schizophrenics interpret death as birth. For philosophy of religion it is crucial to distinguish the delirious opinions of schizophrenics from the mature religious experience.

236

the celebrated example Freud used in his article on "Negation,"[13] I have just told myself that I do not know who this woman represents, but that it is certainly not my mother–I find fault with another who could have said, perhaps did say, that it does indeed refer to her. My denial always involves the same appeal: I can be right only if the Other verifies that this character does not actually represent my mother. A truth which in principle I alone could know and express is the very definition of error.

This appeal to the Other is not necessarily an appeal to any particular person. For if my speech is not sufficient by itself to constitute the truth, then it is clear that neither Peter's, James' nor John's speech enjoys that privilege any more than mine. As soon as any one of them can be alone in seeing what he sees, he is, by that very fact wrong.(5) He is, like me, subject to the Other.

This transcendent Other is clearly never *given* objectively, but speech is an *appeal to* . . . this Transcendence-as-witness."(6) So, if I want to articulate any truth, I must try to identify with this third as witness, thus overcoming all identification with my contingent interlocutor. Even lying is no exception to this rule. Indeed the rule applies twice. I am certain of lying if I speak against what the third as witness would ratify. But at the same time, it is the belief of this Other–which I have succeeded in creating–that my word coincides with what the third person would ratify which makes my lie efficient.

But since truth is a pursuit, I cannot claim to install myself permanently in the position of the third as witness. In order to do that, I would need to possess absolute knowledge. I know it and it is true: coincidence with the third's position can be only partial, momentary and precarious.[14]

The most fundamental characteristic of the paranoid position emerges here. The schizophrenic–inasmuch as he is schizophrenic–is indifferent to the third person's ratification. He only carries on a pseudo-conversation. It is a conversation in which the "shifters,"(7) the connecting gears, are not really used appropriately.[15] On the other hand, the paranoiac professes to be particularly sensitive to the third person's position. For this reason, he says hardly anything that might seem irrelevant in his eyes, such as talking about the weather

---

[13]   Freud, G.W. XIV, p. 11; S.E. XIX, p. 235.

[14]   This thesis raises naturally the philosophical question of the possibility of truth. Inasmuch as this study of De Waelhens is undertaken within the spirit of the phenomenological movement, it is a testimony to the relevance of Wagner's criticism of the phenomenological method. He contends that phenomenology can in principle not solve the question of truth. Wagner, *Philosophie und Reflexion*, p. 328-29.

[15]   Some crucial publications in linguistics on this subject matter are: Roman Jacobson: "Les Embrayeurs, les Catégories Verbales et le Verbe Russe" in *Essais de linguistique Générale* and Emile Benveniste: "Structure des relations de personne dans le verbe" and "La nature des pronons" in *Problèmes de linguistique générale*. In philosophy, this problem is discussed under the titles: "indexicals" "token-reflexives" or "egocentric particulars."

to begin a conversation, or learning of someone's health by addressing him with the ritual: "Good morning, how are you?" The paranoiac talks almost exclusively *in the name of truth.* He looks to us for indiscriminate acceptance of it; he will even summon us to fulfill his need. But his speech is surprising to listen to. The paranoiac is not looking for the truth, he acts as if he possesses it. He does not strive to coincide with the position of the third. He acts as if he occupies it by right, like a throne. He acts as if he coincides with it constantly by prerogative. He does not understand nor admit that one could doubt this prerogative. Let us recall the paranoiac who, accusing her husband of infidelity, claimed that he pretended to leave for the six o'clock train every day, but did not really leave until seven o'clock, and spent the hour thus gained with his accomplice, a female neighbor. Questioned as to the evidence she possessed–for she admits that she had never actually *seen* this intrigue–she replied that, catching sight of the neighbor through the kitchen window one day, she saw one of her undergarments which "was still lying" on the table at ten o'clock. It was pointed out to her that this was no proof that it was already there at six o'clock, and even less proof that this woman had a lover, or that he was the patient's husband. She replied, with a voice showing certitude and contempt: "It is clear that you don't know women." For the paranoiac, his speech is "true just as this cloth is red and that one green". In one sweep, he stops thinking of his speech as 'signs' referring to a truth transcending them: he makes of his 'utterances' *things.*"(8)

But why does it work like this, and what does this attitude towards speech signify? First, following the author we have just quoted, we can point out that the imaginary is, by its very nature, always a thing, always *something finished.* This can be verified in dreams, where these utterances are similarly "treated as images and not as signs."(9) Above all, the subject relates in a totally different way to the imaginary than he relates to the perceived. If, in the latter case, it is necessary to *learn* and *explore* the object by successive approximations, by *Abschattungen,* 'profiles,' the imaginary object on the contrary is "seen" absolutely, from all sides, and for everything that it is.[16] It is not difficult to discover the prototype of this apprehension of the object: it is precisely the mirror object. I know all it contains and it contains everything I know of it. This leads us to take a further step. The paranoiac's world is a world composed of images, in which the subject sees himself as an imaginary object. The subject does not organize his speech to express himself, and represent himself to himself by what he says. And since in his opinion we are blind, he *translates, reflects, photographs* for our use the complete and closed world which is

---

[16]   In an article where De Waelhens compares Husserl and Hegel from the point of view of philosophy of the unconscious, De Waelhens gives a decisive advantage to Husserl, precisely because of his theory of "approximation." "Refléxions sur une problématique husserlienne de l'inconscient, Husserl et Hegel," in *Edmund Husserl* (Phenomenologica, 4), p. 221-237.

his, as it appears to him, i.e., immutable. His world is without transcendence or mystery, a place where all meaning is spoken, and none is yet to come. It is also, as regards its truth, a world without risk. Likewise, the Other's transcendence is excluded from it, since the imaginary other has no background, no inaccessibility, and no consistency of his own. The other is only the other-as-persecutor, the double of the mirror relation, identical in appearance to the self, as is made clear in our description of the mirror phase. But let us go further. In fact, when the paranoiac says "I," he cannot really identify with the subject in question in his speech, since he is only, as has been said, an object, and moreover, an imaginary object. Furthermore, his speech is not really addressed to any real person: it does not call on any third who could testify, in the sense that testimony is intended to collaborate in the common attempt to establish the truth. According to the paranoiac's conception, testimony would be completely futile here, since the other's opacity is non-existent, and he had no role or function to perform, except to be allowed to repeat what the paranoiac saw in his imaginary world and what he said about it. Of this static imaginary world the paranoiac naturally believes to be the infallible interpreter. He believes that its meaning is, in effect, presented to him, once and for all, in the image he has put into words.

Apparently, however, someone spoke, and at least pretended to address another, just as he pretended to ask this other to constitute the truth with him, even if, at a deeper level, all this is illusory and constitutes a pseudo-speech coming from a pseudo-subject, destined for a pseudo-other. For, after all, the legal action brought by Mme. T. against her husband and the neighbor is perfectly real, as is the fact that she asked us to guarantee before the police commissioner the "arguments" and "proof" she had put forward, evidently taking our objections as null and void. The question remains: who is acting and who is speaking in such a case? The answer is the same again. It is the "mirror ego," who contemplates his image in the mirror, the proto-, or pre-subject, and who has discovered himself in his mirror-reflection and in the other, as a unity hitherto lacking in his experience. This hypothesis may allow us to understand paranoia a little better. An interpretation of Mme. T.'s statements and actions seems coherent when one allows that, for this patient, the subject, others, and the world have the meaning and the status of the mirror image. Let us recall that for the schizophrenic, regression and fixation take place in the period before the mirror phase. During that period the "subject" conceives of himself as *being* the mother's phallus. Whether the child is accepted or rejected as such by the mother, he is doomed to exist as a partial object. For the paranoiac, regression and fixation are less archaic, since he has attained an ideal unity and a self-identity corresponding to that unity. However, this paranoiac subject, the others he encounters and the world he lives in, remain all mutilated and truncated if one measures them, for example, with their corresponding structures at the level of the Oedipal experience. In no sense is this a subject who has *to become;* he simply is, as an image. The other is not *different* at all from the self; his otherness is really sameness: i.e., a projection of the subject, sustaining an ambivalence whose extent and origin we are already aware of. The world is not transcendent either. The world is not seen as having an inexhaustible horizon and thus need not be indefinitely explored. On the contrary, the world is regarded as a photograph without depth or mystery. Its "reality" is limited to setting the scene for the subject's aggression against the incarnation of his double. This aggression is then turned about by the paranoiac into persecution undergone. This last mechanism is but a defense against the original "I love her," which Freud explained in his study on Schreber.[17]

The example mentioned before provides an excellent illustration of this whole interpretation. Indeed, in accordance with the psychoanalytic point of view, the principal character in the drama experienced by Mme. T. is not her husband, but her rival, the neighbor. The former is described by the patient as an odd individual, unlikely to arouse passion, but naturally also unlikely to resist it if by chance another made her believe that she was someone's love-object. So Mme. T. thinks that it is out of pure perversity, without any feeling except the inextinguishable hatred towards her, that the neighbor seduced her husband. She has no objective but to steal him from the rightful owner, just as one steals an object. And the purpose is not to enjoy him, but to deprive the other of him. Moreover, Mme. T. readily acknowledges that she has never had any prior cause for complaint about her husband–whom she actually rules with an iron hand and treats as completely insignificant. However, everything has changed since the intrusion of the fatal neighbor (and intrusion is the correct word). The neighbor does not limit her persecution to stealing the husband. She continually disturbs Mme. T. in every way, particularly by throwing rubbish in her garden, or leaving it in front of her door (which forced Mme. T. to do the same, which in turn led to her confinement). So the patient had to be continually on her guard to prevent her enemy's enterprises. Although her deepest desire is just to mind her own business and live in peace with her neighbors ("ah, if it only depended on me . . ."), she is thus forced to continually spy on her rival, to "keep an eye on her" by watching her through the kitchen window. It was this spying that allowed her, as we have mentioned, to surprise the same neighbor who that morning changed clothes rather late. This in turn allowed the patient to gather her "evidence" of the adultery.

There is no need to comment on or to interpret this exemplary story. It gives a picture of all the clinical characteristics of paranoia. But one also sees how much they are clarified if read in the light of the intrusion complex, as described by Lacan in his article in the *Encyclopédie française*. There Lacan describes the intrusion complex as the disturbing correlative of and at the same time the test of the mirror phase. Aggression concerns another who is the same, the double in the mirror. If Mme T., to avenge herself, "replies" with

---

[17] See beginning of Ch. V of this study for a detailed explanation of this thesis of Freud.

cruelty, one can describe it as a display of sadism as much as of masochism. She also inflicts on herself (and on her husband as a secondary gain) an unbearable life. The obligation to vigilance is continual, uninterrupted by day or night. Her husband is worn out; the neighbors–for the neighbor has a husband, who never arises except as someone "to inform"–are driven to reprisals, and finally complain and obtain her confinement. There is no way to decide whether she strikes at the other or at herself or strikes herself through the other or the other through herself. Rather, there is an immediate transitivism between striking and being struck. Between the patient and her double, the degenerate bearer of the phallus to which the patient lays claim, there is a third, the marital object, a stake more symbolic than real, which is only there to ensure the "gravity" of the struggle. No less clear is the ambivalence of the aggression, and the camouflage of love as hatred. The homosexual desire associated with narcissism is perfectly evident, even if the person in question has not the least awareness of it (which is proper for unconscious mechanisms).[18] But no less significant is the existential horizon of the drama, if we may use this expression. Nothing is in doubt; everything is certain, proven, established. The meaning of every possible occurrence is clear, complete, given, not waiting for anything to come which might make it clearer, or diminish its importance, or obliterate it, or make it more serious; in the patient's view, it is perfectly evident to all of good faith. And nevertheless, none of the protagonists in the drama, as they are represented by the patient, and notwithstanding her unbounded passion, has any real existence; all embody images, good or bad, like caricatures. They have no consistency other than the one they draw from the meaning given them in her account. They can have no intentions but those they must display by virtue of this account; thus there is no mystery, no opacity, no shadow. There is no testimony which is expected from others which could verify, corroborate, a fortiori modify, complete or contest, whatever it may be as is evident from her often used final argument: "Because I tell you so . . . ." And there is no issue about her being *able* to tell the full and definite truth. As for us, our only role is to put an immediate end to the conspiracy plotted by the two lovers, who have had their victim locked up in a place where people try to make her appear mad. Our duty as gentleman, in the eyes of the patient, is to use our credit and "power" to convince the police commissioner, blinded by the charms and, "no doubt, the money" of her rival of the truth of her account.(10)

---

[18] The homosexuality discussed here is different from what De Waelhens calls "perverse homosexuality." See later under section V of this chapter: "Schizophrenia and Paranoia."

V. Schizophrenia and Paranoia

The previous descriptions of paranoia and its interpretation suggest a valid structural distinction between schizophrenia and paranoia. Although at first sight a paranoiac might appear to be like a psychotic, nevertheless, only one of the five constitutive elements of schizophrenia appears in the paranoid picture. This does not prevent that picture from also acquiring an intelligible structure as soon as it is related to the mirror phase. This is indeed the level at which the patient is fixated or towards which she has regressed. The one characteristic which is typical of schizophrenia and which seems also typical of paranoia is bisexuality. This should not be surprising. To begin with we know that, according to psychoanalysis, homosexuality is an essential element of paranoia. As has been explained, this homosexuality, or more precisely, this bisexuality is related to the mirror phase. It is clear that we are not discussing real, perverse homosexuality here. When Lacan stood up against the tendency displayed by some commentators (who were preceded on this point in some respects by Freud himself) to explain and understand, at least partially, Schreber's psychosis as a defense against homosexual drives, he hit upon an argument that we are concerned with here. Lacan's commentary on the case of Schreber made it clear that Schreber did not situate himself in relation to the difference between the sexes, that he thought of himself as a man and a woman at the same time. We have tried, following Lacan's view, to explain the possible meaning of this (implicit) affirmation on Schreber's part. For if reaching the Oedipal stage is the condition *sine qua non* for the subject to orient himself in relation to the difference between the sexes, it is clear that a fixation or return to the mirror phase excludes this orientation. Indeed, the mirror phase occurs prior to the establishment of the Oedipal constellation.

In conclusion, there remains one major difficulty. Is the concept of foreclosure, the key-concept of any interpretation of schizophrenia, applicable to paranoia or not? The question seems best approached through what has been said of the problem of the third as witness. Posed in relation to schizophrenia, the answer is evident: from the nature of the illness itself springs the nonexistence of a third as witness who is the guarantor of truth.

In principle, all reference to this third must be excluded from the experience of the schizophrenic. But we have seen that, at least in appearance, it is not quite the same for the paranoiac. For him, the reference is there, but it is also hopelessly distorted and truncated. The Other is not asked to collaborate in the search for, and establishment of truth, he is called to the *duty* of *ascertaining* it, as it is communicated to him by the patient, who systematically confuses his own position with that of the third–the third as witness of the truth. But if we accept, on the other hand, that the normative role of the third person which establishes the truth, finds its original prototypical guarantor in the father, as legislator of the Oedipal prohibition, our difficulty will become clearer. For we will find as a result of this comparison not only that this function can have no meaning for the schizophrenic–which only confirms a thesis already taken for granted–but also that this same function can only receive its full and complete scope through the Oedipal drama. Consequently, what intermediate status should be attributed to it in paranoia? This status can only be that of a witness as it is manifested specifically at the level of the mirror relationship, i.e., a witness without real otherness, without transcendence, who cannot embody the law of the other, because it does not come from a real other, but from another who is the same, who rejects all opacity. This other is ultimately the "subject" himself, or more precisely, his mirror-image.

VI. Paraphrenia

The term *paraphrenia* has even a vaguer meaning than the ones just considered. Nevertheless, no writer rejects it, and it turns up almost as often as the previous ones. Thus, we should try to find a useful and valuable meaning for it. One point will direct our efforts. However diverse its accepted uses may be, one constant factor appears in its use. No one employs it as a term for a psychosis of recent origin. To speak of paraphrenia is always to recognize or affirm that the patient to whom it is applied is not someone who has recently become psychotic. The term is used in this sense even if the circumstances of his admission do not provide biographical proof, not even provisionally. We conclude from this that the age of a psychosis must be ascertainable–as it in fact is–and that it plays a role in the definition of the specific traits of paraphrenia. How and why is this so? Let us proceed with the–apparently–well known concept of *deterioration,* which ordinarily carries great weight in the determination, the length of the illness. The fact is precisely that paraphrenics are, among longstanding psychotics, those who have–relatively speaking–undergone the least deterioration. In fact, what is decisive for the diagnosis is, on the one hand, the listless appearance of the delirium, the patient's relative indifference with regard to it, and its more or less total encystment. But on the other hand, just as decisive is its marked coherence–verging on systematization–the richness of its elements, and the *diplopia* which accompanies it. Indeed, the patient identifies himself fully with the role he has in his delirium, but this identification in no way prevents him from also being *somebody else,* i.e., the man as we see him.

Mme. van R., thinks that at the beginning of time she has cast down from heaven, God the Father, the "one called Mary," her spouse and their son Jesus. She succeeded in doing so only after a terrible struggle which remained undecided for several centuries. It was with the woman, wrongly called a "holy Virgin," that she experienced the most difficulty, to the point that she nearly gave in. Since her victory she owns heaven and rules the earth "in the name of heaven." This is an overwhelming and terrible task, which never gives her rest or respite, especially an account of the opinionated obstinacy of "great men," who seek to free themselves from her authority and to do only what they themselves decide. The most arduous task is to force General de Gaulle into submission, and she is afraid of having to take "extreme measures" against him someday. Mme. Van R. engendered herself by bringing together two leaves of a tree. She cannot name the tree because it involves an atomic secret which is kept in a refrigerator. She used the same procedure to beget her only son. They are the only two beings who were procreated in this way. She revealed the secret to her son so that he could use it on behalf of his daughter, the patient's grandchild. But the son rebelled and disobeyed, preferring to use his wife, "to be like everyone else." She had to punish this insult against heaven and use "extreme measures." So she "had her son die" and buried him in the cemetery at Schaerbeek, in "a new plot" (sic), until he would consent to procreation by leaves, of which he would be the sole beneficiary. If he submits, she will resurrect him–something he has no need of, since he is in perfect health. The Jews constitute another major concern. She must prevent them from gaining an unfair advantage because of the reactions of sympathy brought about by the excesses of antisemitism which in her eyes they themselves provoked with this aim in mind. In fact, the patient's husband is a Jew, and it seems that the marriage has brought her no satisfaction.

This extravagant account, considerably abbreviated here, had a more prosaic, but no less surprising conclusion. When the interview was at an end, the doctor heard her say: "Doctor, please help me. If only I could sleep. My rheumatism makes me suffer terribly–day and night. I think that at the time of my last attack, salicylate gave me some relief."[19] Some time later, the patient was informed that her husband, stricken with cancer, was at death's door. She appeared to be greatly affected by this, asked to visit him and spent a few days at home, although the same husband, at least in delirium, had always been represented as a detestable and detested character. She showed him great tenderness and was deeply sorrowed by his death. During his last days she made no allusion to the heavenly government. When the funeral ceremonies were over, everything reappeared just as before, and she had to be readmitted to the hospital immediately.

This person, having a long psychiatric past, was unanimously considered paraphrenic, and it is easily seen how everyone accepting such a concept will agree in applying it to her. But, on the other hand, it would be correct to add that she fulfilled the criteria of schizophrenia, as they have been described above, equally well; the account we have given is certainly enough to make this assertion very plausible. And, nevertheless, those two terms are not simply synonymous. Schizophrenia is different from paraphrenia. But why and how is this so?

[19] The realism displayed in this quote shows that Mme. von R. lives in two worlds: the one of her physical pains which she can relate to in a realistic way, and the other world of her delirium. She is a split person.

First let us point out that the patient's statements are presented in the form of an organized and, if we may say so, coherent *account*. By this, I mean that the most fantastic actions and facts are given motivation, are connected, explained, and justified in it. On the other hand, all apparent reference to some founding and "fertile moment" which would have made the illness suddenly irrupt is absent. And in all probability it would have been very difficult to find a trace of it. In any case, we did not have the opportunity to attempt to find it. The account, apart from a few details, does not change. It is more like a fantastic story more or less learned by heart, than the expression of someone in full delirium. The patient's affective "participation" in her speech is relatively slight, though not nonexistent.(11) "She is more moved by the account she gives of her rheumatic pains than by speaking of the centuries-old struggle she must wage, in a long and doubtful combat, to clear heaven of its first occupants. Her posture is more like that of a naive popular actor performing a scene than like the behavior of the speaker herself relating a serious event not yet reduced, or elevated to the level of legend. The best example would be a very popular, rather stereotyped ballad, full of ready-made expressions (borrowed) from sporting or military jargon, picturesque though banal. Frequently, real elements are inserted: General de Gaulle's "obstinacy," and the fact that burial in the old cemetery at Schaerbeek is forbidden are amusing examples.

The general effect of this discourse is thus noticeably different from that of a similar account produced by a patient in the acute stage of schizophrenia, or who has recently emerged from it. Making allowances for the patient's intellectual level, her pathological "situation" seems close enough to Schreber's at the time his book was written. At that moment, Schreber had passed beyond the time period in which his delirium was created. But if Schreber happened to correct some of his former convictions he is no longer quite certain of having died and thinks rather that his persecutors gave him the idea that he was dead while in reality he was not–we have not been able to establish anything similar in Mme. Van R.'s case.

In fact it appears as if the paraphrenic is trying, with varying degrees of success, to *encyst* his delirium, without however repudiating it. This creates the appearance of diplopia with regard to the paraphrenic's attitude towards people and things. Needless to say, the paraphrenic is not and cannot even be surprised at this diplopia. For there is little sense in asking oneself how the mistress of Heaven and the Universe can suffer from rheumatism, or why she, who could kill and revive her own son to teach him obedience, is nonetheless bound to observe a communal regulation concerning burial. It is no more amazing than the story of a former tribunal president who believes himself called–and proclaims it in a book–to regenerate the universe by procreating together with God a new race of men, but who proves to be a pleasant conversationalist at meals, and who rules correctly on the legal disputes arising in his family.

No doubt the delirium persists and performs the dual function which, thanks to Freud's findings, we have attributed to it: first, it restores, although only in an imaginary way, some investment in reality, and second, it assures the subject's narcissistic satisfaction. But the alleviation of anguish has to some extent (greater for Schreber than for Mme. Van R.) allowed the reestablishment of what we have called *learnt,* as opposed to *understood*[20] speech. The *learnt* speech comes from a world where one worries about rheumatism, and reads in the newspaper that General de Gaulle is an inflexible man. And the patient also applies the formal rules of this *learnt* speech to her delirium, in a way comparable to the secondary elaboration of a dream which is designed to make the dream itself as coherent as possible. But it would be mistaken to conclude that what is involved in this learnt speech is the common world we are in. For to the patient there is no I, no other, no world or reality, in the *proper* sense of these words. To put it simply, repeating Mme. Dolto's image, the schizophrenic talks about the real the way a blind man talks about colors. This does not necessarily imply that what he says about it is false, but, in any case, he does not know the truth of the matter, because truth has disappeared for him. So he sees no antimony between the learnt discourse or set of discourses he holds, and the inapplicability of the rules of this discourse to his delirious "discourse." The patient "knows," for example, that all discourse must be subject to the judgment of the third as witness, that is, that it must be presented as in principle susceptible to verification. She "knows" that if someone says it is raining, everyone else is equally bound to say it is raining. But as the patient is completely situated outside the dimension of testimony, to which she pretends to submit, this means only that she *believes* the others agree with her remarks, which they repeat, or ought to repeat, just as she makes them, without otherwise being in the least concerned with the world. The dialectic of the third as witness of the truth, and guarantor of the spoken word does not operate at all here, and an occasional reference to it only points to *learnt discourse.*

VII. Manic-Depressive Psychosis

The reader may decide whether the preceding pages have contributed some useful details for a systematic and structurally defined use of the terms schizophrenia, paranoia and paraphrenia.

At this point one could move on to study what is undoubtedly another of the so-called non-organic psychoses: the manic-depressive psychosis. We are not going to do this, but will reserve the subject for another publication. Our restraint is dictated by lack of certainty. We do not feel able to satisfactorily justify an idea that we would like to defend, i.e., the manic-depressive psycho-

---

[20]   Italics of 'understood' is ours (W.V.E.).

sis must be explained quite differently from the way we have explained the other forms of psychoses. Whereas the other psychoses challenge, in the most radical fashion, a person's being-in-the-world, this is not quite the case with the manic-depressive psychosis. Certainly, in order to understand this latter psychosis, Freud made reference to the pre-Oedipal phases of the subject's development, in a way similar to those references he made with regard to other psychoses. But what seems at stake are not the ultimate, decisive moments of the constitution of the subject. The melancholic and the manic seem to live in a world which is identical to our world. The radical fault we believe we have revealed in the other forms of psychosis (schizophrenia, paranoia, paraphrenia)–the failure of primal repression, the failure to gain access to the symbolic, the foreclosure of the name-of-the-father, and the exclusion or distortion of the third as witness (so many different approaches to the same failure) is, no doubt, absent in the manic-depressive. We would see his condition rather as being above all a change in the *Befindlichkeit,* '(ontological) disposition,' and in certain modes of temporalization. It puts *thumos,* 'the spirited part of the soul in Plato,' in question. This is questioning more than *thymie,* 'the state of being angry', in the narrow sense, but perhaps less than questioning the being-subject as such (at least if we mean by this the absolutely ultimate constituents of being a subject).

It is very possible that Binswanger has revealed the essential features of the manic-depressive personality.

Now we can begin the final part of our task, which consists of reflecting on the possible contribution of the foregoing to a philosophical anthropology.

NOTES

(1) It is clear that a phrase as "I have been dead a thousand years" can receive conjointly the interpretation which Freud and Lacan give when commenting on the section of Schreber's book in which he reports his death and funeral as a past event.

(2) We know that Freud, in speaking of Schreber, used almost interchangeable the terms schizophrenia, paraphrenia, and paranoia. We have already considered this point, and we will deal with it even more later on in connection with a comparison of the latter two concepts.

(3) We are using the word metaphor here in a more general sense than the one employed by Lacan or the linguists. We mean by it the *transferral (metaferein)* inherent in the usage of all linguistic behavior, as it is described, for instance, in Freud's example of the child with the spool.

(4) Mme. Gisela Pankow, whose remarkable works on the therapy of psychotics are well-known, works wich make great use of the concepts of the dismembered and disassociated body, writes in regard to the image of the body: "The dissociation of the body image can appear in different ways: either a part plays the role of a whole body in such a way that it (the body can still be recognized and experienced as a limited body; or one finds the confusion, proper to psychosis, between the interior and the exterior.

Hence, parts of the body-image might appear in the external world in the form of voices or visual hallucinations. *Therefore, I define the term dissociation as the destruction of the body-image in such a way that its parts lose their connection with the whole and reappear in the external world.*

This lack of correlation between the interior and the exterior is a characteristic of schizophrenia; there are no associative links which permit the rediscovery of meaningful connections between the fragments of such a splintered world. For example, the methods which are used to help the neurotic to understand the conflicts which he has, so to speak, projected onto his environment, cannot be employed in the case of the schizophrenic. For, prior to being able to recognize an interior conflict at the heart of his projection onto the external world, the schizophrenic would have to be capable of knowing *who* he is. That is to say, he would have to know that he must recover his fragmented body and unify it." *L'Homme et sa psychose*, p. 121-2.

(5)   We are well aware that one cannot deny the fact that I can be alone in knowing certain truths. On the contrary, it is unthinkable that such a truth must be, in principle, inaccessible to others.

(6)   P. Demoulin. *Névrose et Psychose*, p. 125.

(7)   We have explained above the sense in which linguists understand this term.

(8)   Demoulin, *op. cit.*, p. 126.

(9)   *Ibid.*, p. 127.

(10)   The analysis of the following case gives another exemplary illustration of our understanding of paranoia. The patient T. is a young man, twenty-two years old, employed by a heavy construction firm. He comes to the interview voluntarily because he expects to receive some medicine which will give him the psychic power to prevail in the face of the persecutions to which he is being subjected, and to which he is at the point of succumbing. He adds that, if he doesn't receive help, he will kill his persecutor rather than give up the struggle.

This all began about eight months prior to his visit. He was then a member of the parish choir. At one point, the position of the parish organist became vacant. The patient proposed his candidacy because, he said, "he had *the right* to play the pastor's organ." The pastor didn't consider him at all for the position, for the apparently valid reason that he couldn't play that or any other instrument. His pretentiousness surprised us. "I was," he says, "all set to learn how to play, since I have the right to play the pastor's organ." There was no other basis for that right than the *fact* that he *had* the rights! He was furious at not being appointed and therefore quit the choir. This, however, did not bring him good luck, for, at the end of several weeks, he noticed the "bizarre" attitude of people towards him. This gave him the idea that he pastor had undertaken a campaign to discredit him. Notably, (since he was, at the time, in the service), he read on the face of his Colonel that the pastor telephoned many times each day to ruin his military reputation. No one said anything to him, nor did he overhear anything explicit. Yet, it was clear, certain, evident: the pastor "discredited" him everywhere, and with success. After enduring this torture in silence for some time, he decided to return to the choir, hoping in this way to disarm the pastor's persecution. For the same end he spent four hundred francs every Saturday socially entertaining members of the parish. Nothing came of this, and it made him, I dare say, quite disappointed. The pastor increased his persecution to the point where, day and night, the parish spoke of him in the most offensive terms. He was the only topic of conversation. At this point in his story, he interrupted himself and addressed me directly: "Professor, I am going to summarize all of this for you. The heart of the matter (*de kern van de zaak*) is this. The pastor is giving me the run around. (*de pastoor spelt met mijn kl . . .).*" I remarked that, in effect, this summarized everything, but he had the *right* to play the pastor's organ. He didn't react to my remark. I then made one more attempt to learn what the pastor could say about him. He pretended to absolutely ignore this, but I didn't know whether he was sincere or whether the truth was so shameful in his eyes that he loathed to repeat it to me. I inquired whether it had to do with his attitude towards some female member of the congregation. He answered, in a haughty fashion, that he wasn't dreaming of getting married yet. From all appearances, as I expected, there was nothing to look for along that line. As I continued to press him, he answered briskly: "You know that the pastor can always invent something new." (*De pastoor kan toch alle dagen iets anders uit zijn duim zuigen*).

(11) Where someone made the remark that he had no children and that he intended to make use of the method of the two leaves, she reacted vividly and said: "I am sorry. Although you give the impression of being a gentle person, you have just signed your own eternal damnation because of your sacrilege."

Chapter Seven

EXISTENTIAL ELUCIDATION OF THE
UNCONSCIOUS AND OF PSYCHOSIS

De Waelhens

I. Introduction
The Disappearance of the Primacy of Consciousness
(Kant, Hegel, Husserl, Heidegger, Merleau-Ponty)[1]

Whenever a philosopher asserts that a human being is in the world as a king in his kingdom, it must be regarded as a pious wish expressing the most tenacious illusion of the mind and of the rationalist tradition, or from another standpoint, perpetuating a more archaic illusion. Such omnipotence, if it existed at all, could only result from the absolute primacy of reason. Should this primacy itself be an illusion, nothing will ever make a human being omnipotent. It is thus that philosophy confronts the problem of the status of reason.[2]

For a long time, more obscurity than light was shed upon this problem. For it is perhaps not quite accurate to say that modem philosophy has been dominated by the notion of consciousness, if this notion is held to be univocal. For most of the classical authors until Kant, the idea of consciousness hides more or less a dualistic position which distinguishes sensibility on the one hand and understanding or thought on the other.[3] This concealed dichotomy, insofar as it generates confusion and equivocation, favors the sense of imperial primacy that philosophy has given to the human person. For sensibility, in the twofold sense of the term, will constitute what one might call the low ebb of consciousness, which thus becomes ill suited for a majestic and overpowering navigation, for which an empire of the seas is better suited. It is undoubtedly said: *"nihil est in intellectu quod non prius fuerit in sensu,"* but the modern philosopher hastens to add, if he accepts the adage, *"praeter intellectum ip-*

---

[1] In this introductory section, De Waelhens discusses the development of European philosophy since Kant. The purpose of this survey is to show that discourse is replacing the Cartesian cogito as the crucial concept by which philosophy characterizes human consciousness. The introduction of the concept of discourse means that philosophy discovers and affirms that a human being is always and necessarily present to unrevealed levels of meaning.

[2] For an interesting survey of the relation between the central themes of psychoanalysis and the important philosophical systems since Descartes, see: G. Lantéri-Laura, "Les problèmes de l'inconscient et la pensée phénoménologique."

[3] Kant made this dichotomy explicit: see: *Critique of Pure Reason*, A 137 1 10-17; A 141 1 1-2: A 142 1 7-9.

sum."[4] "It can be seen already that the best stimulus for an illusion is the obstinate contempt of origins."[5] Therefore, it is not surprising that the historically most important school of philosophers in the Kantian tradition would have taken upon itself the task of reducing, as much as possible, the split of consciousness which Kant had made manifest and unavoidable.

It is remarkable that the author of the first attempt directed at recovering the origin was Hegel. There is an explicit clarification of this issue in the *Phenomenology of Mind,* where he shows that consciousness, Spirit, and knowledge shall only be truly unified once every dichotomy of the sensibility and of the concept is ruthlessly rejected at the level of the totality.[6]

It is Hegel then who truly grounds and justifies the primacy of consciousness in modern philosophy. He has done this, however, by explicitly bringing together consciousness and discourse, one of the outcomes of which is an identification of ontology with dialectic.[7] Such reconciliation provides invaluable advantages but is loaded with pitfalls as well. Its value is to consecrate the final downfall of the dualism of sensibility and of thought. In the strictest sense, discourse is in effect the interplay of both, the infinite return from one to the other. It is also, but this will only appear after Hegel, the attribution of an essential form of ambiguity to consciousness. For discourse, insofar as it has not yet been transformed into absolute knowledge, cannot and should not ever be absolutely transparent for the person who holds it. The danger lies in that the identification of the human person with consciousness (meant to become self consciousness and then spirit), and that of consciousness with discourse, leads to the dismissal of everything "outside" such discourse and unavoidably results in the promulgation of absolute knowledge. Within the Hegelian perspective, however, this is certainly not a risk but rather a truth which is to be made evident–a position for which Hegelianism is fa-

---

[4]   The first part *"Nihil est in intellectu "* is part of the philosophical tradition as it was transmitted in textbooks. Arguing against Descartes, Locke, and others who are using this proposition within a different philosophical framework than the ancients, Leibniz wrote: *excipe: nisi ipse intellectus (Nouveaux Essais sur l'Entendement,* Livre II, Ch. 1, 12).

[5]   Arguing against Locke and the British empiricists who confused thoughts with the psychological processes which allow thought (sensible impressions, associations, etc.) Leibniz argued for the autonomy of thought and in the process made it impossible to ask developmental questions about the possibility of thinking.

[6]   Indeed, Hegel argues dialectically for his own philosophical position; this requires that he presents the main philosophical positions and cultural views of the Western civilization; it further requires that he shows these views or positions to be onesided in the sense that their thought is different than their actual experience; finally, it requires that Hegel show how the history of thought comes to an end with Hegel's "Absolute Knowledge," because thought and actual experience coincide. Hegel, *Phenomenology*, p. 97, 133, 135, 140, 142, 789ff.

[7]   This problem is elaborated upon in: Mortimer J. Adler; *Dialectic,* Part 11. 3, p. 200ff.

mous. If we speak of risk, then, it is only because certain authors,[8] whom we will later discuss, and who have resumed the identification of the human person with discourse with a different meaning than the Hegelian one, have great difficulty in avoiding the transformation of this discourse into a new version of the absolute knowledge which conflicts with their anthropological position.

The temporary disappearance of the Hegelian star from the philosophical firmament since 1840[9] does not, however, entail the obliteration of a certain primacy of consciousness, although the dull ambiguities of the epistemology prevailing during this period obscured this primacy. For the latter exists only because of the emphasis on the concept of subjectivity. This concept, however, was strongly undermined in all its aspects by the world of science, which alone was considered true and fully real.

From this standpoint, the appearance of phenomenology constitutes a new and essential mutation.[10] Under its Husserlian form, it confirms, although on grounds very different from the Hegelian ones, the elimination of the dualism we have discussed. This elimination is made by means of a radical modification of one of the oldest concepts used in philosophical reflection: perception. The notion of perception is completely "de-psychologized" by Husserl; it is detached from the distinction between the sensible and the intellectual, and provided with a central function in the relation of the conscious subject to reality.[11] One could go as far as saying that in a sense, it *is* this relationship itself, and that it defines it. Perception is not to be "controlled" by a more eminent function of the real; on the contrary, it posits the norms for all possible controls to which other modes of our relation to reality should be subordinated.

One is therefore justified in maintaining that this broadening of the concept of perception prepares the way for the introduction of the typically Heideggerian notion of being-in-the-world.[12] Equally important, both for itself and

---

8   It is not unlikely that De Waelhens has Lacan in mind. See Lacan's statement: "The omnipresence of the human discourse will perhaps one day be embraced under the open sky of an omnicommunication of its texts" (Wilden, *The Language*, p. 27).

9   For a history of the appreciation and interpretation of Hegel since his death in 1831, see: Avineri: "Hegel revisited."

10   On this point see De Waelhens: "Réflexions sur une problématique Husserlienne de l'inconscient, Husserl et Hegel."

11   Indeed, for Husserl perception is seen to be the ultimate foundation for all kinds of conscious acts. Thus, memory is founded upon past perception; imagination is an "as if perception;" judgment is tributary to perception for its truth. For good examples, see his: *Experience and Judgment*. This same idea is present under a different form in the *Cartesian Meditations*, p. 38. There he argues that any active synthesis of consciousness must be grounded in a prior passive synthesis (=perceptual activity).

12   Two excellent book-length commentaries on Heidegger's philosophy are: A. De Waelhens *La philosophie de Martin Heidegger*, W. Richardson, *Heidegger*. De

for its consequences, is the mutation imposed on the idea of time or temporality. We will essentially retain two elements from it. First, temporality ceases to be conceived as external to that-which-is-temporal–before Husserl, Hegel and Bergson are almost the only ones to take some steps, although uneven ones, in this direction[13]–and becomes the unfolding itself of that which is being temporalized: thing, perception, image, project, or world. The correlate which follows is that there are as many modes of temporalization as there are types or modes of being which become temporal. Finally, all temporalization is derived from an original temporality which is that of the conscious subject, or, in Heidegger, of the Dasein. The idea of time is thereby endowed with a role no previous philosophy had ever ascribed to it, and, particularly, it ceases to be the index of all distinction between the being which is totally or partially "spiritual"and the one which is qualified as material. In contrast, Husserl's phenomenology represents a relative regression of the notion of discourse, at least insofar as discourse is distinguished from logos. Finally, intentionality, just as much as the primacy of perception, confers upon that which one still calls the subject, a proximity to things unparalleled in the history of philosophy.

Nevertheless, it is still true that, according to Husserl, the change in perspective to which we previously alluded, concerns primarily the problem of knowing. It is also on this point that the subsequent investigations of this philosophical reform, known as phenomenology, shall essentially concentrate.

For this purpose we can limit ourselves to the Heidegger of *Sein und Zeit*, and some of the other early writings. Nevertheless, from another point of view, Heidegger's subsequent work would be very relevant for the study of our problem. We shall abstain from using this source for the moment, since the later Heidegger remains little or badly known by the authors who have played an active role in the confrontations we intend to consider.

There are at least three theses of *Sein und Zeit* which must be stressed here. The first is the eclipse, or rather, the disappearance, of the notion of consciousness. The philosopher's reflection centers instead upon the Dasein, or, as it is expressed in certain texts of the *Kantbuch,* upon the *"Dasein-in-man."* Consciousness *(Bewusstsein) is* a word almost absent from Heidegger's vocabulary. He replaces it by the expression: 'Dasein' which means disclosedness, revelation *(Erschlossenheit)* or light *(lumen naturale).* This entails simultaneously the explicit abolition of the primacy of knowledge as such, and of its privileges.(1)

Waelhens wrote also an article describing Heidegger's development "Reflexions on Heidegger's Development." Richardson wrote an article "The place of the unconscious in Heidegger."

[13] A very clear and useful article on the problem of time in Husserl is the one by J. Brough: "The emergence of an absolute consciousness in Husserl's early writings on time-consciousness."

The second thesis is the identification of Dasein with discourse, which is strongly emphasized by Heidegger. And if this discourse is essentially *logos*, it is only indirectly the conceptualizing and judging *logos* favored by a certain Aristotelian tradition. Furthermore, revealing discourse, which is typical for human beings, entails different modalities of disclosure, of which truth in the classical sense, is only one possibility among others. The non-transparency of discourse for him who holds it is again preeminent. This is why the constitution of a hermeneutics of discourse is a major task for the philosopher. In order to begin to understand the meaning of 'revealing discourse' one can compare it with two very different conceptions of truth as "αληΘεια," i.e., originating disclosure opening up the possibility of saying anything whatsoever. On the other hand, there is the conception of truth as adequacy of judgment with the thing judged. This adequacy is but an application made possible by the first conception of truth. One knows that the theory of adequacy, as understood for instance by the mediaeval period, is liable to serious confusion.

Finally, we can cite the well known fact that Husserl's intentionality is transformed by Heidegger into care *(Sorge)*. Indeed, Heidegger considers care as being the prime characteristic of Dasein.

These acquisitions are sustained and sometimes reinforced in the works of Merleau-Ponty. This is particularly evident in the way in which the author of the *Phenomenology of Perception* conceives of the idea of behavior, even if the term, in the context of contemporary psychology can lend itself to unfortunate ambiguities.[14] The notion of behavior, according to Merleau-Ponty, further stresses the identification of a human person with discourse as well as the non-transparency of this discourse for the one who delivers it. The idea that the meaning established by a discourse is not necessarily, and in a certain sense never, the meaning uttered, leads us into the core of contemporary anthropology. Even if the metapsychological foundation of this non-transparency can be differently understood, the fact itself suffices to demolish the alleged omnipotence of consciousness, for whose defense the philosopher has been so bitterly reproached.

Nevertheless, what Merleau-Ponty shows us about the behavior discourse diverges considerably from the classical *logos*, and even from the Heideggerian logos. Indeed, discourse for Merleau-Ponty is *embodied* logos. This embodiment is to be related to his concept of 'flesh,' which shows that embodiment is an essential characteristic of discourse, *not just an 'alleged' one.*

If it is therefore typical for the human Dasein to be always, and under all circumstances, meaning-giving and meaningful (namely, he speaks and he provokes speech), this does not amount in the least to claiming that such being

---

[14] For a short sketch of the relation between the two books of Merleau-Ponty: *Phenomenology of Perception* and *The Structure of Behavior*, see the Foreword of A. De Waelhens to the latter, p. XXIVff. This passage also delineates Merleau-Ponty's usage of the word "behavior."

is aware of what it signifies. Whence the tasks of a dialectic between actual and intended meaning are announced, or, according to the language commonly used after Freud, between latent meaning and manifest meaning. One will obviously avoid holding these two pairs of expressions to be simply synonymous. The distance between their components, between the actual and the intended, on the one hand, the latent and the manifest on the other, is not of the same nature. In the first case it is the disparity between speech and word which is constitutive of all language and related to the difference between the verb and the concept. In the second case, there is a distance which originates in the need to mask an unconscious that can neither be repressed nor uttered. In each case the elaboration of the meaning, which has its limits, is only the outcome of a dialectic and of a complementarity.

In addition, the constitution of the behavior-discourse as well as its interpretation can only take place through the insertion of the speaker into a language which dominates him to a greater extent than it is mastered by him. The question of the status of subjectivity, of the subject, of the speaker, arises then. Merleau-Ponty–and with him all the authors inspired by phenomenology–will henceforth refuse to separate the use of language from a tension between language and the speaking subject, wherein, precisely, discourse, insofar as it is *my* discourse, appears.

* * *

We are led to believe that the philosophical theses which we have briefly alluded to–they are, in effect, well known–may constitute a valid starting point for the reflections we shall presently undertake.

II. Preliminary Considerations on the Unconscious, Language, and Reality

1. The Unconscious and Language

A. Freud

Freud himself considered the discovery of the unconscious and the affirmation of its priority to be the most fundamental contribution of psychoanalysis. Subsequent developments have sufficiently shown that these theses are liable to different interpretations. Some have been willing to find in them the assertion of the radically illusory character of consciousness.[15] However, how can one

---

[15] Ricoeur compares the work of Freud with that of Marx and Nietzsche *(The Conflict of Interpretations, p.* 148ff). All affirm the illusory character of consciousness. They replace its primacy by the unconscious (Freud), the economic order (Marx) or the will to power (Nietzsche). One could add Lohmann who argues for the primacy of language *(Philosophie und Sprachwissenschaften).*

maintain that psychoanalysis is a therapy, or a method of investigation, or a body of doctrines related to metapsychology–and psychoanalysis is all of these–and maintain that the unconscious retains always and in every respect its absolute opacity?

B. Politzer

Another interpretation–made famous by Politzer–attempts to reduce a text to its meaning, and the unconscious to its conscious apprehension. In this view the unconscious would be comparable to the rules of grammar and syntax in ordinary discourse. In a sense, one must recognize that there are in effect rules which direct, constitute and dominate our utterances, without, however, our being aware of applying them when we speak. We believe that we say what we like to say, although it is the mechanism of language which forces us to say what we say. But this unconscious is only provisional, and, in a way, operational. I can know, or at least, one can know the rules of grammar and of syntax. The unconscious is thereby recovered, and represents nothing but a moment of discourse or of behavior. It is unnecessary to believe in the reality of such an unconscious, to make of it a real instance of psychic life.

This interpretation accounts for everything by eliminating the problem. But in the first place, it is not certain that we can be exhaustively aware of the mechanism of discourse. Politzer's thesis assumes that such mechanism is a system of fixed rules, and, at least provisionally, a closed system, the knowledge of which would guarantee our mastery and our possession of it. In fact, this is not at all the case, and the mentioned knowledge is only knowledge of its common use at a given moment, without normative character for the use of these rules or for their future development. We therefore do not understand them absolutely. Besides, and in spite of even more serious objections, Politzer's conception is based upon the cleavage of thought (or discourse) and its form. But there is no content of discourse which is not already completely engaged in the activity of the grammatical and syntactical mechanism of the language in which we think. Such breach is literally inconceivable: there is no thought without language, and the rules of discourse are always already operative in every thought.

On the basis of such equivocal arguments, Politzer would like to persuade us that the unconscious–insofar as it is the real locus of the psychic universe–*"is but an abstraction of psychoanalysis which concrete psychology allows to survive."*(2)

The unconscious is then nothing but a thought actually unavailable to the subject. This interpretation, however, misses the essential point of Freud's theory. The Freudian unconscious is preoccupied with something other than the form, and cannot be confused with the preconscious. The unconscious is not merely reducible to the dialectics of meaning or to the unavailabilities entailed by this dialectical interplay.[16] We have repeatedly stressed it: beyond or prior to meaning in language there is the letter which is the carrier of this meaning. And the system of letters is regulated by strict requirements which are simply unavailable in the same way as the meaning itself. The question then becomes whether the only alternatives for explaining discourse are: a theory for which the discourse unfolds at the level of the thing or a theory for which the discourse unfolds in the first person? Freud's discovery, is it not precisely– under the term of thoughts of dreams– a discourse which can un- fold "in person" without being, however, in the form of the first person but rather under the alienated forms of the second or the third person? The subject of discourse, even if it is just a grammatical subject, is nevertheless still a subject: when "the id speaks" in the unconscious, one certainly finds again the dramatical unity cherished by Politzer, although the drama does not necessar- ily unfold in the "first person." One wonders whether perhaps it is not charac- teristic of unconscious structures to include other voices than that of the "first person."(3) There is also, besides the dialectic of meaning, an intrinsic move- ment of the one or many signifiers–just as in conscious discourse words take us beyond the meaning we would like to limit ourselves to give them–and which prevents the passing over of the latent meaning and the manifest meaning into one another completely, as is the case–and this is again an ex- ample given by Politzer–with the theme of a play in its text. The rejection of Politzer's interpretation does not, however, imply the dismissal of all dialectic in the relations between the conscious and the unconscious. It must neverthe- less be differently conceived.

C. Lacan: Two Definitions of the Unconscious
To this effect, and by way of introduction to the following pages, we would like to refer briefly to two of Lacan's well known theses, which we have dis- cussed already with regard to other issues: the unconscious is structured like a language; the unconscious is the discourse of the Other.

a. The Unconscious is the Discourse of the Other
Both the conscious and the unconscious stem from language. Indeed, dis- course which includes my spoken and unspoken communication to the Other, in order to gain recognition from him, embraces not just my conscious dis- course but also my unconscious discourse, as is clear from Lacan's definition of the latter when he writes that: "the unconscious is that part of concrete dis- course, insofar as it is transindividual, which is not at the disposition of the subject in order to reestablish the continuity of his conscious discourse."(4)

A human person can be defined as a being capable of speaking. As such he

---

[16] A similar argument is used against phenomenologists who want to see the Freudian unconscious as an extension of the "unthematized horizon" of phenomenology. For a survey of that debate, see: Ricoeur: *Freud and Philosophy*, p. 375ff.

is not anything, in the sense that one says the table is round, or the meadow is square.[17] A human person must talk in order to signify himself. But if he truly speaks, he cannot do so in order to give himself permanent content or to give himself being through the bias of the word. Since therefore the subject does not attain, as subject, any quality or determination, all the meaning that discourse establishes of myself requires, in order to be true, the recognition of the other.[18] This is the starting point of the concern for truth and of the threat of a trap as well. We know that the subject may attempt to use his discourse fallaciously in order to construct a certain image of himself, which makes him determinate, like the sky is blue. He then transmits this image, and expects the other to authenticate it by returning it back to him such as he had imagined it. In this way, he shall finally be "as eternity formed him." This is a deadly illusion, for "in this effort that he (the speaking subject) makes of reconstructing it (the glorified self-image) for another, he finds again the fundamental alienation which has made him construct it (the image) as another, and which has always predestined it to be taken away from him by another."(5)[19]

By identifying himself with the image he constructs of himself, the subject mistakes himself for another, since we are not an image for ourselves. Indeed, only the other is properly an image for us. Finally, the subject, already alienated in his own image, prepares himself for the certainty of additional alienation which consists in binding himself in advance to the image which the other will reflect of him. The paradigm example of this would be offered by a phenomenological study of a "celebrity" or a "star."

It may happen that the silence of the other, refusing thereby the seal of authentification, forces the subject to further 'objectify' himself, to exhaust himself in the exhibition of his own and disowned image, in order to impose at all costs this recognition which he hopes will free him from the difficulty of existing. But this will have a disastrous result (which could, however, prove redeeming by its very excess), namely, that the speaker will get increasingly entangled in those parts of the discourse which break the continuity of his utterance and the beautiful harmony of his image, which he does not understand and the disposition of which he lacks, since they are in him the discourse of another. The liar is thereby forced to multiply his lies—and their incoherence as well—for he is progressively confronted with the verification of the real and

---

[17] This difference between the human-being-as-subject and things has been stressed even to the point of exaggeration by the German idealists or the contemporary existentialists. The human subject was in these traditions thought of as being self-constituting.

[18] This idea goes back to Hegel in the famous analysis of the master-slave dialectic of the *Phenomenology,* (especially p. 231).

[19] The importance of the other in the construction of one's life is developed in: W. Ver Eecke: "Symbol as a philosophical concept." The defensive relation towards the other leads to imaginary constructs. The positive relation leads to the symbolic order.

with the demands of truth–these are for him the discourse of the other–until the final collapse occurs. "Isn't the subject engaged in a progressive dispossession of this being of himself. Indeed, the sincere pictures he tries to give of himself fail to present a coherent idea of him. Furthermore, the rectifications fail to disengage his essence, because butresses and defenses cannot prevent his statue from tilting, and thus his narcissistic embraces become his animating breath. Finally he must end up by recognizing that this being never was anything other than his construction in the imaginary, and that this construction deceives every certainty in him."(6)

This would be one way–even though a preliminary one–of understanding that the unconscious is the discourse of the other.

Strictly speaking, however, this discourse of the other in us superimposes different layers which have to be accurately relocated.

The 'other' is still, as we have already mentioned, the "transindividuality" of discourse, in the sense that the subject is accessible to himself only through a universal which he can never hope to master or to dispose of. One could, on the other hand, insist on the fact that all discourse or behavior whereby the subject signifies himself (which means all discourse or behavior) can only be constituted in the element of the universal, and is consequently grounded on bereavement and frustrations. To point to oneself as "I" is to acquire the means to posit oneself as a pole of unification or of identity to which all of my experience can be related. However, in saying it, I identify myself with what is most universal as well, since everyone else uses this same pronoun in order to identify himself.

Furthermore, one could take this "transindividuality" to express the predominance of the signifier over the signified which will carry my discourse (turned thereby into a discourse of the other) beyond that which conscious thought desires to give it as meaning. "The signifier needs no cogitation, not even the least reflexive one, in order to strikingly transform the significations which dominate the life of the subject; further yet: the signifier manifests itself in the patient through this alienating intrusion which in psychoanalysis is appropriately designated by the concept of symptom. This latter concept thus testifies to the existence of a relation between the subject and the signifier."(7) This primacy will make us admit that a psychoanalyst must hold fast to what is evident, i.e., that, already before his birth and still after his death, a human being is caught in the symbolic chain which has founded the lineage before history is embroidered on it. The psychoanalyst must get used to the idea that a human being is indeed in his very being, in the totality of his personality, caught as a whole, but in the manner of a pawn, in the game of the signifier, and caught before the rules are transmitted to him, even if he eventually discovers them. These priorities must be understood as logical ones, that is, priorities which are always actual."(8)

The preceding observations do not yet exhaust the truth which relates the unconscious to the discourse of the other. This "discourse of the other" is also

260

the sediment, in the speaker, of the real or imaginary (but censured) vicissitudes of his relationship to constituting others.

These vicissitudes are symbolically imprinted in the symptoms "–in the monuments: and this is my body, namely, the hysterical kernel of neurosis where the hysterical symptom shows the structure of a language and is deciphered as an inscription which, once it is assembled, can be destroyed without serious damage;–in the archival documents also: and these are my childhood memories, just as unfathomable as the former when I do not know their origin;–in the semantic evolution: and this corresponds to the stock and to the acceptions of the vocabulary peculiar to me, as well as to my life-style and character;–in the traditions, namely, in the legends which, under a heroic form, carry my hope;–finally, in the traces which unavoidably include distortions, necessitated by the fitting of the adulterated chapter with related events. Only my effort of interpretation will be able to reestablish the real meaning."(9)

One can obviously not choose between these interpretations. A study of the unconscious must remain attentive to these different dimensions.

b. The Unconscious is Structured Like a Language

The assertion that the unconscious is structured like a language requires also a serious effort of interpretation. First of all, this assertion poses the question of whether or not the language of consciousness and the language of the unconscious simply are one and the same? This is certainly what Lacan means.[20] However, the first issue of *La Psychanalyse,* where Lacan defends the texts we have been discussing, also contains an article by E. Benveniste questioning such identification, or, at least expressing serious reservations towards it.[21]

Benveniste starts by rejecting Freud's statement according to which the absence of all avowed contradiction in oniric language, as well as the fact that every element of this discourse may signify both itself and its opposite, would reproduce a characteristic of the most ancient languages known. Freud relies for this thesis upon the authority of a contemporary linguist, Karl Abel. But then, Benveniste unequivocally writes: "Freud's authority might lead us to take this demonstration for granted, or at least, it propounds the idea that it contains possibilities leading to fruitful research. An analogy would have been discovered between the mechanism of dreams and the semantic of "primitive" languages where the same term expressed equally well both a certain thing and its opposite. The way would be open to an investigation searching for the structures common to both collective language and individual psychic activity. Faced with these perspectives, it is useful to indicate that factual reasons deprive Karl Abel's etymological speculations of all validity."(10) But, besides

---

[20] See Lacan, *Ecrits*, p. 269 or Wilden, *The Language, p.* 32 (Also, ibid, p. 115-116, note 70; 249-51).

[21] Benveniste, E.: "Remarques sur la fonction du language dans la découverte freudienne" in *Problèmes de linguistique générale, p. 75-87.*

stating his thesis, Benveniste also explains the reason for it. The reason is that all collective language attempts a systematization of a particular configuration of the world, and that, consequently, the elimination of contradiction is a constitutive requirement for it. In this regard, the example of the Latin 'altus' means nothing. For, from a certain standpoint, height and depth are not contradictory but identical.

"Assuming there is a language in which 'big' and 'small' are identically expressed, it would be a language where the distinction between 'big' and 'small' has literally no meaning, and where the category of dimension does not exist, rather than a language admitting of a contradictory expression of dimension.(11)[22]

Nevertheless, this does not imply that all analogy between the two languages should be rejected. Benveniste believes that this relative identity should be based on mythical and poetic language (surrealism in particular), rather than on the language of communication. These former kinds of expressions "can be related to dreams; they can introduce in ordinary forms of language the suspension of meaning projected by dreams upon our activities. Their structure is similar."(12)

On the other hand, it is still true that what characterizes all language, both conscious and unconscious, is symbolism, and, in the etymological sense of the term, metaphor. But, again, this symbolism is not the same for the language of communication as for poetic or oniric language. The former, as opposed to the latter, is planned, and *learned:* "it is coextensive with a human being's acquisition of the world and of intelligence with which it is ultimately unified."(13) Such symbolism is subordinated to the reality principle, and is at its command. Its usage is bound to things, and it must remain as much of a direct substitute for them as possible.[23] The shorter the distance between it and these things or our experience of them, the better the symbol shall be. It is made to "become master (of these things) to the extent that it discovers them as realities."(14) Freud, and this is not always mentioned, was not unaware of this aspect. He takes it up, together with other certainly more important traits, in his interpretation of language in connection with the analysis of the game of the child who throws away and picks up his bobbin.[24] One cannot neglect, *because it is impossible,* the effort of mastery over things which every language constitutes and *also* implies. It follows then, that the symbolism of conscious language will be infinitely diversified, and that, for all practical purposes, there are as many systems as there are modes of apprehending the uni-

---

[22] A similar thesis is defended in general by a philosopher: P.F. Strawson: *Introduction to Logical Theory, p. 5.*

[23] Wittgenstein's *Tractatus Logico-Philosophicus.* The author defends a picture theory of language (the two's, from 2.1 on). He then defends the theory that the logic of description is similar to the logic of pictures (the three's).

[24] See Freud, G.W. XIII, p. 11 Iff; S.E., XVIII, p. l4ff.

verse. According to Freud, unconscious symbolism is, on the contrary, universal.[25] It is, furthermore, usually misunderstood and not recognized by those who produce it. Also, adds Benveniste– and this shall give rise to our reservations: "the relationship between these symbols and what they refer to can be typified by the fact that there is a multiplicity of the signifiers and only one signified."(15) Finally, and this is only a consequence of the above, the sequence of elements in symbolic discourse "is not subordinated to any logical requirement."(16)

We do not think that it is merely false to say that the unconscious symbolic discourse has only a unique signified, but thus formulated, the proposition only touches upon a very general truth. It is accurate to say, undoubtedly, that this unique signified is the desire of the subject. Such an assertion is, however, on the same level as the one which recognizes in all dreams the fulfillment of desire, even if it is only the desire to preserve the continuity of sleep. The real issue then becomes that of the diversification of desires and their articulation with the symbols which signify them. At this point, universal symbolism is of little or no avail, and it is then that–if I may say so–the primacy of the signifier over the signified is truly at stake. This means that because of historical and contingent facts specific signifiers play the role of key signifiers in a particular unconscious. We have given various examples of this (particularly with regard to the Wolf man), and we shall see some more soon in connection to the Rat man.[26]

Also the claim that unconscious discourse does not obey the rules of logic is ambiguous. It is true that conscious discourse is different. Conscious discourse is informative or cognitive discourse and must be systematic since it ultimately aims at revealing all that exists. Therefore, it cannot avoid being subordinated to the requirements of that which makes possible the expression and mastery of the totality of what is. This is precisely what we mean by logic. From this standpoint, then, it is absurd and defeating to think that what is there can also not be there at the same time. But does this imply that there can be no logic of desire? Not at all, and it is enough to read Freud to be convinced. Nevertheless, this logic evidently snaps the possibility of a discourse with other ends than those of cognitive discourse. The identity of hate and love, of a thing and its opposite, is perfectly suited for these other ends. It even gives a specific coherence to this new form of discourse.

---

[25] See Freud, G.W. XI, p. 150ff; S.E. XV, p. 149ff, i.e., Lecture X: "Symbolism in dreams" in *Introductory Lectures on Psycho-Analysis*.

[26] De Waelhens discusses the example of the Wolf man in note 14 of Ch. IV. He will discuss the example of the Rat man in Section IV of this chapter: "Transcendence in Human Beings and its Absence in the Schizophrenic" (A.D.W., p. 194ff). A third example, not mentioned here, is described in note 13 of Ch. IV.

2. Language and Reality

Before discussing what is the proper object of this chapter, we shall raise certain questions, more difficult yet, but of great relevance to what follows.

Beyond the distinction between the conscious and the unconscious lies the distinction between language and reality. But what is it to be real, and what is it to say the real? Assuredly one cannot claim that this question presents itself identically to both the conscious and the *unconscious* because of a peremptory reason: the real and the unreal are not distinguished in the unconscious. The problem of the relation between the unconscious and consciousness can only be approached from the conscious reality. Indeed, the structures of the oniric world can only be described and analyzed within the waking universe. However, an interpretation referring to the unconscious must be able to be true, valid and real since we accept that it sometimes can be false, unreal, and invalid. If there are any false desires at all, they are only so relative to a true desire they mask.

It is a generally accepted thesis that nothing "real" takes place during analysis. We shall not contradict it, and we recognize with everyone that the love involved in transference is simply, 'not' true love. However, it comes about by aiming at another love, and by repeating, for *instance,* an Oedipal love. Besides, it is not certain whether this Oedipal love itself is more true (or at least has always been more true). What is certain, however, is that this Oedipal love, whether true or false, has in one way or another, by itself or through its derivatives and symptoms, been registered in what must naively be called the real. It even must have been registered in a manner sufficiently disturbing to make it good and urgent for the person involved to inform us about it. Without the inscription in the real there would have been neither analysis, nor analyst, nor analyzed. We shall here sustain what Merleau-Ponty, after Husserl, says about the certainty of perception: one can always question each one of its elements, but one can only question it to the advantage of another element, so that the existence of the perceived world, or, in the present case, of the real, is affirmed before and after all possible questioning. "Each perception, though always capable of being 'cancelled' and relegated among illusions, disappears only to give place to another perception which rectifies it. Each thing can, after the event, appear uncertain; but what is at least certain for us is that there are things, that is to say, a world. To ask oneself whether the world is real is to fail to understand what one is asking, since the world is not a sum of things which might always be called into question, but the inexhaustible reservoir from which things are drawn. The percept taken in its entirety, with the world horizon *which announces both its possible disjunction and its possible replacement by another perception,* certainly does not mislead us."(17)

It has been repeatedly asserted, and we are very convinced of it, that there is no sense in attempting to treat the problems of delirium in terms of the real.

We shall therefore not imitate the old master who used to interrupt his patient thus: "Come on, my friend, let's go back to reality."   However, just as Mr. Teste, like every poet who writes only for himself, would be completely unknown to us if Valery had not communicated the remarks he attributes to him, in the same way, a delirious person capable of holding all the discourses we hold, and only those, would never appear to be delirious. Once again then, oniric structures, even though they are constituted in dreams, are only known and discussed in waking life.

One must therefore inevitably speak of the word, at the same time that one speaks of the real, without, in any way, confusing them.

We shall not lose too much time with the following serious objection because in the last analysis it leaves matters untouched. One may indeed say: the only way you can come in contact with the real, or aim at it, is *in* and *through* language; one is therefore never outside language. If this statement limits itself to establishing that, in effect, the real could only appear to us somehow in relation to discourse, one is stating an irrefutable truth. But this truth is quite similar to the famous "a beyond of thought is unthinkable" in its equivocal implications. However, does it follow from this that there cannot be an Other of language (if this Other is caught in language), to which language is bound as a shadow to the body but without being confused with it? Today, we can only reach Napoleon through discourse on Napoleon. Does this mean that there is nothing concerning Napoleon other than discourse on Napoleon, and that, for instance, the statements of the historian and those of the madman who takes himself for Napoleon are identical except, perhaps, for the coherence of the former and the incoherence of the latter? Such a line of argumentation, turned against the speaker and no longer applied to the "object" of his discourse, leads to disputing the very existence of the speaking subject.[27] Indeed no word is identical with a subject. A subject must be signified (we have sufficiently insisted on this point). Therefore, no subject coincides with his discourse.

However, in order to explain as clearly as possible what we mean, we would like to refer for a moment to some of the introductory pages of Heidegger's *Being and Time*.

There is, in our experience, only one type of being who questions. And although his questions do not necessarily refer to himself, they always lead to and sometimes begin by putting himself in question. In addition, this unique questioner is presented as necessarily endowed with "Jemeinigkeit,"[28] that is,

---

[27]   Here De Waelhens uses a method of refutation, known as self-referential inconsistency. It has some similarity with aspects of the "ad hominem argument." De Waelhens' argument runs as follows: Person A holds that Napoleon is but the discourse on Napoleon. Person A would then have to accept that he is but the discourse on Person A, which he clearly cannot hold.

[28]   *Jemeinigkeit* means literally: the fact of being mine.

according to the translation we have proposed even if it is not unobjectionable, as "being-mine."

This brings us back precisely, although in a different philosophical vocabulary, to the problematic discussed in connection with language. It is true that the *Dasein,* since this is what the questioner is called, is essentially capability to question, to interrogate. It is not true that there is no distance whatsoever between his question and that which is being questioned. It is therefore through the concept of distance that the distinction between language and its referent might be approached. Certainly, this other will not manage to express himself at all without language; this is precisely what we have verified in pointing out that only one being had the privilege of asking questions. This privilege coincides with the power of making distinctions where there were none and thus where Being and non-Being remained still and differentiated. However, this last expression is, strictly speaking, contradictory, since it aims at qualifying a situation preceding all qualification whatsoever. For night is only conceived through day to which it is the prelude. Expression is set up in Being; what precedes it is inexpressible. But nothing precedes it, and the inexpressible is not inexpressible. The expressive act which merges with the very appearance of the Dasein, separates the heavens, the earth, and the waters.

Let us try to specify, if possible, this contribution of the expression. It brings things together in the unity of the 'world' by relating them to each other, by making them appear in this relation. This is how each thing ultimately discloses all the others and is disclosed by them, because they are all placed together in the disclosedness of being, correlative to the emergence of the Dasein.(18) The "organizer"– who is the questioner– delimits then a space which constitutes (in the active sense) everything in its being. In this space everything holds, and this in the twofold sense of "upholding" and of "holding together." Furthermore, he maintains himself in this space of disclosure and is therein revealed such as he is. The questioner elucidates himself by elucidating the other and elucidates himself as the other of that which he elucidates.[29]

Let us leave aside the point of deciding in what sense and where this elucidation starts to belong specifically to the domain of philosophy. We like to

[29] Although ultimately Hegel holds a quite different philosophical position than Heidegger, here Hegel's *Phenomenology* can serve appropriately to illustrate the Heideggerian thesis. In Hegel's *Phenomenology,* the subject adheres to a theory of the world and a corresponding theory of the self. When the subject recognizes that what he holds to be true is not what he does or experiences, he is forced to create a new theory of the world and a new corresponding theory of the self. Thus when the slave realizes that what counts is not the capability to order, but the ability to execute, the slave has ceased to be slave and he has become a stoic. In relating to his body and its needs, to his work and to his master, the slave has discovered something about himself. At the same time he has achieved a new form of selfhood and autonomy. For an abstract statement of this insight, see Hegel, *Phenomenology,* p. 142 (Hegel's definition of "Experience").

start by explicitly emphasizing that there is an irrevocable difference between Heidegger and Hegel on this point. For the latter, *the Presence,* raised to the level of the absolute Spirit, must ultimately radically coincide– under the form of absolute knowledge– with *what is present.* For Heidegger such coincidence is forever and in principle excluded: the original flaw is irretrievable because it is from it, from the finitude it creates (and from it alone) that the *lumen naturale* emerges.[30] If the gap were really bridged, then it would amount to the return of the non-sensical.[31] The choice thus presented to us, sends us directly back to our debate on language, because the above mentioned problem is a problem of discourse.

How can this reference to Heidegger be pertinent to it? We hope it has allowed us to reformulate both the problem of the genesis and of the development of the speaking subject on the one hand, and that of the relation between language and its other on the other hand. We hope that it shall further allow us to restate the problem in such a way that it can do justice to the demands of a problematic of the unconscious.

III. An Existential Interpretation of the Unconscious and of Psychosis

1. Psychoanalysis, Scientific Method and the Origin of Meaning

We shall not again continue a dispute often raised in reference to Freud but which in fact extends to the whole problematic which is the object of the present work. The new type of intelligibility inaugurated by psychoanalysis–and which could or should inspire both anthropology and psychiatry–was established by a man whose thought was guided by a biologically oriented naturalism that he never completely overcame. It was even less overcome by the majority of his immediate followers. But this naturalism, literally understood,

---

[30] *Being and Time,* p. 171.

[31] That there is a distance between language and its referent can be seen by the fact that different authors give a different interpretation of a language event. Striking is the difference between Fromm's interpretation of the Adamic myth and the Christian interpretation. *(The Heart of Man, p.* 19ff). Nevertheless, both approach the reference of the myth through the language of the event. Language is thus responsible for the very existence of its other. The problem becomes more difficult if one accepts that a concept of language has multiple meanings; it can mean linguistic discourse just as well as the symbolic gesture. Is the restless behavior of monkeys before an earthquake already sufficient to say that it constitutes the earthquake? If the answer is positive then the Heideggerian thesis that there is but one type of being that questions is in doubt. If the answer is negative, how can one then explain that the behavior of monkeys will soon become the legally valid signal for civil authority to order people to leave their homes in anticipation of an earthquake.

contradicts the project of intelligiblity built upon it.[32]

Such a situation is not unparalleled in the development of scientific thought. Every epistemological mutation–for this is what is involved–is set up within a framework of thought which it questions and which hinders it, while it is also this framework that alone makes it possible.[33] At a second stage, and this is where we are today, this intelligibility deepens, reflects upon itself, returns upon its framework and accommodates it to the outline itself of its progress.

Regardless of the difficulties it presents for the contemporary interpreters of Freud, the *Project of a Scientific Psychology* is still the work that started a revolution in the human sciences, even if this revolution requires that the theses of the *Project* be revised. One could make similar remarks with regard to *Gestalt psychology* or in reference to other examples, namely, Kraepelin or Bleuler. Our purpose will be rather to try to understand this new intelligibility and to discover its implications as well as its ultimate meaning.

Mr. Maldiney–in an article which we will quote more than once–(19) is right in saying that the step from a human being as a natural reality towards "anthropogenesis and a human's being's becoming of a first person ... is made in a twofold way, already seen by Hegel: by negation, and by the act of desiring desire."(20)[34] As a matter of fact, this step is also the one from one language to another. It is the step from objectifying language which considers a human being as a product of nature to a discourse whose essence, covertly or explicitly but immutably aims at signifying the world and the human person himself. Such a discourse can only be sustained "by the perpetual renewal of its signifiers."(21) Let us point out, however, that in a sense the first language is not any more or less mythical than the second since it presupposes as solved the ambiguity and equivocation connected with making sense emerge from nonsense. Or, as we wrote elsewhere, it provides a "genetic theory of the human psyche which aims at tracing the birth and becoming of the human subject *starting from the state of nature.* The hope is to trace the development until a full human personality is reached. Such a personality would include

---

[32] Freud's naturalism is very evident in an early work, never published during his life: *Project for a Scientific Psychology,* S.E. I, 281ff. This naturalism is also apparent in Freud's belief in a primal scene. Even when doubting this, he can not but again express his belief in the same footnote. See his remark on the case of the Wolf man: G.W.; XII, p. 156, note 1; S.E. XVII, p. 120, note 1.

[33] For a philosophical essay on the dialectic relations involved in scientific research, see Feyerabend, P.K., "Consolations for the Specialist," particularly p. 197, 202, 205.

[34] See Hegel's analysis of the master-slave relation in *Phenomenology.* The affirmation that one transcends nature and is thus in some sense unique demands that one is *recognized* as such. Transcendence of nature is an intersubjective enterprise (desire of desire). The theme of negation (sublation) is mentioned on p. 225-26, 229; the theme of transcendence being an intersubjective enterprise is mentioned on p. 226, 231.

both consciousness and unconsciousness. This operation proves to be, in the eyes of the phenomenologist, contradictory, since it attempts to posit the origin of all meaning and of all understanding as starting from premises and hypotheses already meaningful themselves and rendered so by the power of intelligence alone which they are supposed to generate. What they claim to explain (the genesis of meaning) can only be explained by starting with what has already been explained (including nature). In other words: for man, the problem of his own origin can only arise *within* his own history—I locate, and everyone else does too, my birth only beyond the 'always-already-born' which is not a contingent character but rather a structural dimension of human existence. My origin, and that of humanity, are not presented to me as facts to be explained, but rather as signifiers in which the signified can be searched through other signifiers. They are not the first signified. No one can doubt this thesis after he has heard psychotics asking themselves about their origin ten or a thousand times."(22)[35]

2. The Ambiguous Position of Meaning in Psychoanalysis

There is therefore in Freud—and no one questions it—a problem of meaning. In order to discuss it, let us continue for a moment the issue on dreams to which we have already alluded. That dreams have a meaning does not imply in any case that this meaning would appear somewhere as *given.* Indeed, this meaning does not appear as a given in the lived experience of the dreamer telling his dream. Neither does it appear in an "objective concept" discernable only by the trained knowledge of the interpreter who would guess it sooner or later depending on the complexity of the case and the range of his experience or the degree of his ability. In fact, this meaning comes to be constituted in the dialectic of latent and manifest meaning which is never closed as is shown by the well known fact that one can successfully work over the same dream at different periods, and, consequently, at different levels of the therapy. This dialectic can be condensed by pointing out that it expressed "the meaning of an existence which hides, and which hides in its appearance."(23) But this appearance is itself a problem. The dream is communicated in a *narrative*. This narrative, however, does not belong as such to the manifest meaning of the dream dreamt. This leads M. Dumoulin to say that every dream, once it is communicated thereby places itself in indirect discourse. This discourse or narrative is then a production of the dreamer *returned to the waking state.* The hyletic matter or the images of the dream find themselves thereupon transformed, since it was neither their nature nor their aim to be incorporated to the inten-

---

[35]   That the problem of origin (of humanity for instance) must be approached by analyzing a system of signifiers, is an insight that Ricoeur used when he analyzed the problem of the origin of evil in *The Symbolism of Evil.*

tionality of a narrative. In itself, the dream is not even a *signifier* it unfolds, in effect, under the system of *confusion* between the signifier and the signified. This is brilliantly shown by Silberer's example often referred to by Freud.[36] The writer who thinks, before going to sleep, that he must still polish the style of his essay, sees himself suddenly polishing a piece of wood.(24) Once they are expressed, nevertheless, these images are presented and aimed at as signifying an intentionality of meaning, of discourse.[37] It is not that the narrative would be, as is said, "invented"; rather, it is perfectly adapted to the dream. However, the status of what is seen is bound to be modified by the mutation of the horizon in which it is presented. Oniric space and the universe of waking discourse do not at all coincide. The former is a closed theater, exempt, for instance, of all reference to the effective motor activity of the perceiver, an activity which sleep, at least. in principle, cuts off. The same is not true for the narrative. Here the images appear to a waking consciousness and regain what they had lost in the dream and for the dreamer: their quality as signifiers. How then can one conceive of the step from one level to the other without it implying the alternative of an equally devastating (or impossible) choice between images lost or inaccessible in the status they had for the one who saw them in dreams, and, on the other hand, a discourse which has dismissed the oniric order? "The Freudian procedure of the seemingly arbitrary fragmentation of the narrative leads in fact to placing each partial meaning in direct relationship with its mode of expression, that is, with the verbal and image-making structures that signify it."(25) Such fragmentation will have as a result "the self-establishment of meaning . . . and the fact that the signified is forged in the signifier."(26) The mobilization of meaning is, in effect, guaranteed by the splitting up of the dream. This fragmentation protects or establishes the opposite emergence of images, sustains or begets the hiatus of meaning between the different fragments of the discourse. Thus one finds preserved, not the dream dreamt–which is simply impossible–but a certain analogy of functioning.

We have frequently stressed the difficulty involved in fixing the images of the dream. In fact, such fixation is impossible; for precisely, it would assume that an immanent meaning is set up in the images just as an immanent meaning is set up in waking discourse. The dreamer is torn between the fluidity of the images in the dream, their continuous passage from one into the other, and, on the other hand, this type of fascinating rigidity–"surrealistic," says Maldiney–of each in the isolated moment of its appearance. It is this opposition rather than the plurality of the images or the vagueness of their relationship that generates for the dreamer a meaning always to be recreated, always in its

---

[36] A particularly instructive example can be found in Freud's Interpretation of Dreams, G.W. II/III, p. 350, S.E, V. p. 345.

[37] Remember that for the schizophrenic, signifiers have lost their capability to be ... signifiers of. Worse, they often replace the signified and become imaginary real.

"original moment." What is involved therefore, are sketches of meaning which all point in the same direction, rather than a series of superposable or hierarchical structures. The development of images, the organization of them in different levels, the explicitation of inserted possibles in each of them can be achieved without reduction or mutilation because of the technique of fragmentation of the narrative. This technique also prevents the narrative from flowing away into a univocal meaning and from solidifying therein as waking discourse tends to do.

One should not therefore hypostatize–as if they were comparable in their respective status–the latent meaning and the manifest meaning. Their opposition cannot be compared to the relation between an original text and its translation into another language even if this latter is truncated by censorship.[38] To quote Maldiney again: "The elaboration of latent meaning is the unveiling of manifest meaning itself. This is done by giving the latent content the function of signifier through its status of signified. Manifest meaning and latent meaning are the poles of the same meaning which is nowhere actualized and which can only be grasped as the direction of meaning pertaining to an individual history. The revealing and constitutive dialectic of this history is only achieved through the vicissitudes of the analytic cure.(27)

3. Psychoanalysis and the Theory of Presence

The goal of this repetition of well-known themes is to prepare a confrontation between the Freudian notion of meaning and the one used by a philosophy of phenomenological inspiration.

It is obvious that both recognize the role of intentionality (this word being understood in its phenomenological significance) in the experience of the subject. There is in both an effort to transcend the hyletic (or even the noetic) towards another that signifies it. But for us it is evident that the Freudian conception goes beyond the intentionality of the phenomenologist.[39] Indeed, an interpretation, such as the one used in Freudian psychoanalysis, aims to unveil "a crooked transcendence where the intentionality of a consciousness aiming at its object, is continually cast adrift by the game of the *transcendences of the Ego*."(28) Let us stress that neither the object aimed at, nor the "subject" aiming at the object remains unalterably identical to themselves in the unfolding of the

---

[38] In the translation the following text is left out, which De Waelhens used to illustrate a false comparison between latent and manifest dream context: "This is similar–and we hereby stay within the spirit of a Freudian metaphor–to the Germans who translated in a distorted way a British war communication with a sole purpose: to prove by such a publication the objectivity of German information.

[39] The relation between phenomenology and psychoanalysis is surveyed in Ricoeur, *Freud and Philosophy*, p. 375ff.

analysis and of the interpretation which takes place in it. It is this constant modifying of one and the other, and of one by the other, that will permit the patient, as soon as he has begun the cure, to surmount the naive and alienating illusion, which very often seduced him to start therapy. This alienating illusion is the fact that the patient hopes finally to discover in the therapy who he is, and even *what* he is. Let us express this in another way by saying that Freudian analysis is very little, if at all, concerned with a phenomenology of consciousness, but is rather concerned with a phenomenology of presence.[40] Let us explain this. Maldiney, who supports this thesis, illustrates it by referring to the phenomenon of *resistance*. Resistance, in effect, doesn't seek so much to camouflage, to deform, to forget–or at least this is not what is essential about it–as it seeks to elaborate "a system of anchorages and of successive horizons."(29) And every time that the subject is expelled from a particular position, he tends to reestablish his position on another basis in order to safeguard the illusion of defining himself as this or that. This is in effect what becomes equally evident in the case of Dora, in that of the Rat man, and in that of the Wolf man. If "subject" and "object" undergo a constant change of presence, the patient nevertheless searches every time to rediscover beyond these modifications "horizons" and "anchorage." This is also clear in the example that we cited in the previous pages. If one enters into analysis in the hope that one will hear the gratifying confirmation of a *truthful self-portrait,* then one is undisputedly trying to establish oneself in a type of presence to oneself and others that confirms the existing alienation. Furthermore, one wants to give this alienation the appearance of truth with the help and the mediation of others. Psychoanalysis should not demand of the patient, should not provoke in him, the rectification of this or that trait, nor even of all traits (personality, character, temperament, etc.), because this would only confirm him in his alienation. Psychoanalysis should require that the patient can want himself or can accept himself without any self-image but as existing in the mode of the presence of a historic figure, or as Merleau-Ponty puts it, of a style. It is true that psychoanalysis denounces illusions, false significances, affections which are also false or are misplaced relative to their real object. But this denouncement does not have as its goal the substitution of traits and objects which this time would be "true" instead of being, like the former, imaginary. One would thus replace a decoy by a more prestigious decoy, and, thus, a worse one. It is this that the subject "will resist" the most. Indeed, this denouncement wants to inscribe the "subject" in another level of existence. At that level, being and objectivity, for example, are no longer considered simply synonyms or absolutely complimentary; furthermore, the subject must give up the attempt to place a certain image of himself as the origin and the pole of all his actions.

Thus, there is something one has to accept, i.e., "the identity of signifiers

---

[40] This is appropriately illustrated by Freud's statement that the purpose of therapy is to achieve that "Where id was, there ego shall be," G.W. XV, p. 86, S.E. XXII, p. 80 (End of Lecture XXXI of New *Introductory Lectures on Psychoanalysis*].

and existential structures."(30) This reveals *a meaning* which, contrary to that of phenomenological thought, coincides at every level for its good as for its ill, in illusion as in truth, with the existence of the one who expresses it. "The same transcendence that founds existence as . . . *presence towards* . . . is constitutive of meaning."(31) From this derive the peculiar problems of interpretation in psychoanalysis. An historian or a philologist would not trouble himself to investigate whether it is opportune to publish or suppress the interpretation that he proposes of a fact or of a text; he will not wonder either *how* he would say it, or rather he would only be worried to formulate his ideas as clearly as he can while stripping them as much as possible of all risk of ambiguity. The psychoanalyst's problem is quite different. He very often does better by remaining quiet or by presenting his interventions, at first, in such a way that their meaning is perceived dimly rather than really understood. This is done in order that the insight gained by the patient would appear as if it came from himself rather than as a communication addressed to him. This is why, again, it is sometimes useful to present the interpretation in a context that connects the new theme with others already elucidated. Such a connection creates ambiguities which often prove to be beneficial. To take a chance, to expose oneself, to show oneself are moments which are inextricably intertwined with the act of speaking. This isn't the case, or not necessarily so, in ordinary or scientific language. In psychoanalysis, language is always discourse. "Understanding does not join itself from outside like an adjacent characteristic. It is a constitutive element of presence."(32)

This explains the agreement–which is very rare–between the authors and practitioners of psychoanalysis on the following point: there is a narrow link between regaining presence in the world by the sick person and the acquisition, the return or the progress of some understanding of himself. The autistic person, for example, who in the limiting case, is no longer present in the world, does not reign in the separate and inaccessible fortress of his "Ego." He has no more knowledge of himself than he does of things around him. He ignores the role that he is playing, the impression that he creates. Both dimensions refer to a same emptiness. Let us remember, with Maldiney, the popular expression: "he seems absent." The double meaning of this expression illuminates the dialectic tie that unites presence in the world with presence to oneself, as it links the understanding of the one to that of the other.

The articulation of presence and understanding is seen likewise as soon as one reflects upon that which happens precisely at the time of the recovery. The latter, in effect, manifests a paradox that gets to the heart of the psychoanalytic mystery. For, finally, this recovery cannot be accomplished simply from the inside. A subject cannot change himself at all by self-examination or by introspection. In this case consciousness would have to depend on itself to rectify its own helplessness. This would be a kind of new Munchhausen who gets himself out of the marsh pulling himself up by the hair! However, the recovery is also not purely the result of a work from the outside, as if the action of the psychoanalyst could be compared to the action of a drug that produces its effect without the patient having any other role to play but to absorb it. Let us say in passing that this already suffices to show the perfect futility of all the methods that use any form of suggestion. This is so if one is concerned with true cure. Indeed, methods using any form of suggestion simply seem to want to abolish discourse in the process of using discourse.

But if it is not the one nor the other, what is it? The answer is that the dialogue implements the covenant of the discourse which, as such, is not at the pure and simple disposal of the subject or of the other and which dominates them more than they dominate it.

This is what Freud implicitly thinks when he writes about little Hans: "In the course of psychoanalysis, the doctor always gives the patient, to a greater or lesser extent, the anticipated conscious representations with the aid of which the patient will be able to recognize and to grasp that which is unconscious. Different patients have respectively more or less need of this aid, but none can entirely do without it. A patient can master alone less serious troubles, but he can never overcome a neurosis alone because neurosis is something which stands in opposition to the Ego as a foreign element. In order to master it, it is necessary to have help from another person and the extent to which this other person can be helpful is the same extent to which the neurosis is curable."(33)

But this help does not consist of transmitting information to the patient about that which is going on inside him, just as a doctor communicates his diagnosis of an organic illness and the treatment implied by it. Giving such information, would imply that the psychoanalyst knows the *true* and *definite* meaning of the action of the patient. It is important to deny that the psychoanalyst possesses similar knowledge or that he has to transmit it to the patient. Furthermore, of what use would this insight and this message be? Could one imagine that Freud–to take a famous example– in listening to the patient who said to him that he did not know the person seen in his dreams but was certain that it could not be his mother,[41] would have answered him: "You are wrong, I tell you that this was certainly her." Even if this certainty existed–which is not the case–to what would his supposed revelation have led? To nothing else but to discourage the patient and confirm him in his illusionary and alienating conception he held of psychoanalysis. And let us recall that ending this illusionary hope should be the first result of the therapy.

Psychoanalytic interpretation will propose, then, neither an account nor an explanation of the conflicts under scrutiny, but an expression that articulates them and with which the patient may agree because it repeats certain of its own sayings.(34) Freud tells us this himself: there will be some resemblance between that which the patient understands and that for which he is looking.

[41] The reference is to the patient in Freud's study on "Negation": G.W. XIV, p. 11; S.E. XIX, p. 235.

This similitude will put him in a state where he can discover the truth. "In this way he will be induced to articulate them (his conflicts) in another way than he has done up until then."(35)

"If we speak of agreement and of inference it is because we do not want to leave the domain of language, which is the domain of the signifier. That the patient becomes conscious of his conflicts through our words does not signify a fortunate co-incidence between a meaning and a discourse which are alien to each other. On the contrary, it manifests the essence of the word which is precisely to speak at the moment when the speakers are quiet or when, breaking the dialogue, they must assume in solitude the meaningful work of words. 'It is not me that you should listen to, but Logos', said Heraclitus. Similarly, Freud teaches the psychoanalyst that his words are wiser than he himself; that their meaning transcends his consciousness. If the word of the psychoanalyst surpasses him it is because the word does not belong to him. It belongs to a dialogue in which every moment is articulated even if it entails several planes of meaning that mask each other. This dialogue expresses urgent demands, the meaning of which is not yet clear to anybody, neither analyst nor analyzed, because, strictly speaking, it does not yet exist."(36)

Although this quotation is long, it condenses in a couple of sentences the real knot of the problem. What Ricoeur said of the symbol, we can say here of the signifier: it gives rise to thought because it gives something to talk about. It gives signs.[42] "Certain words, certain bodily organs are the crossroads of signification. Repression brings about the shifting of meaning that only an interpretation can clarify or uncover. Thus, because there is an archeological language of the lived body and of the verbal chain, an expression whose symbolic aim is not clearly recognized is possible. To interpret a dream, a symptom, a lapsus, is to restore to metaphors the meaning that had been repressed, to give it the right to citizenship in the human universe."(37)

But let us pursue the matter. If the word of the psychoanalyst, or if the psychoanalyst through his word opens to the patient a way that may lead him towards his own truth–a way until then blocked to him–it is evident that this word has priority over him, over that which he may recognize of himself, and even (if one remembers that which was said) over his being and his presence in the world. How has the word such a priority. How can this reign of logos that, I repeat, isn't to be confused with the reign of knowledge, be better explained? The psychoanalyst cannot *know* all that he says and furthermore it is better that he keeps quiet that which he does know.

Ordinarily, we make a clear distinction between that which comes to us through rational understanding and that which is available to us through the empirical activity of perception. Someone communicates to me this or that information. Hearing that which he says to me, I grasp its meaning, I under-

---

[42]   Ricoeur, *The Symbolism of Evil*: Conclusion.

stand it. Simultaneously, I perceive his personality, the sound of his voice, his gestures. The scientist, like the businessman, will take all possible care to avoid that these perceptions interfere with the meaning of his remarks. There is even, between one and the other, a certain incompatibility which is exemplified by the infamous absent-mindedness of the scientist incapable of noticing one or another peculiarity (physical or other) of the speaker which would not fail to attract the attention of a witness who is not such an involved participant in the discussion as the scientist.

And yet this scission has its limits. When I would be concerned about thinking to such a degree that I would no longer care about words, but only be interested in meaning, then discourse would disappear. At no level would such thought really speak. But, inversely, if I am absorbed completely in pure perception or in pure hearing, discourse disappears as well. If it happens that we hear a conversation in a language that we do not understand at all, as is the case for us with Arabic or Chinese, the linguistic phenomenon disintegrates or is even annihilated; the sounds heard communicate no sense at all.

Meaning, thus, never exists without some perception. This perception aims at the one who speaks and who starts to unveil himself in his discourse. We would say that he expresses himself in it. "The dimensions of meaning and the intertwining of these dimensions, the terms, the tone, the volume of the voice, the gestures, the silences, the repetitions, the discourse of the speaker show that he is situated in his words and that through them he is situated in the events that he recounts."(38) But, let us admit it, this analysis and these considerations, however interesting in other respects, hardly further our present purpose. Indeed, this expression of the self, perceived in the saying of meaning, constitutes in turn a meaning. But the link between the one and the other continues to escape us. And it is precisely in this link that the problem of discourse is hidden. If someone lifts a fist, would I say that I understand his gesture or that I perceive in it anger and menace? In fact, I cannot say one or the other. Because, if I understand a gesture–of anger, for example–that does not imply that I understand also its full significance for the angered person, nor consequently that I understand it as an expression of his total being.

Let us stress, therefore, that to resolve our problem we have to undo the distinction that has just been made. We have to think about that moment where gesture and language are united. For it is in such a moment that both meaning and discourse originate.

As Binswanger observes in a particularly illuminating and all the more significant example, since it is as valid in German as in French [or English],[43] "that which one calls perception is inscribed in a larger field, that of apprehension, where apprehension and comprehension refer both to the primary structure of "prehension" . . . of *nehmen bei Etwas,* prehension of something. . . ."(39) To

---

[43]   [or English] added by us. W.V.E.

be taken at one's word, this is to be taken at the word that one has just said. This is also to take the Word as that which gives prehension. Literally, one can say I grasped it or him. That means that to grasp (to prehend) applies as well to the expression "to grasp an idea" as to "grasp a suspect." A being incapable of grasping with his hand or with his teeth, would not be able to grasp with the look either. The expression here refers, then, to an attitude, *to the taking of a position*, to a fundamental mode of being in the world where the word is still, as it were, confused with the very mode that it expresses. It appears, on reflection, even more fundamental than it appears at first sight. The grasping, (prehension) in effect, does not concern only the hand–which is an "articulated- articulating" grasp. It applies also to the grasp by the teeth, the tongue, the neck, or the feet. The archaic meaning of the concept "to grasp" is not regional, but pertains to the whole body, or better, even to embodied man. This is such an archaic meaning that it underlies everything. This is true even when we believe it to refer only to its abstract or intellectual transpositions, as in "comprehension, apprehension, etc.," where prehension or grasping in the first and physical meaning is no longer noticed by the speaker. This concept of "prehension" . . . "constitutes a kind of anthropological burden of which no imagination can free itself even in its most bizarre fictions."(40)

Traum und Existenz by Binswanger[44] offers us an analysis of another example of this same collusion. "Tomber des nues" (literally to fall from the clouds, metaphorically: to be taken aback) is not a simple literary image borrowed from the experience of the fall. He who, as we say, "falls from the clouds" in discovering the reality of that which he holds to be impossible and unthinkable, is lost. We can interpret that to mean that the person in question loses the foundation upon which and the framework within which he judged or presumed something to be true or false. Thus, he is in a void, without aid, and breaks down. He falls as falls the bird struck down by the hunter's bullet, as falls the aviator in distress whose parachute is ripped. These lines are written some hours before, for the first time, a being of flesh and blood, exactly like all of us, will tread the soil of the moon. For the first time a man will perceive that which no one else ever has perceived. He will confront the imperatives of action for which no pattern, no analogue exists in the age-old treasury of the memory. He will have to decide, without the benefit of the oldest and most assured instructions of perceptive knowledge and in immediate peril of his life. This astronaut is going to "fall from the clouds" (to be taken aback) in all senses of the expression without even knowing in advance if, on this occasion, to fall will mean that which it always meant. Also clouds, horizon, and sun may receive a new meaning which could have nothing common with what these words have always meant to everybody. For this astronaut, it is the word that leads to the thing, for alone, as a matter of fact, it is the "psychic" experience that refers to "falling from the clouds" that

---

[44]   In *Ausgewählte Vorträge und Aufsätze,* Band I.

alone could orient him towards perceiving that which takes place. Thus, we see a striking verification of a universal law.

IV. Transcendence in Human Beings and its Absence in the Schizophrenic

One sees thus that there is a grasp of language and a language with a grasp on the world which transcends all opposition between knowing and perceiving. Such discourse is carried by a more ancient and original language because this discourse is more rooted in the flesh than the one which seeks to enunciate–in order to transmit them–the products of a thought which imagines itself to be released from the body, and thus to be incorporeal. Each of us remains caught up in this archaic speech, even if our consciousness does not recognize it any more, or not yet explicitly. It is such discourse that the psychoanalyst uses, even if sometimes he does not know it. And certainly one can say that the psychoanalyst does not always calculate exactly its total scope. This discourse permits him to be understood by the patient, because such discourse is beyond rational discourse, which justifies, calculates, asserts. The possibility of such language eliminates the paradoxes which seem to question both the notion and the practice of psychoanalysis.

Thus the unveiling of truth cannot be the exclusive prerogative of informative or scientific discourse. For the most primordial unveiling comes about just at that point where speech still holds together two aspects of human existence: first, the fact that the world is apprehended by the ego and second, the fact that the ego is lost in that same world. Thus, it is understandable that such language can never be exhaustively made explicit. No interpretation succeeds in exhausting all the senses of a dream, all the senses of an oracle. This is so because such a discourse articulates our " 'pathetic' rapport with things, with beings, with the world. It consists in a structuring of space, of temporality, of communication, that is to say, of the constituting modes of presence. It expresses the style of a situation."(41)

It is similarly evident that this kind of discourse escapes every thematic transposition because it is connected with the existential that it evokes. The temptation to thematize is nevertheless great. The psychoanalyst as well as the patient is constantly exposed to this temptation. And a third party who would have access to the therapeutic dialogue would be tempted even more. This temptation to thematize is the result of the modern tendency of objectification; and this latter is not distinguishable from the illusory but, perhaps invincible, desire for complete possession, even in human relations. This desire is illusionary because the subjectivity of another person is always beyond language, even though this subjectivity is rooted in and structured by language.[45] Sub-

---

[45] This form of perpetual transcendence of the ego is well documented in an article by J. Hyppolite: "Hegel's Phenomenology and Psychoanalysis."

jectivity must be expressed by language, although no word can succeed fully to lay bare this subjectivity. This is why something always remains to be said and that in a sense, as Freud noted, all psychoanalysis is interminable. This is similar to the case of the object which always escapes perception. Indeed, the object is always more than the different points of view in perception, although those points of view *are* the object. Similarly, a subject is really his discourse, but also is more than the sum of his discourses since no one discourse finishes the task of meaning creation of this subject. That is why discourse is conducive to understanding and not to possession. We have already said how possession is a term hardly adequate for alluding to the carnal act to which everyday language ordinarily relates it. Likewise, it is not a suitable concept for labeling that which the other by his discourse gives us of himself. Truly there is no possession except of an idea or at least, of certain ideas: one admits, for example, that the analytic geometer possesses the formula of the figure described by it. For there is nothing about the figure that he does not know implicitly; and the figure is nothing but the knowledge of this formula. On the contrary, subjectivity, even if it be present in each of its expressions, is also and always above them. We say that subjectivity can be apprehended but never possessed. "It is this active transcendence which is in a human being 'the task of the human person.' The recognition of transcendence is the condition for any authentic apprehension of the human condition. Through it and it alone, all human expressions are seen as rooted in subjectivity."(42)

Thus, there is only a true comprehension of another if, at the same time this active transcendence has been recognized as the essence of the other. Without the recognition of this transcendence, the comprehension of another would become immediately imaginary. This recognition implies also the definitive ruin of all hope and all illusion of equating comprehension to possession.

It goes without saying that this recognition prevents all recourse to any form of *Einfühlung* 'intuition.' There cannot be any doubt about this. We do not even have to use a radical criticism of intuition because all authentic psychoanalysis distrusts intuition. For how can it be doubted and it has been explained well enough–that language by nature and purpose undermines any *feeling* a fortiori *Einfühlen*, 'intuition.'

Thus, in order to speak again of disease, one will have neither to transport oneself into the world of the patient, nor to transport him into ours. The first way would result in sanctioning the disease; the second would lead the diseased person to feign a normality. This would inevitably lead to failure which in turn would risk sooner or later to provoke aggression against the very norms of this normality. "Thus it is necessary to . . . know (the diseased person) on *his own terms* in a world which may be neither his nor mine.(43)

Now this common world, which belongs to no one, is exactly the world of language.

"The common world is only there in the communicative situation, where I perceive the person not on my own terms but on ours. Perception of others is possible only because and when, according to the saying of Hölderlin 'we are a dialogue.' Every dialogue has its forum: a public square which is completely open to all through this natural communal instrument: meaning-giving speech where each is linked with all the others in the meeting place of meaning."(44)

This may be true. But even if we know what the forum of common discourse is, the question arises or arises again: what is the forum of psychoanalytic discourse?

Everyday discourse ordinarily, and scientific discourse at all times, is the exchange of notions and of words which tend to be rational. The ideal is that the sense in which they are understood by the two interlocutors is identical. If, by chance, the identity is lacking in some respect, this incident will result from that which one calls, justly, a misunderstanding; one will do one's best to eliminate it as soon as possible.

The procedure is not quite the same in psychoanalytic discourse. To be sure, it also contains informative parts. One speaks in it with the words everyone uses and which mean what they mean for everyone, with words which bear, or are believed to bear upon the real. Freud learns, and we learn from him, that the 'Rat man,' a reserve officer, has forgotten his eyeglasses while leaving for maneuvers.[46] He lets his optician send him a new pair. In his absence, someone else receives the package and pays the delivery charge. Later, he succeeds neither in reimbursing nor in not reimbursing this debt, because all sorts of circumstances hinder the payment. Nevertheless, he does not decide to dodge it. During a stop, a Czech captain, mixed up in the imbroglio concerning the payment, told the patient about a certain Chinese torture, which moved the patient very much. We learn further that this patient's father, being in the regiment, did not pay his gambling debts, that he had married, without love, the daughter of an industrialist, forsaking for her a beloved, but poor, financée. Etc., etc. . . . Everybody understands without equivocation all the "facts" as Freud understood them when he heard them from the 'Rat man.'

And nevertheless in this psychoanalytic discourse more meaning is conveyed than merely an enumeration of *events.* For the words, the sentences, the story, carry, moreover, a meaning of a different nature. Why does the patient, for example, remember suddenly that in the regiment his father was an unscrupulous gambler? The puzzling thing is that he remembers this while he reveals the vain and bizarrely complicated efforts that he displayed to repay his debt to the postal clerk, to another reserve officer, or to the Czech captain– for neither he nor anyone else managed to find out exactly to whom he owed it. Furthermore, why was he so deeply upset by the story of the Chinese torture, which consisted of introducing living rats into the anus of the condemned? And finally, why did he become alert to the double sense of the

---

[46] The title of this case study by Freud is "Notes upon a case of obsessional neurosis," G.W. V11, p. 379ff; S.E., X, p. 151ff.

German morphemes *Rat–Rate* which signify at the same time *rat* and *rate* (of a debt), the coming together of which seems absurd.

Let us remark, first, that this *other* sense always has some relation to the patient. It is for him that there exists a relationship, and an essential one at that, between the torture and the debt. "The word of the patient is at once situation and expression of situation."(45) And, so it is indeed. The 'Rat man,' by submitting to or by creating an inextricable situation which prevents both his repaying and his not repaying his debt, is expressing something. He expresses his incapacity to either imitate his father (if he doesn't pay), or to disavow him (if he pays). In addition, he admits not being able to decide whether to break off his engagement to a young girl who was not very rich or on the contrary to marry her. Once again this problem has also a different meaning than the obvious one. For the question for him is not at all to know whether or not he loves this girl although this is what consciously motivates his hesitation to marry or to break off. The real question reveals itself to be either to accept giving blame to his father by getting married or, on the contrary, in not getting married, to approve of this father and his marriage–a marriage for which the father repudiated a poor young girl. But this approbation would be in bad faith since he knows quite well that it is wrong to renounce a girl that he loves because she is without dowry. Thus even the choice which would indirectly approve of the father would still repudiate him partially.

It thus appears that the 'Rat man's' romantic situation, although it is really just what it is–a problem of love–serves also as an expression of another conflict: that of whether to condemn or to imitate his father. Nevertheless, as it has already been revealed, this conflict masks yet another one which is even more fundamental. This conflict concerns not *a* debt or *a* (moral) law but debt and law in general. The fear or anxiety of placing himself in judgment on his father hides ill the repressed desire to really judge him. For the 'Rat man' is ill from contesting the law of the father, the debt of prohibition and of castration. It is really upon the latter that the revolt bears which he desires and cannot dare, even though he is not aware of it as he is aware of his romantic uncertainty. This revolt expresses itself in the homosexual desire for the father, which in turn is expressed and fought in the horror that the rat torture inspires in the 'Rat man.' Freud tells us that the'Rat man' relates this torture-story to him with "a complex and bizarre expression, an expression which I could not interpret otherwise than as *horror about unbeknownst enjoyment.* The 'Rat man' then continued with many difficulties, saying: 'at this moment *the idea* crossed my mind *that this was happening to someone who was dear to me.'*"(46)

He began by recognizing that this person was the girl of his dreams. Then, in speaking of the imaginary tortured victim he inadvertently used the plural. Freud made him notice it and asked if someone else could not equally be alluded to. He answered that, in his imagination, the torture could also apply to his father.

Thus one sees clearly that the discourse of the patient has many dimensions, many levels, which I dare say, look for each other and anticipate each other. His hesitation to pay his debt and to marry the young girl mean also something else, as also something else is meant by his fear of tarnishing his memory of a tenderly cherished and venerated father.(47) Similarly, the horror which the rat torture inspired has multiple meanings, as does the thought that the young girl could be the victim of this rat torture. The actual experiences and real events of which the patient speaks to his therapist permit one to discover other words and other conflicts, unknown to him, but not totally unknown. Each word, each thing, in addition to its immediate and certain sense, "reaches beyond itself toward a sense that it seeks."(48)

Also the behavior has multiple meanings. The rats–no more than those which Proust used to transfix with knitting needles–are not simply rats, nor is the money simply money. His hesitation to marry is also related to something other than marriage. Horror, love, and veneration are not only horror, love, and veneration.

Now these secondary and tertiary significations, etc., are no longer simply rational in the usual defined sense. To call a rat a rat would mean here to call it a penis. Let us then ask our question again: in what forum can transmutations of this order take place? And what are its rules?

Let us begin with an observation. It is quite clear that the conversations between Freud and his client would have soon and definitely collapsed if either one had not exercised this "active transcendence," characteristic of human beings, of which Maldiney was speaking in the text cited above. If either one of them had failed to follow this movement of transcendence which leads each expression beyond itself, toward another expression and thus something other than the expression, where the subject could also be (since a subject is nowhere in an absolute sense), then the dialogue collapses. The existence or the maintenance of this transcendence thus is the first condition of psychoanalytic discourse. One can verify this first condition negatively in the case of schizophrenia where its absence makes a real psychoanalysis unfeasible. The confusion between signifier and signified, such as we have described and clarified it, provides a typical example of the importance of transcendence. Certainly, we believe that a schizophrenic discourse, for example, the delirium of Schreber–reveals also another meaning than the one which comes through immediately. But it is simply impossible to make the patient become aware of this other meaning since precisely for him that movement of transcendence has stopped or was never available to him. When the patient admits having been his mother's lover one hour after his birth and claims that he remembers it perfectly, we catch the hidden meaning of these remarks, over and above their evidently absurd primary meaning. But the patient sees in it with certainty only a real event. He certainly recognizes it as surprising, but he interprets it as a good witness to the exceptional personage that he is.

Let us add here this other remark, although our thesis must appear shocking to many: this transcendence is also a transcendence toward the world, at least in a certain sense, but one which should not be minimized. The normal person and the neurotic cannot escape the commerce with and the involvement in the world. Let us remember what has been said about 'grasp, prehension." From this world the patient draws not only what he says, but also the means by which he says it. The silence of the hebephrenic is also his absence from the world, as is also the echolalia of the catatonic. For how, otherwise, would the symptom be able to speak. And it is in the world, ours and his, that the hysteric is paralyzed. Certainly, it is true, in a certain manner, to say that the symptom, by its stereotyped repetitions (at least in certain cases), witnesses to a certain blockage of this transcendence. But the psychoanalytic discourse, and the transference in which it culminates, have the effect of reestablishing the transcendence. This is possible only because outside of the symptomatic zone, this transcendence has been maintained, in contrast to what takes place with the schizophrenic where its abolition is, in the limit, total; it is for the same reason that, in this regard, we have spoken previously of the non-existence or the extinction of the subject-being.

Indeed, one must accept that if it is true that psychoanalytic therapy tries to make the language which structures the unconscious speak openly, it is equally true that it tries to promote "the emergence of the symbolic world into the world of reality."(49) If, as it has been said many times, notably following Lacan, that nothing *real* happens in psychoanalytic therapy, it is true also that the patient has undertaken it in order that something will happen in the real. This, however, will be his business and not that of the psychoanalyst. Indeed, the patient will have to introduce the truth found in the psychoanalytic therapy into the real. If the unveiling of the different relationships which link the 'Rat man' to his father, to the concept of debt, to his fiancée, have been tested, and if they were valid and hence something more than a vain play of the mind or an existential illusion, certain results will follow.

Among other things, the 'Rat man' will henceforth find himself able to decide, and *knowing* what he decides, to carry out the proposed marriage or not; he will stop pretending to pay a debt in order never to pay it, whether he finally settles the debt or he refuses to do so. In this we rediscover transcendence toward the world. It, and it alone, promotes this emergence of the symbolic world into reality. Furthermore, it permits us to understand, with Maldiney, that "the methodological and deontological rules of psychoanalysis all converge in this fundamental purpose of making the psychoanalyst the center of a *normal* domain in the *pathological* world of the patient."(50)

This means that if the psychoanalyst would act as a partner or as an effective foil to the transference desires of the patient, he would get involved in the pathological world which created these desires. But the psychoanalyst should not explore the real surroundings of the patient either, since the patient does not belong to these surroundings and has no place in them. The rules creating neutrality, proscribing abstention, and prohibiting all significant worldly relations with the patient–and they go as far as forbidding to look him in the eyes–aim precisely at making possible for the patient the movement of transcendence toward his world. This movement passes through the psychoanalyst but will not stop with him since in this world the psychoanalyst is a stranger, and he must not and also cannot give the patient any support in that world.

One should not seek to deny that this dialectic and this procedure brings to the psychoanalytic relation a certain ambiguity. On the side of the patient, this ambiguity finds its origin in the fact that if the patient establishes an authentic relationship of communication with the therapist, he achieves this only by building this relationship from the most diverse kind of identifications. And those identifications certainly are not authentic.

One will notice, in addition, that this double relation to the other has for foundation a double type of relationship to oneself that the first relation incarnates and symbolizes at the same time. Indeed, the patient is present in his history in two different manners "which imply two temporalities or rather two temporalizations."(51)

According to one form of temporalization the patient is prisoner of his identifications and he exists in the world as it were with a "closed past" which can only be indefinitely repeated. According to the other, produced in his discourse, "time opens itself out into the future" because already in his psychoanalytic discourse the patient anticipates, as we have seen, the new and true sense of his existence.

The fact that psychoanalysis is at least partially analysis of transference, means, as a matter of fact, that psychoanalysis carefully and progressively leads the patient to become conscious that the inclinations and phantasies directed by him toward the psychoanalyst are, in fact, re-workings and repetitions of a past which is buried but not abolished, a past which is unchangeable and compelling. This return and this progress manifests well to what point it is natural for psychoanalysis to refer as much to the past as to the future, and that in an in-dissociable manner. That which is successively unveiled is only uncovered in the perspective of a future which promises a still more radical unveiling and in light of a transcendence toward the world. In one sense, it is perfectly right to say that what thrusts the "Rat man" into psychoanalysis, and also that which is going to end it, is the problem of the final meaning of his love. In his own eyes, this love for his fiancée is ambiguous in that he does not know whether he should marry or repudiate her. In yet another sense, the whole development of the therapy is contained in the deepening of these two questions as they are linked to the question of the father and the question of the debt. We have seen that the answers to these questions come back from the farthest past, just as they anticipate the most decisive future. A psychoanalytic therapy is thus certainly a kind of history, even if, taken in themselves, all the materials of which it is constructed, are not historic. This is so because the factual material is not as such taken up in historical growth. Rather this material constitutes its frozen deposit.

But, then, from where does progress come in the therapy and what does the psychoanalyst do in order to assure it? "The inaugural act of psychoanalysis is the decision of the patient to take away from himself and to give to the psychoanalyst the responsibility for the care of his existence (in the sense of *Sorge* in Heidegger). The final act of the cure is the fact that the patient takes this care in his own hands again. Between these two termini, the psychoanalyst has not been simply the witness to the patient's expressions, the pole of his identifications, nor even essentially the questioner. He has been above all the respondent: he whose words assume the meaning of the other, the patient, in order that this other can assume the meaning of these same words, and thereby become himself his own respondent."(52)

The psychoanalyst is the guardian of meaning and it is only in the realm of meaning that he exercises his expertise. It is up to him "to discover in the immediate linkings of transitions and expressions the real or true order."(53) This true order appears first as masked, twisted, and deformed. Nevertheless, this order is in some manner already avowed, perceptible to the good listener, even though always unknown to the one who utters it. This is also why distance and neutrality are so essential to the psychoanalytic activity. If the therapist abandons them, he will but be confused by superficial agitations which have as purpose to shuffle the cards and obliterate this true order. The psychoanalyst remains thus constantly attentive to this transcendence of meaning; outside of this attention, the transference produces only one more repetition, as perfectly useless and sterile as the preceding ones. Thus one can understand to what extent the cure, correctly understood, must remain aloof from all real or pretended psychological penetration, from all forms of *Einfühlung,* 'intuition,' as also from all desire or anxiety to normalize or adapt, because psychoanalytic therapy takes place at another level. Centered on language, psychoanalysis finds there, according to the celebrated title of an article by Lacan, its field and the only one that it may have to conquer or to work in.[47] But this language is also, as all language, a language which points toward the real.

It is thus not at all a matter of finding out–less still of tracking down–some sort of motivations, or even some sorts of "complexes." It is a matter, if I dare say, of listening to a meaning which goes against another meaning and which manifests itself first as a non-sense. Indeed, this non-sense is not at all deprived of meaning. Simply this meaning contradicts the lines of comprehension which, at first, seemed to impose themselves. The tortuous and complicated maneuvers by which the 'Rat man' attempts at the same time to pay his debt and not to pay it are, on first sight, pure non-sense and absurdity. At any

---

[47]   The article referred to is: "Fonction et champs de la parole et du langage en psychanalyse." This has been translated by Wilden in *The Language of the Self* as: "The Function of Language in Psychoanalysis." Even more pointed is the title of Section II of the article; "Symbole et langage comme structure et limite du champ psychanalytique," translated by Wilden as: "Symbol and Language."

rate, they manifestly contradict the ordinary conduct of a debtor. The latter has a choice between two attitudes: either to reimburse that which he owes or, if he is less scrupulous, to try to extricate himself from this obligation by some means or other, good or bad. On the contrary, it seems insane to want to do both things at the same time.

Indeed, it seems insane, unless one knows that it was not a matter in the first place, notwithstanding the appearances, of paying to an obliging third person the amount due on a postal parcel accepted by him in the patient's name. It seems insane, unless one learns little by little through the discourse of the 'Rat man' the following facts: first, that his father was as his son a reserve officer; that he was a dishonest gambler who, in the course of a stay in the military, acquired and got rid of a "pot" that his mess mates had given him to hold. Second, that the son has a secret and unconscious hate for his father (hate which became slowly apparent in the course of the therapy); that he desires to disavow the conduct of his father by himself showing the strictest honesty; third, that a powerful repression of this hate impelled him, on the contrary, not to pay in order to be as his father was and not to want to be better than he; finally, and above all, that behind these stories of little debts in youth, there stands out the debt–really unpayable–due by every son to his father in return for the name that he has given him. This debt requires the son to renounce the first object of love. But this non-payment is, however, totally unacceptable to the consciousness of our patient since it really means disowning a father that he identifies with and wants to love and honor.

In the light of this insurmountable conflict, the apparent contradictions in the conduct of our patient no longer are at all meaningless, nor incoherent, nor incomprehensible. They only insinuate this same fundamental conflict into facts chosen unconsciously for their symbolic bearing. They insinuate that the patient seeks to resolve the conflict at all cost but without success, because he makes impossible compromises which become that many symptoms and that many unconscious discourses.

These symptoms express the conflict in the style proper to obsessional neurosis and thus in the materials provided by the personal history of the patient. Although the behavior of the patient is absurd on the practical level, it has nevertheless a meaning at a deeper level for whoever knows how to listen, i.e., for whoever is capable of making speak the being itself of him who acts in this absurd way.

Thus we are here faced with discourse, with meaning and with communication. But we are also faced with intersubjective relations since the "problem" (as one says) of the 'Rat man' is a possibility for each of us and thus poses a question about our own being. Indeed, the question of the Debt is posed to each of us. And if the response of each of us differs from the one which the 'Rat man' wrote by means of his bodily symptoms, we can nevertheless understand his response since it is a response to a question which is posed to all of us. Certainly the 'Rat man's' response is pathological. It is pathological since it takes away the dynamic aspect of *meaning*-creation in a whole sector of the 'Rat man's' life. And since the dynamic aspect is characteristic of being of human existence, it is clear that the whole sector is henceforth blocked, bound to stereotype, to rigidity, to sterile repetition. But a congealed or dead meaning is not nonsense, and is thus not empty of all significance.

Previously we have shown how and why psychoanalysis, in unveiling this significance, can restore the dynamic aspect of significance by reopening it to the plasticity and nourishment of a once more creative history.

Precisely this turning about, this redirection of congealed significance onto the path of meaning-creation is, in the case of the psychotic, held to be impossible. Therefore, with regard to the psychotic, there cannot be a psychoanalysis in a rigorous and Freudian sense of the term. For the psychotic, in effect– and we take up again here a fundamental distinction of Heideggerian thought– the meaning of the word is not only congealed: the word itself is transported from the order of the *Zuhandenheit,* 'instrumentality,' to that of the *Vorhandenheit* 'thinghood.' Under these conditions, words are confused with existing things, apprehended in perception, and acquire the status of things.

Roland Kuhn(54) presents the case of a schizophrenic who possessed a collection of cartons on each of which he writes one of the words which he uses. For this patient, "words are not just the titles of a sort of catalogue of the world. They possess, in the cellular rectangle on which they are written, a special extension. They hereby become literally the places for the things, for the arts, and for the sciences. These latter, the patient views as "models" comparable to those which one sees 'exhibited in museums.'"(55) Here there is no need to seek a place for an eventual psychoanalysis. There is none since its place, the "domain" of language, has evaporated. Indeed, as we have tried to describe it in another part of this work, the psychotic confuses signifier and signified. This confusion abolishes all meaning-creating relationships. This meaning-creation cannot be restored, as can happen with a petrified meaning. Indeed, the petrified meaning is restored to life by making it once more communicate with the living sectors of the patient's existence. But when the meaning-creation is abolished there is no longer any passage possible from one meaning to another meaning because significations are traded like pieces of money with unchangeable value. Worse, these significations are treated as money whose value would reside in the value of the raw material of the coin. In this case the coin is not used any longer to pay debts. Similarly the schizophrenic does not use words to speak: he presents words as if they were things. And these words speak of themselves; they are not spoken by he who emits them. This is why they can transform themselves for him into anonymous "voices," as we have explicated it in studying the commentary of Lacan on the case of Schreber.

This allows us to give a new interpretation of what the authors generally call the "mannerisms" of schizophrenics. One says of an individual with mannerisms that he "poses." One means by this that he sets himself up in the attitude of a "model." This is an act without action, Maldiney tells us, because it is an act which does not open up or which does not aim at the world. "The model does not dwell in the surrounding-space." The model does not dwell at all, it appears; and it appears as an apparition without presence. One will understand in the same way the incapacity of numerous schizophrenics to find, when they do speak, the correct tone. They murmur or they cry, they recite as if by heart or make the words follow each other without putting any intonation in them. This is because they do not really address themselves to him who seems to be their interlocutor. Their discourse has only a literal meaning, and no reference is made to the context and thus to the listener. Indeed, words have for these patients none of the connotations that they draw from their insertion in a living experience and a living language. Whatever their language may be, these patients only speak dead languages. Here is, for example, a classic response, heard time and time again. At the moment when the patient entered the anteroom of the clinic, I asked her, after some introductory exchanges: Madame, how long have you been here? "For just twenty seconds, sir" [she replied]. For "here" can have only its literal sense: the precise place in which one finds oneself. *Here* could thus not designate the clinic, still less the city of Louvain or Belgium. This is different from the case where we run by chance into a friend who has been absent, and say to him, "what a surprise, old chap, since when have you been here?" He understands right away that he is not being asked how long he has occupied the portion of the sidewalk on which he stands.

This is why, furthermore, it appears to the schizophrenic as simple and as natural to invent a new word as for a mathematician to change the symbols or letters in his proofs or figures. One schizophrenic speaks constantly of "poulpets"; he really means a hermaphrodite human individual. "Priests are poulpets, since they are men inside and women outside: they wear dresses"–This person had been hospitalized for twenty years! Another one called his "voices," which are loud and suddenly surging, "Boeing"; a third, who makes frequent journeys in the sky, uses for this purpose a vehicle which she denominates the "panamericanairvese." This name, articulated as if it were a single word and stripped of all resemblance to English pronounciation, appeared to me to mean nothing and this pearl would have escaped me without the perspicacity of a doctor familiar both with the large airlines and with Franglais.

Now, it is precisely the tone, the melody, the mimicry, certain accentuations which have as purpose to *engage* a discourse, to insure that the speaker addresses himself to ... and, already, by that, makes sure that he transcends the literal meaning of his words toward new meanings which are still partially hidden. Because speech is incarnated and inserted into the entire world of meanings, it can never be reduced to a geometrical demonstration or to the communication of an informative message.[48] This insertion permits the per-

---

[48] A famous and suggestive article on the multiple levels of language is: R. Jakobson: "Linguistics and Poetics."

petual encroachment of speech on itself. This encroachment and this insertion are destroyed in the schizophrenic. In the neurotic though they are only interrupted. Furthermore they are interrupted only in certain sectors of his experience and of his discourse. Returning to the phenomenon of the pose, we see that it is quite analogous.

"If one attempts to approach the concept of schizophrenia from the point of view of time, affective rapport, communication, language, etc., with the aid of the notions of closure, repetition, spiritlessness, estrangement, ambivalence, we see that each of these traits refer to all of the others and that all converge in *thematisation*. When the *in* severs itself from presence in the world, 'the being of the *Umwelt* receives a strict delimitation. The totality of the *Vorhanden* becomes Theme.'"(56)

The central core of all schizophrenia seems thus to rest in the rupture of all exchanges between presence and meaning. Where the latter ceases to root itself in the former, meaning loses all power of transcending itself. It congeals and, in some manner, substantiates itself, hypostatises itself. This is what Maldiney means by using, more or less fortunately, the phenomenological notion of *thematisation*. For, in effect, it is just in the non-thematic that meaning and presence can continually come in contact with one another, can pass into one another. By the interruption of this osmosis, it comes about that meaning is torn from its existential moorings, is abandoned to itself, and is thus transformed into a proliferating and more or less caricaturing usurper of presence. This is what is meant by speaking of the confusion of the signifier and the signified. This is carried to its maximal intensity in hallucinatory delirium. We find a perfect illustration of it in the story already cited, of Serge Leclaire concerning sparrows.(57)

From this point of view, one can risk an interpretation of autism which adds some traits to those of which we have already spoken. It is characterized, according to Freud, by the withdrawal of all the libidinal investments directed toward objects and the world and the transfer of these onto the subject. From this point of view, autism and narcissism are synonymous terms. Yet, there is no sense in thinking that this loss of the world and this reflux of the subject toward himself safeguards or purifies this subject. In fact, the subject is no less lost than the world, in which the exchange of presence and sense ceases. And that which we witness in autism is the thematization that has just been described, this time bearing on the ego itself. Autism "expresses the thematization of the ego whose behavior is not founded in the *in* of being-in-the-world."(58)

Thus it will be in the *in* of the being-in-the-world, that is to say, in the spatialization proper to human existence, that we will have to seek the primordial place of the exchange and participation of which we have just spoken. The *Stimmung,* 'mood,' is a kind of judgment about the way of being-in-the-world.[49]

[49]   See also Joseph H. Smith: "The Heideggerian and Psychoanalytic Concepts of Mood."

Indeed the presence of *"Stimmungen"* is an indication that a human being has a grasp on his relation with the totality of being. Although this grasp is not necessarily conscious, it is certainly "felt." The *"Stimmung"* could thus be said to be a judgment upon the total lived space in which one dwells. Clearly, this space is different from the space in which one represents things. And this space is even more different from the space of geometry. "There is a similarity of meaning suggested in the words ascension and illumination and in the words darkening and fall. Each pair of words creates a similarity in meaning-connotation which lights up an identical pathos. Still this last term has the default of evoking only the ideas of passivity although the pathetic moment requires in fact activity."(59) The pathetic dimension constitutes a rapport to the totality of beings. It is rooted in and communicates with the things as they are present. But it also changes or transforms the meaning- creating organization imposed on space. The fatigue of the athlete, for instance, who is at the end of his strength, who is totally depleted and who pulls himself along–more than he runs–the last kilometers of a marathon, this fatigue also transforms the distance to the finish– which is getting objectively smaller and smaller–into a murderous, interminable space of inexorably insuperable distance.(60) This is even more dramatic if one sees that the fatigue is going to make him lose the marathon he had all but won. When this communication has been broken, then the movement of meaning-creation also stops. This does not mean that the significations disappear as well, but they no longer "touch" reality or are no longer "touched" by it. This is similar to the figures which the geometer draws. They are assuredly not deprived of meaning, but they "tell" us nothing of things. This can explain the estrangement, the discord, the mannerism, the "morbid rationalism" which are all part of the clinical picture describing the behavior of the schizophrenic.

V. A Structural Interpretation of the Oedipus Complex

These considerations were intended to show how a problematic of the unconscious, expressed in concepts of meaning, structure, historicity, and situation, can escape the naturalistic context which was effectively the one of Freud. We think it can be done without relinquishing anything that a naturalistic context is capable of doing. Such an interpretation has as its purpose to show that the structure of a human being as seen by psychoanalysis is in accord with the account given by the philosophers of being-in-the-world. It can even complete their view and renders superfluous the inflexibility, sometimes close to mythology, which characterizes Freudian realism, without, however, falling into Politzerian intellectualism.

One could sketch a tentative analogue with respect to the Oedipus complex. If instead of attaching oneself to the scenic dramaturgy of the *Oedipus* complex, one is attentive to its structure, one notices that the Oedipal triangle is strictly speaking the typical form of the being-in-the-world of the child, of the style of his communication with others, with things, and with himself (*Mitwelt-Umwelt-Eigenwelt*).(61)

There is no doubt, indeed, that the Oedipal moment marks in the development of the subject the coming of a new mode of existence. This new mode secures the subject against the risk or the temptation to abandon himself to two antithetical, but similarly ruinous, possibilities. This temptation is the greater since certain stages of the subject's anterior development strongly disposes him to these two possibilities which are: the role of *They* and the wish to be an *Absolute Ego*. For, on the one hand, the "maternal space," as it is created in the period of the dual union, is the prototype of all fatherlands, of all future "Homelands." It is a space which sets up a universal presence without limits which has nothing outside itself and ignores all distinction between the same and the other. The period of the dual union makes presence and the All reciprocal: it is, exactly, the primordial participation such as it is defined by a thinker such as Szondi.[50] But it is also a nocturnal absolute, where all cows are black, because such a presence necessarily lacks differentiations.

Clinical experience shows us well enough to what ravages all fixation at and all regression towards this maternal union are leading. One such patient maintains that he expresses himself through the voice of all the lecturers, of all the professors, of all the politicians and even of all the revolutionaries whose discourse appears to him to merit some interest. He gives the name A to this ego who knows everything, thinks everything, is acquainted with everything, and besides can hypnotize anyone. Indeed, the speaker from whom A borrows the speech organs does not realize what happens and thinks that he is speaking even though he remains quiet or, at least, when what he says is but the thought of another. Our patient recognizes, however, that he is ill and beseeches imperiously that he be cured. But he does not at all want to be delivered from his omniscience and from the unceasing migration of A. Quite on the contrary, he expects from the treatment that it will make his ego and A fully coincide. He is now A, but for the moment he does not have full and free disposition of A, in the sense that A can speak with the voice of M. Pompidou or of Kohn-Bendit. The patient knows it only once these voices have started to talk and he cannot predict today what they will make the subject of their next discourse. It is this–and this only–this perpetual *Nachträglichkeit,* 'deferred action'–that he judges to be pathological in his case. "I would be cured when I will have totally mastered A, when consciously and constantly, A and 'I' will be identical; at this moment, I would be truly everything and I would truly know all."(62)

But the reduction to the role of "They" is as dangerous.[51] For another such patient, all the truths have been completely said. Only, it is impossible to know who says them. No need of proofs, of verifications, of witnesses, of

---

[50]   L. Szondi: *Ich-Analyse*, p. 34, 179, 524.

[51]   See Heidegger's analysis of the failing of Dasein where he treats the same problem: *Being and Time*, p. 210ff.

experiments to know, for example, if it is true that his daughter had been thrown by his son-in-law from the top of one of the towers of the St. Gudule cathedral; it has been said, thus it is true. God exists, the Jews are C . . . . It has been said, thus it is true. But this truth doesn't involve anyone, doesn't concern anyone, is addressed to no one and implicates no one. For example, the patient in question is perfectly happy to receive a visit from this "assassin" son-in-law and is not at all astonished that he is accompanied by his granddaughter whom he supposedly had killed. Speech runs around like a sleuth ("he runs, he runs . . . "). Furthermore language is self-sufficient.

The paternal figure such as it is encountered in the Oedipus complex restructures such a world from top to bottom. This figure changes all the landmarks in the pre-Oedipal personality or rather this figure provides the pre-Oedipal personality with landmarks of which it was deprived. This does not mean that this figure brings about the abolition of omnipotence. But henceforth this omnipotence is *other* and exists in another way than it did before. "The father is the husband of the mother, master of the external world and judge."(63) The father is not only *one* of the three terms of the constellation. He is the term which radically modifies the internal relationships, previously obtaining between the first two. This is done by separating these first two, by situating the one relative to the other in a world which in turn has been changed.

This does not mean at all that one must look upon the father as a monolithic figure. Quite to the contrary. Indeed, the father introduces distinctions throughout, both in himself and elsewhere. As has been explained above when we analyzed the problem of the name, he ratifies the rise of the subject to the order of the symbolic and he situates himself at least partially in this order as well as in the real order. And although he has a repressive function he is also, and perhaps to a greater extent, an ideal that the child identifies with.[52]

One can thus follow Maldiney, when he underlines the fact that the father is not only, nor even in the first place, an impressive personality in our most ancient legend. One must say of him that he is a *figure*, in the Hegelian sense of the *Phenomenology of the Mind*. By this we mean that the father by his mere appearance remodels, as does every figure in Hegel's *Phenomenology*, all presence and, by that, all experience. For Hegel, "The Unhappy Consciousness," "The Law of the Heart," or "The Course of the World" are moments which question everything and give a new dimension to the concepts of presence and of the real, and furthermore allow the Spirit in successive levels to march toward the full possession of itself.[53] Similarly, the paternal figure

---

[52] See Ch. IV, II: "'The Elements of the Oedipus Complex" (A.D.W., p. 88ff). See also the article by A. de Waelhens: "Vaderschap en Oedipuscomplex."

[53] Hegel himself calls such a moment which questions everything: Experience *(Phenomenology, p. 142)*. Such experience involves frustration. Hegel calls it: doubt or despair (p. *135*).

questions, gives new dimensions and allows the development of the child toward subjectivity and identity. It is this structuralizing role which psychoanalytic language wants to put in evidence when it speaks of the paternal image.[54]

And this is why the notion of *identification with the father,* which is one of the favorable sequels of a successfully liquidated Oedipal phase, is not exempt from problems nor ambiguities. If this identification were carried out literally "the significative role of paternity" would be confused with and exhausted by the concrete person that the historic father is. This in turn would result in the child being fixated in his infantile situation. Indeed, whenever identification results in imitating a concrete personage, it "misses the mark." There are two reasons for this: first, no one, ever, can be himself by copying another, even if this other be the father. Second, it is clear that if this exemplary father is reduced to his concrete and anecdotal reality, it will be a father with infantile characteristics. The concrete father can only have those characteristics that young children can perceive.

On the contrary, the identification will be successful and will be fruitful if the child refuses total identification with the historical father but instead identifies "non-thematically" with the action of the father. We borrow together with Maldiney the term "non-thematic" from phenomenology. This term seeks to express the structural and symbolic bearing of the paternal figure, and includes the three functions mentioned above, i.e., father is the husband of the mother, he is the master of the exterior world, and he is the judge."[55]

At the level of the non-thematic, the domination of the father over the exterior does not mean that he behaves like an absurd all-powerful tyrant but that by his presence a *world,* at the same time *real* and *true,* is constituted for the child. And that the father has the role of judge means on the same level that the child is asked to place his desire under the guidance of the law incarnated by this father. It means further that if the child does not do so willingly he will be compelled to do so.

The identification of the child with his father does not mean that the child will retain until the end of his days all the "tics" of his father, that he must stick to the preferences and the dislikes of his father, nor even that he has to choose his father's profession, nor finally that he has to take over his moral commitments. But, *first of all,* it means that he enters into the system of rules that legislates and constitutes the world. It means, *second,* that when the moment comes, he will assume this same role with respect to his own descendants.

---

[54] For a definition of the psychoanalytic usage of the concept "imago," see Lacan, " La Famille" p. *8.40-5;* Laplanche and Pontalis: *The Language of Psychoanalysis,* index word: imago, p. *211.*

[55] The negative consequences of the absence of the father (related to the second function: being the master of the exterior world) are described very well in Pettigrew: *A Profile of the Negro American, p. 15-24.*

Only such an identification will assure the present and future independence of the child. This independence, however, would, on the contrary, be definitively compromised by a copy-identification.

In particular, a successful identification will permit the child to incorporate in his existence the world of play and of magic which he has so much need of. Such a child will be able to take this world of play and magic seriously, *but without ever seeking to substitute the first world for the real world.* The child who would have lacked all identification would have no other world than this magical world, which is not a world but something *imaginary,* which, in these conditions, would soon produce psychosis. Inversely, the young subject who gets tangled up in copy-identification, will be only a caricature of an adult, a mature child. And before long such a child will be a childish adult.

VI. Central Role of Language

One can see that our way of understanding the meaning and the place of psychoanalysis results in linking this latter much less (or not at all) with psychological mechanisms than with the concepts of "being-in-the-world" and "language." Furthermore, it calls into question the customary distinction between an interior and an exterior world. This bears as yet no relation to the unconscious. Simply, contrary to certain psychologizing interpretations, it does not seek to place the unconscious where it is not.

Instead of the classical distinction between an interior and an exterior world, we have substituted the idea that a human being has several ways of occupying and inhabiting the world. This diversity can be reduced to the following three essential ones: (and we take up here a terminology that Binswanger borrowed from Heidegger) the *Eigen-Welt* or world of the self; the *Umwelt* or the surrounding world, and, finally, the *Mitwelt* or world of encounter. " Being-in-the-world is unveiling in it under the triple form of being-oneself, of being present to . . . , of the being-with. These three modes of being are concerned with one's own body, the thing, and the other."(64) It is evident, moreover, and it has been sufficiently shown in the course of this work, that these modes, however distinct, are also related one to the other.

For a long time, indeed, phenomenological thought has familiarized us with the idea that the difference in status of things is founded in the spatiality and the mobility of the body itself. Such a typical difference is that between a tool, which can be used practically *(Zuhandenes),* and a thing which is simply there, is looked at through a theory and subjected to theoretical calculations. The concepts of spatiality and of mobility of the body also influence, as it is shown in *Being and Time,*[56] the "vicissitudes of the relation near-far, (of)

[56]   The crucial work of M. Heidegger.

exclusion and of inclusion in unknown space."(65) And with respect to the Other, did psychoanalysis not convince us that the encounter with the other, just as also the way the other himself appears is tied to the manner in which the patient inhabits his world and his body; furthermore, did psychoanalysis not convince us that the degree of otherness of the Other specifies for the "subject" his manner of being in his world and in his body?

How, in this regard, can we avoid pointing out once more the exceptionally revealing bearing that language has for the comprehension and evaluation of pathological modes of existing? One can–and one must–disclose in the pathological the "reflection and anticipation of all other forms of conduct."(66)

For language constitutes the most complete expression of mental illness. It is at the same time the instrument that permits the patient to communicate something and is also the instrument that opens him up in order to direct him to the possibility of real communication. But this requires that one can make the patient speak and that one knows how to listen. "Concrete terms treated as complete sentences or as gestures are the most significant ones. The particularities of these words and above all of neologisms, borrow more from the past and from the actuality of pathological existence than from the ordinary and codified intentions of language. It is not rare, for example, that repetition of certain words or alteration of the meaning of them suffices to reveal the key to a delirium. Such was the case with the patient who spoke of a cousin. The patient had lively but ambiguous feelings of jealousy towards this cousin. Needless to say, she did not admit of having these feelings. The patient told us on several different occasions that this cousin adopted "humiliating" behavior with respect to her. We had the impression that she wished to say "haughty" and this is, indeed, the translation that she gave us in Dutch (hoogmoedig). The patient's mother tongue was Dutch, but she refused to speak any other language than French. Her excellent knowledge of this language would appear to exclude her being able to confuse 'humiliating' and 'haughty.'[57] In fact, she used the phonetic similarity to express that which she refused to think openly about but which her unconscious betrayed: her cousin inspired humiliating feelings in her and, according to the mechanism of projection which Freud explains to us in the case of Schreber, she judged the attitude of her cousin to be humiliating. The same patient claimed that the physical approaches of her relatives to her as well as their feelings about her had "changed and were bizarre." At the same time she called herself "the wom-orphosis." This neologism clearly indicated to everybody that this change, this metamorphosis, had its source in herself.

These examples show that certain words or certain representations can "crystallize" and also condense certain facts, certain real or fantastic objects,

---

[57]   The French words are: "honteux" and "hautain".

on which the delusion hinges.

Nevertheless, what characterizes schizophrenic existence is that these symbolic and stereotyped words and representations have no longer any *hold* on the world. They have ceased to signify their signification and have become the *imprisonment* of signification. We explained this mechanism when we studied delirium, hallucination and the confusion of signifier and signified.[58] This could be expressed by a spacial metaphor as Maldiney did when he wrote that, for the schizophrenic, "being at a distance is abolished."(67)

No object any longer points at another object and the patient has ceased to weave this net of references which is for us the life and the continuity of experience. In affirming this, I do not mean to deny certain appearances: the patient makes associations, sometimes even does not stop seeing relationships: the blushing of the face proves the infidelity of the husband; the mineralogical plaque 49R47 shows, by this R, that it belongs to a royal automobile, etc. But these pseudo-relations, if I dare to say so, are gratuitous and are self-made. They do not have their source in an anticipatory and projective movement toward things, but in the relationships between words or in abusively substantivised qualities. It is true that in certain circumstances blushing of the face can betray sexual emotion or the confusion of being surprised in a delicate situation. It can, however, in certain contexts only be truly attributed to other causes. Indeed fever, bad circulation of the blood, or physical effort, and many other causes can equally make the face blush. It is false that facial blushing must *forcibly* establish the infidelity of the blusher.

NOTES

(1) Note that, for Heidegger, theoretical knowledge (*theorein*), scientific knowledge, and even the knowledge which is detached knowing of things, remain subordinate to a primordial understanding from which they derive. This primordial understanding cannot be distinguished from existence as disclosure.

(2) *Critique des fondements de la Psychologie*, Paris, 1928, quoted from the 1968 edition, p. 156.

(3) J. Laplanche and S. Leclaire, "L'inconscient, une étude psychanalytique," in *L'inconscient*, Paris, Desclée de Brouwer, 1966, p. 97 (English translation, Yale French Studies, 48, 1975, p. 119).

(4) *Écrits*, p. 258 (E: p.49). Wilden, p. 20.

(5) *Écrits*, p. 249 (E: p. 42). Wilden, p. 11.

(6) *Écrits*, p. 249 (E: p. 42). Wilden, p. 11.

(7) *Écrits*, p. 467.

(8) *Écrits*, p. 468.

(9) *Écrits*, p. 259 (E: p. 50).

[58] See Ch V. III (This book, p. 202)

(10) *Problèmes de linguistique générale*, p. 79.

(11) *Ibid.*, p. 82.

(12) *Ibid.*, p. 83.

(13) *Ibid.*, p. 85.

(14) *Ibid.*, p. 85.

(15) *Ibid.*, p. 85.

(16) *Ibid.*, p. 86.

(17) M. Merleau-Ponty, *Phenomenologie of Perception*, p. 344.

(18) It should be noted that these reflections are only inspired by the Heidegger of *Being and Time*.

(19) H. Maldiney, "Comprendre" in *Revue de Métaphysique et de Morale*, 1961, no. 1 and 2, p. 35.

(20) *Ibid.*, p. 35.

(21) *Ibid.*, p. 35.

(22) Introduction to the book of P. Demoulin *Névrose et Psychose*, p. 9-10.

(23) *Ibid.*, p. 36.

(24) The difference between dream and psychosis is that in the former the images *might* be able to become signifiers because the dreamer, in waking, can reintegrate them for himself into the finished order of discourse while the psychotic whose life is dominated by foreclosure could never do this. Therefore, his "discourse" will only be a discourse "in itself" (de facto) or "for us," not "for him." The terms in quotation marks are used in their Hegelian sense of *in itself, for itself* and *for us*. [Underlining of last three expressions is ours. W.V.E.].

(25) Maldiney, p. 37.

(26) *Ibid.*, p. 37-38.

(27) *Ibid.*, p. 38.

(28) Maldiney, *op. cit.*, p. 38.

(29) Maldiney, *op. cit.*, p. 39.

(30) Maldiney, *op. cit.*, p. 39.

(31) Maldiney, *op. cit.*, p. 39.

(32) Maldiney, *op. cit.*, p. 39.

(33) Freud, G.W. VII, p. 339; S.E., X, p. 104.

(34) Maldiney, *op. cit.*, p. 40.

(35) Maldiney, *op. cit.*, p. 40.

(36) Maldiney, *op. cit.*, p. 40.

(37) W. Huber, H. Piron, A. Vergote, *La Psychanalyse, science de l'homme*, p. 174-75.

(38) H. Maldiney, *op. cit.*, p. 43.

(39) H. Maldiney, *op. cit.*, p. 44.

(40) H. Maldiney, *op. cit.*, p. 45.

(41) H. Maldiney, *op. cit.*, p. 52.

(42) H. Maldiney, *op. cit.*, p. 57.

(43) H. Maldiney, *op. cit.*, p. 57.

(44) *Ibid.*, p. 57.

(45) H. Maldiney, *op. cit.*, p. 58.

(46) S. Freud, G.W. VII, p. 392; S.E. X, p. 167.

(47) At the moment when the 'Rat man' enters into analysis, his father has been dead for

nine years. Now many months pass before Freud learns this, since the patient speaks of his father as if he were still alive.

(48) H. Maldiney, *op. cit.*, p. 58.

(49) H. Maldiney, *op. cit.*, p. 59.

(50) H. Maldiney, *op. cit.*, p. 59.

(51) H. Maldiney, *op. cit.*, p. 59.

(52) H. Maldiney, *op. cit.*, pp. 60-61.

(53) H. Maldiney, *op. cit.*, p. 61.

(54) R. Kuhn, *Daseinanalytische Studie über die Bedeutung von Grenzen im Wahn. Monatschrift fur die Psychiatrie und Neurologie*, 1952, nr. 4/5/6.

(55) H. Maldiney, *op. cit.*, p. 74.

(56) H. Maldiney, *op. cit.*, p. 76. The text cited by the author is a sentence of *Sein und Zeit* (p. 362).

(57) "Outside of this communication, we have certainly to deal with objective facts, but the moment of reality is wanting. Also this moment of reality fades away in the schizophrenic in whom communication remains blocked in hyper-objectivity. Even his compensatory delusion–the 'healing' as Freud calls it–which attempts to mobilize and reanimate the perception of this congealed world is progressively blocked, after the phase of the 'atmospherization' of the 'theme'." (Binswanger, *Der Fall Suzanne Urban*) Maldiney, *op. cit.*, p. 76.

(58) H. Maldiney, *op. cit.*, p. 77.

(59) H. Maldiney, *op. cit.*, p. 75.

(60) "The pathetic dimension of feeling is that of a communication with the being of things as they are given. It is as if these things themselves are shaken when the foundations of man are shaken." Maldiney, *op. cit.*, p. 76.

(61) H. Maldiney, *op. cit.*, pp. 77-78.

(62) After these lines were written, the patient became aware of the delusional character of these affirmations. He, therefore, corrected them appropriately.

(63) H. Maldiney, *op. cit.*, p. 78.

(64) H. Maldiney, *op. cit.*, p. 81.

(65) H. Maldiney, *op. cit.*, p. 87.

(66) *Ibid.*, p. 81.

(67) H. Maldiney, *op. cit.*, p. 81.

CONCLUSION

De Waelhens

I. Delirium and the Problem of the Real

This conclusion will be brief since, if the preceding pages have attained their goal, the conclusion will follow by itself.

Philosophical anthropology is no longer conceivable without serious study of the unconscious and of mental illness. This claim entails among other things, that the normal is not intelligible without the pathological. This does not mean that we hold that one passes from mental illness to normality by a continuous transition. Quite on the contrary, we accept an irreversible developmental theory of mental illness. We believe that the principal modes of pathology can be described, differentiated and articulated in such a way that the difficulties at the different levels of behavior of the patient become understandable. This can be done because the pathological structures are related to fixations in some stage of the constitution of the subject. Such a fixation completely structures the mental illness which results from it.

One knows, indeed, that the constitution or the becoming-subject of a human being passes through a series of crises which cause a total restructuring of what will ultimately be called the self, the world, and the other.[1]

If, for reasons that we have tried to bring out before, one of these crises does not get resolved or if, by hypothesis, the subject, for some reason regresses to a previous stage, we maintain that he could only apparently reach the latter stages or retain the benefits of them. As a consequence the relationships of the "subject" to himself, to the world, and to the other (which includes, needless to say, the relationship to the body, to sex, to love, to one's parents, to one's name, to the real, and to death) will be marked, in their meaning and in their status, by the phase where the individual has failed or where the failure is situated.

We have earlier given a description of these crises and of the risks of failing to overcome these crises to which each person is exposed. We have also given a description of the consequences which can result on the pathological level because of such failures, both with respect to the possibility for such a person to become a subject and with respect to the meaning of such a person's experiences. It is superfluous to repeat these descriptions here.

The fact that philosophical anthropology must take into account pathology and the study of the unconscious finds its justification in the fact that the con-

---

[1]   This is an essential thesis of Lacan, accepted by De Waelhens, and presented by Lacan in his article "La Famille."

stituting crises of subjectivity unfold totally, or almost totally in the unconscious. Furthermore, they appear in the open only because of their non-resolution in the diverse pathologies, which carry, in each instance, the imprint of the crisis which was unresolved.

From this point of view, psychoanalytic theory and research provides means for understanding pathology. Pathology, in turn, confirms certain psychoanalytic insights. No doubt, there is mutual influence here, which is to say there is a circle, however, this circle is a *hermeneutic* one.[2] It does not consist of giving gratuitous principles, from which one then claims to draw consequences, which are really already fixed in advance by the very choice of principles. As always when one questions human existence, it is a matter of a double and reciprocal *explication* of meaning and not a matter of a causal explanation. In this reciprocal explication, there is a mutual clarification of principle and of data. However, one cannot hope to find the type of certitude which characterizes the formal sciences. That attempts have been made to bring about a rapprochement with the latter is another matter. We do not have the competence to judge these attempts, but we have the impression that an eventual gain in formal rigor can hardly compensate for the obvious impoverishment of the content.

But let us return to our main argument. Since philosophical anthropology is willing to learn from a study of the unconscious and of the pathological, one has to recognize a primacy which philosophy has only recently acknowledged: the primacy of language.[3] We have already seen in what sense language structures the unconscious.[4] We have also seen how the failure of what Freud calls the original or primal repression, makes access to a full symbolic language impossible.[5] We also learned to see in this inaccessibility to symbolic language the core of the most radical psychosis. We hope that we also succeeded in showing why and how this failure of the primal repression is identical with the foreclosure of the name of the father ("The failure of the paternal metaphor" of J. Lacan) as well as identical with the preservation of or the regression to a fragmented body-image and finally with the incapacity of situating oneself with respect to the difference between the sexes. This latter

---

[2]   This aspect of hermeneutics is not different from the problem encountered in philosophy of science under the name of: "Theory-laden observation." See Carl Kordig, "The Theory-ladenness of observation." For a good study on hermeneutics, see Richard E. Palmer: *Hermeneutics, interpretation theory in Schleiermacher, Dilthey, Heidegger and Gadamer.*

[3]   K.O. Apel's program is to show the central place of language for philosophical reflexion. He shows it among others by indicating how philosophers have overlooked in a crucial moment of their reflexion the function of language. Several of his studies have appeared in the book: *Transformation der Philosophie.*

[4]   See Ch. VII, II, 1. C, b, p. 261ff.

[5]   See Ch. III.

situation (in the active sense of the word) is directly linked to the entrance into the Oedipus complex. Indeed, this entrance is itself rendered impossible by the failure of the paternal metaphor.

There are also important consequences if things are considered from another point of view or if other questions are asked. Philosophers have always asked themselves about "the experience of reality." But they have not often suspected that the study of insanity–at the various levels through which we have tried to understand this concept–could raise their insight into this problem substantially. Heidegger writes somewhere that nothing is more difficult than to see the glasses one wears on one's nose. The experience of reality is so "natural" for us and so "evident" that we can hardly discern its components, how it works and how many levels it has. Here again pathology makes manifest what the normal tends to hide under a veil of self-evidence. For example, the study of pathological cases shows very clearly that the opaqueness, the stability, and the distance of the object are not self-evident, but are strictly correlative to the constitution of the necessary structures of the subject's development. Furthermore, it is not the case that the real is either experienced or not. The common world in which the "normal people" live can be gradually eroded. The degree of erosion depends upon how early in the development of the subject the failure occurred. The nature of these failures, as well as the consequences which result from them for the subject's degree of participation in the common world can be made *intelligible*. At the same time, we are able to distinguish between diverse modalities or levels of experience of the real. We have mentioned this, for example, when we analyzed the question of truth and of the third as witness in schizophrenia or paranoia.

It is also very rewarding to study the very complex problems connected with the notion of delirium. As everyone knows, the etymological root of delirium is the Latin word *lira*, which means 'furrow' and the prefix *de* which signifies 'to leave, to go out of (as in 'deliver, derail, derive' etc.).[6] Someone who is delirious could thus be said to be someone who leaves the furrow of reality. However, for the reasons just mentioned, it is not always easy and it is rarely fruitful to define a delusion in reference to reality. The proof of this thesis is the fact that there are many jealous people, who are without a doubt delirious, but who have in fact been deceived by their wives or husbands. And let us remember Lacan's former teacher who made his interns laugh when, after having allowed a patient to speak, retorted "you see, my friend, all this is not serious, all this is not true, let us get back to the real." Yes, but which real? And how must we interpret the fact that such an invitation to return to the real never succeeds, whether this invitation be a friendly, an imperative or, as happened in previous decades and centuries, a forced one. The classic thesis defined the hallucination as a perception without object and delusion as the un-

---

[6]   The three words chosen as examples are not literal translations of the French examples. The English examples were chosen to convey the meaning of the prefix *de*.

shakeable conviction in the truth of events manifestly false. But this thesis cannot be valid because it cannot explain the fact that the patient never confused the hallucinated object and the perceived object and, moreover, never confused his conviction concerning the real events (the fact that it is raining) with the events of his delusion (the fact that you want to kill the patient). Let us consider, then, two particularly significant examples. A young girl accuses her doctor of burning her face during the night. She is asked if, when looking in the mirror the next morning, she can observe traces of these burns, to which she answers "That would truly be the last straw." Another girl pretends to give birth each week to several children. Reacting to this story in a different way than the teacher just mentioned, I remarked in an indifferent tone that she must spend a fortune in expenses for gynecologists and baptisms! I received this surprising response, which gets to the bottom of the problem of delirium: "You are deceiving me, you always believed what I told you and now you no longer believe me." The classic theory should have expected an opposite response. Indeed, in placing the delusion in the framework of the real, I should have received the patient's gratitude, at least if the classic postulate is right, i.e., that the conviction concerning these repeated births is of the same order as her conviction concerning the weather. Well, this is not so.

Once again it seems that the ideas presented in this book offer the hope of a better understanding of these difficulties. Let us recall briefly two comments made by Lacan in an article called "Propos sur la causalité psychique" (Écrits, pp. 151-193). The first declares that all hallucination and delusion essentially implies a phenomenon of *belief* and not perception in the real sense. The difference between Napoleon and the madman who thinks he is Napoleon is that Napoleon does not *think* himself to be Napoleon, while the madman does. Indeed, a king who is not crazy creates some distance between himself and his role of king. He does not identify totally with this role but takes it for what it is: a burden and a duty to fulfill, a role to play for the good of the State, but which cannot define him exhaustively. The madman, on the other hand, "believes" strongly and completely in this role. Now such a conviction cannot be situated relative to reality because the *referential* and *incomplete* character that is essential for all reality excludes any such identification. Even General de Gaulle did not believe that he was completely General de Gaulle because he tells us that he is also an old man who is exhausted by his trials and tribulations, who is detached from undertakings, who feels the approach of death, but who is never weary of watching in the shadow the gleam of hope.

The remarks of our patients can be interpreted quite well in this framework. For them there is no sense in placing, situating, or inserting the delirious events among the other events. For these delirious events would then become, like the others, relative, dependent, contingent, variable, indifferent at least to a certain extent, subjected to the ebb and flow of reactions and of interactions, as is the case for all reality; in short, they would be condemned to losing this absolute, unequivocal, certain, exemplary imaginary meaning (I mean relative to the order of the image) that is theirs and in light of which, alone, they were unconsciously created.

This thesis is confirmed by another argument which is built upon the second comment of Lacan. In the delirious event, whatever it may be, the patient always has a crucial role. The delusion has something to say to him even if it remains as yet unknown to him. Even if the delusion has a cosmic character, it transmits a message, it expresses a privilege or a damnation, exalts or ruins the subject and his abilities. It is this peculiar characteristic of the delirious event which makes it superfluous that anyone, the doctor, for example, should know it or should be informed of it. No patient will claim that you hear the voices that abuse him and, even if he claims them to be thundering, he will take no offense at the fact that you ask him if he hears them, while you talk to him.

One may recognize a double function in the delusion. First, like the dream, it fulfills an unsatisfied and generally narcissistic desire. This is why delusion can justifiably be interpreted using the same method as those used for the interpretation of the dream. Their application will even frequently be easier than in the case of the latter. If, as Freud said, psychosis is characterized by more or less total submersion of the ego by the unconscious, and by a repression of reality, one can see that this ego will no longer have any strength to disguise the language of the unconscious and to inflict on it the distortions which the latter undergo in dreams or in the narrative of the dream.

Although this first function is important and clearly apparent, it is not the only one. As Freud explains when analysing the case of President Schreber, delusion is also, strangely enough, the beginning of a kind of cure. We know that in its most radical sense psychosis may be understood as an almost total withdrawal of *objective* libidinal investments and their subsequent introjection into the ego. This corresponds to the secondary narcissism of psychoanalysis and to the autism of psychiatrists. It is possible for the patient to try to get out of this deadly hypercathexis of himself and of this situation resembling "the end of the world" (see once more, the discussion of the case of Schreber on this point) by re-establishing another world on the ruins of the former. He thus rediscovers the possibility for libidinal investment of objects. But the new objects offered to his libido will no longer be those that the principle of reality offered; they will be those that are fabricated by his feeling of narcissistic all-powerfulness. The essential materials for the construction of the new world will very frequently be furnished in a way more or less recognizable, by the contents that were foreclosed from the unconscious. This foreclosure came about through the failure of the primal repression. At the beginning of the delirium, these contents often emerged or reappeared "in the real." The Schreberian discourse as it is analyzed by Freud and Lacan, furnishes a clear and typical illustration of these phenomena.

There is therefore no paradox in claiming that delusion is in some respects a limitation or a rupture of autism. This is confirmed by the different diagnoses that every psychiatrist, even those unfamiliar with these ideas, will make concerning the present and future prognosis of a hebephrenic who has no de-lusions and that of a paranoid schizophrenic. On the other hand, one sees here that the double function attributed to delusion conforms perfectly to the con-cept of *compromise* held by Freud as the necessary mark of all psychic *symp-toms*.

II. Philosophy and Mental Illness

In the last part of this book, we have put the principal themes developed ear-lier in a different perspective. We made an effort to repeat them and to inter-pret them in a more directly philosophical context. There, as everywhere, but perhaps more than elsewhere, we have made an effort never to lose sight of the risks of the undertaking. Let us repeat it once more, although it should be self-evident: there is no question of pretending–the idea itself would be ri-diculous–that anthropological and philosophical discourse on human exis-tence, that the psychiatric discourse about madness and the psychoanalytic discourse about the unconscious may be translated into each other or may be substitutable for each other. They can coincide neither in their aim nor in their methods, nor in their subject-matter. However, it remains imperative that they cannot simply ignore each other, nor continue to be alien fields of study. For it would be absurd to pretend that madness is a sickness like tuberculosis or jaundice, that is to say, a series of impairments provoked in the organism by an affliction from outside. Even if it is possible that madness entails an afflic-tion from the outside (at least in certain cases we are not aware of anything of that sort) we have to maintain that in the first place madness is an *intrinsic possibility of human existence*. We believe that, having established this thesis, anthropologists and philosophers must pay attention to it. As for the uncon-scious, we refuse to see it as the unconscious of an organism. We prefer to see it as the unconscious of a psychological being and thus of someone who is forced to become a subject. The problem of the relation between the uncon-scious and philosophy is even clearer if we maintain that this unconsciousness is structured like a language; more specifically like the language of the Other. These views do not have the purpose, either explicitly or implicitly, of bring-ing this unconscious under the control of consciousness or of reason. They also are not meant to take away the dimension of impenetrability of the uncon-scious or to promote the idea that the unconscious can be dissolved. But, on the other hand, it is a mistake to put this impenetrability where it does not belong. Indeed, if human conduct and the development of a human being are totally ruled by inaccessible forces, then what is the status of psychoanalytic method, of psychoanalytic therapy and of Freudian metapsychology.

The philosopher therefore has a duty to reflect on these questions. The reasons for this philosophical reflection will be evident in the following quo-tation from Lacan: "In psychoanalytic therapy one learns that the subject asks himself a question concerning his existence. This question is more than the question of what kind of personality or what kind of ego he is. That is just part of the question. The question is articulated best as: 'What am I?' and concerns his sex, (that he is a man or a woman), and the contingency of his existence (that he might not have been). These two aspects of the question have a mysterious dimension which is evoked by the symbols of procreation and death. It is clear that such a question must provoke more anxiety than a simple question about one's personality. This bigger question about his existence bathes the subject, supports him, overruns him, rips him from all sides, is seen in the tensions, the suspenses, the fantasies that the psychoanalyst encounters. But the importance of this question is revealed only in parts of the concrete discourse where this unconscious question is articulated. It is because these phenomena arrange themselves as the figures of this discourse that they have the fixity of symptoms, that they are readable. It is also for the same reason that these symptoms are resolved when they are deciphered."(1)

III. Philosophical Results

The last part of the book is thus devoted to an interrogation of the status of meaning, intelligibility and intentionality that is typical respectively for the discourse of philosophical anthropology, of psychoanalysis and also of the unconscious itself. It goes without saying that this study was more an introduction, a clearing away of questions, an invitation to further enquiries (of which, however, it clearly marks the direction) than a system of fully elaborated answers. This effort forced us to attempt to articulate the relations between discourse, expression, and presence, it seemed to us that these three concepts are ultimately rooted in the fact of "being-in-the-world." This should be understood as that level of human development where language, the body and the "real" are not yet differentiated. "It is because there is an archeological language of the lived body and of the verbal chain that a verbal expression which is not recognizable in its symbolic aim is possible.[7] To interpret a dream, a symptom, or a lapsus, is to restore the full meaning of those metaphors that had been repressed. It is to give to this repressed meaning the right to citizenship in the human universe."(2) For the same reason, a word connected with this repression can nevertheless be circulated between the partners of the psychoanalytic dialogue.[8] Such a word goes beyond itself, since it pre-

---

[7] The example given by De Waelhens for the language of the lived body is "*prendre*, to prehend" (p. 276-77). An example of a verbal chain is "W" of the Wolf man (p. 189, note 14).

[8] See for instance the case of the Wolf-man, who had sadistic problems. Freud mentions that one of the first questions the Wolf man told him he asked his Nanya was "whether Christ had had a behind too. " G.W. XII, p. 93, S.E. XVII p. 63.

sents or may present the conscious meaning that the other partners in the dialogue immediately associate with. Such a discourse articulates our emotional
relation to things, to beings, and to the world. It consists of structuring space,
temporality, communication, i.e., the essential modes of presence. It expresses
the style of a situation."(3) Such a discourse, we would say, can hardly be
exhaustively translated into explicit themes. This discourse arises at and
evokes the existential dimensions of life. That leads us to admit and to recognize a double transcendence of discourse: transcendence of discourse in relation to itself and transcendence of discourse towards the world. Without the
first, it would not be able to progress from that which has been said towards
that which has not been said. That this is the essence of psychoanalytic discourse is shown by our reflections on the analysis of the case of the Rat-man.[9]
But the second dimension of transcendence is just as necessary. Certainly,
although nothing real happens in psychoanalysis, the analysis has been undertaken so that something could happen in the real.[10] From the point of view of
this double transcendence the neurotic is almost as different from the psychotic (of whom we have spoken) as he differs from the normal man. That is
to say, with the psychotic these two functions of transcendence do not work
any longer or they work only automatically without the control of one by the
other. Now both are required so that "the emergence of the symbolic world in
the world of reality" may be assured.(4)

One could propose, without being too far off, analogous considerations
relating to the problems of the Oedipus complex. Whatever may be, in the
most archaic past of each one of us, the characteristic events that have marked
the Oedipus complex, its essential character remains the triangular structure.
This structure is the constitutive form of being-in-the-world.[11]

The entrance into, and the resolution of the Oedipus complex protects the
subject against the risk of catastrophic impasses to which certain of the more
archaic moments almost predispose him. The first of these threats is the possibility of remaining at the level where one expects that Presence is equal to
Total Presence; a level which is characteristic of the maternal space. This is a
universe (rather a pseudo-universe) of unconditional participation, which creates a dual unity without any limits, and where there is no place at all for the
distinction between interior and exterior or between the self and the other. A
different threat, but related to the first, is the reign of discourse without truth.
This is a discourse which is thought to be unquestionably universal, and which
neither engages nor calls on anyone because it suffices by itself. Such is dis-

---

[9] See p. 280ff.

[10] This is possible because comprehension is in a certain sense prehension of the real
and thus restitution of presence to the real.

[11] If one wants to reflect on whether the triangular structure is constitutive of the human
person in general, or only of the Western person, it is useful to read: Georges
Dumézil: *L'idéologie tripartie des Indo-Européens,* especially p. 11.

course before the Oedipal agreement and before the Oedipal law. It is sometimes like a whisper, and sometimes like a tumult of an ocean without a bottom.

The father figure such as it appears in the Oedipus complex, modifies through its presence from top to bottom, this reign. Provided henceforth with references, this so-called universe becomes a real world, i.e., *the* world. Indeed, the father is not just *one* of the three terms of the constellation. He is above all the one who radically modifies the internal relations which previously tied the first two together. In separating them, the father situates one in relation to the other and makes possible the fact that mother and child mutually confer identity, opacity and the depth of a true autonomous subject in the world. The world too has become totally different because it now confronts a desire that has agreed to be marked by the seal of the law and the test of truth.

NOTES

(1)   *Écrits*, p. 549 (E: p. 194). This is a passage from Lacan's study on Schreber with as title: "D'une question préalable à tout traitement possible de la psychose."

(2)   W. Huber, H. Piron, A. Vergote, *La Psychanalyse, science de l'homme*, p. 174-75.

(3)   H. Maldiney, *op. cit.*, p. 52.

(4)   H. Maldiney, *op. cit.*, p. 59.

BIBLIOGRAPHY

References Used, Augmented by Recent Publications on Schreber, and on and by Lacan

Adler, M. J. (1927). *Dialectic*. New York: Harcourt, Brace & Co.

Alanen, Y. (1958). *The Mothers of Schizophrenic Patients* (Vol. 33 (Supplement 124)). Acta Psychiatric Scand.

Alanen, Y., et al. (1966). *The Family in the Pathogenesis of Schizophrenic and Neurotic Disorders* (Vol. 42 (Supplement 189)). Acta Psychiat. Scand.

Allison, D. B., Prado de Oliveira, E., Roberts, M. S., & Weiss, A. S. (1988). *Psychosis and Sexual Identity: Toward a Post-Analytic View of the Scheber Case*. Albany: State University of New York Press.

Andrès, M. (1987). *Lacan et la Question du Métalangage*. Paris: Point Hors Ligne.

Andreasen, N. C. (1999). Understanding the causes of schizophrenia. *New England Journal of Medicine, 340*(8), 645-7.

Apel, K. (1973). *Transformation der Philosophie*. Frankfurt/a Main, Suhrkamp.

Apollon, W. (1990). Psychanalyse et traitement des psychotiques. In W. Apollon, D. Bergeron & L. Cantin (Eds.), *Traiter la psychose* (pp. 77-110). Québec: Gifric.

Apollon, W., Bergeron, D., & Cantin, L. (1990). *Traiter la psychose*. Québec: Gifric.

Aronen, E. (1993). The effect of family counseling on mental health of 10-11-year-old children in low-and high-risk families: A longitudinal approach. *Journal of Child Psychology and Psychiatry and Allied Disciplines, 34*(2), 155-65.

Aronen, E., Kuosa, M., Tailila, M., & Arajärvi, T. (1995). Kotikäynteihin perustuvan perheneuvonnan vaikutus nuoren psyykkiseen terveyteen- 15 vuoden seurantatutkimus. *Duodecim, 111*, 505-9.

Aronsson, B. (1994). *Norrgårdens behandlingenshem-6 år, en utvädering*. [TIPS-report October 1994]. Umeå University: Department of Applied Psychology.

Aronsson, B. (1999). *Behandling av schizofrena patienter--en utvärering av Norrgårdens behandlingshem* [TIPS-report nr 51]. Umeå University: Department of Applied Psychology.

Aulagnier-Spairani, P. (1964). Remarques sur la structure psychotique. *La Psychanalyse, 8*, 47-67.

Aulagnier-Spairani, P., Clavreul, J., Perrier, F., Rosolato, G., & Valebrega, J. (1967). *Le désir et la perversion*. Paris: Éditions du Seuil.

Avineri, S. (1972). Hegel Revisited. In A. MacIntyre (Ed.), *Hegel*. New York: Doubleday.

Awad, G. A. (1995). Quality-of-Life Issues in Medicated Schizophrenic Patients. In C. L. Shriqui & H. A. Nasrallah (Eds.), *Contemporary Issues in the Treatment of Schizophrenia* [Chapter 31.] (pp. 735-47). Washington, D.C.: American Psychiatric Press.

Baumeyer, F. (1956). The Schreber Case. *International Journal of Psychoanalysis, 37*, 61-74.

Baumeyer, F. (1970). Noch ein Nachtrag zu Freud's Arbeit über Schreber. *Z. Psychosomat. Med., 16*, 243-245.

Bär, E. (1974). Understanding Lacan. *Psychoanalysis and Contemporary Science, 3*, 473-544.

Bär, E. (1975). *Semiotic Approaches to Psychotherapy*. Bloomington: Indiana University Press.

Bélanger, B., & Riou, L. (1990). Délimitation du discours délirant et lien social. In W. Apollon, D. Bergeron & L. Cantin (Eds.), *Traiter la psychose* (pp. 195-203). Québec: Gifric.

Bebbington, P., Bowen, J., Hirsch, S., & Kuipers, E. (1995). Schizophrenia and psychosocial stresses. In S. Hirsch & D. Weinberger (Eds.), *Schizophrenia* (pp. 587-604). Oxford: Blackwell Science.

Bechgaard, B. (1990). En kritisk gennemgang og metodeanalyse af follow-up undersøgelsen fra Chesnut Lodge. *Agrippa, 12*, 123-147.

Bechgaard, B. (1994). *A Critical Review and Methodological Analysis of the Follow-up Study from Chesnut Lodge*. Paper presented at the XIth International Symposium for Psychotherapy of Schizophrenia, June 1994. Now expanded. (pp. 1-22). Manuscript.

Benedetti, G. (1995). *La mort dans l' âme. Psychothérapie de la schizophrénie*. Ramonville Saint-Agne: Erès.

Benjamin, W. (1972). Bücher von Geisteskranken. In *Gesammelte Schriften, IV/2* (pp. 615-619). Frankfurt and Main.

Benveniste, E. (1966). *Problèmes de Linguistique Générale*. Paris: Gallimard.

Benveniste, E. (1971). *Problems in general linguistics* (M. E. Meek, Trans.). Coral Gables,Fla: University of Miami Press.

Benvenuto, B., & Kennedy, R. (1986). *The works of Jacques Lacan*. New York: St.Martin's Press.

Berthold-Bond, D. (1995). *Hegel's Theory of Madness*. Albany: State University of New York Press.

Bertilsson, G., & Berggren, E. (2000). *Utvärdering av de Första 46 Jagstrukturerande Psykoterpiera vid Psykiatriska Kliniken I Skellefteå*. Skellefteå: Psykoterpienheten.

Berze, J. (1929). *Psychologie der Schizophrenie*. Berlin.

Binswanger, L. (1955-1961). *Ausgewählte Vorträge und Aufsätze* (Vol. I, II). Bern: Francke.

Binswanger, L. (1957). *Der Fall Suzanne Urban*. Pfullingen: Neske.

Blatt, S. J. (1995). The destructivenss of perfectionism. Implications for the treatment of depression. *American Psychologist, 50*(12), 1003-20.

Blatt, S. J., Sanislow, Zuroff, D. C., & Pilkonis Paul A. (1996, December). Characteristics of Effective Therapists: Further Analyses of Data from the National Institute of Mental Health Treatment of Depression Collaborative Research Program. *Journal of Consulting and Clinical Psychology*, pp. 1276-84.

Blatt, S. J., & Ford, R. Q. (1994). *Therapeutic Change. An Object Relations Perspective*. New York and London: Plenum Press.

Bleuler, E. (1912). Rezension von Freuds "Psychoanalytischen Bemerkungen." *Z. Psychonoal.*, *2*.

Bleuler, E. (1911). *Dementia Praecox: Oder Gruppe der Schizophrenien*. Leipzig: Deuticke.

Bleuler, M. (1978). *The Schizophrenic Disorders: Long-Term Patient and Family Studies* (S. Clemens, Trans.). New Haven: Yale Unversity Press.

Blomberg, J., Sandell, R., Lazar, A., & Schubert, J. (1997). *Stability of Therapeutic Effects in Terms of Relapse-Rate in the STOPPP-Study*. Paper presented at the 28th Annual Meeting of the Society for Psychotherapy Research. June 26, Panel: Findings of the Stockholm Outcome of Psychotherapy and Psychoanalysis Project (STOPPP), Geilo, Norway, June 25-29.

Borch-Jacobsen, M. (1991). *Lacan. The Absolute Master* (D. Brick, Trans.). Stanford: Stanford University Press.

Borst, C. (Editor). (1970). *The Mind-Brain Identity Theory*. New York: St. Martin's Press.

Bowie, M. (1991). *Lacan*. Cambridge, MA: Harvard University Press.

Bracker, M., Alcorn, M., Jr., Corthell, R. J., & Massadier-Kenney, F. (1994). *Lacanian Theory of Discourse: Subject, Structure, and Societry*. Albany: State University of New York Press.

Braunstein, N. (1992). *La Jouissance. Un Concept Lacanien*. Paris: Point Hors Ligne.

Brough, J. B. (1972). The emergence of an absolute consciousness in Husserl's early writings on time-consciousness. *Man and World*, *5*, 298-326.

Calligaris, C. (1991). *Pour Une Clinique Différentielle des Psychoses*. Paris: Point Hors Ligne.

Cancro, R. (1969a). Clinical prediction of outcome in schizophrenia. *Comprehensive Psychiatry*, *10*, 349-354.

Cancro, R. (1969b). Prospective prediction of hospital stay in schizophrenia. *Archives of General Psychiatry*, *20*, 541-546.

Cancro, R. (Ed.). (1971). *The Schizophrenic Syndrome; An Annual Review*. New York, London: Brunner/Mazel.

Canetti, E. (1960). Der Fall Schreber. In *Masse and Macht* (pp. 500-553). [München]: Carl Hanser.

Carpenter, W. T., Jr., & Buchanan, R. W. (1995). Schizophrenia: Introduction and Overview. In H. I. Kaplan & B. J. Sadock (Eds.), *Comprehensive Textbook of Psychiatry. Vol I-II* (Sixth, Vol. I, pp. 889-902). Baltimore:

The Williams & Wilkins Company.

Carr, A. (1963). Observations on Paranoia and their Relationships to the Schreber Case. *International Journal of Psychoanalysis, 44*, 195-200.

Castoridoris-Aulagnier, P. (1981). *La violence de l'interprétation. Du pictogramme à l'énoncé.* Paris: Presses Universitaires de France.

Chauvin, R. (1941). Contribution à l'étude physiologique du criquet pélerin et du déterminisme des phénomènes grégaires. In *Annales de la Société Entologique de France* (Vol. CX). 133-272.

Clark, M. (1988). *Jacques Lacan: An Annoted Bibliography. 2 Vol.* New York: Garland Press.

Clement, C. (1983). *The Lives and Legends of Jacques Lacan* (A. Goldhammer, Trans.). New York: Columbia University Press.

Conrad, J. (1965). *Lord Jim.* New York: Harper and Row.

Corveleyn, J. (1998). Délire à thème religieux: La psychose et l'hystérie. In D. Devreese, Z. Lothane & J. Schotte (Eds.), *Schreber Revisité* (pp. 185-209). Louvain: Presses Universitaires de Louvain.

Darves-Bornoz, J., Lempérière, T., & Degiovanni, A. (1995). Sexual victimization in women with schizophrenia and bipolar disorder. *Social Psychiatry and Psychiatric Epidemiology, 30*, 78-84.

Davoine, F. (1998). Communication at the Lacan Clinical Forum, Oct 31-Nov 1, 1998. Stockbridge, MA: Austen Riggs Center.

Deleuze, G., & Guattari, F. (1972). *L'Anti-Oedipe.* Paris: Éditions de Minuit.

Demoulin, P. (1967). *Névrose et Psychose.* Paris-Louvain: Nauwelaerts.

Devreese, D., Lothane, Z., & Schotte, J. (Editors). (1998). *Schreber Revisité* [Colloque de Cerisy]. Louvain: Presses Universitaires de Louvain.

Devreese, D. (1989). *De Waan Lezen. Een Hermeneutisch-psychoanalytische Ontleding van de Paranoïde Waan van D.P. Schreber* [Doctoral Dissertation] (Vol. I-II). Leuven.

de Beauvoir, S. (1967). *Tous les Hommes sont Mortels.* Paris: Gallimard.

De Waelhens, A. (1978). *Schizophrenia. A Philosophical Reflection on the Structuralist Interpretation of J. Lacan* [Introduction, Explanatory Footnotes and a Bibliography by W.Ver Eecke] (W. Ver Eecke, Trans.). Pittsburgh: Duquesne University Press.

De Waelhens, A. (1959). Réflexions sur une problématique Husserlienne de l'inconscient, Husserl, et Hegel. In *Edmund Husserl (Phenomenologica, 4)* (pp. 221-237). La Haye: Nyhoff.

De Waelhens, A. (1961). *La Philosophie et les experiences naturelles.* La Haye: Nyhoff.

De Waelhens, A. (1963). Foreword. In *The Structure of Behaviour by Maurice Merleau-Ponty.* Boston: Beacon Press.

De Waelhens, A. (1965). La force du langage et le langage de la force. *Revue Philosophique de Louvain, 63*, 591-612.

De Waelhens, A. (1965). Reflections on Heidegger's Development. *International Philosophical Quarterly*, 475-502.

De Waelhens, A. (1967). Préface. In *Névrose et Psychose by P. Demoulin*. Paris-Louvain: Nauwelaerts.

De Waelhens, A. (1970). Vaderschap en Oedipus complex. In M. Renaer et al. (Ed.), *Liefde en Seksualiteit* (pp. 155-173). Tielt: Lannoo.

De Waelhens, A. (1971). *La philosophie de Martin Heidegger*. Louvain: Neuwelaerts.

De Waelhens, A. (1972). *La psychose. Essai d'interprétation analytique et existentiale*. Louvain/Paris: Nauwelaerts.

Diamond, D. B. (1997). The Fate of the Ego in Contemporary Psychiatry with particular Reference to Etiologic Theories of Schizophrenia. *Psychiatry, 60*, 67-88.

Dingman, C., & McGlashan, T. (1989). Chapter 11. In A. Bellak (Ed.), *A Clinical Guide for the Treatment of Schizophrenia* (pp. 163-81).

Dor, J. (1983). *Bibliographie des travaux de Jacques Lacan*. Paris: InterEditions.

Dor, J. (1985). *Introduction à la lecture de Lacan*. Paris: Denoël.

Dufresne, T. (Ed.). (1997). *Returns of the "French Freud." Freud, Lacan, and Beyond*. London and New York: Routledge.

Dumézil, G. (1958). *L'ideologie tripartie de Indo-Européens*. Bruxelles: Latomus.

Edenius, B. (1999). *Om en Teori för psykos utveckling av en behandlingsmetod* [Medical Dissertations, New Series nr 597]. Umeå: Umeå University.

Edwards, P. (Ed.). (1972). *The Encyclopedia of Philosophy* (Vol. 1-8). New York: Macmillan Publishing Co., Inc. & The Free Press.

Erikson, E. H. (1950). *Childhood and Society*. New York: W.W. Norton.

Evans, D. (1996). *An Introductory Dictionary of Lacanian Psychoanalysis*. London and New York: Routledge.

Ewens, T. *Essay on the Ground of an Interrogation: The Theme of Schizophrenia in Freud* [Doctoral thesis]. Louvain.

Fairbairn, W. (1956). Considerations arising out of the Schreber Case. *British Journal of Medical Psychology, 29*, 113-117.

Farmer, A., McGuffin, P., & Gottesman, I. (1987). Twin Concordance for DSM-III Schizophrenia. *Archives of General Psychiatry, 44*(7), 634-641.

Farmer, A., McGuffin, P., & Gottesman, I. (1988). In Reply. *Archives of General Psychiatry, 44*(7), 877-878.

Felman, S. (1987). *Jacques Lacan and the Adventure of Insight*. Cambridge, MA: Harvard University Press.

Fenton, W. S., & McGlashen, T. H. (1995). Schizophrenia: Individual Psychotherapy. In H. I. Kaplan & B. J. Sadock (Eds.), *Comprehensive Textbook of Psychiatry. Vol I-II* (Sixth, Vol. I, pp. 1007-1018). Baltimore: The Williams & Wilkins Company.

Feyerabend, I. (1970). Consolidation for the Specialist. In I. Lakatos and A. Musgrave (Eds.), *Criticism and the Growth of Knowledge* (pp. 197-230).

Cambridge: Cambridge University Press.

Fink, B. (1995). *The Lacanian Subject. Between Language and Jouissance.* Princeton: Princeton University Press.

Fink, B. (1996). The Subject and the Other's Desire. In R. Feldstein, B. Fink & M. Jaanus (Eds.), *Reading Seminars I and II. Lacan's Return to Freud* (pp. 76-97). New York: State University of New York Press.

Fink, B. (1997). *A Clinical Introduction to Lacanian Psychoanalysis. Theory and Technique.* Cambridge, MA: Harvard University Press.

Fink, B., Feldstein, R., & Jaanus, M. (1995). *Reading Seminar XI: Lacan's Four Fundamental Concepts of Psychoanalysis.* Albany: State University of New York Press.

Fink, B., Feldstein, R., & Jaanus, M. (1996). *Reading Seminar I & II: Lacan's Return to Freud.* Albany: State University of New York Press.

Fisher, S., & Greenberg, R. (1996). *Freud Scientifically Reappraised.* New York: Wiley.

Fonagy, P., Steele, H., & Steele, M. (1991). Maternal representations of attachment during pregnancy predict the organization of infant-mother attachment at 1 year of age. *Child Development, 62,* 891-905.

Fort, D. C. (1990). Parent-Child Effects on Performance, Thinking, and Communication in Families of Normal and Schizophrenic Sons. In A. S. Silver & Cantor Morton B. (Eds.), *Psychoanalysis and Severe Emotional Ilness* (pp. 73-98). New York: The Guilford Press.

Fox, R. (1967). *Kinship and Marriage.* Harmondsworth: Penguin.

Freedman, A. M., Kaplan, H. I., & Sadock, B. J. (1975). *Comprehensive Textbook of Psychiatry. Vol I-II* (Second). Baltimore: The Williams & Wilkins Company.

Freud, S. (1968-). *Gesammelte Werke* [Quoted as G.W.]. Frankfurt/a Main: Fisher.

Freud, S. *Psychoanalytische Bemerkungen über einen autobiographisch beschriebenen Fall von Paranoia [Dementia Paranoides].* In *G.W. VIII.* Frankfurt am Main: Fisher.

Freud, S. (1911). Psycho-Analytic Notes on an Autobiographical Account of a Case of Paranoia (Dementia Paranoides). In *S.E., XII.* London: Hogarth.

Freud, S. (1953-74). *The Standard Edition of the Complete Psychological Works of Sigmund Freud* [Quoted as S.E.] (J. Strachey, Ed.) (J. Strachey, Trans.) (Vol. 1-24). London: Hogarth.

Fromm, E. (1968). *The Heart of Man.* New York: Harper and Row.

Fromm-Reichmann, F. (Edited and Introduction by A-L.S.Silver). (1990). The Assets of the Mentally Handicapped: The Interplay of Mental Illness and Creativity. In A. S. Silver & Cantor Morton B. (Eds.), *Psychoanalysis & Severe Emotional Ilness* (pp. 47-72). New York: The Guilford Press.

Gabbard, G. (1997). More is more. Review of Sidney J. Blatt and Richard Q. Ford. The Therapeutic Change. An Object Relations Perspective. *Contemporary Psychology, 42*(12), 1103-04.

Gallop, J. (1985). *Reading Lacan*. Ithaca: Cornell University Press.

Gardiner, M. (Ed.). (1971). *The Wolf-Man*. New York: Basic Books.

Gaudillière, J. (1998). Communication at the Lacan Clinical Forum, Oct 31-Nov 1, 1998. Stockbridge, MA: Austen Riggs Center.

Gear, M. C., Liendo, E. C., & Prieto, L. J. (1975). *Sémiologie Psychanalytique*. Paris: Éditions de Minuit.

Godderis, J. (1998). The Elderly Paranoid Patient in Front of the Mirror. Reflections on the current relevance of psychoanalytic and phenomenological criteria of psychosis for the clinical psychiatrist (pp. 1-18). Leuven: Unpublished talk given in "Second Symposium on Anthropology, Psychoanalysis, and Psychiatry : Psychosis." Feb 26-27, 1998.

Gottesman, I. (1991). *Schizophrenia Genesis: The Origins of Madness*. New York: W.H. Freeman.

Gottesman, I. I. (1993). Origins of Schizophrenia: Past as Prologue. In R. Plomin & G. E. McClearn (Eds.), *Nature, Nurture and Psychology* (pp. 231-44). Washington, DC: American Psychological Association.

Granon-Lafont, J. (1985). *La Topologie Ordinaire de Jacques Lacan*. Paris: Point Hors Ligne.

Grosz, E. (1990). *Jacques Lacan. A Feminist Introduction*. London and New York: Routledge.

Grotstein, J. S. (1990). The "Black Hole" as the Basic Psychotic Experience: Some Newer Psychoanalytic and Neuroscience Perspectives on Psychosis. In A. S. Silver & Cantor Morton B. (Eds.), *Psychoanalysis and Severe Emotional Ilness* (pp. 29-46). New York: The Guilford Press.

Harding, C. M. (1995). The Interaction of biopsychosocial Factors, Time, and Course of Schizophrenia. In C. Shriqui & H. Nasrallah (Eds.), *Contemporary Issues in the Treatment of Schizophrenia* [Chapter 27] (pp. 653-681). Washington, DC: American Psychiatric Press.

Harrow, M., & Marengo, J. (1986). Schizophrenic thought disorder at follow-up: Its persistence and prognostic significance. *Schizophrenia Bulletin, 12*(3), 373-393.

Hartmann, E., Milofsky, E., Vaillant, G., Oldfield, M., Falke, R., & Ducey, C. (1984). Vulnerability to Schizophrenia. *Archives of General Psychaitry, 41*(11), 1050-1056.

Hegel, G. (1967). *The Phenomenology of Mind* (J.B.Baillie, Trans.). New York: Harper & Row.

Heidegger, M. (1950). *Holzwege*. Frankfurt/a Main: Klostermann.

Heidegger, M. (1962). *Being and Time* (John Macquarrie and Edward Robinson, Trans.). London: SCM Press.

Huber, W., Piron, H., & Vergote, A. (1964). *La psychanalyse, science de l'homme*. Bruxelles: Dessart.

Husserl, E. (1960). *Carthesian Meditations*. New York: Humanities Press.

Husserl, E. (1973). *Experience and Judgement*. Evanston: Northwestern

University Press.

Huttunen, M., & Niskanen, P. (1978). Prenatal loss of father and psychiatric disorders. *Archives of General Psychiatry, 35,* 429-431.

Hyppolite, J. (1971). Hegel's Phenomenology and Psychoanalysis. In Warren Steinkraus (Ed.), *New Studies in Hegel's Philosophy* (pp. 57-70). New York: Holt, Rinehart, Winston.

Israëls, H. (1989). *Schreber: Father and Son.* Madison, CT: International Universities Press.

Jablinsky, A., Sartonius, N., Ernberg, G., Anker, M., Korten, A., Cooper, J., Day, R., & Bertelson, A. (1992). *Schizophrenia: Manifestations, incidence and course in different cultures: A World Health Organization ten-country study.* In *Psychological Medicine. Monograph Supplement 20.* Cambridge: Cambridge University Press.

Jakobson, R. *Essais de Linguistique Générale.* Paris: Editions de Minuit.

Jakobson, R. "Closing statements: Linguistics and Poetics. In T.A. Sebeok (Ed.), *Style and Language.* New York.

Jessner, L. (1966). On Becoming a Mother. In R. M. Walter von Baeyer, Grifith (Ed.), *Conditio humana* (pp. 102-114). Berlin, New York: Heidelberg, Springer (NY).

Jessner, L., Weigert, E., & Foy, J. C. (1970). The Development of Parental Attitudes during Pregnancy. In Anthony and Benedick (Ed.), *Parenthood* (pp. 209-244). Little, Brown, and Co.

Journal of European Psychoanalysis. (1995-6). *Lacan Today I.* New York: Telos Press Ltd.

Julien, P. (1994). *Jacques Lacan's return to Freud: The real, the symbolic, and the imaginary.* New York: New York University Press.

Juranville, A. (1984). *Lacan et la Philosophie.* Paris: Presses Universitaires de France.

Kafka, J. S. (1990). On the question of insight in psychosis. In A. S. Silver & Cantor Morton B. (Eds.), *Psychoanalysis & Severe Emotional Ilness* (pp. 18-28). New York: The Guilford Press.

Kant, I. *Critique of Pure Reason* (Norman Kemp Smith, Trans.). New York: St. Martin's Press.

Kaplan, H. I., & Sadock, B. J. (1995). *Comprehensive Textbook of Psychiatry. Vol I-II* (Sixth). Baltimore: The Williams & Wilkins Company.

Karno, M., & Norquist, G. S. (1995). Schizophrenia: Epidemiology. In H. I. Kaplan & B. J. Sadock (Eds.), *Comprehensive Textbook of Psychiatry. Vol I-II* (Sixth, Vol. I, pp. 902-927). Baltimore: The Williams & Wilkins Company.

Karon, B. P. (1999). The tragedy of schizophrenia. *The General Psychologist, 34*(1), 1-12.

Karon, B. P., & VandenBos, G. R. (1981). *Psychotherapy of Schizophrenia. The Treatment of Choice.* New York: Jason Aronson.

Karon, B. P., & Widener, A. J. (1994). Is there really a schizophrenogenic parent? *Psychoanalytic Psychology, 11*(1), 47-61.

Katan, M. (1950). Schreber's Hallucinations about the `Little Men.' *International Journal of Psycho-Anal, 31*, 32-35.

Katan, M. (1952). Further Remarks about Schreber's Hallucinations. *International Journal of Psychoanalysis, 33*, 429-432.

Katan, M. (1953). Schreber's Prepsychotic Phase. *International Journal of Psychoanalysis, 34*, 43-51.

Katan, M. (1959). Schreber's Hereafter. *The Psychoanalytic Study of the Child, XIV*, 314-382.

Katan, M. (1949). Schreber's Delusion of the End of the World. *Psychoanalytic Quarterly, 18*, 60-66.

Kendler, K. S. (1995). Schizophrenia: Genetics. In H. I. Kaplan & B. J. Sadock (Eds.), *Comprehensive Textbook of Psychiatry. Vol I-II* (Sixth, Vol. I, pp. 942-957). Baltimore: The Williams & Wilkins Company.

Kendler, K. S., & Diehl, S. R. (1993). The Genetics of Schizophrenia: A current genetic-epidemiologic perspective. *Schizophrenia Bulletin, 19*(2), 261-85.

Kitay, P. (1963). Introduction and Summary to the Symposium on "Reinterpretation of the Schreber Case: Freud's Theory of Paranoia." *International Journal of Psychoanalysis, 44*, 191-193, 222-223.

Klein, M. (1962). Bemerkungen über einige schizoide Mechanismen. In *Das Seelenleben des Klein-Kindes* (pp. 124-126). Stuggart.

Knight, R. (1940). The Relationship of Latent Homosexuality to the Mechanism of Paranoid Delusions. *Bull. Menninger Clin., 4*, 149-159.

Kojève, A. (1947). *Introduction à la Lecture de Hegel*. Paris: Gallimard.

Kordig, C. R. (1971). The Theory-ladenness of observation. In *The Review of Metaphysics* (pp. 448-484).

Kuhn, R. (1952). Daseinsanalytische Studie über die Bedeutung von Grenzen in Wahn. In *Monatschrift fur die Psychiatrie und Neurologie*.

Lacan, J. (1959). Desire and the Interpretation of Desire in Hamlet. *Yale French Studies 1977, 55/56*, 11-52. Also in S. Felman (Ed.), *Literature and Psychoanalysis: The Question of Reading: Otherwise.*

Lacan, J. (1938). La Famille. In *Encyclopédie française* (Vol. VIII, pp. 8.40.5-8.40.16; 8.42.1-8.42.8). Paris: Larousse.

Lacan, J. (1966). *Écrits*. Paris: Éditions du Seuil.

Lacan, J. (1966). Sur une question préliminaire à tout traitement possible de la psychose. In *Écrits* (pp. 531-583). Paris: Éditions du Seuil.

Lacan, J. (1977). *Écrits. A Selection* (A. Sheridan, Trans.). New York: W.W.Norton & Company.

Lacan, J. (1977). On a Question Preliminary to any Possible Treatment of Psychosis (Sheridan Alan, Trans.). In *Écrits. A Selection* (pp. 179-225). New York: W.W. Norton.

Lacan, J. (1988). *The Seminar of Jacques Lacan. Book I . Freud's Papers on Technique. 1953-1954* (J. Miller, Ed.) (J. Forrester, Trans.). New York:

W.W. Norton.

Lacan, J. (1993). *The Seminar of Jacques Lacan. Book III. The Psychoses. 1955-1956* (J. Miller, Ed.) (R. Grigg, Trans.). New York: W.W.Norton.

Lacan, J. (1957-58). *Les Formations de l'inconscient.* Typewritten.

Lafon, R. (1963). *Vocabulaire de Psychopédagogie et de Psychiatrie de l'Enfant.* Paris: P.U.F.

Lang, H. (1997). *Language and the Unconscious. Jacques Lacan's Hermeneutics of Psychoanalysis* (T. Brockelman, Trans.). Atlantic Highlands, NJ: Humanities Press International, Inc.

Lantéri-Laura, G. (1966). Les problèmes de l'inconscient et la pensée phénomenologique. In Henri Ey (Ed.), *L'Inconscient* (pp. 387-407). Paris: Desclée de Brouwer.

Laplanche, H. (1970). *Vie et Mort en Psychoanalyse.* Paris: Flammarion.

Laplanche, J., & Leclaire S. (1970). The Unconscious: A Psychoanalytic Study (P. Kusell, & J. Mehlmann, Trans.). *Yale French Studies 1972, 48,* 118-75.

Laplanche, J. (1969). *Hölderlin et la question du père.* Paris: Presses Universitaires de France.

Laplanche, J., & Leclaire, S. (1966). L'inconscient.: Une étude psychanalytique. In H. Ey (Ed.), *L'Inconscient* [VI Colloque de Bonneval] (pp. 95-130). Paris: Desclée De Brouwer.

Laplanche, J., & Pontalis, J. (1968). *Vocabulaire de la Psychanalyse.* Paris: Presses Universitaires de France.

Laplanche, J., & Pontalis J-B. (1973). *The language of psychoanalysis* (D. Nicholson-Smith, Trans.). New York: W.W. Norton & Co.

Laplanche, J., & Leclaire, S. (1961). L'inconscient. Une étude psychanalytique. In *Les Temps Modernes* (pp. 81-177).

Lévi-Strauss, C. (1969). *The Elementary Structure of Kinship* (J. Bell, J. H. von Sturmer, & R. Needham, Trans.). Boston: Beacon Press.

Leclaire, S. (1958). A propos de l'épisode psychotique que présente l'homme aux loups. *La Psychoanalyse, 4,* 83-110.

Leclaire, S. (1958). *Psychanalyser.* Paris: Editions du Seuil.

Lee, J. S. (1990). *Jacques Lacan.* Amherst: The University of Massachussets Press.

Lehman, A. F. (1995). Schizophrenia:Psychosocial Treatment. In H. I. Kaplan & B. J. Sadock (Eds.), *Comprehensive Textbook of Psychiatry. Vol I-II* (Sixth, Vol. I, pp. 998-1007). Baltimore: The Williams & Wilkins Company.

Lehman, A. F., & Steinwachs, D. M. (1998). At Issue: Translating Research into Practice: The Schizophrenia Patient Outcomes Research Team (PORT) Treatment Recommendations. *Schizophrenia Bulletin, 24*(1), 1-10.

Leibniz. (1962). *Sämtliche Schriften und Briefe. Vol VI: Nouveaux Essais sur l'Entendement* (Vol. VI, pp. 39-527). Berlin: Akademie Verlag.

Lemaire, A. (1977). *Jacques Lacan* (D. Macey, Trans.). London: Routledge &

Kegan Paul.

Lewis, G., Andreasson, S., & Alleback, P. (1992). Schizophrenia and city life. *The Lancet, 340*(7), 137-140.

Lidz, T. (1978). A developmental theory. In J. Shershow (Ed.), *Schizophrenia: Science and Practice* (pp. 69-95). Cambridge: Harvard University Press.

Lidz, T., & Fleck, S. (1985). *Schizophrenia and the Family*. New York: International Universities Press.

Lidz, T., Fleck, S., & Cornelison. (1966). *Schizophrenia and the Family*. New York: International Universities Press.

Lipton, A. A., Cancro. (1995). Schizophrenia: Clinical Features. In H. I. Kaplan & B. J. Sadock (Eds.), *Comprehensive Textbook of Psychiatry. Vol I-II* (Sixth, Vol. I, pp. 968-987). Baltimore: The Williams & Wilkins Company.

Loeb, F. F., & Loeb, L. R. (1987). Psychoanalytic Observations on the Effect of Lithium on Manic Attacks. *Journal of the American Psychoanalytic Association, 35*(2), 877-902.

Loewald, H. (1951). Ego and Reality. *International Journal of Psychoanalysis, 32*, 10-18.

Loewald, H. (1971). On Motivation and Instinct Theory. *The Psychoanalytic Study of the Child, 26*, 91-128.

Lofts, S. G., & Moyaert, P. (1994). *La Pensée de Jacques Lacan. Questions historiques-Problèmes théoriques*. Louvain-Paris: Éditions Peeters.

Lohmann, J. (1965). *Philosophie und Sprachwissenschaften*. Berlin: Duncker and Humblot.

Lothane, Z. (1992). *In Defense of Schreber. Soul Murder and Psychiatry*. Hillsdale, NJ: The Analytic Press.

Lothane, Z. (1998). Pour la défense de Schreber: Meurtre d'âme et psychiatrie. In D. Devreese, Z. Lothane & J. Schotte (Eds.), *Schreber Revisité* (pp. 11-29). Louvain: Presses Universitaires de Louvain.

Macalpine, I., & Hunter, R. (1955). *Schreber: Memoirs of my Nervous Illness*. London: Dawson and Sons.

Macey, D. (1988). *Lacan in Contexts*. London: Verso.

Maldiney, H. (1961). Comprendre. In *Revue de Metaphysique et de Morale* (pp. 35-89).

Mann, J. A., and Kreyche. (1966). *Approaches to Morality*. New York: Harcourt, Brace and World.

Mannoni, M. (1970). *Le Psychiatre, son 'Fou' et la Psychoanalyse*. Paris: Éditions du Seuil.

Mannoni, M. (1969). *Clefs pour l'Imaginaire ou l'Autre Scène* (pp. 75-99). Paris: Éditions du Seuil.

Mannoni, M. (1970). *The Child, his "Illness," and the Others*. London: Tavistock Publications.

Mannoni, M. (1972). *The Backward Child and his Mother* (A.M. Sheridan Smith, Trans.). New York: Random House.

Marini, M. (1986). *Jacques Lacan*. Paris: Pierre Belfond.

Matthews, L. H. (1938-1938). Visual stimulation and ovulation in pigeons. In *Proceedings of the Royal Society of London*. B, vol. 126.

McGlashan, T. H. (1988). A Selective Review of recent North American Long-term Followup Studies of schizophrenia. *Schizophrenia Bulletin, 14*(4), 515-542.

McGlashan, T. H., & Hoffman, R. E. (1995). Schizophrenia: Psychodynamic to Neurodynamic Theories. In H. I. Kaplan & B. J. Sadock (Eds.), *Comprehensive Textbook of Psychiatry. Vol I-II* (Sixth, Vol. I, pp. 957-968). Baltimore: The Williams & Wilkins Company.

McGuffin, P., Reveley, A., & Holland, A. (1982). Identical triplets: Non-identical psychosis? *British Journal of Psychiatry, 140*, 1-6.

McKenna, P. (1994). *Schizophrenia and Related Syndromes*. Oxford: Oxford University Press.

Medina, A., & Malone, K. (1980). Book review: A. De Waelhens, Schizophrenia; A. Lemaire, Jacques Lacan. *Man and World, 13*, 447-458.

Mehlman, J. (1972). The Floating Signifier: From Lévi-Strauss to Lacan. *Yale French Studies, 48*, 10-37*Also in: French Freud: Structural Studies in Psychoanalysis*.

Meissner, W. W. (1976). Schreber and the Paranoid Process. *The Annual of Psychoanalysis, 4*, 3-40.

Merleau-Ponty, M. (1962). *The Phenomenology of Perception* (Colin Smith, Trans.). London, New York: Routledge and Kegan Paul.

Merleau-Ponty, M. (1963). *The Structure of Behaviour* (Alden L. Fischer, Trans.). Boston: Beacon Press.

Meyer, R., & Karon, B. (1967). The Schizophrenogenic mother concept and the TAT. *Psychiatry, 30*, 173-179.

Miller, G. (Ed.). (1987). *Lacan*. Paris: Bordas.

Minkowski, E. (1927). *La Schizophrénie; Psychopathologie des Schizoïdes et des Schizophrènes*. Paris: Payot.

Mischler, E., & Waxler, N. (1968). *Interaction in Families: An Experimental Study of Family Processes and Schizophrenia*. New York: Wiley.

Mitchell, K. (1968). An analysis of the schizophrenogenic mother concept by means of the TAT. *Journal of Abnormal Psychology, 73*, 571-574.

Mojtabai, R., Nicholson, R. A., & Carpenter, B. N. (1998). Role of Psychosocial Treatments in Management of Schizophrenia: A Meta-Analytic Review of Controlled Outcome Studies. *Schizophrenia Bulletin, 24*(4), 569-587.

Mooij, A. (1975). *Taal en Verlangen, Lacans theorie van de psychoanalyse*. Boom: Meppel.

Mortensen, P. B., Pedersen, C. B., Westergaard, T., Wohlfahrt, J., Ewald, H., Mors, O., Andersen, P. K., & Melbye, M. (1999). Effects of family history and place and season of birth on the risk of schizophrenia. *New England Journal of Medicine, 340*(8), 603-8.

Moyaert, P. (1993). Schizophrénie et paranoïa. In *Psychanalyse. L'homme et ses destins* (pp. 255-281). Louvain/Paris: Peeters.

Muller, J. P. (1980). Psychosis and Mourning in Lacan's Hamlet. *New Literary History, 12*(1), 147-165.

Muller, J. P. (1988). Lacan's Transmission. *Psychoanalysis and Contemporary Thought, 11*(3), 483-533.

Muller, J. P. (1989). Lacan and Kohut: From Imaginary to Symbolic Identification in the case of Mr.Z. In D. Detrick & S. Detrick (Eds.), *Self Psychology: Comparisons and Contrasts* (pp. 363-94). Hillsdale: The Analytic Press.

Muller, J. P. (1996). *Beyond the Psychoanalytic Dyad. Developmental Semiotics in Freud, Peirce and Lacan.* New York and London: Routledge.

Muller, J. P. (1999). Modes and functions of sublimation [To be published in]. *The Annual of Psychoanalysis. Chicago Institute for Psychoanalysis*, 1-36. Hillsdale, NJ: Analytic Press.

Muller, J. P., & Richardson, W. J. (1982). *Lacan and Language. A Reader's Guide to Écrits.* New York: International Universities Press.

Myhrman, A., Rantakallio, P., Isohanni, M., Jones, P., & Partanen, U. (1996). Unwantedness of a Pregnancy and Schizophrenia in the Child. *British Journal of Psychiatry, 169*, 637-640.

Nancy, J., & Lacoue-Labarthe, P. (1992). *The Title of the Letter. A Reading of Lacan* (F. Raffoul & D. Pettigrew, Trans.). Albany: State University of New York Press.

Nichols, N. (1970). *The relationship between degree of maternal pathogenicity and severity of ego impairment in schizophrenic offspring* [Doctoral Dissertation]. Michigan State University.

Niederland, W. (1951). Three Notes on the Schreber Case. *Psychoanal. Quarterly, 20*, 579-91.

Niederland, W. (1959 a). Schreber: Father and Son. *Psychoanalytic Quarterly, 28*, 151-169.

Niederland, W. (1959 b). The 'miracled-up' world of Schreber's childhood. *Psychoanalytic of the Child, 14*, 383-413.

Niederland, W. (1960). Schreber's Father. *Journal of American Psychoanalytic Association, 8*, 492-499.

Niederland, W. (1963). Further Data and Memorabilia Pertaining to the Schreber Case. *International Journal of Psychoanalysis, 44*, 201-207.

Niederland, W. G. (1974). *The Schreber Case: Psychoanalytic Profile of a Paranoid Personality.* New York: Quadrangle.

Nunberg, H. (1952). Discussion of Katan's Paper on Schreber. *International Journal of Psychoanalysis, 23*, 454-464.

Nydes, J. (1963). Schreber, Parricide, and Paranoid-Masochism. *International Journal of Psychoanalysis, 44*, 208-212.

Ortigues, M., & Ortigues, E. (1966). *L'Oedipe Africain.* Paris: Plon.

Pally, R. (1998). Bilaterality: Hemispheric specialization and integration.

International Journal of Psycho-Analysis, 79, 565-78.

Palmer, R., & Colton, J. (1970). *A History of the Modern World.* New York: Alfred A. Knopf.

Palmer, R. E. (1969). *Hermeneutics, interpretation theory in Schleiermacher, Dilthey, Heidegger, and Gadamer.* Evanston: Northwestern University Press.

Palmier, J. (1969). *Lacan.* Paris: Aubier-Montaigne.

Pankow, G. (1969). *L'homme et sa psychose.* Paris: Aubier-Montaigne.

Pao, P. (1979). *Schizophrenic Disorders. Theory and Treatment from a Psychodynamic Point of View.* New York: International Universities Press.

Parfit, D. (1971). Personal Identity. *The Philosophical Review, 80,* 3-27.

Pelman, C. (1903). Rezension zu den Denkwürdigkeiten. *Dtsch. Z. Nervenheilk, 27,* 352.

Peraldi, F. (1987). Krake/Krakra: A Case Study. *PsychCritique, 2*(1), 55-63.

Pettigrew, T. F. (1964). *A Profile of the Negro American.* Princeton: Van Nostrand.

Pettigrew, D., & Raffoul, F. (Eds.). (1996). *Disseminating Lacan.* Albany: State University of New York Press.

Pfeiffer, R. (1904). Rezension zu den Denkwürdigkeiten. *Allg Z. Psychiatrie, 60.*

Politizer. (1968). *Critique des fondements de la Psychologie.* Paris: Presses Universitaires de France.

Portin, P., & Alanen, Y. (1997). A critical review of genetic studies of schizophrenia. I. Epidemiological and brain studies. *Acta Psychiatrica Scandinavica, 95,* 1-5.

Prado de Oliveira, E. (Ed.). (1979). *Le Cas de Schreber: Contributions Psychanalytiques.* Paris: Presses Universitaires de France.

Prado de Oliveira, E. L. (Ed.). (1996). *Schreber et la Paranoïa. Le meurtre de l'âme.* Paris: L'Harmattan.

Prado de Oliveira, E. L. (1997). *Freud et Schreber. Les sources écrites du délire, entre psychose et culture.* Ramonville Saint-Agne: Erès.

Radke-Yarrow, M., Cummings, E., Kuczynski, L., & Chapman, M. (1985). Patterns of attachment in two- and three-year olds in normal families and families with parental depression. *Child Development, 56,* 884-893.

Ragland-Sullivan, E. (1986). *Jacques Lacan and the Philosophy of Psychoanalysis.* Urbana: University of Illinois Press.

Richardson, W. J. (1965). The place of the unconscious in Heiddeger. *Review of Existential Psychology and Psychiatry, 5,* 265-290.

Richardson, W. J. (1967). *Heidegger. Through Phenomenology to Thought.* The Hague: Nyhoff.

Richardson, W. J. (1983). Lacanian Theory. In A. Rothstein (Ed.), *Models of the Mind: Their Relationships to Clinical Work* (pp. 51-74). New Haven: Yale University Press.

Richardson, W. J. (1988). Lacan and the Problem of Psychosis. In D. B.

Allison, P. de Oliveira, M. S. Roberts & A. S. Weiss (Eds.), *Psychosis and Sexual Identity: Toward a Post-Analytic View of the Schreber Case* (pp. 18-29). Albany: State University of New York Press.

Ricoeur, P. (1967). *The Symbolism of Evil* (E. Buchanan, Trans.). New York: Harper & Row.

Ricoeur, P. (1970). *Freud and Philosophy* (Denis Savage, Trans.). New Haven: Yale University Press.

Ricoeur, P. (1974). *The conflict of interpretations* (D. Ihde, Ed.). Evanston: Northwestern University.

Rifflet-Lemaire, A. (1970). *Jacques Lacan*. Bruxelles: Dessart.

Rosenbaum, B., & Sonne, H. (1986). *The language of psychosis*. New York: New York University Press.

Rosolato, G. (1969). Paranoia et Scène Primitive; Repères pour la Psychose. In *Essais sur le Symbolique* (pp. 199-241, 315-334). Paris: Gallimard.

Roudinesco, E. (1990). *Jacques Lacan & Co.: A History of Psychoanalysis in France, 1925-1985* (J. Mehlman, Trans.). Chicago: University of Chicago Press.

Rutter, M. (1985). Resilience in the face of adversity: Protective factors and resistance to psychiatric disorder. *British Journal of Psychiatry*, *147*, 598-611.

Samuels, R. (1993). *Between Philosophy & Psychoanalysis. Lacan's Reconstruction of Freud*. New York and London: Routledge.

Sandell, R., Blomberg, J., Lazar, A., Carlsson, J., Schubert, J., & Broberg, J. (1997). *Self-reported outcomes and their clinical significance after psychotherapy and psychoanalysis in the Stockholm Outcome of Psychotherapy and Psychoanalysis Project (STOPP)*. Paper presented at the 28th Annual Meeting of the Society for Psychotherapy Research. June 26, Panel: Findings of the Stockholm Outcome of Psychotherapy and Psychoanalysis Project (STOPPP), Geilo, Norway, June 25-29.

Sandell, R., Blomberg, J., Lazar, A., Schubert, J., Carlsson, J., & Broberg, J. (1998). *The importance of time in treatment and follow-up. Long-term outcomes of psychoanalysis and long-term psychotherapy in the Stockholm Outcome of Psychoanalysis and Psychotherapy Project (STOPPP)*. Paper presented by Rolf Sandell at confernce "Problèmes methodologiques posés par l'évaluation des psychothérapies psychanalytiques et de la psychanalyse." Organized by l'Association de Psychanalyse et Psychothérapies, l'Assciation de Santé Mentale du 13ème Arrondissement de Paris et le Département de Psychiatrie de la Salpètrière, Paris.

Sartorius, N., Jablensky, A., Korten, A., Ernberg, G., Anker, M., Cooper, J., & Day, R. (1986). Early manifestations and first-contact incidence of schizophrenia in different cultures. *Psychological Medicine*, *16*, 909-928.

Sartorius, N., Gulbinat, W., Harrison, G., Laska, E., & Siegel, C. (1996). Long-term follow-up of schizophrenia in 16 countries: A description of the international study of schizophrenia conducted by the World Health

Organization. *Social Psychiatry and Psychiatric Epidemiology, 31,* 249-258.

Sartre, J. (1957). *The transcendence of the ego* (F. Williams & R. Kirkpatrick, Trans.). New York: Noonday Press.

Sartre, J. (1966). *Being and Nothingness* (Hazel E. Barnes, Trans.). New York: Washington Square Press.

Sass, L. (1992). *Madness and Modernism. Insanity in the Light of Modern Art, Literature, and Thought.* New York: Basic Books.

Sass, L. (1994). *Paradoxes of Delusion. Wittgenstein, Schreber, and the Schizophrenic Mind.* Ithaca, NY: Cornell University Press (Recommended by Suzanne Bernard).

Sass, L. (1999). Schizophrenia, Self-experience, and the so-called "Negative Symptoms." *Paper for the Fifth Internationl Conference on Person, Thursday August 5, 1999. Santa Fe.*

Schatzman, M. (1973). *Soul Murder: Persecution in the Family.* New York: Random.

Schneiderman, S. (Editor & Translator). (1980). *Returning to Freud: Clinical Psychoanalysis in the School of Lacan.* New Haven: Yale University Press.

Schneiderman, S. (Ed.). (1993). *How Lacan's Ideas are used in Clinical Practice.* Northvale, NJ: Aronson.

Schofield, W., & Balian, L. (1959). A comparative study of the personal histories of schizophrenic and nonpsychiatric patients. *Journal of Abnormal and Social Psychology, 59,* 216-225.

Schore, A. (1994). *Affect regulation and the origin of the self.* Hillsdale, NJ: Lawrence Erlbaum.

Schore, A. (1997). Early organization of the nonlinear right brain and development of a predisposition to psychiatric disorders. *Developmental Psychopathology, 9,* 595-631.

Schreber, D. (1988). *Memoirs of My Nervous Illness* [with a new introduction by Samuel M. Weber] (I. Macalpine & R.A. Hunter, Trans.). Cambridge, MA: Harvard University Press.

Schreber, D. P. (1903). *Denkwürdigkeiten eines Nervenkranken.* Leipzig: Oswald Mutze.

Schultz, S. C. (1995). Schizophrenia: Somatic Treatment. In H. I. Kaplan & B. J. Sadock (Eds.), *Comprehensive Textbook of Psychiatry. Vol I-II* (Sixth, Vol. I, pp. 987-998). Baltimore: The Williams & Wilkins Company.

Scott, G. R. (1958). *Phallic Worship.* Westport: Mental Health Press.

Searles, H. (1961). Sexual Processes in Schizophrenia. *Psychiatry, Supplement to Volume 24,* 87-95.

Searles, H. (1965). Schizophrenia and the inevitability of death. In *Collected Papers on Schizophrenia and Related Subjects* (pp. 487-520). New York: International Universities Press.

Searles, H. F. (1986). *My Work with Borderline Patients.* Northvale, NJ: Jason Aronson Inc.

Shenton, M., Solovay, M., Holzman, P., Coleman, M., & Gale, H. (1989). Thought disorder in the relatives of psychotic patients. *Archives of General Psychiatry, 46*(10), 897-901.

Shoemaker, S. (1963). *Self-Knowledge and Self-Identity*. Ithaca: Cornell University Press.

Shriqui, C. L., & Nasrallah, H. A. (1995). *Contemporary Issues in the Treatment of Schizophrenia*. Washington, DC: American Psychiatric Press.

Silver, A. S. (1991). Indications for long-term psychodynamically oriented hospitalization. *Directions in Psychiatry, 11*(21), 1-7.

Silver, A. S. (1992a). Intensive psychotherapy of psychosis in a decade of change. *The Psychiatric Hospital, 23*(2), 49-54.

Silver, A. S. (1992b). Treating the hospitalized borderline patient: Reworking trauma of toddlerhood. *Journal of the American Academy of Psychoanalysis, 20*(1), 114-129.

Silver, A. S., & Cantor, M. B. (Eds.). (1990). *Psychoanalsyis & Severe Emotional Illness*. New York: The Guilford Press.

Simiu, D. (1986). *Disorder and early alienation: Lacan's original theory of the mirror stage* [Doctoral Dissertation]. Washington, DC: Georgetown University.

Simon Silverman Phenomenology Center. (1988). *Phenomenology and Psychoanalysis* [The Sixth Annual Symposium]. Pittsburgh: Simon Silverman Phenomenology Center.

Simon Silverman Phenomenology Center. (1992). *Phenomenology and Lacanian Psychoanalysis* [The Eight Annual Symposium]. Pittsburgh: Simon Silverman Phenomenology Center.

Slater, L. (1998). *Prozac Diary*. New York: Random House.

Smith, J., Pao, P., & Scheig, N. (1972). On the Concept of Aggression. *The Psychoanalytic Study of the Child, 28*, 331-346.

Smith, J. H. (1970). The Heideggerian and Psychoanalytic Concepts of Mood. *Review of Existential Psychology and Psychiatry, X*, 101-111.

Smith, J. H., & Kerrigan W. (1983). *Interpreting Lacan*. New Haven: Yale University Press.

Sontag, S. (Editor). (1976). *Antonin Artaud: Selected Writings*. New York: Farrar, Straus, and Giroux.

Spiegelberg, H. (1972). *Phenomenology in Psychology and Psychiatry*. Evanston: Northwestern University Press.

Spitz, R. A. (1965). *The first year of life*. New York: International Universities Press.

Spring, W. (1939). Observations on World Destruction Fantasies. *Psychonalytic Quarterly, 8*, 48-56.

Stencranz, A. (1998). *Jagstrukturerande psykoterapi--förändringar hos fyra unga psyykotiska patienter, del 2* [TIPS-report nr 50]. Umeå University: Department of Applied Psychology.

Stencranz, A., & Malmgren, B. (1997). *Jagstrukturerande psykoterapi med fyra schizofrena patienter, del 1--en processbeskrivning* [TIPS-report nr 49]. Umeå University: Department of Applied Psychology.

Straube, E. R., & Oades, R. D. (1992). *Schizophrenia. Empirical Research and Findings*. San Diego: Academic Press.

Strauss, M. (1987). La vraie fonction du père, c'est d'unir un désir à la loi. In G. Miller (Ed.), *Lacan* (pp. 59-76). Paris: Bordas.

Strawson, P. (1952). *Individuals. An Essay in Descriptive Metaphysics*. London: Methuen.

Strawson, P. (1952). *Introduction to Logical Theory*. London: Strand, Methuen and Co.

Sullivan. (1953). *The Interpersonal Theory of Psychiatry*. New York: Norton and Co.

Szondi, L. (1956). *Ich-Analyse*. Bern: Stuggart.

Taylor, M. (1992). Are Schizophrenia and affective disorder Related? A Selective Literature Review. *American Journal of Psychiatry, 149*(1), 22-32.

Teixeira, M. A. (1997). *Problematics of Specificity and Assessment of Psychosocial Risk Factors in the Pathogenesis, Course, and treatment of Schizphrenia (and Affective Disorders)*. Paper presented at the 12th International Symposium for the Psychotherapy of Schizophrenia.London, October 12-16, 1997.

Tienari, P. (1992). Interaction between genetic vulnerability and rearing environment. In A. Werbart & J. Cullberg (Eds.), *Psychotherapy of Schizophrenia: Facilitating and Obstructive Factors* (pp. 154-178). Oslo: Scandinavian University Press.

Tienari, P., & Wynne, L. C. (1995). Subtypes of schizophrenia: Diagnostic and conceptual issues. In S. Mednick & J. Hollister (Eds.), *Neural Development and Schizophrenia* (pp. 177-189). New York: Plenum Press.

Tienari, P., Wynne, L. C., Moring, J., Lahti, I., Naarala, M., Sorri, A., Wahlberg, K., Saarento, O., Seitamaa, M., Kaleva, M., & Läksy, K. (1994). The Finnish Adoptive Family Study of Schizophrenia. Implications for Family Research. *British Journal of Psychiatry, 1994(Suppl)*(23), 20-26.

Tort, M. (1966). De l'Interprétation ou la Machine Herméneutique. *Les Temps Modernes*, 1461-1493, 1629-1652.

Turmel, F. (1990). Psychopharmacologie et utilisation de la médication dans un Centre psychanalyque de traitement des psychotiques. In W. Apollon, D. Bergeron & L. Cantin (Eds.), *Traiter la psychose* (pp. 161-169). Québec: Gifric.

VandenBos, G., & Karon, B. (1971). Pathogenesis: A new therapist dimension related to therapeutic effectiveness. *Journal of Personality Assesment, 35*, 252-260.

Vangaard, T. (1972). *Phallos: A Symbol and Its History in the Male World*. New York: International University Press.

Van Hautte, P. (1989). *Psychanalyse en Filosofie. Het Imaginaire en het Symbolische in het Werk van Jacques Lacan.* Leuven: Peeters.

Vergote, A. (1973). Raisons de la déraison. *Revue Philosophique de Louvain, 71,* 772-85.

Vergote, A. (1984). Phenomenology and Psychoanalysis; Reflections in reference to the book of Alphonse De Waelhens, Schizophrenia. *Journal of Phenomenological Psychology, 15,* 1-19.

Vergote, A. (1993). Dépression et mélancolie. In J. Florence, A. Vergote, J. Corveleyn, R. Bernet, P. Moyaert & L. Cassiers (Eds.), *Psychanalyse. L'Homme et ses Destins* (pp. 109-129). Louvain: Peeters.

Vergote, A. (1998). Le plaisir destructeur transfiguré en hiérogamie. In D. Devreese, Z. Lothane & J. Schotte (Eds.), *Schreber Revisité* (pp. 223-243). Louvain: Presses Universitaires de Louvain.

Ver Eecke, W. (1969). Vers une Philosophie de la Psychose. *Man and World, 1*(4), 44-49.

Ver Eecke, W. (1971). Myth and Reality in Psychoanalysis. *Proceedings of the American Catholic Philosophical Assoc., 45,* 158-166.

Ver Eecke, W. (1974). Freedom, Self-reflection and Intersubjectivity or Psychoanalysis and the Limits of the Phenomenological Method. In A.-T. Tymieniecka (Ed.), *Analecta Husserliana* (Vol. 3, pp. 252-270). Dordrecht: Reidel Publishing Company (l).

Ver Eecke, W. (1975). The Look, the Body, and the Other. In D. Ihde & R. M. Zaner (Eds.), *Selected studies in Phenomenology and Existential Philosophy. Vol 5: Dialogues in Existential Philosophy* (Vol. 5, pp. 224-246). The Hague: Nyhoff.

Ver Eecke, W. (1975, March). Symbol as a Philosophical Concept. *International Journal of Symbology,* pp. 20-30.

Ver Eecke, W. (1977). *Negativity and Subjectivity. A Study About the Function of Negation in Freud, Linguistics, Child- Psychology, and Hegel.* Brussels: Paleis der Academiën.

Ver Eecke, W. (1984). *Saying 'No'* [Expanded and Revised Edition of Negativity and Subjectivity]. Pittsburgh: Duquesne University Press.

Ver Eecke, W. (1988). Phenomenology and Paternal Metaphor in Lacan. *Phenomenology and Psychoanalysis. The Sixth Annual Symposium of the Simon Silverman Phenomenology Center,* 91-119. Pittsburgh: Simon Silverman Phenomenology Center Duquesne University.

Ver Eecke, W. (1993). Lacan and Schatzman: Reflections on the Concept of Paternal Metaphor. In *Tradition and Renewal. Philosophical Essays Commemorating the Centennial of Louvain's Institute of Philosophy* (Vol. 2, pp. 75-92). Leuven: Leuven University Press.

Ver Eecke, W. (1995). Schreber and Hölderlin: The Concept of "A-Father." In B. Babich, E. (Ed.), *From Phenomenology to Thought, Errancy, and Desire. Essays in Honor of William J. Richardson, S.J.* (pp. 473-82.). Dordrecht: Kluwer Academic Publishers.

Ver Eecke, W. (1997). Review of Muller, John P. Beyond the Psychoanalytic Dyad: Deveopmental Semiotics in Freud, Peirce and Lacan. New York: Routledge, 1996. *Clinical Studies. International Journal of Psychoanalysis, 3*(1), 115-119.

Villemoes, P. (1989). *Hur jaget struktureras (How the ego becomes structured).* Härnösand: Internet.

Villemoes, P. (1994). *Jagstrukturerande psykoterapi. Senare rön (On egostructuring psychotherapy-New experiences)1989-94.* Internet.

Villemoes, P. (2000). E-mail, June 24. Internet.

Wachs, T. (1983). The use and abuse of environment in behavior-genetic research. *Child Development, 54,* 396-407.

Wagner, H. (1967). *Philosophie und Reflexion.* München: Ernst Reinhardt Verlag.

Wahlberg, K., Wynne, L. C., Oja, H., Keskitalo, P., Pykäläinen, L., Lahti, I., Moring, J., Naarala, M., Sorri, A., Seitamaa, M., Läksy, K., Kolassa, J., & Tienari, P. (1997). Gen-Environment Interaction in Vulnerability to Schizophrenia: Findings from the Finnish Adoptive Family Study to Schizophrenia. *American Journal of Psychiatry, 154*(3), 355-362.

Walsh, F. (1978). Concurrent grandparent death and birth of schizophrenic offspring: An intriguing finding. *Family Process, 17*(12), 457-463.

Walters, O. (1955). A Methodological Critique of Freud's Schreber Analysis. *Psychoanalytic Review, 42,* 321-342.

White, R. (1961). The Mother-conflict in Schreber's Psychosis. *International Journal of Psychoanalysis, 42,* 55-73.

White, R. (1963). The Schreber Case Reconsidered in the Light of Psycho-social Concepts. *International Journal of Psychoanalysis, 44,* 213-221.

Wilden, A. (1968). *The Language of the Self.* Baltimore: Johns Hopkins Press.

Wilson, E., Jr. (1979). Madness and Philosophy. *Contemporary Psychology, 24*(5), 423-5.

Winnicott, D. (1953). Transitional Objects and Transitional Phenomena. *International Journal of Psychoanalysis, XXXIV,* 89-97.

Wittgenstein, L. (1955). *On Certainty.* New York: Harper and Row.

Wittgenstein, L. (1955). *Tractatus Logico-Philosophicus* (p. 207). New York: Harcourt, Brace, and Co.

Wright, G. v. (1972). Wittgenstein on Certainty. In G. v. Wright (Ed.), *Problems in the Theory of Knowledge* (pp. 47-60.). The Hague: Nyhoff.

Wyatt, R. J., Kirch, D. G., & Egan, M. F. (1995). Schizophrenia: Neuro-chemical, Viral, and Immunological Studies. In H. I. Kaplan & B. J. Sadock (Eds.), *Comprehensive Textbook of Psychiatry. Vol I-II* (Sixth, Vol. I, pp. 927-942). Baltimore: The Williams & Wilkins Company.

Wyschogrod, E., Crownfield, D., & Raschke, C. A. (Eds.). (1989). *Lacan & Theological Discourse.* Albany: State University of New York Press.

Zizek, S. (1991). *Looking Awry. An Introduction to Jacques Lacan through Popular Culture.* Cambridge, MA: MIT Press.

INDEX

132; 188; 191; 198; 200; 203; 235; 242; 253; 254; 262; 264; 266; 275; 276; 287; 291

Dopamine, 41; 42; 43; 44; 59

Dreams, 21; 26; 64; 189; 199; 233; 238; 258; 261; 262; 263; 265; 269; 274; 281

Dscourse, 113; 118; 125; 126; 137; 142; 145; 153; 157; 165; 166; 170; 183; 186; 206; 207; 210; 223; 245; 246; 252; 254; 255; 256; 257; 258; 259; 260; 261; 263; 265; 267; 268; 269; 270; 273; 274; 275; 276; 278; 280; 282; 284; 286; 288; 291
  psychoanalytic discourse, 280; 282; 283; 284

dual union, 32; 151; 153; 168; 214; 218; 219; 222; 223; 224; 291

Dual, dualism, 28; 32; 33; 37; 39; 40; 51; 63; 72; 76; 97; 98; 100; 101; 102; 151; 153; 168; 181; 206; 214; 218; 219; 222; 223; 224; 245; 291

Dual, dusalism, 39; 45; 252; 253

Dyad, dyadic, 56; 94; 96; 213; 224

Edenius, B., 116; 121

Environmental, 38; 40; 52

Epressed emotions, 54; 103; 107

Erikson, 32; 33; 36; 84

Erotomania, 192; 226

Evans, D., 74; 75; 119

Ewens, T., 188; 228

Ey, H., 171; 233

Failure, 23; 28; 29; 37; 56; 70; 71; 74; 75; 77; 79; 80; 85; 94; 96; 97; 101; 105; 106; 118; 130; 134; 141; 147; 149; 150; 160; 170; 195; 205; 214; 215; 216; 218; 220; 226; 231; 233; 247; 279

Family dysfunction, 107; 108

farmer, A., 56

father, 22; 25; 26; 27; 30; 31; 32; 33; 34; 37; 41; 48; 52; 54; 71; 72; 74; 75; 77; 78; 94; 96; 99; 109; 114; 118; 156; 157; 168; 176; 177; 179; 180; 181; 188; 189; 197; 205; 210; 211; 212; 215; 216; 218; 219; 220; 221; 222; 224; 230; 231; 242; 280; 281; 282; 283; 284; 286
  A-father, 221; 222

Finitude, 73; 74; 77; 110; 267

Fink, B., 54; 61; 74; 75; 77; 81; 89; 119

Fisher, S., 53; 67

Fixation, 33; 162; 189; 191; 194; 196; 198; 239; 242; 270; 291

Fonagy, P., 54

Foreclosure, 28; 29; 30; 34; 35; 71; 74; 81; 96; 118; 130; 149; 150; 156; 159; 171; 172; 177; 188; 203; 204; 220; 221; 222; 224; 228; 231; 242; 247

Fort, D.C., 49; 50; 51; 103; 109; 143; 145

Fort-da (Freud's grandchild), 28

Freedman, A.M., 35

Freud, S., 12; 22; 23; 28; 33; 35; 63; 67; 76; 95; 96; 110; 111; 127; 128; 136; 139; 143; 144; 146; 147; 148; 149; 154; 163; 165; 171; 173; 183; 185; 187; 188; 189; 191; 192; 193; 194; 195; 196; 197; 198; 199; 200; 201; 202; 203; 204; 205; 210; 212; 216; 218; 225; 226; 227; 228; 237; 240; 242; 246; 247; 256; 257; 261; 262; 263; 267; 268; 270; 274; 275; 279; 280; 281; 282; 289; 290

Fromm-Reichmann, F., 91; 92; 120

Fulfillment, 147; 152; 263

Fundamental disorder, 16; 77; 128; 131; 132; 133; 134; 138;

FIGURES OF THE UNCONSCIOUS

(Hors série)

- D. DEVREESE, Z. LOTHANE, J. SCHOTTE (éds.), *Schreber revisité*
  1998, 243 p., ISBN 90 6186 908 0, BEF 1250 - € 30,98

1. PH. VAN HAUTE, J. CORVELEYN (eds.), *Seduction, Suggestion, Psychoanalysis*
   2001, 128 p., ISBN 90 5867 127 5, BEF 850 - € 21,07
2. A. DE WAELHENS, W. VER EECKE, *Phenomenology and Lacan on Schizophrenia, after the Decade of the Brain*
   2001, 338 p., ISBN 90 5867 160 7, BEF 1250 - € 30,98
3. J. CORVELEYN, P. MOYAERT (eds.), *Psychosis: Phenomenological and Psychoanalytical approaches*
   Forthcoming: autumn 2001

Drukkerij en Binderij
SCHEERDERS van KERCHOVE
9100 ST.-NIKLAAS